Alimentary Tracts

NEXT WAVE

NEW DIRECTIONS

IN WOMEN'S STUDIES

A SERIES EDITED BY

INDERPAL GREWAL,

CAREN KAPLAN, AND

ROBYN WIEGMAN

Alimentary Tracts

APPETITES, AVERSIONS,

AND THE POSTCOLONIAL

Parama Roy

 DUKE UNIVERSITY PRESS

DURHAM AND LONDON 2010

© 2010 Duke University Press
All rights reserved
Printed in the United States
of America on acid-free paper ∞
Designed by Amy Ruth Buchanan
Typeset in Quadraat and Quadraat
Sans by Keystone Typesetting, Inc.
Library of Congress Cataloging-
in-Publication Data appear on the
last printed page of this book.

IN MEMORY OF

Ramola Roy

AND

Amalendu Roy

Contents

Acknowledgments

This book has been a long time in the making, and whatever thanks I can render at this point to the colleagues, friends, and institutions who have aided me over the course of its prolonged gestation are necessarily inadequate. As always, my most acute interlocutors have been Carole-Anne Tyler and Sandhya Shetty; I am grateful to them for their gifts of rigor and imagination. I am grateful as well to Sangeeta Ray and Ajay Skaria, who read the manuscript in its entirety with a remarkable mixture of incisiveness and generosity. Anjali Arondekar and a second, anonymous reader for Duke University Press gave it the kind of meticulous scrutiny that proved immensely useful in defining the stakes of the project. I have also benefited immeasurably from the critical stimulus provided by a host of other scholars: Lalitha Gopalan, Bishnu Ghosh, Sudipta Sen, Lawrence Cohen, Catherine Robson, Sukanya Banerjee, Caren Kaplan, Piya Chatterjee, Inderpal Grewal, Raka Ray, Amitav Ghosh, Barbara Metcalf, Vasudha Dalmia, Bhaskar Sarkar, Jenny Sharpe, Frances Hasso, the late Meenakshi Mukherjee, Maria Couto, Margie Ferguson, Fran Dolan, Liz Constable, Geeta Patel, Jennifer Brody, Suad Joseph, Omnia El-Shakry, Karl Britto, Minoo Moallem, and Marisol Cortez. For their unsurpassed collegiality I am deeply appreciative of Kim Devlin, Deborah Willis, George Haggerty, Steve Axelrod, Carole Fabricant, Georg Gugelberger, Katherine Kinney, and Joe Childers, my erstwhile colleagues at the University of California, Riverside.

Versions of several chapters of this book were presented at UC Berkeley, UCLA, UC Irvine, UC Santa Barbara, UC Santa Cruz, UC Riverside, UC Davis, the University of Minnesota, the University of Wisconsin, Milwaukee, the University of Colorado at Boulder, Stanford University, the University of London, and the Subaltern and the Popular Multicampus Research Group conference at Cairo. I am indebted to those who extended the invitations—Simona Sawhney, Vinay Lal, Arnab Chakladar, Susan Koshy, Rachel Dwyer, Lalitha du Perron, Suzanne Daly, Ross Forman, Peter Abraham, Julie Carr, and Swati Chattopadhyay—and to the superb audiences at these venues who engaged my work. The project was supported by the Center for Ideas and Society at UC Riverside; the University of California President's Research Fellowship in the Humanities; the Rockefeller Foundation's Bellagio Study and Conference Center; the University of California Humanities Research Institute; and UC Davis faculty research grants. The members of the Eating Cultures research group at UCHRI in fall 2007, Melanie Dupuis, Julie Guthman, and Carolyn de la Peña in particular, provided a congenial forum for working through some of the ideas in this book.

I owe a special note of thanks to Ken Wissoker, the best of editors, and to Courtney Berger, Leigh Barnwell, and Mark Mastromarino at Duke University Press. I am indebted to Larry Kenney for copyediting the final manuscript and Ryan Fong for preparing the index to this book.

To my parents, Ramola and Amalendu Roy, both of whom passed away while this volume was being written, I owe a debt for which no words can suffice; this book is dedicated to their memory. For urging me to get it done and for long-term sustenance beyond my deserts, my thanks go to Bharat Trehan.

. . .

Earlier versions of the material in chapter 2 appeared in *Gender & History* 14.1 (April 2002), 62–91, as "Meat-Eating, Masculinity, and Renunciation in India: A Gandhian Grammar of Diet," and in *Pacific Coast Philology* 42.2 (2007), 133–55, as "Transits, Transformations, and Transoceanic Dialogues: Gandhi's Passages from India." A small portion of chapter 3 appeared in *Women of India: Colonial and Postcolonial Periods*, edited by Bharati Ray, 392–423 (New Delhi: Sage, 2005), as "Women, Hunger, and Famine: Bengal, 1350/1943." An early version of the material in chapter 4 appeared in *positions: east asia cultures critique* 10.2 (fall 2002), 471–502, as "Reading Communities and Culinary Communities: The Gastropoetics of the South Asian Diaspora."

Introduction

I repeat: the pepper, if you please; for if it had not been for peppercorns, then what is ending now in East and West might never have begun. Pepper it was that brought Vasco da Gama's tall ships across the ocean, from Lisbon's Tower of Belem to the Malabar Coast: first to Calicut and later, for its lagoony harbour, to Cochin. English and French sailed in the wake of that first-arrived Portugee, so that in the period called Discovery-of-India—but how could we be discovered when we were not covered before?—we were "not so much sub-continent as sub-condiment," as my distinguished mother had it. "From the beginning, what the world wanted from bloody mother India was daylight-clear," she'd say. "They came for the hot stuff, just like any man calling on a tart."

—SALMAN RUSHDIE, *The Moor's Last Sigh*

The question is no longer one of knowing if it is "good" to eat the other or if the other is "good" to eat, nor of knowing which other. One eats him regardless and lets oneself be eaten by him. The so-called non-anthropophagic cultures practice symbolic anthropophagy and even construct their most elevated socius, indeed the sublimity of their morality, their politics, and their right, on this anthropoph-agy. . . . The moral question is thus not, nor has it ever been: should one eat or not eat, eat this and not that, the living or the nonliving, man or animal, but since *one must* eat in any case and since it is and tastes good to eat, and since there's no other definition of the good [*du bien*], how for goodness sake should one eat well [*bien manger*]? And what does this imply? What is eating? How is this metonymy of introjection to be regulated? And in what respect does the formulation of these questions in language give us still more food for thought? In what respect is the question, if you will, carnivorous?

—JACQUES DERRIDA, "'Eating Well,' or the Calculation of the Subject: An Interview with Jacques Derrida"

Men who come out here should have no entrails.

—JOSEPH CONRAD, *Heart of Darkness*

Hunger

As a child in India I tended to dream of what I considered to be British food. Improbable as it seems now, I dreamed of potted meats (especially Spam), tinned tongue, jam tarts, ginger beer, pork-pies, and éclairs. I dreamed of gastronomic surprises nestled in tuck boxes and hampers of food, poised to reveal their bounty in the midnight feasts I read about but never experienced in my own life. I longed especially for the singular delectation of eating my food out of a tin—to me the very sign of gastronomic avant-gardism, situated as I was in a global backwater and largely innocent of what I was to learn later were called "industrial foods."[1] My mother's vision of the British table, however, did not accord with mine. When I asked her, at seven or eight, what sahibs (for me as well as for others a shorthand for white, usually British people) ate, she said, "They take a hunk of meat, put salt and pepper on it, and stick it in a hot oven. They boil potatoes and a head of cabbage. When everything is cooked through, they sit down to eat. This is what I have read." Despite a childhood and adolescence spent in colonial India, she had only a textual knowledge of the alimentary habits and rituals of the Anglo-Indians resident there—quite unsurprising, given the nonexistent social contacts, except at the very highest levels, between colonizer and colonized. Shocked and disbelieving—nothing in her description accorded with my sense of the rituals of cookery or even the character of food—I concluded that she had read the wrong sources.

My own sense of the delights of British cuisine was the result of reading the works of Enid Blyton, the best-selling children's author in the world, notwithstanding her death in 1968, until the meteoric rise of J. K. Rowling. Read widely in Britain as well as in countries of the so-called Commonwealth, especially India, Pakistan, the Caribbean (as the evidence of Jamaica Kincaid's *Annie John* suggests), Australia, New Zealand, Singapore, South Africa, and (what was then) Rhodesia, these tales of children's adventures celebrated juvenile autonomy, comradeship, a breezy and self-assured Englishness, and the joys of eating often and abundantly. Written largely during the period of wartime and postwar rationing in Britain in the 1940s and 1950s, the books invariably featured rhapsodic descriptions of glorious feasts, usually eaten in farmhouses, in the outdoors, or in boarding-school dormitories after lights were out. The primary involvement of Blyton's juvenile characters with the world was salivary, or so it seemed. The books made me salivate too, especially because the foods they lovingly blazoned seemed as desirable and unattainable as the adventures the characters casually attracted; even biscuits and hard-boiled eggs, which we consumed routinely in the postcolony, appeared on the page to be infused with an exoticism quite novel to me. Much later, in my teens, a reading of E. M. Forster's acerbic summary of the mock-English menu at the Anglo-Indian club of Chandrapore— "Julienne soup full of bullety bottled peas, pseudo-cottage bread, fish full of branching bones, pretending to be plaice, more bottled peas with the cutlets, trifles, sardines on toast: the menu of Anglo-India. A dish might be added or subtracted as one rose or fell in the official scale, the peas might rattle less or more, the sardines and the vermouth be imported by a different firm, but the tradition remained; the food of exiles, cooked by servants who did not understand it"—sealed my sense of the impassable gulf between proper British cuisine and the Indian context.[2] But it also gave me a slightly different understanding from the one I had harbored earlier of the pleasures and investments of British cooking. The Anglo-Indians dreamed of British food too, it seems; their mistake lay in their literal-mindedness in translating their dreams of ingestion into the stuff of everyday life in a remote and unpromising colony. Now that Indian food is, in the early twenty-first century, the most popular food in Britain (at least where opinion polls about public dining are concerned), and chicken tikka masala the British national dish, the content of the food fantasies of westward-looking Indian children must be considerably unsettled.

In my own life, other revelations had occurred before my encounter with Forster's astringent gloss on the Anglo-Indian palate. My history classes had taught me about other, more consequential historical hungers, ones that looked east rather than west as I did; had it not been for pepper, as Rushdie notes in his witty conjoining of the events of 1492 and

1498 (the latter being the year of Vasco da Gama's arrival in Calicut on the Malabar coast), the world as we know it today might not have come to be.[3] Medieval and early modern Europe, one learned, hungered for the spices of the subcontinent and of southeast Asia. Used in a variety of ways—for embalming, magical rituals, cooking, and preservation as well as in medications, aphrodisiacs, cosmetics, and perfumes—spices were endowed with considerable glamour and value, their possession and use being a mark of conspicuous consumption and of discriminating taste among European elites seeking to consolidate their claims to refinement. Indeed, Wolfgang Schivelbusch suggests that eastern spices were a stimulant to the imagination at least as much as they were a spur to elite modes of social competition. The taste for spices, he argues, implies "a peculiarly medieval longing for faraway places—the longing . . . for the Paradise they thought could be tasted in the spices. . . . Something of this notion survives in the censer-swinging of the Catholic mass."[4] This gustatory fantasy, Schivelbusch postulates, was the engine that made Europe what it is today, launching it from medievalism to modernity through its long sea voyages and subsequent colonial conquests. For over three centuries the lucrative European spice trade with the East was dependent upon land routes across Asia and the Middle East and upon numerous intermediaries, primarily Arab and Venetian. But by the sixteenth century improvements in navigational techniques had led the other European powers to seek the fabled spices directly. Sea captains like Ferdinand Magellan and Vasco da Gama were instrumental in opening up the sea routes to the East and ensuring Portuguese monopoly over the spice (primarily pepper) trade until other European powers decided to challenge its hegemony. The Dutch were the first to break the Portuguese monopoly and to replace it in the Moluccas with a near monopoly of their own. This they enforced with ruthless brutality for two centuries, garnering profits from the clove trade not just with Europe but also with other parts of Asia, notably northern India.[5]

The Dutch were in turn challenged, though unsuccessfully, by the British East India Company, established by a royal charter from Elizabeth I on 31 December 1600. The arrival of the East India Company in India was not planned; it was, rather, the consequence of bungling. The Company's ships arrived at the western port of Surat in India in 1608 only after failing to make significant progress against their Dutch rivals in the Moluccas. Over the course of the next century, however, the Company's agents made considerable headway against their Portuguese rivals in the subcontinent. Their own trade there was in textiles, indigo, saltpeter, and tea, though they made inroads into the Dutch monopoly of the spice trade in the Moluccas as well.[6] But by the mid-eighteenth century, when the East India Company had begun to establish its paramountcy in the subcontinent, subduing its French rivals as well as numerous Indian rulers, the European taste for spices that had driven the race to the East was in decline, being replaced by a taste for coffee, tea, opium, and sugar (the last item was classified with spices in the European Middle Ages). Yet spices held on to their value in another register. As Timothy Morton notes, spices retained their status as fantasy objects and as ideologically charged substances long after their economic value had declined.[7] The commercial and fantasmatic traffic in spices is an early modern historical lesson in the magical realism that forms the idiom of colonial hunger. Rushdie instantiates this beautifully in The Moor's Last Sigh through the code switching that allows the lost Moorish paradise of Al-Andalus to dissolve into the newly discovered spice groves of European fable.

British interest in the subcontinent shifted to other, more profitable commodities. The most successful of these ventures was the Company's cultivation of opium as a monopoly crop in the subcontinent. Carl A. Trocki and James Hevia suggest that opium should be accorded the status as "one of the most empire-friendly commodities circulating in the global economy."[8] The work of Sidney Mintz in the Caribbean has persuasively established the importance of the global commodification of sugar for thinking about connections among the Atlantic slave trade, plantation economies in the Americas, proto-industrial forms of production, the tempo of the working day in the factory, and new patterns of mass consumption (and consumer boycotts).[9] The significance of opium to the East India Company in particular and to the empire in general belongs to a similar anthropology and history of world systems, far exceeding what might appear to be the parochial contexts of British opium smuggling into China and the resulting Opium Wars of the nineteenth century. "Without opium the British global empire is virtually unthinkable," notes Hevia, reviewing the work of Trocki. "By the early part of the nineteenth century, British Indian opium had stanched the flow of New World silver into China, replacing silver as the commodity that could be exchanged for Chinese tea and other goods. By the 1830s, silver was flowing out of China to India and beyond. . . . Opium revenues in India not only kept the colonial administration afloat, but sent vast quantities of silver bullion back to Britain. The upshot was the global dominance of the British pound sterling until World War I."[10]

The extraordinary scale and importance of this traffic have led Hevia to describe the British empire as itself a figure of addiction, one whose character is to be understood in terms of its "drug dependency."[11] An arresting figuration of global-colonial capitalism—a figuration that calls to mind Karl Marx's more famous formulation about vampire capitalism in *Capital*—drug addiction places the empire tropologically not so much in the standard neoclassical economic languages of efficiencies of scale, good bookkeeping, and responsible work practices that have been used to explain British colonial success as in an appetitive and phantasmal one, underlining the nonutilitarian, debilitating, and uncontrollable cravings it simultaneously incites and exploits. Trocki's term for the opium-driven empire is "drug cartel"; while gesturing toward a corporate logic of exploitation rather than toward a medicalized and moral one of pathology, the term does not altogether abolish the frisson engendered by the strange figure of the addict. Rather, it absorbs the addict into the larger figure of parasitism, of unhealthy feeding, that Marx accentuates in his critique of the vampiric form of nineteenth-century political economy, including a colonial political economy.[12] Addicted to addiction itself, the character of colonial hunger, in this formulation, calls for what Avital Ronell has called a "narcoanalysis," one that would register the wild, fabulous character of its appetites.[13]

Arguably such a narcoanalysis could also be brought to bear upon the empire's more salubrious and health-giving commodity, tea, given its vectoring through opium smuggling in the nineteenth century—just as sugar in an earlier period was yoked to the economy of Caribbean slave production. But if there was a noteworthy appreciation in Britain in the late eighteenth century and the early nineteenth of the moral and sometimes even bodily taint of "blood sugar," there was little corresponding indignation about tea after the eighteenth century, and the commodity chain that linked sugar, opium, and tea was not one that drew particular remark.[14] Ironically enough, tea production in Indian plantations, established from the 1830s on to compete with Chinese tea, took off on the world market just as Britain won trading concessions as a result of the Opium Wars. Less surprisingly, these plantations borrowed forms of coercive labor, corporal punishment, and legal exceptionalism from the sugar and cotton plantations of the Americas.[15]

Feeding

As all these instances of the psychopharmacopoeia of empire—spices, opium, sugar, and tea—demonstrate, colonialism was in important respects a reconfiguration of the fantasmatic landscapes and the sensorium of colonizer and colonized, generating new experiences of desire, taste, disgust, and appetite and new technologies of the embodied self. Such a reconfiguration comprised a crucial part of what Gayatri Spivak has denominated, adapting Martin Heidegger, the "worlding" of the (now Third) world in terms of the subject-constituting imperative of nineteenth-century colonialism. For her this imperative is to be understood as "soul making," or "the imperialist project cathected as civil society-through-social-mission." For Charlotte Brontë's Jane Eyre, and for all those who were willing to shoulder the white man's—or, in Jane's case, the white woman's—burden, this involved the monumental but necessary task of transforming "the heathen into a human so that he [could] be treated as an end in himself."[16]

Details both grand and vulgar of colonial history make it eminently clear that the projects of epistemic overhaul involved in making heathens human occurred in several registers concurrently. For one thing, they were irreducibly somaticized; souls in the making were more often than not incarnated in bodies whose appetites, expressions, and comings and goings had to be rigorously fashioned. Soul making and body shaping, physiology and epistemology were intimately conjugated. The body was both a figurative reservoir, generating tropes of encounter—such as cannibalism or even caste—with abandon, and the materialist locus of transformation. Colonial politics often spoke in an indisputably visceral tongue: its experiments, engagements, and traumas were experienced in the mouth, belly, olfactory organs, and nerve endings, so that the stomach served as a kind of somatic political unconscious in which the phantasmagoria of colonialism came to be embodied. "Men who come out here should have no entrails," remarks the manager of the Central Station in *Heart of Darkness*, in a telling comment on the enteric manifestation of empire's troubles. This alimentary habitus, one that included not just the mouth but also skin, sinew, and gut, was the banal yet crisis-ridden theater for staging questions central to encounter and rule, questions of proximity, cathexis, consumption, incorporation, digestion, commensality, and purgation. As the very title of David Arnold's study of imperial medicine, *Colonizing the Body*, suggests, the body of the colonized subject was the fecund and hotly contested terrain of soul making, with medicine, hygiene, diet, evacuation, vestments, exercise, sex, and childbirth serving as the major vectors of remaking and self-fashioning.[17]

In many ways the shock of encounter with colonialism manifested itself very signally in the production of new forms of appetite, new notions of health and hygiene, and new modes of disgust. Thus one might note that while Western forms of scientific and humanistic learning and English literary instruction passed without comment and, indeed, were welcomed with eagerness by the Bengali Hindu bhadralok of the nineteenth century, these very subjects were dismayed by the departures from culinary and commensal orthopraxy practiced by some of the students of this new knowledge.[18] The orthodox Bengali Brahmin scholar Bhudev Mukhopadhyay, a critic of the imitative ways of westernized Indians, noted with disgust the conduct of his fellow students at Hindu College in Calcutta in the 1840s: "Open defiance of Hindu social conventions in matters of food and drink was then considered almost de rigeur [sic] by the avant garde students of the College. To be reckoned a civilized person, one had to eat beef and consume alcohol."[19] An acute cultural physiognomist, Bhudev recognized that to be in the vanguard of an order of colonial modernity—to be "avant garde," in his terms—involved not just a new freedom from orthodoxy but a new orthodoxy of taste and disgust, now "almost de rigueur," to replace older Brahminical ones. It also involved a certain stylization of the relationship between interiority and a public persona; eating, as well as not eating, became part of a novel, aggressively visible political theater.

Clearly Bhudev felt himself classed among the backward ones, those who were failing to pass the test of historically appropriate embodiment. This was an important consideration in a period that, under the pressure of colonialism, saw the induction of new norms of corporeal propriety and normality. Palate, sinew, and stomach came to assume a certain historical charge through featuring prominently in debates about the forms of colonial modernity in the subcontinent. Henceforth alimentation would be an indispensable element in thinking about the forms of colonial, anticolonial, and nationalist virtue—and not only for bhadralok males being drawn inexorably into the circle of westernization. The fact that the Indian Mutiny of 1857 is popularly believed to have originated in the introduction in the Native Infantry regiments of the British Indian army of greased cartridges for the new Enfield rifles, cartridges that were rumored to be, and in fact may have been, coated with beef tallow and pork fat—offensive to the religious sensibilities of both Hindu and Muslim sepoys (infantry soldiers)—makes clear the degree to which Bhudev's terrors about alimentary outrages against caste and religious integrity were shared by several sectors of the colonized population and not confined to its elite or westernized constituencies. For many kinds of subjects of colonialism, including upper-caste bhadralok men, high-caste but economically vulnerable sepoys, aspiring nationalist males, women seeking orthodox sanction for unorthodox forms of public and professional life, diet was configured from the nineteenth century on as a terrain for encounter, challenge, transformation, and consolidation. It was the ground on which the constitutive terms, limits, and concrete possibilities of a modern colonial order came to be assimilated and sometimes repudiated. Mohandas Karamchand Gandhi's public turn to vegetarianism in his early manhood in Britain, for instance, was much more than conformity to a familial and regional vegetarian tradition: it was carefully chosen and symbolically freighted. A pragmatic contrivance at the outset to win passage out of provincial existence—his mother would not permit him to leave Gujarat for England unless he vowed to remain faithful to vegetarianism—it came to be converted in short order into a more elevated thinking about the sacrifice necessary to triumph over the relentlessly consumptive, even parasitic, order represented for him by colonial modernity.

Indians responded to what seemed to be a new prescription to consume in a number of ways. Some, like the Young Bengal rebels castigated by Bhudev, turned with gusto from an antiquated alimentary regime conspicuous for its prohibitions on consumption and commensality. Others of bhadralok origin sought to remake colonized masculine subjects into properly nationalist ones through modes of somatic and psychic self-cultivation.[20] Still others, much lower on the social hierarchy and not particularized with proper names, capitalized on the new world order emerging in 1857 in order to mock Brahminical rules of caste purity and caste hierarchy. The low-caste khalasi (worker) who, in one of the stock tales about the start of the Mutiny, gleefully reported the news of the greased cartridges to the high-caste sepoy surely was one of them (see chapter 1).

For others yet, the response to the alimentary challenge inaugurated by colonialism assumed a different bodily investment, one that can be described as sacrificial and ascetic and more uneasily as nationalist. The twelve-year-old Bhudev, newly admitted to Hindu College, was bound by a vow to his father to avoid all prohibited food and drink. It was a vow to which he was zealously faithful. As in the case of Gandhi, the vow as a long-established form of moral regulation takes on added resonance in the new sensory worlds opened up by colonialism. The exceptionalism of the achievement of Anandibai Joshi, the first Hindu woman physician to receive a medical degree in the West, went hand in hand with, indeed was guaranteed by, her vow to adhere to dietary and vestimentary propriety during her sojourn at the Women's Medical College of Pennsylvania. "I will go as a Hindu and come back to live as a Hindu," she famously declared in her address at the Serampore College Hall on the eve of her departure for New York. Dying early of a tuberculosis apparently strained or even precipitated by cold winters and dietary restrictions, she was to achieve fame not so much through professional achievement—she did take her degree but died before assuming her post at the Albert Edward Hospital in Kolhapur—as through the aberrant contours of the brief life she led. For the Christian missionaries who had supported her ambition and eagerly expected her conversion, there was more than a trace of bafflement at her willed sacrifice of her body as a recalcitrant, morbid tribute to antiquated habits. To a Hindu orthodoxy in India, on the other hand, it was precisely these putative perversities of diet and dress, manifestations of a patriotism and homesickness that had produced an alimentary heroism unto death, that were to be celebrated; especially in the case of women, passing the test of suitable embodiment could entail abnegating life itself when required.[21]

As the examples above demonstrate, an alimentary investment for the (caste-privileged) body poised precariously between colonialism and nationalism could be quite complex. Conceived above all as a principle of asceticism, this investment sets itself against what it sees as the insatiable feeding of the West, even as it acknowledges that such renunciation might militate against a colonially inflected and even an empirically verifiable sense of somatic fitness. In this it affirms an alimentary ethics that seeks a more expansive definition of fitness, something more than, and something that might be in opposition to, a bodily health measured by strength and efficiency. At the same time, though, at least for Gandhi and Anandibai, such renunciations are very much oriented toward a West marked by carnivory and other forms of alimentary voracity.[22] Vows of alimentary abstinence make possible the passage into the West in the first place; they are recontextualized and brought to a pitch of moral perfection by being practiced there, outside of and alienated from their putatively proper contexts. Dietary belonging is no longer tied to a place or context but becomes part of the portable apparatus of embodied practice that actually has the greatest effect by being set adrift in the world. Diaspora (usually in the West), as the arena of temptation, testing, and sacrifice, is in many ways the most appropriate theater for the turn, or return, to practices of dietary belonging and dietary fidelity. If diaspora features largely in three of the four chapters in this book, it is precisely because of its favored place in an alimentary discourse engaged with the always vexed questions of interiority, belonging, and alienness and with the entailments of dining with strangers.

Body talk about colonialism has tended to focus, perhaps understandably, on the bodies of the colonized and on the coercive and subtle modes through which their phenomenological existence came to be understood and often reconstellated in the new world order of colonialism. But, as increasing numbers of studies of Englishmen and Englishwomen in the tropics have come to show, colonizers themselves were not immune from the embodied obligations of biopower, which surely has something of a relationship with soul making, even though the two are far from identical. For them, as much as for the colonized, politics in the colony could not help but be a bodied, carnal politics; carnality, including alimentation, was an important theater for the soul making of Indians as well as for the self-making of Anglo-Indians.

What, however, constitutes food and ingestion or eating, especially in the colony? What substances can be considered necessities in the sense of meeting a biomoral minimum of ingestibility? and for whom? Which ones are considered natural to eat? What forms of violence are involved in ingesting them? and what are their somatic effects? And what or who is assimilated in the process of procuring, cooking, sharing, and ingesting them? As Claude Lévi-Strauss and others after him have emphatically recognized, cooking has the contours of a language, with gustemes that correspond analogically with the phonemes that organize linguistic meaning. As in the case of language, which mocks the notion of private property, there can be no eating or digestion that is strictly one's own.[23] Besides, as Lévi-Strauss suggests in "The Culinary Triangle," cooking, however defined, is universally a means by which nature becomes culture and categories of cooking are always apt symbols for social differentiation. Hence foods and totemic species are "goods to think with" rather than only "goods to eat," as Edmund Leach observes in his reading of Lévi-Strauss.[24] To feed, as Derrida implies in the above epigraph, is invariably to be inserted into relationship, a relationship with an other, though not always or necessarily a human one.

But what is one to think of the mutual feeding by and upon humans that for Derrida constitutes one's irreducible communication with the other? It is not reducible, for one thing, only to the parasitic ingestive order that is commonly used to describe the operations of colonialism, as for instance in the narcopolitics of opium. Neither is it the same as the vampirism Marx invokes as a figure of monstrous gastronomy, of voraciousness without limit. In the literature on vampirism, vamping is by definition destructive absorption in the service of cloning oneself, Diana Fuss noting that vampirism is "both other-incorporating and self-reproducing."[25] In such a scene of ingestion, one assimilates the other totally to reproduce oneself without being altered or disturbed in any degree by this consumption; the other loses its character of otherness, if it can be said ever to have possessed it, in this process. Consumption never displaces or confuses self-reproduction but simply and straightforwardly supplements it. Thus, in his well-known reading of Bram Stoker's *Dracula*, Christopher Craft calls attention to the indistinguishability between the Count and the other vampires in the novel, those whom he has vamped in order to recreate them in his image: "[We] must remember that the vampire mouth is first of all Dracula's mouth, and that all subsequent versions of it . . . merely repeat as diminished simulacra the desire of the Great Original, that 'father or furtherer of a new order of beings.' . . . Dracula himself, calling his children 'my jackals to do my bidding when I want to feed,' identifies the systematic creation of female surrogates who enact his will and desire."[26] As an eating without digesting, a consumption without remainder and without conflict, vampirism encompasses a single, self-sufficient end of the alimentary tract. It is an instance of what Derrida has named an exemplary orality, or "exemplorality," the process by which a (fantasmatic) mouth "transforms everything into auto-affection, assimilates everything to itself by idealizing it with interiority, masters everything by mourning its passing, refusing to touch it, to digest it naturally, but digests it ideally, consumes what it does not consume and *vice versa*."[27]

Cannibalism has often been conflated with vampirism and imagined therefore as an ingestion of the other that results in undisturbed replication. To be sure, it has functioned variously for many thinkers from at least the early modern period on, sometimes as an emblem of appetite carried to its unbearable logical and ethical limit and just as often, but not necessarily contrarily, as an emblem of unassimilable civilizational otherness.[28] The crude ideological function of the latter reading is perhaps all too demonstrable: thinking of Amerindian societies as irremediably committed to the consumption of human flesh permitted their enslavement and even extermination by their European colonizers. Geoffrey Sanborn notes the way the description of an appetitive, unbridled cannibalism came generally to be accompanied by the expression of a (normatively European) "humane" horror. Cannibalism thus came to be opposed to and therefore constitutive of humanity as such: if to be human, and humane, was to be of the party that loved humanity, it was also consequently to disavow the possibility of love for those humans who ate other humans.[29] For those who avowed the existence in certain parts of the world of a cannibalism practiced by social sanction, rather than a situational cannibalism resulting from extremity of circumstance, this humanity came to have an emphatically racialized character. The popular tales of shipwreck cannibalism among European crews in the first half of the nineteenth century consequently distinguished between "the reprehensible desire of dark-skinned beings and the piteous need of whites."[30] Even for those who dismissed the possibility of cannibalism outside the context of famine, and therefore of the existence of the cannibal qua cannibal, the rhetorical figure of cannibal consumption was immensely productive for its capacity to stage a certain imaginative and ethical limit. Even for those authors who came to locate cannibalism within Europe itself, the act lost little of its character of civilizational otherness in this relocation, being used, for instance, in Britain at the end of the eighteenth century to highlight the differences between British moderation and French barbarousness.[31] Edmund Burke's turn to the rhetoric of cannibal appetites to describe the predations of the revolutionaries in France served as the most apt figuration of the event as moral extremity.[32]

A resonant concept-metaphor with a long history in the production of colonial difference and racial and sexual panic, cannibalism has also featured more counterintuitively in another strain of cultural critique, now centuries old. This has tended to invert the terms of the commonsensical racial-civilizational logic of cannibalism, emphasizing among other things what Alan Bewell has termed "imperial *geophagy*" rather than anthropophagy.[33] Cannibalism comes in this inversion to be not the consumption of human flesh but asymmetrical extraction and exploitation. This permits the Jonathan Swift of "A Modest Proposal" to satirize English maltreatment of the Irish, and the Joseph Conrad of *Heart of*

Darkness to portray the cannibalism of a Kurtz, a cannibalism that is an ironic supplement to an oratory both disembodied and lofty and a contrast to the self-restraint of the cannibal crew of the *Nellie*. In such a reading cannibal culture is now the peculiar property and the continuing patrimony of a West that has produced slavery, colonialism, and capitalism and their forms of rapacious consumerism.[34]

In the instances cited above, the identity of the cannibal might change, attaching itself variously to colonized or colonizing subjects, but the meaning of cannibalism itself remains more or less axiomatic and uninterrupted. For Derrida, on the other hand, anthropophagy has quite another resonance, one involving a form of incorporation of the other that is not reducible only to the violent reproduction of sameness. In this he follows in the wake of those like Michel de Montaigne and Sigmund Freud, for whom anthropophagy has functioned less as an abomination than as a parabolic instantiation of unexpected somatic and ethical engagement with the other. For Freud the mythic narrative of the primal horde that engages in cannibalism is an explanation of the origin of civilization and the emergence of a social contract among males through the deferred incorporation of the father's prohibitions. Anthropophagy becomes for him a figure of the idealization, incorporation, and mourning of and for the other that founds community.[35] As such, anthropophagy functions quite as effectively, Derrida suggests (though without specific recourse to Freud), as a rendition of the ethical and affective organization of nominally nonanthropophagous communities as of anthropophagous ones. The question is not whether one should ingest the other but how this should done, since all feeding involves humans in economies of hospitality of a sort, of giving to and receiving from the other, of the interiorization of the other as well as a submission to incorporation by the other; that is what "eating well" is. It follows that the refusal to partake with or of the other is an important breakdown in or rejection of ethical reciprocity with the other.

Aversion

Such communion, which involves both a partaking with others and a transubstantiation of food or rather trope into flesh, is more often than not a vexed affair. In fact, communities are perhaps as frequently built on principles of distaste, distance, and avoidance as on taste and consumption; there is a primordial violence that inaugurates group bonds. Catherine Gallagher's analysis of the place of the potato in late eighteenth-century political economic discourse and in the bread riots of hungry English working folk considers one instance of the modes of rejection that are generative of community. She notes that E. P. Thompson's assumption, in his famous essay on the clash between an extant moral economy and an emerging cash nexus, about "the reasonableness of popular action and its conformity to an implied human norm" leads him to overlook the place of the potato and its status as a "limit food" or nonfood in the representation of food, hunger, entitlement, and grievance. Reintroducing the potato into the alimentary economy of the rioters gives a somewhat different inflection to their actions. Reacting as much against the possibility of having to turn to the potato, the freely available food of the Irish peasantry, as they were avowing and maintaining the "bread nexus" of long institutional and social standing in England, English workers demonstrated their aversion to Irish modes of consumption even as they rejected a further proletarianization of their own condition.[36]

In the subcontinent, as we shall see in chapter 1, Anglo-Indians were similarly, if somewhat less excusably, anxious to draw a *cordon sanitaire* between their own pristine bodies and local practices of feeding and digestion. But in some cases alimentary mingling and even dependence were unavoidable. The most striking case was that of the Indian wet nurse, routinely hired to nurse white infants in a nineteenth-century context in which metropolitan middle-class norms of outsourcing infant care and nourishment coincided with medical prohibitions against Anglo-Indian nursing in the colonies.[37] Anglo-Indian mothers were utterly dependent on these wet nurses for the health of their babies in a country in which they felt incapacitated by the "debilitating climate" and in which infant mortality was higher than in Britain. They were nonetheless often ambivalent about the "economy of the borrowed breast," as Sara Suleri has felicitously described it.[38] This ambivalence was generated not so much by the fact that the wet nurses, nursing mothers themselves, sometimes lost their own babies in order to nurture their Anglo-Indian charges; at least, this is rarely mentioned.[39] Occasionally, wet nurses were suspected of feeding opium to the infants in their care in order to pacify them. But even when such dangerous supplements to the breast were not suspected, there was a vexed character to maternal milk itself, Flora Annie Steel noting with some exasperation that "some Anglo-Indians feared that the milk of 'native women' might contaminate an English child's character."[40] The problem was generally not a lack of care but the all-consuming nature of it, one that inducted the yet-unformed child into native languages, alien food habits, precocious sexual knowledge, and strong affective ties across the racial divide in ways that could not but subtract from his future Englishness. The *pharmakon* that was the wet nurse's milk thus had the potential to make a stranger of the English child, to disturb the genealogical transmission of identity.[41] Notwithstanding its crucial role in physical sustenance, milk was an emphatically nonutilitarian, prosthetic food, incapable of being an entirely innocuous component of a colonial domestic economy. More than any other substance in the Anglo-Indian alimentary economy, it highlighted the lability involved in ingestion; for the vulnerable Anglo-Indian child, feeding, especially at the breast, was to put on a form of dangerous and ethically transformative knowledge, to be changed rather than simply fortified. Hence the familiar phenomenon of dispatching very young Anglo-Indian children, some as young as three, to native lands they had never seen, of which Rudyard Kipling writes with such pathos in "Baa, Baa, Black Sheep."[42]

Anglo-Indian anxieties about the particulate, divisible, and racially unstable character of their somatic identity and about the biomoral substances that tended to recast it should make one rethink to some degree at least the received wisdom about the ingestive orders of the subcontinent. Generally speaking, the alimentary and digestive economy of the British who came to South Asia has always been considered to be worlds apart from the ones they encountered in the subcontinent. Indeed, the context of social dining was routinely posed as one exemplary instance of what kept rulers and subjects firmly segregated, orthodox Hindus and dietarily circumspect Muslims, who eschewed pork and alcohol, refusing the pollutions that dining with casteless, omnivorous, hard-drinking Europeans and Christians would entail. Indian men, both Hindu and Muslim, were marked by an economy of withholding, of a refusal of the homosocial traffic in food, here accorded the same status as the traffic in women— "We cannot dine with you and we cannot see your women, and therefore there can be no real friendship between us" was the charge commonly leveled by British men at Indian men—and therefore outside any kind of social or ethicopolitical economy.[43]

Indeed, it was a commonplace in the colonial period, as it still is to a significant degree today, that ideas about food and the rules governing the ways in which it is handled and exchanged are formulated with extraordinary minuteness in a Brahminical Hindu culture of caste purity and pollution.[44] The institution of caste, which traditionally has provided the grammar for such alimentary arrangements, has functioned in Indological literature, from Max Mueller and Max Weber to Louis Dumont, as "the central problematic of Indian society," incorporating and sometimes displacing related categories of identity and difference such as religion and class.[45] As the anthropologists Ronald Inden, Arjun Appadurai, Gloria Goodwin Raheja, Nicholas Dirks, and others have observed, this led to "a substantialized view of caste (reified as India's essential institution) and an idealized view of Hinduism, regarded as the religious foundation of caste."[46] Such an Indological fix on caste as the epistemological key to India's otherness was inseparable from a British colonial policy that had, as early as the eighteenth century, pressed ancient Sanskrit texts of putative Hindu law into service for the governance of India by indigenous rather than foreign value-systems.[47]

From the nineteenth century on, textual evidence of caste rules and practice came to be supplemented with ethnographic information, information that was inseparable from the logic of rule. Bernard Cohn notes, for instance, the interest in scrutability that undergirded colonial administrators' firsthand compendia of caste organization: "In the first instance, a caste was a 'thing,' an entity, which was concrete and measurable; above all it had definable characteristics—endogamy, commensality rules, fixed occupation, common ritual practices. . . . This way of thinking about a particular caste was useful to the administrator, because it gave the illusion of knowing the people; he did not have to differentiate too much among individual Indians—a man was a Brahman, and Brahmans had certain characteristics. . . . India was seen as a collection of castes; the particular picture was different in any given time and place, but India was a sum of its parts and the parts were castes. . . . The 'official' census-based view of caste therefore saw the system as one of separate castes and their customs."[48] This is undoubtedly too censorious a view of the instrumentalization that is an inescapable part of any production of knowledge. But it does underscore the drive toward the schematization and management of forms of otherness, including the other's forms of knowability, that colonial rule generated; it clarifies what one scholar has called "the effective governmentalization of the colonial state by means of caste."[49] This schematization led, as Raheja notes, to a view of castes as "isolable communities with their own customs, histories, and marriage rules" rather than as entities bound in mutual, if unequal, interrelationship.[50] Such a view of caste as uncontested and unchanging could not easily accommodate any sense of the historicity of caste or indeed the considerable histories of *dalit* (untouchable) and non-Brahmin critique, mobilization, and struggle in the nineteenth century and the twentieth (to say nothing of earlier periods).[51]

To suggest, in contradistinction to such received views of the singularity of caste, that purity and pollution or indeed hierarchy are not its invariant, dominant principles, or that vast numbers of people on the subcontinent are not hailed by Brahminical norms, is not to propose that caste was an invention of the colonial order, as Nicholas Dirks sometimes comes close to doing, or that caste has not functioned, historically and in the present, as an instrument of subordination and humiliation, especially of those ranked low in a caste hierarchy. Rather, it is to indicate that within a nonegalitarian order there are "multiple configurations of caste, . . . multiple hierarchies, and multiple perspectives on social life."[52] An atomistic view of the caste subject and caste community has come to be challenged, notably by McKim Marriott, by a somewhat different emphasis upon the permeability, circulation, and transformation that mark caste being and caste relationship rather than an absolutist notion of hierarchy or of purity. Marriott's well-known discussion of the constitution of body and person in Hindu India has described the transactional and transformational logic that governs the relation between persons in India, persons that he consequently characterizes as "dividual" (rather than "individual") and highly permeable clusters of code and substance: "To exist, dividual persons absorb heterogeneous material influences. They must also give out from themselves particles of their own coded substances—essences, residues, or other active influences—that may then reproduce in others something of the nature of the persons in whom they have originated. Persons engage in transfers of bodily substance-codes through parentage, through marriage . . . , and through services and other kinds of interpersonal contacts. They transfer coded food substances by way of trade, payment, alms, feasts, or other prestations."[53] Such traffic, it should be noted, is outside any liberal-egalitarian logic of modularity or likeness. These transactions between "dividuals" or between hierarchically arranged segments such as castes, families, and so on are carefully governed by rules about the direction in which coded substances are permitted to flow, though directions can change with context. Each maintains its identity and uniqueness through forms of exclusiveness (which are also forms of context-specific hierarchization), though these entities are also interrelated and synthesized through complex processes of receiving and giving into increasingly broader social bodies.

Transaction and exchange among like and unlike biomoral subjects were bypassed in a colonial taxonomy of caste by a quite different emphasis: the contrast, implicit or explicit, between the freely choosing moral agent of modern European civilization and the native subject of caste, "incarcerated," in Appadurai's terms, within an intransigent moral and intellectual ecology.[54] Without using the language of incarceration, Dumont's classic text *Homo Hierarchicus* in fact contrasts the *homo hierarchicus* of Hinduism with the *homo aequalis* of the West.[55] Yet the meliorative actions of a putatively liberalizing colonial state sometimes enhanced the rigidity of caste restrictions in the course of enacting legal reforms. The Widow Remarriage Act of 1856, which universalized upper-caste gendered restrictions on inheritance, maintenance, and custody and imposed them on lower-caste women in the course of legalizing Hindi widow remarriage, is a case in point.[56] If, as Anupama Rao observes, the colonial state acted "erratically" in its attempts to expand the freedoms of the historically downtrodden "by bringing them into the domain of Western progress and improvement," this may have been a function both of its failures to anticipate the results of its legislation and of its own desire to maintain caste privileges in at least some instances.[57]

Moreover, as the instance in the preceding section of Anglo-Indian fears about the dangers of the borrowed breast indicates, vigilance over the biomoral substance of unequally constituted subjects was not an exclusively Hindu or Muslim property. If, as Dirks maintains, caste in its present or official form is a modern construction that cannot be fully understood outside the context of British colonialism, it might also be possible to suggest that Anglo-Indians were themselves hailed by caste in unforeseen ways. It is no accident that it is the young "country-born" Irish lad Kimball O'Hara, rather than the Indians, who attends to the landscape of the Grand Trunk Road as a gigantic and endlessly fascinating compendium of caste.[58] But Anglo-Indians did not simply know caste, they also made it their own, both in the sense of formalizing it through the modes of applied law and socioreligious taxonomy and in the sense of submitting to its mandates. That they often used the metaphor to define their own deeply hierarchical society, headed by the Brahmins of the covenanted civil service, is well known.[59] At times they even seemed actuated by a certain form of caste competitiveness with the original subjects of caste; the events of 1857, for instance, make this cannibalization of and by caste visible (see chapter 1).

What these examples help to highlight is the logic of permeability rather than of inviolability that often marks the workings of an alimentary order. In the instance above, Anglo-Indians come to be possessed by caste. Conversely, it is analytically helpful to investigate a South Asian gastropolitics and gastropoetics (to the degree that it can be held apart from an Anglo-Indian alimentary order) not so much in terms of an Indic focus that is historically immutable and restrictively defined—though there is no doubt Indic texts and practices of alimentary and commensal permission and prohibition are entirely crucial to such analysis—as in terms of contingency, encounter, translation, contestation, and amalgamation. At almost all points the purported particularities of a South Asian alimentary grammar are interlinked with and illumined by non–South Asian modes of alimentary discourse. For instance, a consideration of Indian famine needs to be vectored through a broader imperial understanding of poverty and relief policy; famine relief so-called in Ireland thus brings similar endeavors in India into legibility. Likewise, Gandhi's ethics of everyday embodied practice are not really fully explicable except in terms of a global conversation on consumption, ethics, and spiritual and somatic perfectibilism in the late nineteenth century and early twentieth, with its emphasis on the cultivation of technologies of the self-sufficient masculine body. In the case of the celebrated gastronome Madhur Jaffrey as well, questions of citizenship, assimilation, westernization, and authenticity come to be precipitated through the experience of diasporic voyaging in London and through a prior British investment in the glamour of spices.

Even or perhaps especially in the production of states and conditions that supposedly distinguish an Indian alimentary particularity—vegetarianism, famine, spices, even caste practices of proximity and avoidance—there is the trace of foreign encounter, ingestion and occasional indigestion, that is, metamorphosis both expected and unlooked-for. Can one name this encounter or exchange a form of (Derridean) anthropophagy, an inescapable and inescapably violent confrontation with the other into which one is inserted outside the structures of consent? If the bodily intervention that is alimentation involves injury and fragmentation, might it also involve some form of prosthesis, something both alien and critically necessary to function? The examples above are a reminder that nonvampiric, that is to say, nonidealist, eating can suggest new rather than only self-evident and censorious possibilities for thinking about alimentation's promise of assimilation *and* self-derangement.

Eating Well?

If the colonial order described above was marked by forms of disgust and deprivation, then can one think of postcoloniality as the promise of eating well, both in the sense of abnegating dearth and in the sense of partaking in a relationship of hospitality with the other? The question of famine has famously served, as it does for the economist and moral philosopher Amartya Sen, as a paradigmatic instance of the injustices of colonial rule and the promise of redress that its abolition offers; hence his oft-cited claim that famines occur in totalitarian rather than democratic dispensations. Famine was one of the notorious features of colonial rule, British rule in India being bookended by two notable instances, the Bengal famine of 1769–70 and that of 1943–44. At the beginning of the twentieth century Indian critics of the political economy of British colonialism took pains to draw attention to the policies that produced such catastrophes, Romesh Chunder Dutt in particular emphasizing the increased revenue demands made upon agriculturalists in the nineteenth century. They noted that even the Bengal famine of 1770, which caused a loss of ten million lives and the depopulation of severely affected areas, did not impede the work of tax collectors. In 1771, in the aftermath of the famine year, tax revenues went up because of the intense pressures to maximize the profits of the East India Company.[60] Sen does not focus on state policy as much as Dutt, and he does not necessarily use the term *postcolonial* to describe his vision of a just order; his preferred terms are *democracy* and *totalitarianism*. But since he uses the Bengal famine of 1943–44, on the verge of a subcontinental passage out of colonialism, as an exemplary instance of the failure of state responsibility, it is not entirely unjustifiable to see its historical context as exemplary of the totalitarianism he denounces.

The subject of famine brings into visibility in a striking way questions of equity and access as well as questions of normality and anomaly or crisis. Does famine constitute a rupture in the existing moral economy, a breakdown of normal modes of access, entitlement, and redress? Or does it bring into scandalous relief everyday forms of poverty and inequality? Does the definition, by analysts and state alike, of famine as a problem of scale (and subsumable therefore within an idiom of crisis) obscure quotidian experiences of alimentary and medical dearth? Sen has argued persuasively that modern famines are not caused in any fundamental way by simple lack of food or other ecological disturbances such as droughts and floods but can sometimes occur even when there is no diminution in the quantities of food available. Droughts, floods, crop disease, and shortfalls in production might create the proximate conditions for the onset of famine, but they cannot explain why people come to starve, sometimes to death. Indeed, the history of modern famines reveals that these phenomena are often "boom famines." Far from being a leveler, famine has generally tended to exacerbate extant forms of inequality and exploitation, including gendered ones.[61]

If famine was the sign of a colonial, nonrepresentative alimentary and moral order, postcoloniality, or decolonization, was meant to effect its reversal. This was an urgent task, given India's unique status after 1947 as the world's largest democracy that was also home to the largest number of poor people. But the emphasis on food security in the planning of the postcolonial state, especially in its early years—a priority that might seem to accentuate Sen's emphasis on the moral economy of democracy—has failed decisively to curb conditions of alimentary inequality and alimentary violence, including hunger and malnutrition, and its record has been widely understood to be "meager, disappointing, and failure-ridden."[62] The postcolonial dispensation was intended from the start to be the principal, if not the one and only, agent for the material and social uplift of its citizens and for providing relief under conditions of catastrophe. Many of the functions of education, medical services, and social welfare that the colonial state had been willing to leave to voluntarist and associational groups, including political organizations, came now to be the function of the state, which was vested with a representative and a pastoral, or at least meliorative, character toward those it was expected to hail as its constituents rather than its subjects.[63] The desire for political legitimacy thus necessitated a partially welfarist orientation. This was aimed where rural populations were concerned at redressing some of the inequalities in the ownership and use of land, an orientation that was often at odds with the state's alliances with dominant groups in a highly feudalized rural sector and a strong developmental imperative that occasionally sought to sidestep the messier aspects of democracy. As Niraja Gopal Jayal, who describes the Indian state as being interventionist rather than welfarist, notes, "[The] poverty alleviation strategy . . . was a project aimed at ridding society, especially rural society, of acute poverty, rather than any more ambitious project of enhancing, much less maximising, welfare. . . . It sought to fulfil its rather limited aims without in any way touching, much less damaging, the interests of the rural rich, or disturbing the rural power structure."[64]

Besides, as Partha Chatterjee usefully observes, these forms of welfare rarely if ever entailed any active participation by the poor and dispossessed in the name of a moral claim upon the state as its citizens. He makes an important conceptual distinction between citizens and populations. The first is defined as an ideal bourgeois type, vested with the associational powers of civil society and the moral and legal privilege of partaking of the sovereignty of the state. Populations, he says, can be the subjects of governmentality and are "empirical categories of people with specific social or economic attributes that are relevant for the administration of developmental or welfare policies." They can be identified and affirmatively acted upon as the addressees of a welfare based upon a cost-benefit analysis which is often coded as charity rather than rights-based redistributive justice. But such welfare, often of a distinctly ad hoc variety, belongs to a different category of democratic access from the moral legitimacy of the citizen who has the right to have rights, as it were.[65] This weakly and contradictorily welfarist orientation of the state is further compromised by its strong predilection, especially in matters of law and order, for techniques of governance inherited from an authoritarian colonial order. Ranajit Guha has characterized such techniques as the exercise of "dominance without hegemony."[66]

The question of subalternity remains stubbornly lodged within the alimentary and moral economy of the postcolonial order. Mahasweta Devi has written acerbically about the lack of fit between the state's languages of statistical triumph (fueled by the Green Revolution) and the inescapability of famine for the most disenfranchised of India's poor, whose sufferings exceed any available language of sociological realism. If subalternity has been seen, by Antonio Gramsci as well as by the Subaltern Studies group, perhaps most notably by Spivak, as constituting a certain kind of epistemological and representational limit, the work of Mahasweta underlines the imaginative and ethical effortfulness involved in thinking the question of subaltern being and subaltern embodiment. Her work suggests that material on appetite, digestion, and pollution can serve as a remarkably apposite means of examining questions of broad ethical import, including the question of responsibility to non-like others. As we have seen, to eat, to abstain deliberately from eating, or to have to go without eating is to pose questions of identification, desire, differ-ence, and responsibility—responsibility to other humans at the very edge of human/nonhuman being, including the monstrously human or ab-human.[67] It is also to be inserted into responsibility with respect to non-human animals and sometimes to specters and gods, all of whom partake in one form or another in the ethically charged and complex questions of sacrifice—whether self-sacrifice or other-sacrifice—manifest in an une-qual alimentary order.

Alimentary Tracts

How do appetites, hungers, compulsions, excesses, intoxications, aver-sions, and addictions help to institute, enact, or unsettle one's sense of identities and histories in the colonial period and the postcolonial aftermath? *Alimentary Tracts* seeks to underscore the productivity of recu-perating and analyzing often-overlooked social and bodily grammars of colonial encounter and postcolonial development—grammars that can substantially recast existing accounts of events, communities, and per-sons. As I have suggested above, the strong, continuing interest in the forms of embodiment under colonialism has not fully incorporated the ways in which questions of alimentation performed a critical rather than an epiphenomenal role in matters of bodied experimentation, trans-formation, and retrenchment. In thinking of the representational and car-nal economies of the contact zone, whether in colonialism or in postcolo-niality, such scholarship has analyzed brilliantly the psychopolitical and aesthetic entailments of systems of racial taxonomy and spatial and sexual segregation, all of which are frantically policed and regularly breached. What this book proposes is that the alimentary tract is a boundary, a fiercely policed but also a contested and hotly trafficked one, just as much as any dividing line that might separate the *medina* from the settlers' town in *The Wretched of the Earth*. Who eats and with whom, who starves, and what is rejected as food are fundamental to colonial and postcolonial making—and unmaking. It is crucial to examine the nuances of the tropo-logical language of alimentation, especially as it is used to think through the complex entailments of a congeries of articulated concepts: violence, desire, intimacy, assimilation, reproduction, transformation, subaltern-ization, and justice. This is what the book seeks to underline, even as it recognizes that the palate cannot be considered except within a broader consideration of embodiment, one that would involve its relation to other senses or vehicles of incorporation and transformation, including especially olfaction, touch, hearing, and sight. The book thus applies itself to a scrutiny of the mundane and embodied, the aesthetic, and the ethico-political aspects of a colonial and postcolonial alimentary order. Four chapters address themselves to disgust, abstention, dearth, and appetite, which function simultaneously as topoi and tropes of alimentation.

The events and protagonists that instantiate these topoi and tropes also correspond in a very loose way to various historical stages in a chronology of a global modernity: colonialism, nationalism, decolonization and postcoloniality, and diaspora and globalization under late capitalism. They encompass iconic figures and moments of explicit historical crisis but, just as importantly, the banal dietary economies of the everyday. The first station on this very broad historical arc is the so-called Mutiny of 1857, memorable as one of the most spectacular instances of anticolonial insurgency in the nineteenth century. Despite the relatively small number of European casualties sustained during the uprising (the mortality figures on the side of the Indians have never been tallied up in any convincing fashion), especially in comparison with those of other military conflicts such as the Crimean War that was its immediate predecessor, it registered in the popular and official (Anglo-Indian and British) imagination as one of the most terrifying and unforgettable events of an otherwise robustly imperial century.[68] For many commentators, colonial and postcolonial, the syllabaries of caste abomination marshaled by the mutineers and their civilian rebel counterparts were the accents of an increasingly archaic social and ethical order, one that had perforce to give way before the inexorable engine of modernization that was the British empire in India. Caste here is the figure and institution that signifies all that is backward about the Indian as a sociopolitical and material body, marked by improper ingestions, improper aversions, and improper evacuations. And yet, while the Anglo-Indian sought to cultivate an aesthetics of distance and disgust—a modern and rational disgust, grounded in hygiene rather than in the perverse logic of religious pollution—from the Indian, these distinctions came to break down in an event of shared bodily trauma and shared alimentary fantasies. The Mutiny is in some senses a textbook case of the workings of caste fantasy, not simply for the Indians who were scripted as its proper devotees but also, and just as crucially, for Anglo-Indians. The experience of somatic disturbance, including hunger, filth, overcrowding, disease, and decomposition, served to pull the Anglo-Indian into the orbit of the other in a way that disallowed the possibility of remaining himself; it established the Anglo-Indian as the subject of caste at the very moment and through the same events that served to accentuate the hyphen that held apart Anglo and Indian.

Continuities as well as ironic juxtapositions mark the sequence of the chapters. The economies of excess, avoidance, and intimacy that mark the Anglo-Indian experience of distaste and despair are followed by a chapter on abstinence, which is both the obverse of and similar to excess. It speaks in ways expected and unexpected to the hyperbolic performative idioms of one of the twentieth century's most prominent vegetarians, Mohandas Karamchand Gandhi, also known as the mahatma. I should emphasize that vegetarianism is not in itself an instance of alimentary abstinence unless one takes carnivory as the condition of alimentary normality; many millions of people all over the world, but especially in India, inhabit a normal, everyday vegetarianism throughout their lives with no sense that it involves any form of sacrifice of pleasure, health, or indeed variety. But for Gandhi vegetarianism was very emphatically the cornerstone of an ethics of abstinence. The chapter maps a trajectory of his gastropolitics, from the carnivorous mandate of the early years, during which he associated meat eating with nationalist duty, to the diasporic discovery of vegetarianism in London and finally to the carefully elaborated alimentary rigors and public fasts of the later years. All of this stresses how profoundly somatic Gandhi's "experiments in truth" were and how pronounced was his belief that self-rule at a national level was meaningless without self-rule at the most banal and intimate bodily level. The chapter simultaneously scrutinizes the gendered familial and intersubjective entailments of a Gandhian vegetarianism. While his vegetarianism has normally been considered—when it is given any consideration at all—as an instantiation of ahimsaic (nonviolent/noninjurious) virtue, his repeated alimentary crises around the care and feeding of family members suggest that the (self-)sacrificial logic of a consciously chosen masculine vegetarianism is vexed and ad hoc rather than resolved once and for all. The evidence of his biography and his writings suggests that the mouth can function as an instrument of violence, not only in its incorporations but also in its abstinences. Sacrifice here involves a staging of ambiguous effects rather than a definitive refusal of the violence of slaughter and the violence of ingestion.

Chapters 3 and 4 span the extremities of appetite that mark the state that is denominated the postcolonial, encompassing famine on the one hand and gastronomy on the other. The third chapter, on the terrifying logic of hunger, famine, disenfranchisement, and disembodiment in postcolonial India, accentuates the importance of hunger and famine and the fears and fantasies associated with them as decisive, emblematic forces in Indian postcoloniality. This chapter devotes particular attention to Mahasweta Devi's hunger fictions, especially "Shishu" ("Children," 1979) and *Pterodactyl, Puran Sahay, and Pirtha* (1982). Written in the aftermath of the failures of decolonization and the crises of postcolonial state legitimacy dramatized most prominently by the brutal repression of the Naxalite movement against feudal exploitation of the rural poor and by Indira Gandhi's declaration of Emergency (1975–77), these fictions point to some of the most wrenching failures of decolonization.[69] Mahasweta's fictions dramatize the lack of access by the landless low-caste and tribal poor of the Indian hinterland to the bare necessities for survival, including water, salt, and basic food. None of these deficits of food or of justice can even be acknowledged by a postcolonial state that prides itself upon its enlightenment, even as it seeks to act affirmatively upon subaltern subjects who remain stubbornly outside the limits of official legibility and the rational calculus of uplift and charity. A consideration of Mahasweta's work draws attention to the enormous allegorical fecundity of famine, and its capacity to stage questions about responsibility, humanness, and the character of subaltern being. It does so by foregrounding the ways in which figures of the nonhuman—the ghost in "Shishu" and the pterodactyl in *Pterodactyl*—become for Mahasweta the most emblematic and peremptory figures of famine. Realism itself encounters its limit in the representation of famine; ghost stories, science fiction tales, animal allegories, and gothic fictions become the paradigmatic accounts of catastrophe and moral failure. These stories also permit one to ponder forms of witnessing and revelation that cannot be rendered into the usual modes of moral accounting; they compel one to confront the character of one's responsibility to beings who exist outside the limits of a liberal discourse of rights, equality, universality, and intelligibility.

The fourth chapter, which is about the emergence of an Indian gastronomy and an aesthetics of plenitude in a late capitalist diaspora, trains its attention upon the opposite bound of a postcolonial map of alimentation. This bound is marked by a turn away from the aversions, scarcity, and ascetic habitus of a colonial past and a postcolonial present in favor of a metaphorics of abundance. It is marked too by the possibility of auto-ethnography (rather than the unrepresentability that typifies the victims of famine). This chapter examines the writings, screen performances, and iconic status of Madhur Jaffrey, conceivably the greatest popular authority on Indian culinary arts in the United States and in Britain and a person who functions spectacularly as an exemplary figure of the nation in its moment of global emergence. Jaffrey's emergence is keyed in crucial ways to the deployment of an idiom of culinary authenticity and culinary corruption, the latter indexed for her by the ubiquitous association in the West of the terms *curry* and *curry powder* with subcontinental cuisine. Spices, once the raw material for a European vision of resplendent faraway worlds, come to be refurbished for her as a trope of authenticity, sequestered from the satisfactions, both crass and pathetic, of curry powder. As part of the drive to install authenticity, her texts seek to rekindle in her British and North American readers as well as in newly diasporic subcontinental ones an imaginative and culinary investment in spices. Yet if food serves as parabolic national form in her texts, the form through which dramas of national and familial duplicity and devotion are enacted, a careful parsing of the performative idioms of her screen performances and cookbooks supplements and queers a desired logic of nostalgia and authenticity. A sanitized diasporic vision of spices, historical fidelity, and pluralist nationalist longing gives way, perhaps ironically, to the staying power of curry and curry powder, so that the mistress of spices in her latest incarnation cannot but succumb to a British attachment to the institution of curry. A focus on her food writing and on her star image thus serves as an apt occasion for a thickening and rethinking of the historical hungers and the fantasmatic landscapes of alimentation with which the history of colonial expansion commences.

Coda

We went in search of a lonely spot by the river, and there I saw, for the first time in my life—meat. There was baker's [leavened] bread also. I relished neither. The goat's meat was as tough as leather. I simply could not eat it. I was sick and had to leave off eating.

I had a very bad night afterwards. A horrible nightmare haunted me. Every time I dropped off to sleep it would seem as though a live goat were bleating inside me, and I would jump up full of remorse.

—M. K. GANDHI, *Autobiography*

A focus on the alimentary tracts of colonial and postcolonial India has several lessons for students of literary, feminist, cultural, and area studies, some obvious, others less so. It enables us most obviously to scrutinize forms of soul making and self-fashioning that we have come to see as absolutely crucial to colonial transformation as situated simultaneously in theaters of the flesh and of the psyche, rather than the latter alone. Its absorption in banal and ephemeral practice sometimes provides a novel purchase on figures, texts, and events usually framed by less vulgar concerns. Perhaps most importantly, it insists that a scrutiny of a grammar of ingestion and avoidance involves an attentiveness to the complex moral structure of embodiment. And finally, it intimates that a testing of ethics, politics, and aesthetics upon the tongue can sometimes confound our received sense of just what eating, digestion, violence, assimilation, and relationship might be. If all eating is, as thinkers as distinct as Gandhi, the Jain philosophers, and Derrida have contended, a consumption of and with the other (one that is anthropophagic, in Derrida's terms), is such consumption always parasitic, a battening upon the flesh of the other without any form of reciprocity or exchange? If so, the ancient Jain practice of *samadhi maran* (fasting to death as a form of enlightened practice) may be the only form of ethical living—that is to say, ethical living must be a form of ethical dying, at least for humans. Even this inexorably principled stance is predicated on the supposition that the body is properly one's own and can appropriately be devoted to autophagy; but, as we shall see in the following pages, autophagy is not separable in any self-evident fashion from the consumption of or violence against others.

Moreover, abstaining from the consumption of the nonhuman or human animal other may be based on something other or something more than the desire to exist in a relation of noninjury to the ecologies one inhabits. As the instances drawn from the gastropolitics of caste, whether Indian or Anglo-Indian, and the dietary reform movements of the nineteenth century in Britain, Russia, and the United States should show, abstention can be and often is deployed for the purpose of self-purification and the purgation of an abjected other; it is mobilized all too often as a powerful precaution against one's vulnerability to capture or contamination by the other. Thus James Laidlaw, in his study of Jain asceticism, observes that the guarded Jain response to the accidental killing even of microbial life is not so much a safeguard against killing as it is an abjection of excessive life, the teeming world of *samsara* (the phenomenal world) represented by the microbes.[70] If, on the other hand, one's consumption of the other, whether human or nonhuman, is symbiotic rather than only a form of destructive absorption or self-destruction, our sense of who assimilates and who is assimilated and what that assimilation might involve—transformation? dyspepsia?—is profoundly deranged. Consumption may signify mastery over the other, but it may also signify one's subjection to the other, something that cannot entirely be refused. Thus the adolescent Gandhi's forbidden, abortive meal of goat's flesh results in a temporary becoming animal (though through an uncanny and guilt-stricken proximity to cooked butcher's meat more than through any substantive form of ingestion), as he feels and hears a goat bleating in his stomach. Is this a nightmare? An experience of possession? A rendering monstrous of the human body through a rearrangement of its morphology? Is he addressed by the goat? Or does the goat express itself through him? The alimentary tract that speaks in a goat's tongue offers no straightforward lesson but one that has to be strenuously and sometimes counterintuitively learned.

1

Disgust

FOOD, FILTH, AND

ANGLO-INDIAN FLESH IN 1857

Introduction: Traumas of the Mouth

Perhaps there are few revolutions and rebellions in the eighteenth century
and the nineteenth that are not subtended by a belly politics—as witness
the French revolution of 1789, the Taiping rebellion, and the food riots in
late eighteenth-century England that produced E. P. Thompson's famous
formulation about the bread nexus and the cash nexus.[1] Nonetheless,
even when placed within such a concatenation, there is a kind of fantastical excess associated with the gastropolitical imaginary of the event
known as the Indian Mutiny of 1857–58. Historians as well as literary
critics have taken sometimes embarrassed note of the often fantastic
phenomena—tales of greased cartridges, perambulating and encrypted
chapatis, rumors of contaminated foods, and reports of raped and mutilated Englishwomen—that have marked the narrative of the Mutiny. In
practically all the histories, journalism, and fiction of the colonial period
and even of the period after 1947 two objects in particular, the greased
cartridges and the migratory chapati, have played an inescapable if refrac-
tory role. As Homi Bhabha has noted, these have constituted the totemic
foods of the Mutiny and as such require a brief gloss.[2] The proximate
cause of mutiny has typically been understood to be the introduction of
greased cartridges for the new Enfield rifles, cartridges greased with beef
and pork fat that had to be bitten off before being inserted into the
rifles—and that therefore were obnoxious to both high-caste Hindu and
Muslim sepoys of the Native Infantry regiments of the British Indian
army. The cartridges, combined with rumors of contaminated food sup-

plies and a mysterious circulation of chapatis that apparently served as a signal to mobilization, have generally served as the *mise-en-scène* of the events of 1857–58. They have been glossed by many colonial commentators and historians as well as by some postcolonial Indian ones as symptoms of a deeply reactionary, feudal, and outmoded social order struggling against the doctrines of modern social equality and material progress embedded in the reformist impulses of the East India Company in midcentury. Most typically, these irreducibly somatic and vulgar details have been read in terms of a clash of civilizations that finds its most expressive form in the institution of caste, the most striking and non-negotiable sign of a Hindu/Indian difference from the subcontinent's colonial rulers.[3]

Writers of a more critical cast have objected from the beginning to Sir John Lawrence's official finding after the Mutiny that it was caused primarily by the cartridges and secondarily by poor discipline in the army; they have objected as well to the trivialization of the causes of the revolt by reducing them to the opposition between religious fanaticism, represented by mutinous Indians, and modern values and modern technology, represented by the British and the East India Company.[4] In Ranajit Guha's words, they have sought to establish cartridges and chapatis as red herrings rather than as causes of the Mutiny and the civil rebellion that accompanied it.[5] Nonetheless, every tale of the Mutiny must reckon with cartridges, rumors of contaminated flour, and chapatis before proceeding to more seemingly profound causes. They are clearly excessive, absurd, embarrassing even, and in some cases inexplicable; yet no history of the Mutiny can help passing through them. The very ubiquity and narrative force of these trivial details, which are the detritus, indeed the indigestible part, of any sober accounting, are the focal point of this chapter. Indeed I will suggest that the British or Anglo-Indian historian or writer's focus on the Mutiny as a peculiar problem of cartridges and chapatis—and therefore of caste embodiment and caste anxiety—exists in a complex, productive relationship with Anglo-Indian experiences of bodily purity and bodily violation during the Mutiny. The digestive troping of rebellion and counterinsurgency may be something more than accidental or eccentric; like the equally charged trope of the ravished English lady, to which it is occasionally linked, its workings may illuminate one's sense of the irreducibly embodied and irreducibly shared vernaculars of rule and rebellion.

Of the scholars who have taken these illicit or anomalous forms of orality seriously, a few stand out. In *Elementary Aspects of Peasant Insurgency*

(1983), his remarkable work on subaltern modes of understanding and contesting authority, Guha identifies rumor, or orality more broadly, as a mode of communication specific to preliterate peasant cultures.[6] He notes the several aspects of rumor—its anonymity and ambiguity, its improvisatory character as it "leaps from tongue to tongue," its relationship to tale and myth, its unverifiability, its centrality in insurrection, and its creation of comradeship in transmission—that separate it from news.[7] All of these qualities were seen as offenses against rationality, utility, and clarity in the official accounts of the Mutiny and as the part of the adulterations of a native bazaar that trafficked in shoddy goods, illicit sexualities, and loose talk. The chapati—read by some as a time-honored mode called chalawa of using a ritually consecrated animal or object to act as the carrier of an epidemic, cholera in this case, and bear it outside the limits of a designated territory—also functions for Guha as part of this apparatus of preliterate and subaltern transmission of rebel agency. For him, the event of subaltern rebellion involved a form of code switching which permitted an idiom hitherto reserved for the management of disease to be pressed into service for quite another purpose.

Unlike Guha, who reads the chapati as something that came to be transformed from the semiotic of epidemic to that of rebellion in 1857–58, Bhabha reads its agency in more disseminated, less purposive ways, focusing less on its performative intentionality than on its impact upon Anglo-India. For him it is precisely the impossibility of clarifying the cryptic character of the chapatis and the archaic modes of their iteration that produced a blockage in an Anglo-Indian information order; this had a curiously powerful and hystericizing effect upon Company officials. "The organizing principle of the *sign* of the chapati is constituted," he suggests, "in the transmission of fear and anxiety, projection and panic in a form of circulation *in-between* the colonizer and the colonized. Could the agency of peasant rebellion be constituted through the 'partial incorporation' of the fantasy and fear of the Master?"[8]

All these readings gesture toward the indubitably somatic origins and vectors of the Mutiny's affect for Indians and Britons alike. As I noted in the introduction, the contact zone of the colonial period was located quite decisively in the alimentary tract. The events of 1857 in particular laid bare the ways in which the body in its moments of appetite, disgust, pollution, and purification was key to grasping the psychopolitical arrangements of the colonial order. Bread, grease, contaminated food supplies, bazaar gossip, and rumor were not the picayune details of a historically consequential event, but the very grammar—affective, symbolic, material, and political—of that history. This is true, I suggest, not just of the Hindus, Muslims, and other Indians who experienced appetites, incorporations, and aversions as the quotidian facts of colonial rule, but of Anglo-Indians as well. For Indians and Anglo-Indians alike, the experience of the Mutiny was routed through some fundamental questions of somatic and affective integrity: What did it mean to eat? What was food? And what were the dangerous supplements that threatened to metabolize it? What constituted an "eating well" in which one could not but eat the other?[9]

The Mutiny was a stunning reminder to Anglo-Indians of their status as fragile, vulnerable bodies in the subcontinent, subject in entirely unexpected ways to experiences of violence, decay, deprivation, disease, and exhaustion. Their texts of the Mutiny provide both an extraordinarily literal sense of the shock of bodily encounter and a highly charged metaphorics of bodily contamination and dissolution. Their sense of outrage was profoundly tied to the rough handling their hitherto inviolable bodies received at the hands of mutinous Indians bent upon the extermination of the colonial order and of all whites and Christians. The pedagogy of the alimentary canal enacted by these texts intimates that palate, sinew, and gut were central to the self-fashioning of both dominator and dominated in a colonial order. The proliferation of literal and vulgar details like hunger, stenches, drunkenness, flux, and wounding, in addition to cartridges and chapatis, serves to underline the often-overlooked social and embodied grammars of that process that have been described as civilizing. Reading Mutiny texts in relation to midcentury discourses (indigenous and Anglo-Indian) of ingestion, pollution, and purgation lays bare certain insistent somatic tropes, tropes that are metaphorical indices of widely shared cultural fantasies and panics about rule and rebellion, purity and pollution. What this reading proposes is that the event generated an enormous gestural repertoire of intimacy and pollution that encompassed Anglo-Indians and Indians within a shared affective and corporeal circuit and that their dietary and sexual permissions and prohibitions were braided together rather than disjunct.[10] What Bhabha has described as an iterative or mimetic logic and what in this specific case can be described as a form of alimentary circularity works to bind the Mutiny's antagonists in strange intimacies.[11]

A familiar historical event seen from the seemingly anomalous perspective of the belly or, more broadly speaking, of alimentation confirms on a surprisingly corporeal register what one knows of the severe retraction of Anglo-India from intimacy with Indian bodies and modes of life following the Mutiny. But why might this have happened? Certain texts of the events of 1857 might give a semblance of an answer, and I will examine some of them to that end. Some of the gastropolitical tracts I read here are the familiar ones: Hindu and Muslim texts of unwonted and abominated caste intimacies. This is a set of texts altogether familiar to readers of the anthropological literature on the subcontinent, which has tended to emphasize a thematics of purity and pollution. Some of the others, however, are less familiar but equally somaticized texts in which Anglo-Indians reveal themselves to be somewhat like secret sharers of allegedly irrational Hindu and Muslim fears, archaic interdictions, and ritual outrage. The racial, ethnic, and religious gap that presumably divides the Anglo from the Indian into two mutually antagonistic, distanced forces under conditions of normality breaks down under the crisis precipitated by insurgency. In its aftermath one sees Anglo-Indians reassert the boundaries of their breached, fragile subjecthood by processes of abjection and self-purification that, perhaps surprisingly, draw their inspiration from the caste-bound other. The moment of the Mutiny, then, is not so much the well-rehearsed face-off of caste and modernity as an encounter between caste anxiety and something I will denominate as caste envy.[12] This renders a new inflection to the meanings of the hyphen that separates but also welds together the *Anglo* and the *Indian* at the level of the phenomenological body and at the level of ritual and moral-cosmological ordering.

A note about the documentation of the uprising is in order here. The texts of the Mutiny are almost overwhelmingly colonial in their origin and character; even twentieth-century accounts, whether British, Anglo-Indian, or Indian, rely perforce on these. In the existing historical archives there is an insufficiency of material from Indian eyewitnesses.[13] The notable functionary Munshi Jivanlal, a go-between for the governor-general's agent at the Mughal court in Delhi, and the *kotwal* (police inspector) Mainodin Hassan Khan provided accounts of events as they unfolded in the Mughal capital; these were translated and prepared for publication by Charles Theophilus Metcalfe after the writers' deaths.[14] Of the other prominent residents of Delhi, the famous poet Ghalib left a personal account of the siege of the city and of the expulsion of its Indian population once it was retaken by British forces in September 1857.[15] Sir Syed Ahmed Khan, then a subjudge, wrote an analysis in 1858 of the causes of the Mutiny and, later, the only Indian account of the uprising in

Rohilkhand.[16] In Cawnpore, the primary evidence from the Indian side was produced by the pleader Nanak Chand, an avowed foe of the rebel leader Nana Saheb; his journal came to be regarded by many Anglo-Indian contemporaries and by Indian historians of a later date as the work of a time-server. In addition there were the depositions produced in Cawnpore for the enquiry headed by Lt. Col. G. W. Williams in 1858–59. Williams found his task a difficult one, given the animosity in the region against British rule and a reluctance to testify to involvement in actions against the sahibs; not surprisingly, the testimonies he gathered either overlapped or conflicted with one another.[17]

There are accounts of the Mutiny, though not always from the perspective of the eyewitness, in several Indian languages, especially Urdu, Marathi, and Bangla, though these feature less prominently than they ought to in one's understanding of the events of 1857–58.[18] Recently, the popular writer William Dalrymple has examined the Persian and Urdu documents, including petitions to the Mughal court, paperwork from the secretariat of the Mughal prince and anti-British leader Mirza Mughal, spies' reports, and Urdu newspapers, that comprise the Mutiny Papers in the National Archives of India in order to produce a detailed account of the last months of the reign (however minimally one must gloss that term) of the last Mughal emperor, Bahadur Shah II, and his court at Delhi.[19] While this offers a densely textured sense of developments in court circles in Delhi, it must be remembered that what is called the Mutiny was to a large degree a disaggregated set of events rather than a coherent one, with multiple centers and sometimes multiple targets of rebellion. As yet, there are no comparable or easily available records for the other centers of the Mutiny, in Lucknow, Jhansi, Bundelkhand, and Cawnpore/Kanpur. Ranged against a plethora of Anglo-Indian and British eyewitness accounts, diaries, journalism, histories, and fiction from and on 1857—practically every Anglo-Indian gentleman or lady who survived the Mutiny rushed into print, it seems—and produced, as many of these were, under conditions of the most marked duress, this is often a slender record.[20] A very small number of scholars and writers have turned to folk ballads, popular stories, and other nonelite sources; the best known among these is Mahasweta Devi's biography of one of the most highly regarded leaders of the uprising, Rani Lakshmibai of Jhansi, *Jhansir Rani* (The Queen of Jhansi, 1956).[21] A good deal, though by no means all, of the Indian understanding and experience of the Mutiny belongs to the obscurity of an irretrievably subaltern past. When this experience is recorded, it often comes to readers refracted through Anglo-Indian and British eyes. These entailments haunt any engagement with the materials of the Mutiny, this one included.

This reading is not an analysis of the events of 1857–58 in toto, but of the Anglo-Indian experience in particular. My relatively modest task here is the examination of the tropological figurations of an occurrence that acquired an almost mythic status in the nineteenth-century imagination; such an examination reinforces for us that what we know as history is both trope and event. Moreover, in acknowledgement of the mythopoetic charge with which many of the places and events of 1857–58 have been invested in the colonial accounts, I have retained specifically colonial designations and names such as Mutiny, not rebellion or war of independence, Oudh (not Awadh), and Cawnpore (not Kanpur), bypassing the nominalist questions with which modern accounts of the events almost invariably begin in order to focus on more humble topics like food, filth, and intimacy.

Making Sense of Salt

It is worth rehearsing briefly some of what are considered the important events of the Mutiny of 1857–58. Acting, it was said, under the influence of opium and bhang, a cannabis product, the sepoy Mangal Pandey of the Thirty-fourth Bengal Native Infantry regiment rose in mutiny on 29 March 1857 at Barrackpore, firing at a British officer and calling upon his comrades to join him in revolt. (Mutineers would come to be known as pandies in British Mutiny lore.) Launched in a state of intoxication, the Mutiny apparently began prematurely, ahead of an agreed-upon date for a widespread uprising, one that would coincide, some Anglo-Indian commentators suggested, with the centennial in June of the battle of Plassey, which had marked the first major British military triumph in the subcontinent. A figure of untimeliness and errancy, produced as a rebel not through historically dignified causes but through the ingestion of intoxicants, Mangal Pandey was seen as the locus classicus of a pedagogy of disappointment, one in which the native fails consistently to arrive at the appropriate terminus of historical fulfillment.[22] Rudrangshu Mukherjee describes him as "a rebel without a rebellion" insofar as he acted alone rather than in the name of a collective whose will he could have manifested.[23] When mutiny broke out among the sepoys the mutineers did not claim to have been inspired by him; they turned instead to the Mughal emperor in Delhi, who retained some of the charisma of his royal lineage and stature, notwithstanding the diminution of his power and prestige under British rule. Mangal Pandey's status as the begetter, however inept, of the rebellion was conferred not by his fellow rebels but retrospectively, by historians writing accounts of the uprising and seeking to bring temporally and geographically disparate events within a single narrative arc.[24]

In the weeks after Mangal Pandey's mistimed rebellion, at least two of the regiments that had refused to receive the greased cartridges were disbanded, and eighty-five troopers were put in irons and hauled off to prison in a display of public humiliation. On 10 May 1857, sepoys from three regiments of the Bengal Army in Meerut rose in mutiny against their European officers, killing several of them along with their families and setting fire to their houses and opening up the prisons.

. . .

While the greased cartridge was presented as the trigger for the Mutiny, other causes have been adumbrated by some nineteenth-century commentators and by twentieth-century historians. They point to the egregiously expansionist policy of the Governor-General Lord Dalhousie in the 1840s and 1850s, which led to the forcible annexation of several Indian kingdoms which were bound by treaty to the East India Company. The most flagrant and deeply resented of these was the annexation of Oudh in 1856, a state from which many sepoys were recruited. Related to this were changes in land revenue policy that stripped *talukdars* (traditional landholding elites) of their property, overassessments of property for tax purposes, and widespread unemployment in the region as a result of the dissolution of the Nawab of Oudh's court and army. The anxieties about sustenance and agrarian stability of high-caste but economically vulnerable peasants were inseparable from those of the sepoys who came from their ranks. The sepoys themselves had seen their conditions of employment deteriorate, with low pay, minimal prospects for promotion, the reduction of special allowances, mandatory foreign service, and contemptuous treatment by British officers being the leading causes of discontent.[25] They were the first to rise against the Company's rule. After disposing of their European officers at Meerut, the sepoys marched to Delhi, where they hailed the titular Mughal ruler Bahadur Shah II as emperor of Hindustan and compelled him to lend his authority to the revolt. In the following weeks mutiny spread among other regiments until roughly half of all the sepoys and *sowars* (cavalrymen) in the Bengal

Army joined ranks with the mutineers. These weeks also saw a spate of uprisings in which Indian rulers of princely kingdoms, religious leaders, peasants, and landowners in northern India, especially in Oudh, all played a part. It is worth repeating that there were multiple uprisings, not a single one, and in some cases the wrath of the insurgents was directed against moneylenders, whose existing power was strengthened by the consequences of the colonial state's land revenue policy, and the propertied as much as against Company and Anglo-Indian interests.[26] The latter were sorely beset and had to endure long sieges at Delhi, Cawnpore, and Lucknow. Cawnpore in particular came to have a great resonance in Mutiny lore because it was the scene of two notable massacres. In the first case, Anglo-Indian men and women who had surrendered to Nana Saheb on condition of safe passage out of Cawnpore were fired upon and killed as they were boarding boats at the Satichaura Ghat on the Ganges; in the second case, Anglo-Indian women and children who were prisoners of Nana Saheb and survivors of the first massacre were mercilessly slaughtered by hired butchers and their bodies cast into a well. It was the second of the two massacres, involving the killing of Anglo-Indian ladies and children, that was to make Cawnpore an almost mythic symbol in the British and Anglo-Indian imagination of Indian depravity. Even though Colonel James Neill's "bloody assizes," the slaughter of large numbers of mutinous sepoys, suspected rebels, and civilians around Allahabad in June 1857, predated the violence at Cawnpore, Anglo-Indian and British writers claimed it was the massacres in that city that led to a ferocious policy of counterinsurgency, including military battles, the sacking of cities, the burning of villages, and wholesale hangings, bayonetings, and shootings of sepoys, peasants, and other Indians, whether combatant or civilian, unfortunate enough to find themselves in the vicinity of British troops. The subcontinent was substantially subdued by mid-1858, and the East India Company's rule replaced by that of the Crown.

Even though 1857 was often presented as an extraordinary and anomalous event, one that apparently shocked old India hands who maintained an unwavering faith in the ties of loyalty, affection, and paternalism that bound sepoy and Anglo-Indian officer together, the most casual scrutiny of the historical record demonstrates that 1857 was but the latest and most spectacular and sustained of mutinies that had marked the sepoy–officer relation for well over half a century. Indeed, C. A. Bayly argues that "armed revolt was endemic in all parts of early colonial India. What distinguished the events of 1857 was their scale and that for a short time they posed a military threat to British dominance in the Ganges Plains."[27] Many contemporary commentators on the events of 1857–58 noted its antecedents in earlier mutinies, most specifically in the Vellore mutiny of 1806.[28] The official cause of this early mutiny was the issuance of new headgear in the form of a round hat to the sepoys (to replace their turbans), of a kind that was seen to resemble a European or Christian hat; what sealed its character as Christian insignia was that it sported a leather cockade constructed apparently of the hides of pigs and cattle.[29] The regulations that made the new hats mandatory also forbade other forms of bodily and sartorial marking, including earrings, caste marks, untrimmed whiskers, and beards, that had hitherto been worn with official sanction. Mocked by the locals as *topiwalas* (hat-wearers) and by implication European and Christian, some sepoys attacked white officers and soldiers on the night of 10 July 1806 and ransacked their quarters but were quickly overcome.[30]

The sepoys' misgivings about the refashioning of their outfits and their socioreligious identities were apparently part of a broader spectrum of indigenous discontent about the uniformities and forms of assimilation desiderated by the colonial system, and reports abounded of other affronts by the Company against the Indian social order. J. W. Kaye, the foremost historian of the Mutiny of 1857, discusses some of the "preposterous stories" circulating in the bazaars of Vellore in 1806: "Among other wild fables, which took firm hold of the popular mind, was one to the effect that the Company's officers had collected all the newly-manufactured salt, had divided it into two great heaps, and over one had sprinkled the blood of hogs, and over the other the blood of cows; that they had then sent it to be sold throughout the country for the pollution and the desecration of Muhammadans and Hindus, that all might be brought to one caste and to one religion like the English. When this absurd story was circulated, some ceased altogether to eat salt, and some purchased, at high prices, and carefully stored away, supplies of the necessary article, guaranteed to have been in the Bazaars before the atrocious act of the Faringhis had been committed."[31]

For Kaye these tales of contamination and force-feeding were forms of illicit speech, the predictable emanations of a native bazaar that dealt in fraudulent commodities, especially fraudulent information. The representation of the bazaar as the locus of all Indian abominations is a well-known staple of official documents and fictional renditions of the colonial scene, both before and after 1857.[32] The fact that these "wild fables" and "absurd stories" found purchase among the bazaar's customers was evidence overwheming of indigenous superstition and hysteria, impervious alike to realist forms of narrative and to appropriate modes of getting, spending, and consuming. Kaye's rhetoric is worth some attention here, especially for the way in which it may be set to work for a reading of illicit speech. Taking his lead and reading the account above as a "wild fable" rather than as a realist form allows one to sift through its tropological operations, to see the ways in which its structures of displacement and condensation provide an accounting of the voraciousness of empire. At a broad level the "wild fable" indexed widespread fears that the colonial order was the malicious engine of transformations simultaneously radical and insidious, not just among the sepoys it directly controlled but also among a wider civilian populace; indeed, the recurrence of cows and pigs in the stories of hats and salt suggests that they were versions of the same story and that ingestion belonged to a larger logic of pollution, occurring not just through specifically designated orifices but through the surface of the entire body.[33]

It was perhaps not an accident that the object of pollution was salt. In fact salt, existing as it did in two incommensurable registers—an older one of sacred ties, including those of hospitality and loyalty, and a newer one of commodification and marketization—was to serve in 1806 and 1857 as a brilliantly condensed and extraordinarily visceral sign of the tensions of colonial rule.

• • •

If salt carried a significant affective and metaphoric charge in the colonial period for sepoy and Company, this investment drew upon the already extant connotations of salt in northern and eastern India. Salt was, as Tanika Sarkar notes, "the essential food, the universal property in diet with implications of trust, hospitality, reciprocity, and mutual obligation. . . . a nationalist song compared the salt-earth to the mother's breasts from which no one had the right to take the child away."[34] In the Mughal symbolic ensemble, salt was a highly coded substance, being sprinkled over Mughal troops as a guarantor of their loyalty. The East India Company, which presented itself as the heir to the Mughal empire and assumed many of its idioms of legitimacy, found it convenient to retain the symbolic function of salt to compel loyalty from an alien soldiery.[35] Thus sepoys were said to have routinely described their ties to the Company as the relationship of salt, which made faithfulness an obligation; those who mutinied were described as *namak haraam*, faithless to their salt. This was a usage that evoked the notion of the Company as paymaster, no doubt; the relationship between salt and salary is so well known that it needs no further gloss. But it also evoked the Company as *mai-baap* (mother and father), a patriarchal, protective, quasi-feudal entity to which self-abnegating service was owed and which compelled a fidelity that exceeded the language of contract or the calculus of wages and benefits; it tied the sepoy to the Company through what Thompson in another context has described as a "moral economy."[36] Anglo-Indian commentators often lauded as miraculous "the bondage of the Salt" that kept the sepoy tied in a self-denying relationship to a Company that did. not necessarily reciprocate his generosity: "In an extremity of hunger, he had spontaneously offered his scanty food to sustain the robuster energies of his English comrade. . . . He had subscribed from his slender earnings to the support of our European wars. He had cheerfully consented, when he knew that his Government was in need, to forego that regular receipt of pay which is the very life-blood of foreign service."[37] It seems that even mutinous sepoys were not always immune to the obligations of the "bondage of salt" entered into with the Company. In 1857 a group of them apparently explained the failure of their revolt in a strikingly corporeal idiom that gratifyingly echoed British expectations of servitude, loyalty, and Indian fatalism: "Sahib, it has been all the work of fate. After what we had done, we never could fight. No matter whether your troops were black or white, native or European, we could not stand against them; *our salt choked us*."[38] No rhetoric could have been better suited to the affective premises of British rule, which harped obsessively upon a calculatedly archaized "fidelity to one's salt" as the single measure of Indian worthiness in all accounts of the Mutiny.[39] Thus the shock of the Mutiny was its enactment of alleged disloyalty and ingratitude; popular and official accounts are replete with tales of Anglo-Indian officers who, beguiled by long residence in India and too heedless an intimacy with natives, were massacred by sepoys whose fidelity to their salt they had taken as given. While some rebel leaders, Tantia Topi most conspicuously, contested the terms of loyalty to the British, claiming they were never the Company's vassals to begin with, their claims were rejected. Even the Mughal emperor was tried on charges of treason despite the fact that the East India Company was technically his feudatory. As Ian Baucom rightly notes, the relationship of Britain and India after 1857 would be governed above all by the trope of faithfulness.[40]

In a context in which salt was semiotically inflected in these ways, the rumors of its contamination indexed the most fundamental of betrayals: the incapacity or refusal of the paternalist state to protect its dependents. Worse, the rumors suggested that the very salt that was the symbol of sepoy dependence and sepoy loyalty could be deliberately, maliciously, and duplicitously turned into an instrument of complete subjugation through pollution and conversion. The fall from religious purity occasioned by the ingestion of forbidden foods was the high road to conversion to the Christian faith that was the distinctive mark of foreign rulers and their local stooges. In this scenario, conversion resulted from and was in effect a form of force-feeding, one in which relations between eater and eaten were reversed, turning the subject who consumes into one who is consumed by what she or he eats and turning highly polluting blood and bone into food. The trope of bloody contamination also figured the Company as a rapacious entity, a great maw if you will marked by an insatiable hunger. In this sense, the understanding of the predatory, unnatural, even vampiric character of the Company's acts of incorporation agrees with Marx's diagnosis of British rule in India, which he likened famously to a "hideous pagan idol, who would not drink the nectar but from the skulls of the slain."[41]

The Company's role as duplicitous purveyor of forbidden foods was attributed, however, not to motiveless malignity but to a form of instrumental reason characteristic of colonial governance: "Why should they think the Government wished to convert them? Their imaginations supplied a plausible answer. The white man was bent upon taking away their caste and making them Christians, in order that, no longer hesitating to eat his strengthening food, or to embark in his ships, they might be able to go forth at his bidding, as warriors endowed with new vigour, to gratify his insatiable ambition by fresh conquests."[42] What the Company had embarked on was the calculated commodification of the sepoy body and sepoy labor for a colonial enterprise marked at once by an unappeasable appetite for territory and the lack of European manpower to realize this ambition. In this reading, the sepoy acknowledged that religious and caste restrictions on diet and foreign travel militated against strength and efficiency and therefore made him less than fully useful to a British empire seriously hobbled by lack of homegrown manpower, especially in the wake of losses in the Crimean War.[43] The Company's purpose in tampering with and Christianizing this body was an exercise in efficiency, reforming the sepoy's appetites, producing his body as a robust commodity, and rendering him more malleable for its labors. This was for the sepoy an all too plausible development in an era in which commodification came to define new areas of social life. For instance, the land reforms following the annexation of Oudh in 1856 were theoretically designed to save the peasants from the exactions of talukdars (and to make for more efficient revenue collection). But in effect the new inflexible revenue demands fixed in money terms (in place of the old grain-sharing arrangement) left the peasant vulnerable to the ill effects of bad harvests, price fluctuations, and overassessment without the protections once afforded by his feudal overlord. This deranged the "subsistence ethic" of the Oudh peasantry at the same time that it stripped the talukdar of his earlier privileges, powers of patronage, and lands.[44] A number of estates came to pass into the hands of absentee landlords, mainly urban moneylenders and merchants, through sale and auction at this time. This, combined with the auctions of the effects of the royal houses of Oudh and Nagpur, also annexed in pursuance of the Doctrine of Lapse enforced by Dalhousie, confirmed the Company's character as predatory, callous, and calculating in the eyes of the Oudh populace at large. Much to the shock and dismay of well-intentioned Anglo-Indian officials, many peasants joined hands with their putative oppressors, the talukdars, in the civil rebellion at Oudh.

This clash between the world of patronage, protection, honor, and loyalty and that of tradeable, corruptible commodities also manifested itself in the question of the salt tax. It was impossible in early nineteenth-century India to mention salt without conjuring up at the same time the colonial government's monopoly on salt production and its prohibitively high salt taxes. Salt came to be subject to high taxes for the first time in Indian history under the East India Company's rule, and part of the great fortune of Robert Clive, the conqueror of Bengal and one of the founders of British rule in India, was made through revenues from salt taxes. These taxes were a source of economic distress to common people, and they outraged the sensibilities of those who were accustomed to thinking of items like salt, tobacco, and betelnut as part of a nonmarket economy of hospitality rather than as tradable commodities. In the first decade of the nineteenth century salt became a British monopoly. It became illegal for anyone else to produce, transport, or trade in salt; even scraping salt off the surface of salt flats was attended with severe penalties. Erstwhile salt manufacturers in coastal districts like Midnapore in Bengal came to be reduced to the status of petty criminals as a result of activities now out-lawed.[45] The salt workers of Orissa, the *malangis*, who had been independent salt makers for generations, found themselves working for pitiful wages for the Company's salt department and rebelled on more than one occasion. There was widespread discontent at the heavy taxation of a basic item of food and fierce debates about the amount of salt used or required by Indian families. A member of the Bengal Medical Service testified before a Parliamentary Select Committee in 1836 that the average laborer would need to spend a sixth of his yearly wages to pay for the salt his family required.[46] So when in 1930 Gandhi made the protest against the salt monopoly the center of a widely publicized and immensely successful campaign against British rule, he was not innovating a form of anticolonial protest but following in a tradition of salt-related insurgencies. Mark Kurlansky and Tanika Sarkar affirm that Gandhi's well-publicized campaign was matched by the much more obscure but no less committed campaigns against salt monopolies and salt taxes in Cuttack, Midnapore, and other places.[47]

"Indigestible Edibles"

Sepoy terrors about salt contamination and caste violations, and the Company's sense of the dangerous irrationality of caste orthodoxy, must be contextualized in light of the determined efforts of the Company to recruit high-caste men of peasant stock into the Bengal Army in northern India and to foster their endeavors to maintain caste purity and caste exclusiveness. Seema Alavi notes that Governor-General Warren Hastings quite explicitly foregrounded caste as an instrument of an imperial policy of divide and conquer as well as of legitimizing British rule; he and his subordinates created a "separate religious tradition in the army," taking special pains to promote the "religious, dietary, and travel preferences" of the high-caste sepoys.[48] She suggests that high-caste identity in the army was enabled through a complex, rigid set of permissions and exclusions, mostly related to diet, cooking, and commensality, which allowed Brahmin and Rajput sepoys to mark their high-caste status much more thoroughly than would have been possible in their native villages. "In a sense, then," she observes, "the Company was promoting sanskritization of the military."[49] This institution of ritual rules to maintain the army as a nursery of high-caste Hindu male practice was, ironically, productive of some troubles for the Company, as more than one mutiny in the 1820s was prompted by the sepoys' unwillingness to depart from the ritual observances nurtured by the army.

The heightened alertness to caste purity certainly appears to have been at play in the response to the famous greased cartridges. The encounter that putatively set in train the saga of the greased cartridges is one that is told again and again and incorporates in dramatic ways the Mutiny's somaticized logic of incorporation, aversion, and sexual discomposure.[50] There are several variations on the story, but in most versions it goes like this: in January 1857 a Brahmin sepoy stationed at Dumdum was walking along with his *lota* (water pot), and because, according to some reports, he was proceeding to prepare his food he was in a state of heightened ritual purity. Accosted by a low-caste *khalasi* (laborer) who requested a drink from his lota, he refused indignantly on grounds of the pollution his interlocutor's touch would induce. Whereupon the low-caste man retorted, "You will soon lose your caste, as ere long you will have to bite cartridges covered with the fat of pigs and cows," or "words to that effect," according to the initial report by Captain J. A. Wright, who commanded the Rifle Instruction Depot. A slightly different version is given a little later by Major-General J. B. Hearsey, the commanding officer of the Presidency Division: "The saheb-logue will make you bite cartridges soaked in cow and pork fat, and then where will your caste be?"[51] Note that as the tale ranges from one sahib's mouth to another the cartridges come to be more thoroughly saturated (the difference between "covered" and soaked") with the objectionable grease; in the second telling the sahibs are also made the specific agents of contamination, while in the first no agent is explicitly named.

This parable or versions thereof bookends all accounts of the Mutiny, since it is the moment that best captures the Company's transformation, in the high-caste sepoy's eyes, from provider and protector (the bestower of salt) to the dispenser of grease or poison. Yet it happens not directly but through the perverse conduit of the low-caste male. It is worth remembering, in reading this scene, that food here is a significant vehicle of pollution in a high-caste Hindu gastropolitical order, and eating itself is dangerous, rendering the Brahmin male subject most vulnerable to penetration by polluting agents. Food is a heavily coded substance, and transactions involving food are ineluctably biomoral and hierarchical ones. As the introduction indicates, caste subjects are marked by their susceptibility to transfers of bodily and moral substance.[52] Such fungibility is nonetheless not exempt from a carefully organized hierarchical structure, transactions between "dividuals" being carefully regulated (though always susceptible to disturbance). Thus the first sign of crisis in this phobically charged encounter is the low-caste male's aggressive solicitation, his desire to become one, at least in part, with the high-caste male body by drinking out of his lota; this biomoral outrage is auxiliary to the greater outrage of being forced to consume other abominable substances. The vulnerable Brahmin male is opened to assault and aspersions of emasculation by the low-caste male, an assault incited by the absent but authoritative British male. The lower-caste male's disconcerting role as the bearer of information, pollution, and insult is evidence of a world turned upside down, inseparable from betrayal by the Company. In this three-way exchange the aggressive, emasculating low-caste male becomes the familiar of the white officer, though, ironically, in his zeal to maintain bodily impenetrability the Brahmin sepoy is akin to the sahib.

The message of alimentary pollutions is embedded within a sexually anxious economy: to eat with low-caste males is prophetic of many other forms of bodily vulnerability and promiscuous bodily commingling. It is no surprise therefore to note that these reports of violation proliferated along other, contiguous axes, as outrages against rules of commensality were accompanied by rumors of outrages against connubiality. It was reported, for instance, that Indian landowners would be forced to marry the widows of British soldiers who had perished in the Crimean War.[53] Given that these tales unfolded in the context of the legalization of the marriage of high-caste Hindu widows, it is not difficult to see that they were inseparable from a sense of high-caste masculine sexual violation. The oft-told tales of the taunts of the whores in the bazaars, who, like the khalasi of the cartridge tale, derided the sepoys about their emasculation and apparently incited them to avenge these pollutions, also belong in a familiar continuum of outrages against alimentary and gendered propriety. They also highlight the complex concatenations of a rebellion that involved not only high-caste Hindu sepoys, peasants, dispossessed talukdars, and wronged sovereigns, but also itinerant fakirs, budmashes (rogues or petty criminals), whores, and marauding Gujars, sometimes in tense and antagonistic relationship with one another.[54] Who was rebelling against what or whom was not always clear or consistent. Indeed, as Dalrymple points out, Muslim and Hindu elites in Delhi, including those at the Delhi court, were appalled by the presence in the capital of the mutinous sepoys, whom they regarded as boorish, violent outsiders.

The humbler inhabitants of Delhi were also harassed by the depredations of sepoys, sowars, and Gujars.[55]

While the fears of pollution that were crystallized in the cartridge parable were dismissed by some of the sahibs, others among them were largely persuaded that in fact some grease of polluting origin had made its way into the cartridges. There were suggestions that sepoys be taken to the manufacturing depots to witness the process by which the cartridges were made, but these were not acted upon. The objectionable cartridges were withdrawn, however, and sepoys were permitted to grease their own cartridges, but they remained suspicious of the cartridge paper, whose glaze they suspected was produced by grease; they feared, Kaye writes, that "the paper was little more than 'bladder.' "[56] In an echo of the Vellore mutiny of 1806, there were bazaar rumors among the civilian populace of other alimentary violations, violations that were yoked in most instances to fears of forcible conversion to Christianity: "It was said that the officers of the British Government, under command from the Company and the Queen, had mixed ground bones with the flour and the salt sold in the Bazaars; that they had adulterated all the ghi with animal fat; that bones had been burned with the common sugar of the country; and that not only bone-dust flour, but the flesh of cows and pigs, had been thrown into the wells to pollute the drinking water of the people. Of this great imaginary scheme of contamination the matter of the greased cartridges was but a part, especially addressed to one part of the community. All classes, it was believed, were to be defiled at the same time; and the story ran that the 'bara sahibs,' or great English lords, had commanded all princes, nobles, landholders, merchants, and cultivators of the land, to feed together upon English bread."[57]

In the gastrologic that this passage evidences, sepoys and civilians are bound together by a pollution that is characterized by its pervasiveness and simultaneity. The catalogue of far-flung, malicious, and inescapable pollutions culminates in this passage in an anticipated meal that is not so much an instance of union and fellowship as an obscenely leveling device, a carnival of forced intimacies. The command is that all castes and classes feed together upon "English bread," a substance "optimally defiled," according to Guha, by its use of the five unclean ingredients, flour, salt, sugar, fat, and water, and, in its forms of hyperbolization and condensation, quite clearly a fantastical substance.[58] This simultaneously outrages caste Hindu prohibitions on commensality and Muslim and Hindu dietary prescriptions and mimics a Christian sacramental meal that forcibly makes all Indians into one body, which is an alien because a Christian one. The deployment of the Christian sacrament in the nightmares of anxious Hindus and Muslims is an important index of the ways in which the transformations wrought by colonial encounter manifested themselves through overlapping psychic landscapes and a partially shared repertoire of tropes of incorporation. (It is not insignificant that the public proclamations of Bahadur Shah II and of Begum Hazrat Mahal of Oudh sought to distinguish themselves from Company rule through a counterpolitics of consumption and prohibition. Bahadur Shah endeavored to inaugurate gastropolitics as an instrument of state policy by forbidding the cow-slaughter deemed offensive to Hindus.)[59]

The fact that forms of communal eating had been introduced in the 1840s in a rationalization of the prison system, a change that had caused uprisings within the prisons and discontent outside them, lent some substance to these fantasies of larger social transformations.[60] The prison, a characteristically colonial institution, was also a social laboratory in which the lines between punishment, reform, and experiment were often tenuous and as such was the site of protracted political struggles between colonizer and colonized.[61] In his study of the "lotah emeutes" of 1855 in the prisons of colonial north India, Anand Yang notes that colonial punishment in the nineteenth century was directed at the body in a fairly overt way and that this often conflicted with the colonial state's official policy of noninterference in indigenous religious practices. Penal reforms sometimes involved new forms of bodily regulation or punishment such as messing, rather than monetary allowances or uncooked rations for prisoners, and, in a few instances, the abolition of the ritually purer brass lotas for less acceptable earthen ones; prisoners, regarding the changes as offenses against caste and religion, protested strongly.[62] In many cases prisoners won the energetic support of a broad cross-section of the local inhabitants of the areas where the jails were situated and even of their Indian jailers. Prisoners as well as the nonincarcerated saw developments in prison as a blueprint for larger social reforms, especially at a time when prison populations, augmented in part by the ranks of the sepoys who refused to accept the greased cartridges, were expanding. When the Mutiny broke out, prisons were among the first government institutions to be targeted, and large numbers of prisoners were released.

What was seen as the growing influence of Christian missionaries exacerbated these terrors of somatic and social transformation. Missionary activity, which had been freed from restrictions since the Charter

Act of 1813, had become increasingly visible in the subcontinent. To some people at least missionary activity seemed to have government sanction, since the government gave grants to missionary-run schools and permitted evangelically inclined officers to preach the gospel to their troops.[63] Missionaries were among the strongest critics of the institution of caste and responsible for much of the writing on it.[64] Their success in effecting the passage of the Caste Disabilities Removal Act of 1850, which gave converts to Christianity protection against the forfeiture of the rights of inheritance, was bitterly resented, as inheritance was traditionally seen as entailing the fulfillment of ritual obligations to one's male forebears, obligations that the convert, who had died a "civil death," could not honor.[65] Missionaries tended to be particularly active in times of dearth, such as the great famine of 1837–38 in the United and North-Western Provinces.[66] They came to be associated without difficulty with tales of scarcity and tainted food.

• • •

In the colonial records the Indian, whether sepoy or civilian, is the subject of a double oral obsession—an obsession with what may or may not be absorbed through the mouth and an addiction to malicious, absurd, and proliferating rumor. As we have seen, Guha identifies rumor, or orality more broadly, with preliterate, peasant, and subaltern modes of communication and mobilization. But what is also striking is the degree to which Indians and Anglo-Indians shared a gestural repertoire, both oral and somatic, during the Mutiny. For the Anglo-Indians as for the Indians the colonizer–colonized encounter, and indeed the experience of the Mutiny, was understood in significant ways through tropes of orality and of bodily purity and pollution; they were bound by unexpected forms of somatic, especially alimentary duplication. One might note, for instance, the degree to which rumor played a decisive part in the Anglo-Indian conduct of counterinsurgency and the way in which an Indian fantasy of consuming defiling "English bread" was matched by an Anglo-Indian dream of dangerous Indian bread. One of the tales that haunted the Anglo-Indian imagination was that about the itinerant chapati. It was said that, starting in January 1857, chapatis were passed from hamlet to hamlet through the hands of the village chowkidars (watchmen), without being consumed as food; they were circulated with an injunction to make more and pass them along to adjoining villages. Apparently they were diffused across the countryside "with a rapidity almost electric."[67] The very texture of the metaphor here evokes the speed of the telegraph or of the train that was purported to bind Indian subjects together in unwilling proximity. In fact, though Guha does not articulate it in these terms, the chapati can be seen as a figure itself of rumor and of rumor's mysterious, illicit transmission. Apparently no other message but this injunction to transmission circulated with these gnomic chapatis. Initially the *Friend of India* wondered whether the chapatis were portents or trifles: "Is it a treason or a jest? Is the chaupatty a fiery cross or only an indigestible edible, a cause of revolt or only of the colic?"[68] Many officials speculated that the unspoken message of the chapatis was to warn the peasantry to prepare for some as-yet-unknown event, though the content of the event remained always unspecified, and there is no record of the popular response to the circulation of chapatis. Some officials connected it to other tokens that had circulated in other moments of unrest. No particular secrecy seems to have attached to the circulation of chapatis; at least one Anglo-Indian official, Mark Thornhill, a magistrate at Muttra (Mathura), even received an installment of chapatis, though without being asked to carry on the work of transmission.[69] The chowkidars through whose hands the chapatis passed were also uncertain of their origins, some believing they were circulated by government order as a sign that all would be compelled to eat the same food as Christians. As J. A. B. Palmer points out, the notion that government was responsible for the peregrinating chapatis was perhaps not an entirely outrageous gloss on the phenomenon, given that chowkidars were colonial functionaries, responsible for village security and for filing weekly reports with their local stations of criminal or suspicious activity.[70] A few saw the event as no more than an instance of chalawa for cholera, though there have been disputes about this functionalist explanation.[71] Other English observers, commenting in retrospect, saw it as evidence of a preexisting plot, comparing it to the "fiery cross" of popular mobilization in the Highlands.[72] Given that "the most prominent form of social protest in early modern Europe was the grain riot or the bread riot," and given too the history of famine and agrarian unrest in northern India, it is perhaps not surprising that Anglo-Indian observers connected the itinerant chapati with the portents of rebellion.[73] In these accounts, this common symbol of sustenance in an agrarian landscape came to be converted into alarm both about means of subsistence and about the forms of pollution induced by British rule. The officers presiding over the trial of Bahadur Shah II even suggested ingeniously that the conspiracy against Company rule began with the chapatis but since their circulation was soon proscribed by the authorities, the bone-dust rumor came to take its place as an effective substitute. By this reckoning the chapati displayed remarkably fluid properties, being disaggregated into its component parts of flour, salt, water, ghee, and sugar. From this it was a short step to a transmogrification into another register of orality—rumor. It was through these forms of combination, division, transformation, and transmission that the work of conspiracy proceeded.[74] The speed and almost magical extent of the chapatis' transmission seemed congruous with the spread of rebellion itself, approximating telegraphy or, what seemed more likely, telepathy.[75] In the riddling, occult landscape they traversed, chapatis were part of a chain of displacements that included rumors, mutinous sepoys, incendiarism, and sedition-preaching fakirs. Whatever the initial confusion caused by the chapatis, the recounting of the trauma of 1857 came quickly to be gothicized in the sahib imagination, and this hallucinatory bread became, along with dreams, portents, prophecies, and unspeakable terrors, part of the phantasmagoria of the event itself.

Over the course of a century, the Company had built up an admirable far-flung, well-coordinated information network of approvers, spies, and native informants and had ensured the consolidation of their empire of information through such technologies as the telegraph. And yet their command of the networks of information and surveillance was incomplete in many respects because they either did not have access to or spurned literate women, religious mendicants, pilgrims, shopkeepers, and tribals as sources of information. As a result their information systems were sometimes marked by atrophy. Occasionally they were swamped by data panics when esoteric forms of information (or noninformation) such as the chapatis induced panic without providing edification.[76] The years after the Mutiny therefore saw a boost in the role of intelligence at the administrative and imaginative levels. The gaps in surveillance and knowledge that the Mutiny exposed were to be overcome in post-Mutiny Anglo-Indian fictions, which often fetishize the figure that Gautam Chakravarty names the "spy-hero," who can extend the reach of the colonial state by passing as one of the natives.[77]

Despite or perhaps because of their enigmatic character as food or word or both, the chapatis formed one of the staple foods of the Mutiny tale or account. In a few, mostly nonofficial accounts it was alleged that lotus flowers were distributed along with the chapatis, though the improbability of the lotus surviving transmission probably did its part to put that tale to rest. Mainuddin Khan reported that pieces of goat's flesh were being distributed along with the chapatis, a fact his translator Sir Charles Theophilus Metcalfe invested with a murderous meaning.[78] Some attempts were made, especially in the twentieth century, to decode a chapati numerology that nonetheless failed to add up. Palmer observes that "the number five seems to prevail in the distribution," though he also notes that "there are references to six and four."[79] In the case of Flora Annie Steel, conducting research for the novel that was to become *On the Face of the Waters* (1897) meant gaining rare access to the Mutiny papers of the Punjab government, but only on condition that she exercise her "discretion, judgment, loyalty."[80] She does not hesitate to report that in the course of her examination of these confidential documents she had indeed established that the chapatis were no superfluities but the authoritative writing of mutiny, since she found (perhaps a little improbably) "tiny notes in quills, one in a *chupatti*." By embedding quills, actually carried during the Mutiny by British spies, in chapatis, she makes the Indian chapati the equivalent of the Anglo-Indian secret missive. She says, however, that her sense of patriotic duty ensured that the secret of the chapati would remain in its proper form, that is to say, encrypted: "I don't think I learnt much that was absolutely new in them; only—on both sides— details which I felt must be suppressed."[81] The chapati is here a paradoxical text of revelation: its secret is effectively contentless or at least already familiar, and yet this content must remain concealed. For Steel the chapati can retain its tremendous imaginative power only if it functions as an ellipsis rather than too scrutable a text of the Mutiny.

For the Mutiny to retain its *necessary* character as a mysterious, atavistic, and dreadful event, it cannot be otherwise. Bhabha aptly describes the chapati story as producing "an infectious ambivalence, an 'abyssal overlapping,' of too much meaning and a certain meaninglessness." In an astute reading of the grammatical logic of the historian Kaye's account of Governor-General Canning's understanding of rumor and panic, he notes that the anxiety being ascribed to a native populace is in fact "equivocal, circulating wildly on both sides. . . . What is represented and fixed as native panic at the level of the content or propositionality (*enonce*) is, at the level of narrative positionality (*enunciation*) the spreading, uncontrolled fear and fantasy of the colonizer."[82] Bhabha's trope of contagion highlights the degree to which Anglo-India caught the infection of chapati, bone dust, and rumor; its response to the signs in the Indian landscape gives evidence of a certain parasitic, even cannibalizing logic.

Note, for instance, rumors of the rape of Englishwomen, rumors that in the minds of Anglo-Indians formed one of the staples of the Mutiny. These have a pervasive, indeterminate, and hyperbolic cast to them that may be said to approximate the parables of Indian pollution. Jenny Sharpe has written about the ways in which rape formed a signal part of the mythology of 1857 and became for the first time a figuration of the colonial fear of the colonized but dangerous and uncontrollable masses. Even though investigations found no evidence of systematic sexual assault upon English women, it came to be believed in Anglo-India and England alike that the Mutiny was the work of Indian males who desired white female flesh so desperately as to be driven to rape and murder.[83] Sharpe has detailed the ways in which English newspapers, journals, and pamphlets legitimized tales of the rape of Englishwomen and the mutilation of their bodies by accepting hearsay as fact. These forms of legitimation were supplemented notably by the work of avenging white soldiers who entered the Bibighar in Cawnpore shortly after the massacre there of Anglo-Indian ladies and children by Nana Saheb's hired assassins. The soldiers covered the walls of the Bibighar with inscriptions—inscriptions that were readily believed to have been calls for revenge composed by the ladies before their slaughter. All this was used as sanction for a terrifying orgy of violence that was unleashed upon Indians, whether combatants or noncombatants: Britons believed themselves to be acting to avenge the rape and murder of Englishwomen. But the fetishization of the raped and mutilated female body had, Sharpe suggests, another important effect, separate from that of racial mobilization: it permitted a bypassing of the vulnerable and penetrable British *male* body, itself the victim of insurgent violence.[84] Like Sharpe, Nancy Paxton glosses the rumors of rape as an anxiety-ridden response to colonial crisis, though she submits that they function to foreclose any examination of the brutality of British counter-insurgency.[85] She construes them as an Anglo-Indian answer to the chapati tale, though, as Bhabha suggests, it is unclear whether the chapati was the stuff of Indian dreams or Anglo-Indian ones. Taken together, these stories of betrayal, possession, and bodily pollution speak powerfully to colonial fears of bodily proximity to natives, fears curiously braided together with indigenous fears of caste pollution. The almost delirious character of such tales has some kinship surely to the "wild fables" of the bazaar about the forced, bastardizing intimacies induced by contaminated flour. The sexual subtext that informed the sepoy and bazaar stories of forced touching, forced feeding, and forced marriage may well have found an ironic consummation in the tales of the violated bodies of English women.

Bhabha is utterly persuasive in his mapping of the iterative and uncanny logic that proliferates panic among sahibs at least as much as among natives. But his highly suggestive interpretation of the equivocality of rumor and panic can be pushed even further to account for the ways in which rumors of conspiracy, uprising, and rape can be remarkably generative and even pleasurable for a colonial imagination that seeks to incite crisis rather than forestalling it altogether. Sharpe's work clarifies the ways in which rumor speaks with a forked tongue, with effects that can be productive for the task of counterinsurgency and not just insurgency. Citing "the legitimating function of rumors in the Anglo-Indian communities," her analysis illustrates how rape becomes a figuration of the fear of the colonized but at the same time consolidates the moral authority of colonialism in the management of rebellion.[86] This fertile character of rumor is surely on display forty years after the Mutiny in Steel's story of the encrypted chapati. While Steel eschews the sensational stories of rape, she draws incontrovertibly upon its figuration of the English lady as the moral custodian of the Raj. Further, her story is a parable about the delectation of secrecy and uncertainty. Her self-censorship upon the very threshold of revelation may frustrate, but it also tantalizes and delights, being superior to the certain knowledge that abolishes pleasure. For the Mutiny tale to retain its frisson, it must resolutely keep rumors in circulation.

Pathologics

In the first chapter of The Wretched of the Earth, Frantz Fanon has a well-known description of the Manichaean geographic imaginary of the settler colony: "The colonial world is a world cut in two. The dividing line, the frontiers are shown by barracks and police stations. In the colonies it is the policeman and the soldier who are the official, instituted go-betweens, the spokesman of the settler and his rule of oppression. . . . The zone where the natives live is not complementary to the zone inhabited by the settlers. The two zones are opposed, but not in the service of a higher unity. Obedient to the rules of pure Aristotelian logic, they both follow the principle of reciprocal exclusivity."[87] While Fanon is describing the spatial contours of an early to mid-twentieth-century colonial city, the fact is that these spatial and racial limits had come to be conceived from at least the 1820s and 1830s onward, at least in a colony like India. Although the new East India Company rulers had adopted large elements of the lifestyle of Indian elites in the eighteenth century, maintaining Indian-style retinues and spatial arrangements in their households, adopting Indian garb and culinary habits at home, cohabiting with free and slave Indian women (though rarely marrying them in Christian ceremony), sometimes in polygamous arrangements, and providing for their mixed-race children either through education in Britain or through appointments in civil and military departments in the subcontinent, by the last decade of the century things had begun to change at the level of policy and official recognition.[88] Of course, even before formal shifts in policy, the Anglo-Indian nabob, with his parvenu ambition, decadence, and taint of Asiatic corruption, had been a figure of both derision and moral opprobrium in Britain; the colony, with its corruptions of place, was seen as debilitating to dignity, virility, and moral welfare.[89] The Company began in the 1790s—a decade that saw reforms introduced by the Governor-General Lord Cornwallis as well as Hastings's trial—to discourage marriages and liaisons between Indian women and Englishmen in the upper echelons of civil and military service, to promote the entry of white women from Britain, to bar mixed-blood sons from the services and to dismiss those who were already ensconced in them, to prohibit the payment of educational and other stipends from pension and charitable funds to the orphaned children of European fathers, and to proscribe the dispatch of mixed-race children to Britain.[90] Reacting aversively to the possibility of the emergence of an appreciable creole population in the subcontinent—perhaps, Sudipta Sen postulates, in response to rebellions in the creolized Spanish Americas—the Company took decisive steps to demarcate racial and civilizational distinctions of constitution and entitlement between communities now more decisively marked as native and expatriate or diasporic.[91] Practice did not necessarily accord with policy, especially at the lower ranks, as the presence of a sizeable Eurasian community—targeted, along with Britons and native Christians, during the Mutiny—attested, though these practices enjoyed a much reduced legitimacy and official recognition.[92] While some prominent Englishmen "living on the frontiers" continued, as Durba Ghosh has shown, to maintain relationships with Indian women and to produce mixed-race children into the 1830s without damage to their careers, even they were critically concerned about upholding the Britishness of the children whom they publicly acknowledged as their own.[93] Indeed, there seems to have been a strenuous effort from this point on to unthink the possibility of India as a creole or even as a settler colony and to maintain an Anglo-Indian identity as an avowedly exilic or diasporic one. Anglo-Indians in later decades would no doubt assert an Anglo-Indian identity not entirely reducible to that of metropolitan Britons but cognate with theirs nonetheless.[94] Many besides took pride in an Anglo-Indian ancestry that had bound their families to official service in India through many generations and that came to be embodied in Anglo-Indian cemeteries in the subcontinent; Kipling was to memorialize these generational continuities in "The Tomb of His Ancestors."[95] Nonetheless, the possibility of India as a settler colony was inconceivable to most Anglo-Indians, including writers; of the latter, only Kipling—and only in Kim—was willing to imagine this eventuality, and even he was to speak of it quite emphatically as one best suited for the "country born," rather than those born and raised in the British Isles.

Under these circumstances it is perhaps no surprise that for the better part of a century Anglo-Indians had a profoundly vexing and contingent relationship with the question of their own legitimacy and autochthony in a colony far from a place denominated as home. As Sen notes, sovereignty was "ill defined and jealously guarded in the new regime established in India by the East India Company." In India, the Company saw itself as heir both of the Roman empire and of the Mughal one; and, despite the inconsistency and ambiguity of its relationship with the Mughal emperor, it was unwilling, before the events of 1857–58 (when the Company was violently set aside and the Mughal emperor hailed by the mutineers as the sovereign of Hindustan) to repudiate decisively the notion of a shadow legitimacy derived from their relationship with him.[96] Nicholas Dirks notes further that the Company struggled with the question of sovereignty over several decades and with respect to more than one state entity since its rights and privileges had to be defined not only in relation to the Mughal empire but also in relation to a British Parliament that sought periodically to regulate its proceedings and to manage its unsound finances. "The Company continued in many respects as a rogue state," Dirks says, "in its relation both to the Mughal empire and the British Crown."[97] This led to a continuous tension between the idioms of intimacy and distance that formed the grammar of Anglo-Indians' relationship to their place of rule and long, if sometimes reluctant, habitation.

The Mutiny is construed in most accounts as a moment of crisis for Anglo-Indian self-definition and as a crucial turning point in the racial logics of belonging and alienation.[98] While it is possible to overstate the importance of 1857 in the hardening of racial distinctions, the transformation "from nabob to sahib in India" was certainly dramatized at this juncture.[99] This transformation was marked by its intensely somaticized logic and certain orificial obsessions. If the Indian male was characterized by improper appetites (the lust for white women, opium, and bhang), improper aversion (the refusal to eat meat, or some kinds of meat, and the rejection of commensality), and improper evacuation (the failure to manage bodily waste in accordance with the dictates of civilization), the Anglo-Indian in the nineteenth century sought to distinguish his civilizational status through the "clean and proper" modes of managing food and bodily waste.[100] In this he was analogous to the secular upper-class European so vividly described in Norbert Elias's The Civilizing Process as the end-product of the management over several centuries of such mundane bodily practices as eating at the table, expectoration, farting, urination, and defecation. Elias details the ways in which changes in the management of sexual life and of the alimentary canal, including how, where, and in whose presence one ate, belched, farted, urinated, defecated, and had sex (or not), were transformative of affective structure and response.[101] This historically contingent and socially constructed second nature or habitus was at the same time part of a differential system designed to separate modern from primitive, civilized from uncivilized. Elias suggests that it is an emerging vocabulary of social distinction in the Renaissance that governs the micrologic of bodily and intimate practice and leads to the emergence of what today is designated the private rather than considerations of the medical and hygienic values of cleanliness and changing technologies of waste management.[102]

These transformations of mundane bodily practice, affective life, interpersonal relations, and technologies of waste removal occurred slowly and unevenly in Europe, though the diacritical character of this supposed civilizing process was never in doubt. By the nineteenth century, as the work of Peter Stallybrass and Allon White (among many others) on sanitary reform in Britain has shown us, a middle-class interest in slums and sewers and their products and inhabitants—pigs, rats, bodily wastes, and impoverished populations scarcely distinguishable from them—was the sign of a "reformation of the senses" that established "new thresholds of shame, embarrassment and disgust."[103] A process of transcoding linked these avatars of the low to the "lower bodily stratum" and to uncovenanted sexual behaviors that retained their fascination despite or perhaps because of their relegation to a social and moral periphery.

. . .

The marked sanitary preoccupations and reforms of nineteenth-century London and Paris undoubtedly form one of the contexts for the organization of Anglo-Indian living space in a distant colony, although, as we shall see, caste is inseparable from the thinking of social class formation for Anglo-Indians. Described by Florence Nightingale as a "focus of epidemics," a land of "domestic filth," and a place where plague and pestilence were "the ordinary state of things," India came to be identified by its unremitting filth and stenches.[104] Europeans, as unprotected newcomers in this alien, dangerous landscape, were thought to be susceptible to a variety of fevers, fluxes, and liver diseases to which the natives were largely immune. With the passage of time, however, the susceptibility of Occidentals came to be explained less through the logic of their lack of acclimatization than through the pathologization of the bodies of the Indians they encountered. Long before germ theory gained ground among European and, much later, Anglo-Indian epidemiologists, theories of contagion emphasized atmospheric and moral vulnerability. Contagionists believed that cholera was spread by contact with infected people, food, and objects, while subscribers to the miasmic theory insisted that it rose from the noxious effluvia of slums, which were marked by accumulations of dirt and decayed matter.[105] As in Britain, cholera and many of the other diseases of the subcontinent, such as plague, dysentery, malaria, and enteric fever (typhoid), were associated with the foul odors of contaminated food, drink, and sewage, disseminated among Anglo-Indian populations by contaminated native bodies themselves immunized against infection by long familiarity with filth.[106] This provoked demands for greater physical and social distances between the Indians and sahibs over the course of the century. Anglo-Indians in the nineteenth century came to reside at a marked distance from the miasmas, sexual danger, and disease of crowded Indian bazaars and mosquito-ridden tanks. A public health policy that would involve cleaning up Indian towns was expensive and politically chancy. So European settlements— cantonments and civil stations—were built at a safe distance upwind from the stenches and clamor of the "black town." In these settlements, colonial and household management constituted a single unit, as Rosemary George has demonstrated.[107] Its policies dictated that servants' quarters be situated far away from the bungalow, at the outer limits of the compound, and that vigorous efforts be made to police the bodily and sartorial cleanliness of the servants, from cooks and bearers to the *dai* whose breast milk nourished fragile Anglo-Indian infants.[108] As in high-caste Hindu households the untouchable figure of the sweeper was regarded with particular suspicion and often barred from every place but the latrine.[109] Hill stations were developed in the foothills of the Himalayas and in the southern mountain ranges to provide sanatoria for troops, schools for the European children who could not be sent to Britain for their education, and a refuge, especially for women and children, from the heat and dust of the plains. Consisting of houses and gardens built on the English rural model and enforcing restrictions on the entry of plains-dwelling Indians, except for servants, porters, and shopkeepers, hill stations came to be seen as islands of Britishness in an insalubrious land.[110] Unlike their forebears of the preceding century, Anglo-Indians wore clothing such as flannel underwear, suits, evening dress for dinner, and hooped skirts that made few concessions to the temperatures of the subcontinent, though the Indian practice of daily bathing was readily adopted. Curries, chutneys, kedgeree, and mulligatawny soup were incorporated into the Anglo-Indian diet, but a concerted effort was made in the official community to procure and serve European foodstuffs, above all on official occasions, with tinned foods of dubious quality often substituting for fresh Indian vegetables.[111] These endeavors to eschew tactile, oral, and olfactory contact with Indian bodies were characteristic primarily of the members of the covenanted civil service, the so-called heaven born, the Brahmins of the Anglo-Indian community, and of military officers, second to them in the protocols of precedence. At the lower reaches of this hierarchy there was a not-inconsiderable traffic, primarily sexual, with Indian bodies, as the frequent alarms about the British soldier's health indicated.[112]

For these fragile, anxious, and cosseted bodies, the experience of the Mutiny was overwhelmingly that of a bodily trauma entirely unwonted for them.[113] The outrageousness of the Mutiny lay not only in the betrayals and ingratitude it enacted, but also in the violence and degradation it visited upon hitherto sacrosanct Anglo-Indian bodies. A large part of the Anglo-Indian experience, whether female or male, of 1857 was one of bodily labor, dearth, filth, overcrowding, and captivity and of contact with vermin, corpses, bodily waste, and strange foods (or nonfoods). Account after account of the sieges at Cawnpore and Lucknow, two of the three centers of the Mutiny, stresses a metaphorics of bodily defilement and disintegration, as epidermal and orificial limits were repeatedly ruptured or violated.

. . .

One of the earliest intimations that something was out of joint in the relations of Anglo-Indians and natives manifested itself in the experience of a Mrs. Elizabeth Sneyd, who was traveling through Cawnpore in March 1857. When she stopped at the Old Cawnpore Hotel, the only suitable commercial lodging for a European lady, she learned, disturbingly for her, that the best rooms had been booked by a group of "native princes & chiefs" and their numerous armed retainers. A recent popular account of the Mutiny speculates that these native princes might have been Nana Saheb and Azimullah Khan. Given two shabby little rooms normally occupied by the head clerk, possibly an Indian or a Eurasian, Mrs. Sneyd was dismayed to find that the sepoys outside her rooms laughed and pointed at her rather than showing the deference to which she was accustomed. Worse yet, when, after some delay, she finally received her meal, it consisted of "only a small quantity of the stale remnants of the natives' dinner." At this point she fled the hotel and continued on her journey.[114] The episode has something of a nightmare quality, being marked by an escalating set of encroachments, pollutions, and humiliations: the usurpation of the best rooms by natives, the assignment of rooms normally occupied by native bodies and therefore "dirty and comfortless," the threatening proximity and insolence of armed men, the belated production of leftovers from native tables, and, finally, the flight into the Indian night. At each step the trespasses, proceeding from the spatial to the alimentary, become more intimate and threatening. It is apt perhaps that the tipping point comes for her with the belated arrival of the "stale remnants." How, one wonders, did these come to be identified as "stale remnants" rather than the food proper to an English lady? Was it the circumstance of their late arrival? Or their meager quantity? Or the fact that the meal probably consisted of Indian rather than Anglo-Indian food? Was Mrs. Sneyd indeed served the half-eaten remains of others' food? The narrative does not clarify this, only her dissatisfaction at the leavings that were, like the room, contaminated by Indian usage.

It is instructive to read this anecdote through the lens of a Hindu caste-based gastropolitics, one with which Anglo-Indians were thoroughly familiar, through the concept of *jootha* or *uchhishta*. The concept of jootha, encompassing anything that has come into contact with saliva, is central to understanding caste norms of purity, pollution, and ritually enforced degradation. In normal interactions every effort is made to avoid consuming food or water left over from another's plate or table, especially those of equal or inferior rank, though younger children are often fed from a parent's, usually a mother's, plate. This is because, as Charles Malamoud writes, "leftover food is not only the remains of *some thing*, it is the remains of *some one*; and as such, the more vile and impure the person who might have eaten or touched it, the more impure the leftover" (emphasis added).[115] Consuming cooked food from another's table or plate is consequently an acknowledgment of one's ritual inferiority and may be undertaken or mandated to give concrete form to such inferiority. Thus wives will eat off their husbands' plates, disciples will consume the leftovers of their guru, and everyone partakes of food offered to the gods (*naivedyam*), which returns to devotees as *prasad*, or divine leftovers. Even more significantly, leftovers were and are routinely given to untouchables, such receipt of leavings becoming one of the most explicit reminders of their degraded status. In light of this, one can see that the word jootha is immensely recalcitrant to translation into English, in which it is often rendered as "leftovers" or, occasionally and more accurately but still imperfectly, as "garbage."[116] In a context in which the consumption of high-caste jootha is one of the definitional axes of ritual degradation, the encounter with the Nana's jootha constitutes for Mrs. Sneyd a portent of apocalypse.[117] In an insurgent context marked by the undermining of the prestige of dominant figures and classes through verbal and ritual insults and the forceful inversion of the terms of mastery and subordination, this may indeed have been the import of the lady's reception at the Old Cawnpore Hotel. Many sepoys did commence their commitment to mutiny by throwing off deference to their white officers.[118] Certainly she, as an Anglo-Indian steeped in the caste-based habitus of spatial and alimentary deference and degradation, seems to have read it in these terms.

Once the outbreak was under way, mutineers' alimentary offenses and Anglo-Indian alimentary sufferings took a variety of forms, some of them quite sensational. Alexander Duff for one declared that "in [a] well-authenticated case, *the European servant of a mess was seized and slowly cut up into small pieces, and portions of his flesh forced down the throats of his children*, before they were themselves cruelly destroyed!"[119] Cannibalism became a repeating trope, appearing in accounts of rebel atrocities committed at Delhi, Meerut, and Allahabad and even reported prominently in the London *Times*. It also features quite prominently in Edward Leckey's account of the "fictions connected with the Indian outbreak of 1857."[120] Such abiding interest was perhaps unsurprising given a nineteenth-century European imaginary fascinated with cannibalism as an exemplary instance of the waning or absence of civilization and a centuries-long Christian literary and visual tradition of seeing hell as a giant mouth or kitchen and chewing, digestion, and regurgitation as its punishments for the damned.[121] In a macabre echo of indigenous fantasies of force-feeding, Indians did not turn cannibal themselves but compelled English children to devour their own parents. In other tales, mothers were fed upon children. Occasionally the cannibal fantasy teetered on the edge of comic absurdity—this is perhaps inescapable in the cannibal tale—as in the story of twenty-eight officers slaughtered in an Allahabad mess, their arms and legs cut off to be arranged in dishes like joints of beef.[122] Clearly the Indian butchers were adept, if sanguinary, mimics of British modes of food preparation and service. Yet the hyperbolic improbability of these tales does not obscure altogether the panic they register about the breakdown in the impermeability of once inviolate bodies.

. . .

There were also more banal but no less consequential instances of alimentary privation. In fact a significant experience of the Mutiny for Anglo-Indian women and men involved living in conditions of alimentary dearth, hygienic deprivation, and overcrowding that were entirely undreamed of for them. A number of the accounts of survivors describe the distresses of diminishing rations and unequal distribution in contexts where social hierarchies continued to flourish despite the scope of the crisis. For those living in the beleaguered entrenchment at Cawnpore, the early days of plenty, featuring champagne, rum, tinned herrings and salmon, sweetmeats, and jam, soon gave way to meager rations of split peas and flour. Anglo-Indians unskilled in domestic labors complained of the high prices charged for cooking by the few remaining Indian servants. Even this diet of chapatis and dal (the everyday food of the common folk in northern India) had to be eked out with other anomalous, primitive, and forbidden forms of nutriment. "Food, which in happier times would have been turned from with disgust, was seized with avidity and devoured with relish," says Kaye. "To the flesh-pots of the besieged no carrion was unwelcome. A stray dog was turned into soup. An old horse, fit only for the knackers, was converted into savoury meat. And when glorious good fortune brought a Brahmani bull within the fire of our people, and with difficulty the carcase of the animal was hauled into the intrenchments, there was rejoicing as if a victory had been gained."[123] This picture of the Anglo-Indian turned eater of carrion is not without a sense of irony and even of gusto, though Kaye's account also records that some members of the entrenchment were too consumed with disgust to partake of horse flesh and dog soup. What was more unequivocally troublesome was the lack of water, the well inside the entrenchment being exposed to enemy fire. The hazardous task of drawing water was performed, after the death of the Indian water carriers, by volunteers from the European regiments, who sometimes charged high prices for their services, delegated the task to Indian servants, and on other occasions threatened the water supplies of weaker members of the entrenchment. When water could be procured it was sometimes contaminated by fallen mortar and by human and animal blood.

Those in the Residency at Lucknow were much better provisioned, though many of the memsahibs possessed the most rudimentary domestic skills and were hard put to cook meals and wash clothes and keep themselves cool without the usual contingent of Indian servants. Notwithstanding the crisis under which all inhabitants of the Residency labored, some civilians had access to a stock of gastronomic delicacies, one which could be augmented by purchases at auctions of the supplies of the dead. Women and sepoys received less food than British soldiers, and camp followers even less. Meanwhile their attackers mocked them by dangling chickens and chapatis at the ends of poles while their bands played "God Save the Queen" and "The Girl I Left Behind Me."[124] The experience of subsisting on unfamiliar and inadequate food was exacerbated in both Cawnpore and Lucknow by the health and sanitary conditions that prevailed in the heat and rain. In Cawnpore water was obtained with difficulty and was available only for drinking, not for ablutions; before long the stench in the barracks drove many families to the open air of the trenches. In Lucknow there were no sweepers to empty the latrines, which were soon filled to overflowing. To the stench of these was added that of rotting corpses and animal carcasses. There were vermin of all kinds and a high and often fatal incidence of diarrhea, cholera, typhoid, malaria, typhus, hepatitis, scurvy, and dysentery. In the Residency hospital, patients were surrounded by and sometimes covered in blood, vomit, pus, excreta, vermin, and amputated limbs; gangrene and blood poisoning were common.

These experiences of bodily deprivation and penetrability and the adjacency to dirt, bodily waste, and human remains served in a fashion as a form of Indianization, as hitherto pristine, invulnerable Anglo-Indian bodies became malodorous, pulpy, suppurating containers of blood, excrement, and sweat. In a reversal of the usual relationship of white (or half-white) body to cleanliness, when W. J. Shepherd, a Eurasian member of General Hugh Wheeler's entrenchment in Cawnpore, went into the city in Indian guise, he was almost immediately recognized as one of the English party because he was markedly smelly and greasy and because he was drunk on rum.[125] And Mowbray Thomson, seeking to quell rumors of the rape of the ladies at the Bibighar, provided a grossly corporeal reason for their having been spared such violation: "Such was the loathsome condition into which, from long destitution and exposure, the fairest and youngest of our women had sunk that not a sepoy would have polluted himself with their touch."[126]

This dissolution of bodily boundaries was exacerbated in conditions of captivity. George Otto Trevelyan, the author of *Cawnpore* (1865), one of the classic Mutiny narratives, speaks at length of the numerous bodily indignities visited upon the Anglo-Indian women and children who were the captives of Nana Saheb at the Bibighar.[127] Notwithstanding the privations suffered during the three weeks at Wheeler's entrenchment—weeks marked, as has been noted, by dirt, disease, and a diet of pariah dog and horse soup—Trevelyan stresses the delicacy and privileged status of the victims: "Here, during a fortnight of the Eastern summer, were penned two hundred and six persons of European extraction: for the most part women and children of gentle birth." Their privations included overcrowded lodgings meant for servants, matting in place of bedding, heat, manual labor, such as the washing of one's own linen and the grinding of corn, "coarse Indian food" of lentils and chapatis, and trips to the verandah rather than the rides on horseback to which they had been accustomed. These deprivations are properly glossed, Trevelyan argues, not according to any commonplace understanding of privation or punishment but according to the sensibility of the victims: "If the various degrees of wretchedness are to be estimated by the faculty for suffering contained in the victim, then were these ladies of all women the most miserable."[128] *Cawnpore* as a text functions as the most successful instance of the Mutiny's narratives of sensibility, transforming the sensationalist details of the famous massacre into a finely calibrated representation of the physical debility, emotional vulnerability, and tremblingly delicate responses of gentlewomen and children. As in other examples of the narrative of sensibility, its fetishization of female suffering does more than highlight (or celebrate) a classed feminine susceptibility to physical and psychic pain: it calls out at the same time for male sensitivity and male redress.

Like Kaye, J. W. Sherer, W. H. Russell, Thomson, and other contemporary historians, writers, and eyewitnesses, Trevelyan repudiates the stories of the rape of white women at Cawnpore: "If we except a single case of abduction, it is absolutely certain that our ladies died without mention, and, we may confidently hope without apprehension of dishonour."[129] Nonetheless the expulsion of the Indian rapist from the scene of incarceration and suffering does not do away altogether with other kinds of unseemly and quasi-sexualized proximity. Seventy-five paces from the Bibighar, Trevelyan relates, was a hotel favored by Nana Saheb. Here he lived "in a perpetual round of sensuality" in the company of "priests, pandars, ministers, and minions" and his favorite courtesan, "Oula or Adala." His rooms were the site of nightly entertainments of feasting, music, dance, pantomime, and other all too obvious debaucheries. "The noise of this unhallowed revelry was plainly audible to the captives in the adjoining house," says Trevelyan.[130] More than this auditory link connected the scene of the Nana's noisy libidinal revelries and the ladies' prison, however, as the "Begum," the woman who was the ladies' warden, was a member of the entourage of "Oula or Adala." For the author of *Cawnpore*, there is little question that this was a deeply gendered insult, standing in to some degree by the logic of contiguity for the sexual trespasses he is compelled overtly to disavow.[131]

In the grotesque sensorium that was the Nana's prison every sense came under assault: sight (of jeering sepoys), sound (of the Nana's debaucheries), smell (in cramped and insalubrious quarters), touch, and taste. The "nauseous and unwonted food" served up to the captives was an additional part of the Nana's visceral assault: "They fed sparely on cakes of unleavened dough, and lentil-porridge dished up in earthen pans without spoon or plate. There was some talk of meat on Sundays, but it never came to anything. Once the children got a little milk."[132] Compounding this outrage was the fact that the ladies were served their food by sweepers, outcaste menials who were usually assigned the cleaning of latrines, rather than by high-caste attendants, a detail Trevelyan sees as a very significant component of the English ladies' degradation: "The attendance of such debased menials was in itself the most ignominious affront which Oriental malice could invent: and even these were provided exclusively for the humiliation of our countrywomen, and might do nothing for their comfort."[133] The revulsion caused by having to eat the same food as the Indians is inseparable here from that caused by being served by handlers of excrement; indeed, Trevelyan's narrative hints that to the delicate-stomached English lady Indian food, Indian environs, bodily waste, and low-caste Indian bodies are scarcely distinguishable from each other. Here, eating, digestion, and being served are far from being self-contained; mouth, epidermis, and stomach function as conduits rather into a densely textured series of distinctions and maneuvers. Eating in this narrative functions as a trope for other dangerous interminglings and metabolizations, but it is also risky in the most irreducibly somatic terms. For the ladies it had the expected apocalyptic results. Within eight days, Trevelyan tells his readers, these bodily torments had claimed, notwithstanding the ministrations of an Indian doctor provided by the Nana, twenty-five European lives through dysentery and cholera, an annihilation effected through offenses against nourishment, hygiene, habitation, and deference that anticipated the greater massacre to come. In the weeks and months to come, avenging British troops would register their sense of these outrages at Cawnpore through the digestive troping of their own violent actions: to give a mutinous sepoy or indeed any Indian a "Cawnpore dinner" was to assault him with six inches of steel in the gut.[134]

The Well of the English

We can undoubtedly cleanse this poisoned well.
—EDWARD THOMPSON, The Other Side of the Medal

The imagination of atrocity came most often to rest in the environs of the Bibighar in Cawnpore, where British women and children had been imprisoned by Nana Saheb, and in the well into which their dead and dying bodies were cast. It was no accident that Trevelyan's celebrated account of the Mutiny was entitled Cawnpore or that it read the events of 1857–58 in terms of developments in that city: General Wheeler's entrenchment, the attack at the ghats, and the slaughter of the women. Patrick Brantlinger notes the ways in which Mutiny texts return obsessively to the "well of horror." It is an architectural landmark that tropes in these texts the breach signified by the Mutiny: "The well becomes a widening chasm dividing the forces of absolute righteousness from the demonic armies of the night."[135] The well came to be productive of an immense train of associations, recalling the Black Hole of Calcutta of a hundred years earlier, the polluted wells of Indian rumor, and the besieged wells—one serving as a source of water, another as a makeshift sepulcher—of the entrenchment at Cawnpore. It also opened up, as we have seen in the case of the rumors of rape, a semipornographic portal to an imagined world of raced and sexualized atrocity.[136] It does not take too much imagination to read the well as a giant gullet or as a cloacal opening, drawing unsuspecting British innocents into the unsavory depths of an all-devouring subcontinent (much as Morrowbie Jukes is engulfed into a village of the polluted Indian undead in Kipling's story).

. . .

While it does not focus on the Bibighar as such, the description of the entrenchment and its environs by the *Times* journalist W. H. Russell affords a vivid sense of an encounter with the colonial bowels: "It was a horrible spot! Inside the shattered rooms, which had been the scene of such devotion and suffering, are heaps of filth and rubbish. The entrenchment is used as a *cloaca maxima* by the natives, camp-followers, coolies, and others who bivouac in the sandy plains around it. The smells are revolting. Rows of gorged vultures sit with outspread wings on the mouldering parapets, or perch in clusters on the two or three leafless trees at the angle of the works by which we enter. I shot one with my revolver; and as the revolting creature disgorged his meal, twisting its bare black snake-like neck to and fro, I made a vow I would never incur such a disgusting sight again."[137] Rooms, trenches, and wells here are sewers rather than the monumentalized *lieux de mémoire* they were to become in other Mutiny texts.[138] In an interestingly de-idealizing move, Russell does not, unlike many of his contemporaries, expend too much energy, in the diary at least, on the pathos of helpless, doomed ladies and children and unsuspecting British officers proceeding all unwittingly to their massacre.[139] He can take as given his readers' familiarity with the "devotion and suffering" enacted on this spot. More than anything else, this encounter with one of the scenes of Mutiny atrocity is an intense experience of almost gothicized architectural and natural decay (moldering parapets, leafless trees) and of bodily grossness. The latter is represented by all the most disgusting operations of an alimentary canal open both above and below, gorging, vomiting, and excreting. Human remains and human waste, among the most potent of polluting substances, are powerfully conjoined here.[140] What renders the conjoining most disturbing is that the former (human remains) have been converted to the latter (human waste). What remains here of slaughter and suffering is a great stench and "filth and rubbish" generated by natives indifferent to, perhaps even deliberately contemptuous of, sanctity of place. Excreta and rubbish have both a material and a figural character here. As we have seen, scatology is tied explicitly to the representation of backwardness and underdevelopment, and olfactory and excremental vigilance functions as a marker of civilization.[141] The natives in Russell's account are no longer mutinous or murderous; but odor, of all senses the most akin to animality and mortality and the one which most threatens to engulf us, is the form in which the native body assaults him.[142] "Smell is, so to speak, taste at a distance," says Immanuel Kant, "and other people are forced to share a scent whether they want to or not. . . . Internal penetration (into the lungs) through smell is even more intimate than through the absorptive vessels of mouth or gullet."[143] Hence it induces in Russell a moment of marked cultural and somatic panic, attended by a discharge unusual in a text marked in a great many respects by its deliberative, restrained character. Written in February 1858, well after Colonel Neill's capture of Cawnpore and his widespread slaughter of the local population, the work of cleansing and vengeance is presumably complete and yet, judging from the excretory activities of masses of natives, not quite done. The paragraph moves from excreting native to gorged, revolting vulture in a fashion that cannot but establish the slide as allegorically marked; the repletion of the vultures, who function simultaneously as birds and snakes, exceeds the norms of empirical depiction. Still gorged, presumably upon European flesh, given the affective drift of this tableau, several months after the deaths and massacres of the former Anglo-Indian and Eurasian inhabitants of the entrenchment, the vultures call for an Englishman's violent vengeance, a vengeance that must be withheld (but only barely) from the human objects of disgust.

The revenge Russell deflected to the vultures was to be carried out by Frederick Cooper, deputy commissioner of Amritsar, who slaughtered nearly five hundred unarmed and famished sepoys of the 26th Native Infantry regiment who had surrendered to him, after killing two of their officers, in the expectation of being court-martialed. Thus he was able to conclude, "There is a well at Cawnpoor; but there is also one at Ujnalla."[144]

The real and imagined atrocities of the Mutiny were avenged with a ferocity of which not a few English commentators took note. Christopher Herbert is right to underline the sometimes disconcerting and unhinged mode, rather than an invariably triumphalist one, that marks these accounts of the brutality of counterinsurgency.[145] That Indians were put to death in large numbers regardless of their participation in the uprising against the colonial power is too well known now to bear repeating at any length, though the numerous eyewitness accounts of Anglo-Indian officers still make for sobering reading, as do the accounts of nonrebellious and even in some instances pro-British Indians such as Ghalib and Bholanauth Chunder.[146] In all too obvious ways, as thinkers such as Carl Schmitt and Achille Mbembe have established, these modes of counterinsurgency serve as an elaboration of the racialized supplement to the Westphalian order that established the rules of legitimate war between legitimate enemies. This is the "unbracketed war" that can be waged in the "overseas zone" outside the boundaries of the European state system and against the unjust enemy, whether slave, colonized subject, or the nonwhite subject of the apartheid regime, who does not deserve the considerations accorded the just enemy.[147] Such an antagonist, against whom violence can be exercised free of constraint, is an instance of what Baucom has named "inimical life," one who inhabits a body open to the full force of superior and annihilating might.[148] Further, unbracketed war against such a foe can exercise violence in a mode of performative and pedagogical excess, as Mbembe memorably observes: "Violence, here, becomes an element in manners, like whipping or taking of the slave's life itself: an act of caprice and pure destruction aimed at instilling terror."[149]

What is certainly as important to note, however, about the counterinsurgency is the way in which it fully and inventively incorporated indigenous ideas about ingestion and contamination; its tactics seem driven by the desire to bear out, retrospectively, the logic of profanation and force-feeding in the bone dust and cartridge stories. Such a desire was perhaps not unique to counterinsurgency in colonial India. Colonial and slave-holding forms of punishment did occasionally involve what might be designated "creolization from above," as Diana Paton's work on the punishment of slaves in eighteenth-century Jamaica has demonstrated. Pointing out that floggings and the nailing of severed body parts to silk cotton trees capitalized upon their significance in Afro-Jamaican cosmology, she notes, "The magistrates may have been seeking to displace the power of obeah from the cotton tree by demonstrating their greater power over the bodies of African and African-Jamaican slaves. It is also possible, however, that they recognized the power associated with the tree and aimed to use it to their own ends, . . . The belief in the symbolic importance of the cotton tree was something Jamaican whites were aware of, tried to manipulate, to some extent adopted, and in so doing, probably increased."[150]

In post-Mutiny India, a common punishment for mutineers was to blow them to bits from the mouths of cannon, a punishment that made burial or cremation impossible. In the case of those dispatched by hanging or shooting or bayoneting, the corpses were in most instances not released to the next of kin but left deliberately to feed jackals and wolves. Captives were frequently made to eat beef and pork before being dispatched to their doom. In some cases Muslim corpses were sewn in pigskin or burned and Hindu bodies buried in a reversal of customary funerary practice—acts of desecration that encompassed living kin in their punishments.[151] In a particularly noteworthy instance Indians captured in Cawnpore, who were held culpable in the deaths of women and children at Bibighar simply by reason of their proximity to the place of massacre, were forced to lick clean a square foot of the blood-soaked floor before being taken to the gallows.[152] Those who demurred at this were whipped by mehtars (cleaners of lavatories; untouchables) who had explicitly been recruited, along with other lower-caste men, to serve as auxiliary police forces against the rebels.[153] Colonel Neill, who ordered the blood licking at Cawnpore, made it clear that more was at stake than punishment for crimes committed and that he was as much invested in the gastrologic of pollution as those he was punishing: "To touch blood is most abhorrent to the high caste natives; they think by doing so they doom their souls to perdition. Let them think so."[154] Russell reprobated these "excesses," even as he suggested that the tortures practiced by the English avengers were neither English nor Christian but part of a peculiarly Indian contagion: "All these kinds of vindictive, unchristian, Indian torture, such as sewing Mohammedans in pig-skins, smearing them with pork-fat before execution, and forcing Hindus to defile themselves, are disgraceful, and ultimately recoil on themselves."[155]

What is fascinating here about Anglo-Indian affect and practice is the appropriation of caste against the caste-bound, in a deadly combat in which the servants' tools are used to dismantle the servants' house.[156] The Anglo-Indian borrowing of structures of somatic response suggests, resists, and manages ideas of acculturation and assimilation. As we know, conquest and war in the colonial context produce in their wake anxieties of counterinvasion and reverse colonization; counterinsurgency therefore becomes a way of generating prophylactics against the threat of contamination.[157] We have seen from a reading of the Anglo-Indian texts of Mutiny that these affects have powerful bodily manifestations. What these texts also underline is the way in which the conquerors' identification with their subjects is most inexorable, ironically enough, during the crisis of counterinsurgency. After all, when the enemy has perfected the art of ritual degradation to such an extraordinary degree, what better instructor can one hope to find? One might characterize this peculiar process of identification as a certain caste envy on the part of those who would always be found wanting, despite their long history of imperial conquest and notwithstanding their most sanguinary fantasies, in the endeavor to best or even to match such a richly baroque and stunningly durable apparatus of abjection as caste appeared to be.

Such forms of caste emulation and caste envy could not be practiced, needless to say, without a certain degree of ambivalence. Thus the spectacular and archaic grossness of bloody, ritually degrading punishments sits uneasily, undigested, in the colonial texts. While details of Indian atrocities are described in thorough and often stomach-churning detail there is greater decorousness about English ones in *Cawnpore*. "Of what did take place the less said is the better," says Trevelyan about the vengeance visited on Cawnpore. "Reckless as men . . . half-starved, and more than half-intoxicated, . . . they enacted a scene into the details of which an Englishman at least will not care to inquire."[158] The digestive troping of counterinsurgent ethics reminds one that, for Britons at least as much as for Indians, mouth and stomach were not peripheral but central to understanding the logic and operations of colonialism. As the author's terse summary intimates, the availability of enormous quantities of alcohol made drunkenness among tommies—always regarded as a physical and moral liability because of their uncontrolled appetites—and occasionally among Sikh soldiers a real trial for officers and chroniclers. On occasion drunken troops disobeyed their officers and on others widespread intoxication made military advances impossible. In several cases stores of alcohol had to be destroyed to ensure a minimal degree of sobriety among the ranks of the noncommissioned. Sometimes the wanton looting of Indian cities and indiscriminate slaughter of Indians were also, as in this instance, attributed to the influence of alcohol. Such excesses of appetite and expression made it enormously difficult for English officers to maintain the discipline that supposedly separated English troops from opium- and bhang-stupefied mutineers and fanatics.[159]

Episodes such as these are awkward and unsettled moments in the narrative of mutiny, turning the gastrologic of colonialism on its head and producing white bodies as embodiments of drives, decay, and delirium. The imperative to obliterate these fraught carnalities—carnalities that, as I have suggested, showcased the unexpected and uncanny alimentary and sexual intimacies of Indian and Anglo-Indian—might account at least in part for certain obsessive forms of purification and memorialization that followed the conclusion of the Mutiny. If the tenuous hyphen separating and conjoining *Anglo* from and with *Indian* collapses or at least teeters in the course of the Mutiny, post-Mutiny recovery is an endeavor to overcome self-estrangement and restore decorum to a Britishness lost to itself.

Bernard Cohn for one has described how the fetish of the Mutiny pilgrimage—to Mutiny sites in Delhi, Cawnpore, and Lucknow—became a routine part of English travel to India.[160] This was an extension and reorientation of a decades-long tradition by British travelers and Anglo-Indians of paying homage to memorials to European mortality in the Indian landscape, memorials that seemed to constitute "a kind of 'melancholy' title to India."[161] Moreover, in an Indo-Islamic context that had long used grand tombs as a mode of asserting political power, Anglo-Indians came even to take a certain pride in their stately funerary monuments.[162] But what began as an emulation of the Mughal empire came eventually to be a marker of Anglo-Indian particularity and difference, encouraging distinctly nonindigenous forms of recognition in its Anglo-Indian viewers. "The self-image of the imperial service," notes Robert Travers, "relied heavily on a sense of affiliation with the community of the imperial dead."[163] Such modes of architectural devotion (and a concomitant self-alienation), accentuated in the decades after the Mutiny, were the obverse of the process of architectural destruction that occurred in the great urban centers of the uprising, notably Delhi and Lucknow, in the aftermath of the crisis. The restoration of British power after the capture of Delhi involved what Cohn has called a "desacralization" of the person of the Mughal emperor and of the city that was the seat of his rule.[164] Hence historical buildings within the Red Fort, the residence of the Mughal emperor, and its vicinity in Delhi were vandalized, and mosques were destroyed, sold to Hindu merchants, or converted to military or government purposes.[165] As the implicit counterpart to such annihilation, the Mutiny pilgrimage was as much a memorialization of the martyrdom and the eventual triumphs that characterized British rule in the subcontinent as it was an elaboration of the estrangement of the sahib's body from its place of habitation. In a curious way this very estrangement simultaneously configured India as part of a sacred Anglo-Indian geography, with Anglo-Indians distinguished as the salt of that alien earth. Baucom puts it aptly: "In thus discovering the Mutiny as the pretext for a narrative of imperial belonging, the colonists rendered a visit to the Mutiny sites an act of Ruskinian remembrance and anticipation in which the present and future are subordinated to a privileged past, and memory emerges as the angel of history and the god of the everyday."[166]

Note, for instance, Trevelyan's meditations, from 1865, on the afterlife of the well at Cawnpore, now cleansed and architecturally remade with newly commissioned statuary and a church: "It is interesting to observe the neat garden that strives to beguile away the associations which haunt the well of evil fame, and to peruse the inscription indited by a vice-regal hand. It may gratify some minds, beneath the roof of a memorial church that is now building, to listen while Christian worship is performed above a spot which once resounded with ineffectual prayers and vain ejaculations addressed to quite other ears. . . . For that is the very place itself where the act was accomplished."[167] Less than a decade after the Mutiny the well at Cawnpore is a bucolic spot, purged of all signs of corpses and bodily wastes and presided over by Baron Carlo Marochetti's beautiful marble angel.[168] What makes this picture of innocence possible is the exclusion of all non-Christian Indians from the site of the well and the graves. (They were to be barred from it until the end of British rule in 1947.) This marmoreal shape—not quite a Benjaminian angel of history! —works as an apt figure of a reformed and etherealized Anglo-Indian body, freed finally of appetites, stenches, and emissions.

2

Abstinence

Meatless Days

The topic of M. K. Gandhi's incarnation as a prodigy of alimentary abstinence, a term that includes vegetarianism, fasting, and other forms of
culinary and gustatory discipline, is one that scarcely needs any introduction for scholarly and popular audiences of South Asian studies or indeed for audiences more broadly conceived. Gandhi was almost as noted,
indeed notorious, for his experiments in alimentation and elimination
as for those in celibacy and nonviolent political action; the fact of their
forming a single associative continuum should be by now almost entirely
commonsensical, and commonsensical not simply for modern audiences, with their knowingness about the intimacy between the gastronomic and the libidinal, but for the experimenter himself. Yet while
Gandhi's experiments with sexuality have received some attention, his
experiments with dietetics have, with few and often sketchy exceptions,
been curiously underread, or read as though their meaning is incontestably and reassuringly transparent. They are construed most typically as a
simple extension of a lifelong philosophy of *ahimsa* (nonviolence).

• • •

The seminal work of Susanne and Lloyd Rudolph and Joseph Alter and
the more recent work of Leela Gandhi provides an important corrective to
such unimaginative readings, though much remains to be done by way of
examining the paradoxes and aporias that the consistent practice of a
principled vegetarianism posed for Gandhi.[1] It is to this end that I under-

take an appraisal of the familial and national(ist) economies of carnivory, vegetarianism, fasting, and masculinity in his life and work, especially in his *Autobiography*. A scrutiny of the details and the contexts of his writings and practices on matters dietary demonstrates the profoundly complicated, equivocal, and transitional character of his gastropolitics, which was heavily reliant on the technology of experimentation.[2] The purport of his dietary experiments was quite often unclear to his associates and followers, who had frequently to live with the consequences of his various alimentary trials, and occasionally it was none too clear to Gandhi himself. Alternatively, his enduring interest in diet, dietary reform, and fasting has been read as a fad, extraneous to any serious consideration of his mahatma-hood. Many commentators have been reluctant to grant how consumingly corporeal Gandhian practice and ethics were and how pronounced his belief that the purification of the body was inseparable from the purification of the mind necessary for *swaraj* (self-rule). Gandhi's choice of diet as the terrain upon which his politics would be inaugurated, during his student days in England, is by no means as anomalous as it might initially appear. The fact that he would make salt the center of a widely publicized and immensely successful campaign against British rule in 1930 speaks to the ways in which he had refined a gastropolitics of long standing. The ethics of Gandhi's vegetarianism, its relationship to ahimsa and *brahmacharya* (celibacy), and its relation to a philosophy of bodily administration, representativeness, and leadership—all these merit more attention than they have received. I take up all of these questions here. But I would also like to examine not just the ethics of Gandhi's dietetics (though the question of ethics is irreducible in any consideration of a Gandhian diet) but its style, or the style of a Gandhian dietetic ethics—its gastroaesthetics if you will. My analysis will be directed at least in part to the figure of the body as vegetarian, especially to the production and transubstantiations of the meat-renouncing and sometimes food-renouncing male body. A scrutiny of this figure can help delineate the ambivalent social terrain of vegetarian practice and its modes of gendered self-staging; it can also illuminate the deeply complicated and unsettled ethical logic of a Gandhian vegetarianism.

In this reading of the aesthetics and ethics of embodied gender I am informed by a sense of the transactional and contextual character of Gandhi's body talk and body politics. To this end, I insist that the gendered character of his vegetarianism, fasting, and other modes of bodily discipline cannot be understood without invoking a large, inescapably gendered cast, including his mother, his male friends, his wife, his sons, and his female and male disciples. In particular, the consistently familial contexts of Gandhi's alimentary practices must be highlighted in any consideration of the gendered character of vegetarianism, nonviolence, and sacrifice, including self-sacrifice.

. . .

Gandhi's autobiography, it has often been noted, is marked by an unusual degree of candor, candor that manifests itself most characteristically in the quotidian rather than in the exalted details of everyday behavior. "What is most striking about Gandhi's experiments," says Alter, "is their utterly banal character, and Gandhi's own virtual obsession with seemingly mundane, utilitarian issues of diet, health, and, above all else, the control of sexual passion."[3] The details seem not so much the stuff of the quasi-allegorical end proper to the genre of autobiography: they are too numerous, too repetitive, too generically surprising if not outlandish, and too persistently earthbound for that.[4] For instance, much of his account in the *Autobiography* of his three years in England is given over, in contradistinction to other examples of the genre, not to his encounters with bourgeois English culture, his experiences as a student, his homesickness, or his associations with other Indian expatriates, but to what he describes as his "new religion" of vegetarianism. Sandhya Shetty notes another odd, even perverse, moment later in the *Autobiography*: when providing a narrative of his first Congress meeting in 1901, Gandhi allots a considerable modicum of narrative space to the other end of the alimentary canal, to the description of the delegates' odious sanitary habits: "Some of the delegates did not scruple to use the verandahs outside their rooms for calls of nature at night. In the morning I pointed out the spots to the volunteers. No one was ready to undertake the cleaning. . . . I saw that, if the Congress session were to be prolonged, conditions would be quite favourable for the outbreak of an epidemic."[5] This is a reaction one might expect from the Kipling of "The City of Dreadful Night" but not necessarily from one poised to be a leader of the nationalist movement. (As it happens they were both speaking of Calcutta, which had assumed by this point an emblematic status as the "shock city" of colonial India.) But such a response to Gandhi's sanitary concerns misunderstands, or understands only trivially, a figure who was a virtuoso of the symbolic act; Bhikhu Parekh has remarked upon his immensely successful mobilization of "a new aesthetics" of political behavior.[6] As the Rudolphs point out, the details are intimately related to the specific form of a Gandhian politics, a politics that brilliantly transformed mundane items like salt, caps, and *charkhas* (spinning wheels) into potent political symbols: "The autobiography . . . must be read with a particularly sensitive ear, one that hears what he has to say concerning his diet, or his relations to his wife, and considers what it might mean for his political style and for how that style was received. To relegate these remarks to the category of personal frills and curiosities that constitute the gossip rather than the serious significance of a great man is to miss what was central to his leadership."[7] It is in such a spirit I wish to examine Gandhi's experiments in dietetics, reading the details of his vegetarianism, fasting, and food asceticism, which are related but not necessarily identical with one another, not simply in terms of a ceaseless quest for perfectibility, but also situating them variously within specifically gendered discourses of bodily management and exhibition, within Indian as well as global and diasporic debates about modernity and its countercultures, and within the gendered dynamics of the Hindu vegetarian household. I move from Gandhi's early life in Kathiawad to his sojourns in England and South Africa and then to the ethicopolitical and gendered economy of the great public fasts of the later years. I conclude with a reading of three important moments of crisis around vegetarianism. Gandhi's *Autobiography*, or what he preferred to call *The Story of My Experiments With Truth*, written in 1927 as a series of didactic articles for his journal *Navajivan*, will be a primary object of my analysis, though I shall also have recourse to his other writings and to the compositions of his associates and fellow travelers.

As is well known, Gandhi grew up in a milieu marked by contrary principles of dietetics. His Hindu Vaishnava mother, whose favorite child he appears to have been and upon whose strictures and example (characterized by "saintliness" as well as "strong commonsense") he modeled himself as an adult, is remembered in the *Autobiography* not only for the number and duration of her food-related austerities but also, at least in the admiring grammar of the son's account(ing), for their sheer cumulative ambitiousness and their spectacular quality: "She would take the hardest vows and keep them without flinching. . . . To keep two or three consecutive fasts was nothing to her. Living on one meal a day during *Chaturmas* [the four-month period of the rainy season] was a habit with her. Not content with that she fasted every alternate day during one *Chaturmas*" (2). In later years Gandhi was to say, "I imbibed . . . [fasting] with my mother's milk," a curious locution that conjoins life-giving maternal nourishment with the greater gift of alimentary abstinence.[8] It is also indisputable that Jain principles of dietary discipline, which were widely disseminated in Gujarat, were of considerable and often self-conscious significance in the understanding of dietetic morality that he was to form over the course of his career. Some of the particulars associated with the dietetic philosophy of the adult Gandhi—the emphasis on vows in the chastening of the palate and of the libido; the careful limiting of the number and not just the kinds of food one eats over a given period; the refusal of spices and seasonings, including salt; and the importance of the fast, including, occasionally, the fast unto death, as a mode of regulating the violence of cooking, eating, and living in general—feature in a very fundamental way in Jain thinking about violence and consumption.[9] Perhaps even more than specific details, it was the centrality of diet and abstinence to everyday Jain self-fashioning that provided an important template for Gandhi's thinking about embodied ethics. As James Laidlaw says about Jain forms of asceticism, "The sense of pervasive asceticism which lay Jainism exudes comes not from uniform adherence to a set of socially enforced rules, still less from any sense that its followers live lives of consistent or imposed privation, but rather from the fact that because everyone must make a whole series of decisions for themselves, and adjust their diet continuously for a range of religious reasons, it is always a subject of conscious reflection and practical reasoning."[10]

Gandhi's lifelong interest in the ethics of ingestion, abstention, and elimination constituted an innovative recasting of these modes that vegetarianism assumed in the western Indian milieu of his youth. But, living as the Gandhis did under the aegis, even if indirect, of British rule, the question of diet as indeed of bodily ethics in general was not simply a local or insular one but spoke to the eater's status as a citizen of the world.[11] In emphatic contrast to the renunciatory ethic of the Vaishnava and Jain communities of Kathiawad was another dietary philosophy, conceived at least in part in response to the fact of colonialism and its putative effeminization of Indian and particularly Bengali Hindu males.[12] If the Macaulayan rhetoric of British colonialism had characterized the Bengali and paradigmatically the westernized, English-educated Hindu male as "feeble even to effeminacy,"[13] the object of derision had, ironically, made the stereotype of degeneracy his own;[14] Swami Vivekananda's prescription of "beef, biceps, and Bhagvadgita" as the curative is perhaps only the best known of the Indian responses to such a reproach. "It now seemed," says Milind Wakankar, "as though the gendered colonial subject, the 'lazy native,' but also the white-collar native bourgeois, needed . . . to define a relation to his body, to ensure the 'ascendancy' of his 'race'/'class' on the tree of evolution and the struggle for survival."[15]

. . .

British and Indian commentators agreed substantially not only in the diagnosis of physical and moral inadequacy but also about its positivist and environmental causes: an enervating climate, the precocity and frequency of marital sex that made women out of men through the depletion of seminal reserves, early childbearing and its baneful effects on physical robustness, and a meatless diet. The self-conception of feebleness was perhaps strongest among Bengali Hindu males but was also effectively internalized by colonized males in other parts of India (though, notably, Muslim and lower-class males were rarely hailed by such a characterization).[16] Gandhi recalls a doggerel in fashion among schoolboys in his youth that extolled the preternatural prowess of the Englishman, a prowess conferred by the eating of meat: "Behold the mighty Englishman / He rules the Indian small, / Because being a meat-eater / He is five cubits tall" (17). The carnophilic and carnivorous mandate that resulted from such national disparities in male physical and moral fiber was impressed on him by the tempter of his youth, the persuasive, seductive, and physically compelling Sheikh Mehtab: "We are a weak people because we do not eat meat. The English are able to rule over us, because they are meat-eaters. You know how hardy I am, and how great a runner too. It is because I am a meat-eater. . . . You should do likewise" (17). This piece of folklore about the flaccid vegetarian Hindu appears to have had a persuasive hold on the adolescent Mohandas, despite the fact that meat eating was not then and is not now prohibited to large numbers of caste Hindus; the prevalence of vegetarianism in his immediate household and among the Hindu and Jain communities he knew may account for the narrative's power over him. He appears, after some initial revulsion, to have developed a certain commitment to carnivory that, in common with many of his contemporaries, Muslim and Hindu, Indian and British, he associated with nationalist duty. Meat eating or a kind of culinary masculinity (to borrow a term from the Rudolphs) would nourish, in the most literal sense, not just Indian resistance to British rule but an entry into modernity and a condition of postcoloniality (indeed the two objectives were quite compatible with each other), so that a newly muscular Hinduism could challenge and match a muscular Christianity or a muscular

Englishness on its own terms.[17] More recently Derrida has named this "carno-phallogocentrism," asking, "In our countries, who would stand any chance of becoming a *chef d'Etat* (a head of State), and of thereby acceding 'to the head,' by publicly, and therefore exemplarily, declaring him- or herself to be a vegetarian? The *chef* must be an eater of flesh."[18] Thus, says Gandhi, "I wished to be strong and daring and wanted my countrymen also to be such, so that we might defeat the English and make India free" (18).[19] Meat, in other words, became a sacrificial substance whose introjection and assimilation enabled an address to and a parity with a figure both superior and other. Moreover, meat eating would free Gandhi not just from British rule but from his galling sense of physical inferiority to his wife, Kasturba, as the writer, by no means deficient in a sense of the ridiculous, recalls: "I knew she had more courage than I, and I felt ashamed of myself. She knew no fear of serpents and ghosts. She could go out anywhere in the dark. My friend . . . would tell me that he could hold in his hand live serpents, could defy thieves and did not believe in ghosts. And all this was, of course, the result of eating meat" (17).

"A wave of 'reform' was sweeping over Rajkot at the time," recalls Gandhi; in such a conjuncture, to eat meat was to enter a homosocial community of British and modernizing Indian males. Thus the transgression of caste taboos on meat eating and commensality (with Muslims) constituted the adolescent Gandhi's endeavor to be assimilated into modernity. This was somewhat at odds with his prejudice against the Christian missionaries of Rajkot, who were presumably engaged in analogous virilizing activities; they allegedly induced converts to Christianity to eat beef, drink alcohol, and Europeanize their clothing (29–30). The mature Gandhi would never, despite his heartfelt reverence for Christ and for the New Testament, shake off this sense of the denationalizing character of "Christian" diet and clothing in India. Moreover, the nationalist duty of virilizing palate and sinew was also at odds with the mandate of submission to and transparency with one's parents. He decided therefore to renounce meat eating until after their death. "When they are no more and I have found my freedom, I will eat meat openly," he resolved. Such a renunciation is nothing if not ambiguously phrased: the death of the parents is a release, at least in light of the male's nationalist duty. Further, the fantasy of public carnivorousness underscores the anthropophagic and parricidal scaffolding of meat eating in the manner of the incestuous feast in Freud's *Totem and Taboo*, and anticipates in crucial ways the violence that is an unfailing component of (self-)sacrifice in the Gandhian biography.[20] And yet Gandhi was to render to his dead parents precisely the "deferred obedience" that had been unwillingly extracted from him during their lifetime.

Gandhi's relationship with Mehtab, the dangerously attractive friend and secret sharer of meat, met with the disapproval of his entire family, including his parents, wife, and brother. The young Muslim seems to have functioned as a kind of counterfamily to this accredited family—the family-in-law, if you will, to use Gayatri Spivak's term for familial legitimacy—providing those services, that is, food and sex, usually provided by the wife.[21] He was a purveyor of erotic competition for the sanctioned, yet not guiltless, pleasures of the marital bed, coaxing the adolescent Gandhi into (abortive) encounters with prostitutes, much as he had prepared carnivorous repasts for him. True to the continuing theme of unsanctioned and exorbitant sexuality, Mehtab brought prostitutes into Gandhi's home in South Africa years later. He threatened, tantalizingly, to "expose" Gandhi when he was discovered in *flagrante delicto* and was expelled in consequence.[22]

It is hardly a surprise, given the lineaments of the Hindu national imaginary in the late nineteenth century, that it is the Muslim boy who performs the role of the seducer and intimate enemy for the crisis-ridden Vaishnava lad. This is notwithstanding Gandhi's staunch, unceasing efforts to promote Hindu–Muslim amity in South Africa and India. From the empirical evidence of fasting and other religious practices, the Muslim could just as logically as the fasting Vaishnava mother or the abstemious devotee of Jainism have functioned for him as a figure of austerity and renunciation.[23] But the affective logic of the Hindu response to Muslim dietary practices is not assimilable to the logic of these modes of empirical evidence. Gandhi's older brother Karsandas had himself succumbed to the lures of meat eating; he was also Mohandas's accessory to a petty act of stealing. He, however, is never cast as the tempter in Gandhi's account of his troubled youth.

The erotics of meat eating are accentuated by Gandhi in these particular ways in these early chapters on temptation; but they are also woven in more periphrastic ways into the fabric of his encounters with Mehtab. Indeed, Gandhi's account (at least in the language of the English-language version) of his encounters with the meat-eating Mehtab is governed by the interlaced tropes of secrecy, infatuation, and seduction, in marked contrast to the language of visibility and publicity that marks the narrative of his turn to vegetarianism. He speaks, in a narrative that appears to conjoin the language of religious and erotic temptation, of their rendezvous in secret places, of his being under Mehtab's spell, of his "blind devotion" to him, and of the "infatuation" that nearly ruined him (21, 143). The autobiography makes it clear how difficult it was to disavow Mehtab's appeal, despite the rhetoric, which has been echoed by most biographers, of wishing to reform the reprobate Muslim. Almost alone among the major commentators on Gandhi, Erik Erikson has recognized the powerful affective bond between the yet incipient mahatma and the familiar of his adolescence and young manhood: "It is . . . clear that Mehtab would have had to be invented if he had not existed. . . . For Mehtab played perfectly the personage on whom to project one's personal devil and thus become the personification of Mohandas' negative identity, that is, of everything in himself which he tried to isolate and subdue and which yet was part of him."[24] He also suggests, provocatively, that it was left to Gandhi's oldest son, Harilal, a temporary convert to Islam and therefore to meat eating, an alcoholic, a disreputable businessman, and a frequenter of prostitutes, to live out the potential embodied in Mehtab and disavowed by his father: "It may be that Harilal found in Mehtab the ingredients for that rebellious role with which he later faced his father. At any rate, Harilal later became a Muslim and a derelict who within a year after the Mahatma's assassination, was found in a coma 'in some locality.' "[25]

Diet and Diaspora

If the meat eating of Gandhi's youth had been marked by secrecy, reserve, and the guilt of filial violence, vegetarianism was invested with a distinctly different set of affective lineaments. Vegetarianism's import has a great deal to do with its status as the vehicle of Gandhi's entry into public life during his student years in London. But what is equally if not more significant is the sense that the vegetarian body was, initially in England but later in India as well, a body characterized by its hyperbolic visibility; it was a body characterized by its looked-at-ness and its status, first as freak and then as holy spectacle. This spectacularization of the vegetarian or, more generally, the renunciant male body is most fruitfully investigated perhaps through certain forms of indirection and metaphoric displacement. With that in mind, I turn to the crisis of gendered caste identity provoked by the decision to go to England and to the structure of prohibitions with which the aspiring traveler was faced. After a frustrating and unsuccessful year at college in Bhavnagar, the young and now fatherless Gandhi decided that the quickest road to advancement was to train as a barrister in England. He received the occasionally wavering support of his oldest brother, Lakshmidas, and the conditional blessing of his mother for this enterprise but found himself unable to prevail upon his caste council, which strongly disapproved of overseas voyages as transgressions against orthopraxy, especially its rules of purity and pollution. (He went anyway and was excommunicated for his act.) The strictures of his caste elders and of his uncle when Gandhi announced his desire to journey to England involved, interestingly, the coupling of two forms of transgression—not that of diet and sex as one might expect and as is exemplified in his mother's demand that he forswear meat, alcohol, and sexual relations with women for the duration of his diaspora, but that of ingestion and of clothing. His uncle Tulsidas, the head of his clan, whom he had approached to ask permission to travel overseas, objected thus: "I am not sure whether it is possible for one to stay in England without prejudice to one's own religion. . . . When I meet these big barristers, I see no difference between their life and that of Europeans. They know no scruples regarding food. Cigars are never out of their mouths. *They dress as shamelessly as Englishmen*" (34 [emphasis added]). The strictures here against going native in England, especially through the transgression of dietary taboos, are entirely familiar ones. What gives pause in this passage is that curious detail, which for the uncle is of a piece with dietary pollutions, about the shamelessness of English male clothing. That the rhetoric of male sartorial shamelessness is not entirely accidental is evidenced by Gandhi's response to the English wardrobe procured for him in Bombay: he speaks of liking some of his new clothing, but "the short jacket I looked upon as immodest" (37). What is one to make of these unexpected idioms of modesty and shame? While there was some debate about the appropriate forms of Indian male attire in the colonial context, when conducted between Britons and Indians the discussion focused on "proper forms of respectful behaviour" as indexed by headgear and footwear, as Bernard Cohn demonstrates,[26] on the deleterious economic effects of British rule (as in the *swadeshi* movement against British products, especially cloth from Lancashire mills), and on the uneasy fit of Western clothes into "the existing classifications of appropriate caste, regional or religious styles," as Emma Tarlo notes.[27] There was little sustained discussion that I am aware of about the masculine modesty—or lack of it—of

Western clothing, though one does encounter the stray remark in Indian- and English-language fiction about the inappropriateness of form-fitting English-style trousers.[28] When the Western-attired Indian male constituted a spectacle it was for the most part because of the incongruousness of his garb rather than, as appears to be true in the case of Gandhi, his status as an erotic or a potentially and improperly erotic object. The question of modesty was on another hand foregrounded to a substantial degree in debates about the new forms of women's attire.[29] What can one make then of what seems to be an aberrant, hyperbolic, or out of place modesty? One might pause here to think of Gandhi's quite self-conscious androgyny, recalling his numerous endeavors to "feminize" himself, the Indian polity, and the forms themselves of nationalist politics.[30] Might it be possible to read the language of shame and modesty as the retrospective effeminization of the autobiographer seeking to recast the gendered project of nationalist struggle? (Without recourse to the Gujarati version, it may be hard to speculate on the precise or, more properly, the alternative resonances of the terms translated as "shameless" and "immodest," although it is worth noting that Mahadev Desai's rather priggish English prose was corrected by Mirabehn and approved by Gandhi.)[31] One might recollect Gandhi's well-known identification with his mother's ideals of purity and austerity; "[The] mother-cult of Gandhi's boyhood days remained throughout his life a very strong element in his philosophy," as Nirmal Kumar Bose noted early on.[32] At this juncture there was also the visible inscription upon his body, in the form of dietary restrictions and his necklace of wooden beads, of the maternal signature. In any event, his sartorial shame—or, more properly, his very marked sartorial self-consciousness—is linked through metonymic as well as figurative affiliation with the feminine-inflected vegetarianism of his youth in colonial India. (One should also be mindful of the associations of vegetarianism with feminism in 1880s London [a connection of which Gandhi could not have been oblivious, given his latter-day references to the feminist and suffragist movements in England], and the association of the suffragists with hunger strikes in the early part of the twentieth century.)[33]

The language of modesty returned at another sartorial crossroads in the Gandhian biography, the moment when he decided, as the combined result of deliberation and contingency, to adopt the reduced dhoti that was to be the signature of the "half-naked fakir." He is said to have anguished, as did his colleagues and companions, over the brevity and modesty of his new garb in a mode that resonates to some degree with debates about respectable women's attire in public places.[34] To be sure, his sartorial experiments were the product of powerfully felt ideals regarding simplicity, freedom of movement, and an identification with the poorest among his fellow Indians. And abbreviated forms of clothing have always been permissible among Hindu and Jain male ascetics, who, however, do not generally mingle with the lay public. Nonetheless their ambiguously gendered logic is palpable in the discussions that accompanied this sartorial shift.

Gandhi's insistence upon this novel and radical form of "nakedness" speaks to the ways in which he sought, over the course of a long political career, to convert erstwhile badges of humiliation into symbols of carefully chosen renunciation. Thus he was able to convert the shameful vegetarianism of his early days in London into an ethics of eating appropriately. Likewise, his failure to receive spices and condiments from the authorities during a jail sojourn in South Africa persuaded him of the necessity of a plain, unseasoned diet (291). His abandonment of the garb of the England-trained gentleman was also the fortuitous by-product of an imprisonment during which he was given the prison uniform of a "Native"; "[It] marked the beginning of a period of sartorial experimentation," says Tarlo, " . . . when Gandhi began to convert his own embarrassment at being wrongly dressed into a strategy for exposing injustice and embarrassing others."[35]

In the instance of his fateful voyage to England meatlessness and new forms of clothing were clearly related and were just as clearly associated with certain forms of sometimes shameful and sometimes exciting visibility and publicity, a visibility that has most conventionally attached itself to the feminine body.[36] In fact, vegetarian dietetics was to constitute Gandhi's earliest and perhaps most sustained mode of public performance in political life. While on shipboard, being a vegetarian involved to some degree opening oneself up to public scrutiny so that one could be advised and cautioned and so that one could provide public proofs of one's dietary virtue. Gandhi's voyage appears to have been marked by a series of temptations posed by those fellow travelers who were invested not so much in the transformative ethical properties of meat but in an environmental logic; they argued the necessity of a carnivorous and alcoholic diet after passing through the Suez Canal, that is, in the territory of the West proper.[37] A good part of the young man's sense of apprehension about diet and his resultant sensation of exposure must be attributed to the substantial difficulties that characterized public eating for a vegetarian in England, notwithstanding the availability of vegetarian restaurants in London. Indeed, V. S. Naipaul's sweeping indictment of the dietary focus seems curiously shortsighted in its estimation of the attentiveness required of fastidious vegetarians in contexts where carnivoracity is normative: "That is the voyage: an internal adventure of anxieties felt and food eaten, with not a word of anything seen or heard that did not directly affect the physical or mental well-being of the writer. The inward concentration is fierce, the self-absorption complete. . . . His experiments and discoveries and vows answered his own need as a Hindu, the need constantly to define and fortify the self in the midst of hostility; they were not of universal application."[38] Such a dismissal bypasses the ethicopolitical coordinates of diet; for Naipaul the vegetarians are mere "cranks," and the eminent scholar and translator Edwin Arnold is judged to have "wasted" his time on a vegetarian club started by Gandhi. What he omits to note here is that the culinary theater is the site for the staging of ethical dilemmas of long standing. He also fails to note the distinction between the autobiography and others among Gandhi's texts, such as his "London Diary" and *Satyagraha in South Africa*, which bespeak a lively interest in their surroundings.[39] More importantly, he misunderstands the character itself of *The Story of My Experiments With Truth*, which was intended as a didactic account of certain ethical and spiritual experiments rather than as the exhaustive account of the individual life. In later years Gandhi himself denied he had produced an autobiography and, while one might reasonably be skeptical of such a claim, it will not do to dismiss it altogether; at least it should alert one to the work's occasional deviation from generic conventions.[40]

But Naipaul is quite right nonetheless to note the exorbitant character of the dietary theme. The practical difficulties of being a practicing vegetarian in beef-eating England do not suffice to explain the considerable intellectual and emotional charge that attaches to meatlessness even prior to the account of the departure from vegetarian-friendly India. Besides, Gandhi's parting words on his English sojourn in *The Vegetarian* for June 1891, written though they undoubtedly were for a distinct, circumscribed audience, speak nonetheless to the centrality of an ethic of bodily and dietetic purity to his worldview: "In conclusion I am bound to say that during my nearly three years' stay in England I have left many things undone . . . yet I carry one great consolation with me, that I shall go back without having taken meat or wine, and that I know from personal experience that there are so many vegetarians."[41]

At this point in the autobiography there is some sense not just of the vegetarian body as spectacle but also of the self-staging and self-exoticization of vegetarianism. It appears to be the only topic of social interchange that the mahatma remembered or remembered initiating; besides, he solicited and received from his fellow passengers certificates of his success in the performance of vegetarianism. The publicity associated with vegetarianism was highlighted in London. One of his early acquaintances in London, Dalpatram Shukla, who was, not coincidentally, a man of the world (he taught him "how to behave and how to use the fork and the spoon") and a Benthamite, associated Gandhi's vow of vegetarianism with feminine superstition and feared that his adherence to a meatless diet would disable him permanently for entrance into cultivated English society.[42] In the company of this friend Gandhi does makes a spectacle of himself repeatedly by his failure not only to eat meat but to manage his vegetarianism discreetly; vegetarianism repeatedly emerges as that which by its nature draws attention to itself. In his fairly long account, the longest regarding any of his acquaintances in England, of Narayan Hemchandra, his sense of the Gujarati writer's linguistic and sartorial oddness is inseparable from his vegetarianism. It is tempting to speculate on the mahatma's ironic identification, in the 1920s, with the dhoti-clad but indomitable provincial who was hooted by English children and once arrested for the supposed indecency of his clothing. In fact, Gandhi's famous sartorial flirtations with a modish English garb were prompted by a desire to compensate for the ineptitude his vegetarianism signified: "I decided that . . . I should assure him that I would be clumsy no more, but try to become polished and make up for my vegetarianism by cultivating other accomplishments which fitted one for polite society" (45).

This dandyism, accompanied by extended rituals of adornment and heavy financial outlays, all described in detail by the author, was a development that in its turn did not fail to draw the eye of contemporary observers: "He was wearing a high silk top hat burnished bright, a Gladstonian collar, stiff and starched; a rather flashy tie displaying almost all the colours of the rainbow, under which there was a fine striped silk shirt. He wore as his outer clothes a morning coat, a double-breasted vest, and dark striped trousers to match and not only patent leather boots but spats over them. He carried leather gloves and a silver-mounted stick, but wore no spectacles. He was, to use the contemporary slang, a nut, a masher, a blood—a student more interested in fashion and frivolities than in his studies."[43] This account, written in the retrospect of Gandhi's access to the status of mahatma and his martyrdom, is almost too replete with fascinating superfluities to fit convincingly into a narrative of realism: is it likely the author, Sachidananda Sinha, would have remembered such a plethora of details from a chance encounter with an acquaintance in Piccadilly Circus? Yet it is true that Gandhi was never to lose a marked sense of sartorial and bodily drama and even in his most ascetic phase was meticulously neat about the appearance of his dhoti-clad and oil-massaged body.

But even in a postdandy mode and as a vegetarian among vegetarians in London's Vegetarian Society, Gandhi did not become, in his own perception, less of a public spectacle. Though he wrote regularly for *The Vegetarian* and attended all the meetings of the society, even becoming a member of its executive committee, in his account of the association he enacts repeatedly and publicly in that arena his failure to be a successful public figure; the failure is itself highly public. At his last meeting of the society he "only succeeded in making [himself] ridiculous" (54) when attempting a speech, as though the attentiveness to one kind of regime of orality sabotaged success in another. Only through the wry omniscience of retrospection was he able, in a characteristic move, to convert this awkwardness into moral capital, linking reticence in public speech with other forms of economy and renunciation, including brahmacharya, since the subsequent chapter in the *Autobiography* is devoted to an account of the way in which his reserve kept him from successful sexual escapades with English women.[44] The carefully observed "days of silence" in the days of his mahatma-hood years later were a refuge no doubt from the incessant demands made upon him, but they were no less an exercise in oral discipline, cognate with the chastening of the palate.[45]

If the mahatma in the making was able to translate these pedagogies of shame and embarrassment into ethical self-consolidation, it was a lesson forged in a diasporic context. In his avatar as an "apostle of abstinence" Gandhi has commonly been identified with a certain traditional Indianness or, more properly, Hinduness or Jainness. But his turn to vegetarianism out of moral conviction rather than out of fealty to a filial vow—however strongly it might have been founded in a belief in the biomoral character of various foods, a belief that was not, as is often believed, peculiar only to Hinduism and Jainism—is articulated with his critique of colonial modernity and must be read through the lens of diaspora and against a global horizon, particularly through a consideration of the global vegetarian movement.[46] As is well known, there was substantial support for vegetarianism, pacifism, socialism, new educational systems, and the Swedenborgian church on both sides of the Atlantic in the nineteenth century.[47] If Leo Tolstoy and George Bernard Shaw were the most famous of Western vegetarians at the turn of the century, they were not lone or even pioneering figures. In 1889, the year following Gandhi's arrival in the metropolis, there were thirty-four vegetarian restaurants in London.[48] Among metropolitan vegetarians, vegetarianism was often linked, as it always would be for Gandhi, with an interest in fasting. The Vegetarian carried advice on fasting and accounts of spectacular, forty-day fasts undertaken by members of vegetarian societies.[49] In the United States in the nineteenth century, the health reform movement, led by such figures as Sylvester Graham (of graham cracker fame), William Alcott, and John Harvey Kellogg urged a meatless diet in order to curb the excesses of male libidinality, which were presumed to have the most deleterious physiological effects.[50] Tolstoy himself was sympathetic to the doctrines of these proponents of the science of a Christian male physiology but was less concerned about physiological corruption than about the spiritual decay incumbent upon the gratuitous expenditure of semen.[51] Many of these proponents were also, like Tolstoy, among the most fervent critics of the project of modernity, especially of industrialization, urbanization, and secularization and the refashioning of sexual ideology, bodily discipline, and gendered behavior these developments brought.

• • •

The young Gandhi's happy discovery of a vegetarian restaurant in London—the Central, off Farrington Street—was therefore no haphazard event. In the Autobiography, it is presented as a richly parabolic moment, since it also coincided with the discovery of a gospel, Henry Salt's pamphlet "A Plea for Vegetarianism," which was on sale in the window of the restaurant. Gandhi was to speak of this as a moment of conversion, confirming but also transcending his vow to his mother; the chapter detailing the episode was entitled "My Choice." It was to spark a missionary zeal for the cause that endured during his South African sojourn—in fact he met two of his most important South African associates, Henry Polak and Albert West, in a vegetarian restaurant at Johannesburg—and was further enlarged in India. While in England and South Africa he carefully read the extant Western literature on vegetarianism available in *fin-de-siècle* London, including Howard Williams's *The Ethics of Diet*, Anna Kingsford's *The Perfect Way in Diet*, and the writings of Percy Shelley. This was to be supplemented in later years by cognate works, though of greater philosophical ambition, most notably Edward Carpenter's *Civilization, Its Cause and Cure* (1888), a critique of industrialism and modern medicine, Tolstoy's *The Kingdom of God Is Within You* (1893), an unorthodox interpretation of Christianity and nonviolence), and John Ruskin's *Unto This Last*, a searing critique of Victorian political economy.[52] The seemingly self-absorbed, diet-obsessed young Kathiawadi of late nineteenth-century London was also the inhabitant of a world that encompassed William Morris, Henry George, Sidney Webb, William Booth, Carpenter, Annie Besant, and the Fabian Society. Even though the overt evidence of the autobiographical writing does not always provide direct evidence of his consciousness of some of these figures and movements, its impact is visible in the general tendency and in the details of his response to industrial modernity.[53] His meatlessness must be seen as articulated at least in part in relation to the pronouncements and activities of these figures and to the "web of idealistic thinking of action" that cohered around the vegetarian movement.[54]

One can perhaps speak of Gandhi's encounters in London with vegetarians, antivivisectionists, pacifists, and theosophists as an instance of what Françoise Lionnet and Shu-mei Shih designate "minor transnationalism," the transversal experience of minor and minoritized subjects—one that is not identical with that of the better-known encounters of metropolitan and marginal subjects.[55] More expansively, Leela Gandhi reads Gandhi's friendly encounters with these sometimes politically radical subcultures as an instance of the openness to civilizational otherness that marked the utopian movements of the late Victorian and Edwardian periods. Focusing on friendship as "the lost trope in anticolonial thought," she represents his easy entry into and preeminence within the British vegetarian movement as having been facilitated by the vegetarians' ethical investment in hospitality, xenophilia, and anticolonial cosmopolitanism.[56]

. . .

Leela Gandhi's argument is important for permitting a reading of the encounter in the metropolis that exceeds the conceptual limits of a colonizer–colonized antagonism. At the same time, it is as important to keep in mind the conditions that allowed Gandhi, on his part, to be hailed by such an invitation from the English vegetarians rather than seeing it as an uncomplicated gesture of hospitality, as Leela Gandhi is wont to do. If part of the youthful Gandhi's experience of English vegetarianism, English theosophy, and English naturopaths involved a rethinking of Englishness, provincialism, and the possibility of friendship and dialogue with unlikely fellow travelers, part of it also involved for him a rethinking of Indianness and of his own more privileged relationship to it. As a member and later an officeholder of the Vegetarian Society, he offered testimony as an Indian vegetarian that was eagerly sought and respectfully received. This was unsurprising in a British vegetarian context that inhabited, as Tristram Stuart has demonstrated, an already Hinduized terrain: vegetarians in the British Isles had long looked to the vegetarian cultures of the subcontinent as a model of ethical diet, simple living, and nonviolent coexistence with the animal world.[57] As a newly minted expert on what had been hitherto a source of embarrassment, Gandhi hosted meetings, gave interviews to The Vegetarian, and wrote a dozen articles for The Vegetarian and the Vegetarian Messenger on Indian diet, festivals, and ethnographic types. As it happens, he was solicited not only as a vegetarian but also as a Hindu, most famously by two theosophists, for his putative expertise on the Bhagavadgita. Such solicitations of religious, linguistic, and dietetic expertise, combined with his reading of or face-to-face encounter with people like Besant, Carpenter, Edwin Arnold, and Helena Blavatsky, all of whom had an appreciation of Indian and especially Hindu spirituality, replaced his earlier sense of Indian inferiority and flaccidity with what Richard G. Fox has called an "affirmative Orientalism." As James Hunt puts it, he was "stimulated by this eccentric but lively group of Westerners to value his own heritage."[58] From aspiring to a condition of gastropolitical mimic manhood he had come to be linked in unlikely fellowship with the denizens of a global community marked by antimodern and sometimes anti-imperial critique. Coming to England, he encountered an entirely new vegetarianism, one quite unfamiliar to him from India. Yet the Englishmen and Englishwomen he encountered were also like Indians in diet and in spiritual and political outlook, though not so much so as to displace his newfound authoritative status as Hindu Indian and lifelong vegetarian. In conspicuous counterpoint to the tales of his awkwardness and incompetence in the "London Diary" and the Autobiography is the tone adopted in the essays and interviews for The Vegetarian. For instance, his review of his voyage back to India in 1891 has an assured, knowledgeable cast that departs from the drama of cal-low youthfulness that signaled his maiden voyage from Indian shores. And in an essay entitled "The Foods of India" he slyly ventures to measure his ignorance against that of James Mill, the author of the monumental History of India that was a textbook for all India-bound imperial officials but that famously was produced without any firsthand acquaintance with the subcontinent and without any familiarity with its languages.[59]

If the contexts of the vegetarian traditions of Hinduism and Jainism cannot be deployed exclusively to explain Gandhi's turn to it as a self-consciously chosen ethical program, it is equally true that it cannot be explained exclusively in terms of dietary ahimsa. His abjuration of meat is more appositely seen not so explicitly or exclusively as ahimsa (given that ahimsa cannot be entirely isolated from the other details of a Gandhian program) as a critical response to the project of modernity itself, to which meat eating was, in colonial India at least, a privileged point of entry. As such, it is of a piece with his impassioned arraignment of industrialism, urbanization, modern medicine, and scientific progress in Hind Swaraj (1909). In fact through much of his life Gandhi's critique of modernity often took the form of dietary and medical undertakings. One of the immediate and most far-reaching effects of his reading of Ruskin's critique of the rationality of political economy and industrial modernity in Unto This Last was a program of food production at Phoenix Farm which endeavored to bypass as entirely as possible the reliance on machinery and the appurtenances of the industrial production of food. He also prided himself on being what he jokingly called a quack who cured himself and others through fasting and other dietetic cures and who was a considerable adept at nursing. Indeed, he had hoped in his adolescence to become a doctor, being deflected from it by his parents' disapproval of a polluting contact with cadavers, and he maintained throughout his life a passion for alternative forms of doctoring and nursing that was fully equal to his censure of modern biomedicine. In the mode of Carpenter, he launched a scathing critique in Hind Swaraj of modern medicine's excessive care for the body, its failure to treat the moral and spiritual causes of disease, and the violence of its methods, which included violent forms of ingestion: "Hospitals are institutions for propagating sin. Men take less care of their bodies, and immorality increases. European doctors are the worst of all. For the sake of a mistaken care of the human body, they kill annually thousands of animals. They practise vivisection. No religion sanctions this. . . . These doctors violate our religious instinct. Most of their medical preparations contain animal fat or spiritous liquors; both of these are tabooed by Hindus and Mahomedans. . . . The fact remains that the doctors induce us to indulge, and the result is that we have become deprived of self-control and have become effeminate."[60] Committed as it is to an excessive love of bodily well-being that militates against the practices of self-restraint incumbent on all patients, modern medicine is for Gandhi an exemplary case of the manifold ills of overconsumption. Shetty notes that what might seem like an anomalous focus in *Hind Swaraj* on the "seemingly minor complaint" of indigestion in fact accords well with his "overall conception of the affliction of modern civilization as pre-eminently a distemper of the oral-alimentary tract."[61]

It should be noted that despite the unyielding character of these assertions, Gandhi's practice was more complex and more subtle; he underwent surgery in 1924, permitted Kasturba to undergo surgery in South Africa, urged Chakrayya, a resident of Sabarmati Ashram, to undergo surgery to remove a brain tumor, and took quinine as a prophylactic against malaria. His personal physician, Sushila Nayyar, was trained in Western medicine, though she came to share in large part his belief in the efficacy of brahmacharya and "nature cures,"[62] most of which were derived, as Alter has demonstrated, from nonconventional European rather than from conventional European (biomedical) or Indian (ayurvedic) sources.

I do not deny that Gandhi's turn to a carefully articulated and chosen (rather than an unreflexive) vegetarianism and alternative forms of therapeutics is consistent with a Hindu and Jain dietary and bodily ethics that sees feeding as intimately linked to other features of carnality, including sexual desire, as well as to mental and spiritual health. There is no doubt that some of the religious and affective lineaments of his practice of vegetarianism and fasting are illuminated through an understanding of Indic thought on bodily ethics and on the relation between different kinds of living beings. Interestingly, however, the sense of the biomoral property of food was widely and globally shared at the end of the nineteenth century and was part of a global, not an exclusively Indian, Hindu, or Jain ethical and corporeal culture. Joan Brumberg, for one, has documented the Victorian belief, shared by doctors and patients alike, that meat was "a heat-producing food that stimulated the production of blood and fat as well as passion."[63] Details such as these serve to emphasize the assumptions about the biomoral properties of food that were shared by the cultures and the countercultures of modernity. If the young Gandhi's publicly staged vegetarianism was his primary mode of engagement with the world of politics, he spoke not simply the language of a Hindu or Jain dietary ethics but a sometimes unexpectedly global one.

Prescriptions for Fasting

No account of the characteristically public character of Gandhi's vegetarianism can fail to take into account the public staging of the fasts of his later years. Maud Ellmann has drawn attention to the style of the hunger striker, whose inanition is never self-sufficient but must be supplemented with the visible signature of political intent.[64] Or, as Gang Yue puts it, the modern hunger strike "stages itself so that it might generate a tragic effect upon its audience. It is a mortgage of death as a credit for a better life or lives."[65] One of the texts to which Ellmann returns, however, and from which she draws the title of her book, is Kafka's story "A Hunger Artist." Kafka's protagonist is not so much the hunger striker, whose privation is subservient to recognizably political objectives, but the faster, a figure whose starvation transgresses the relatively simple transactional logic of political or economic rationality. Kafka speaks with considerable acuity of the incalculable delectation of fasting, which actively solicits, indeed exists for, an audience of admirers and worshipers.[66] This occasionally tenuous and troubled distinction between faster and hunger striker and the pleasures, calculations, uncertainties, and travails of each must be borne in mind in a consideration of Gandhi's autophagous politics.

It hardly needs repeating that Gandhi was famous for his fasting. In a period that was, to quote Tim Pratt and James Vernon, "the golden age of the hunger strike in anticolonial struggles," he was the most notable faster of all, undertaking as many as seventeen fasts unto death as well as innumerable fasts of restricted duration during his lifetime.[67] Taken together, they constituted an extraordinary reconstellation of the hypervisible, maladroit, and anomalous vegetarian male body of his early years as a vegetarian convert. His first fasts were undertaken in South Africa, not in the service of overtly political ends, as in India in the 1920s, 1930s, and 1940s, but in the context of maintaining the ideals of austerity and the sexual sanctity of communal life in the Tolstoy and Phoenix Farms, which had been started by him as experiments in communal living. An epicurean at the outset despite his associations with occasionally puritanical English vegetarians, Gandhi had progressively simplified his diet and that of the commune, though not without some discontent on the part of those who were subject to his preferred saltless, spiceless, and notably spartan dietetic experiments.[68] This was the beginning of a lifelong interest in discovering a cheap, nutritious diet, especially for the poorest of his compatriots in South Africa and India. Madhu Kishwar notes that "his experiments were conducted with a view to finding out the most wholesome food and the most sensible way of preparing it, keeping in mind the conditions of poverty in which a majority of people lived. Equally touching is his deep concern for eliminating the drudgery of women as far as possible."[69]

Moreover, Gandhi undoubtedly felt, as, say, did medieval European moralists, that gastronomic overindulgence was not simply unhealthful but a crime against the hungry masses: "In an economic order in which there is not food enough to go around, in which starvation and famine are always lurking about, gluttony's moral stakes ratchet up. . . . Eating was [in medieval Europe] a zero-sum game. The more you ate the less someone else did. And any ingestion beyond what was necessary for the maintenance of life was an act of injustice."[70] In such a context the most innocuous-seeming act of eating could be construed as an incipient assault, not merely upon that which was being ingested but upon the body politic and therefore upon one's fellows as well; indulgence was impossible to uncouple from aggression.[71] The fact that it is now understood, thanks to Amartya Sen, that hunger and famine are caused not by a lack of food resources but by the inequities of distribution does not detract from the moral force of Gandhi's position, even though his scrupulously pursued simplicity was not without its own unforeseeable ironies and extravagances.[72] Gandhi's insistence on discovering cheap, nutritious, easily prepared foods notwithstanding, his own simple meals—he had taken a vow to eat no more than five items of food a day and to eat nothing after nightfall—were often, paradoxically, difficult to prepare so as to meet his rigorous demands for plainness and appropriateness. The poet and unabashed carnivorous gourmet Sarojini Naidu, reputed to have been "the licensed jester of the mahatma's court," is said to have remarked a trifle caustically that it took a millionaire to keep the mahatma in poverty, referring in this instance to G. D. Birla, a prominent industrialist and a major contributor to Gandhi's favorite causes.[73]

Besides, Gandhi's experiments in dietetics, including fasting, are never entirely reducible to pure functionalism or to a simple morality of distribution: they gesture toward other bodily and moral economies simultaneously. Not coincidentally, his turn to fasting as a moral instrument was articulated with his endeavor, pursued with intermittent success from his early thirties and sealed with a vow in 1906, when he was thirty-seven, to practice brahmacharya. While his early and conscious avowals of vegetarianism in England were not explicitly rooted in the desire to achieve *sexual* self-control, they were nonetheless morally and affectively inseparable from it, given the linked character of his mother's prohibitions against meat, alcohol, and heterosexual relations. But later in life, increasingly persuaded of the necessity for brahmacharya for his own spiritual uplift as well as for the good of a public whose powerfully renunciant leader he was, he abstracted spices, salt, cow's milk, lentils, and at times even cooked vegetables from his diet.

The link between continence of the palate and of the libido is elaborated in unambiguous terms in the *Autobiography*: "As an external aid to brahmacharya, fasting is as necessary as selection and restriction in diet. So overpowering are the senses that they can be kept under control only when they are completely hedged in on all sides, from above and beneath. . . . it may be said that extinction of the sexual passion is a rule impossible without fasting, which may be said to be indispensable for the observance of brahmacharya. Many aspirants after brahmacharya fail, because in the use of their other senses they want to carry on like those who are not brahmacharis" (183–84).[74] To understand the importance and the potency of brahmacharya, it is necessary to come to terms with the seminal economy in which it is grounded. For Gandhi, as for many Hindus, sexual activity was perhaps the most energy-depleting of all human male pursuits, as it led to the loss of seminal fluid, the primary source of energy in the human and paradigmatically male body. Semen was and is avowed to be "the distillate of most other body fluids and substances—blood, marrow, and bone, in particular—and is therefore thought to contain the essence of the whole body within itself."[75] The loss of semen through intercourse is computed as the equivalent of one day's mental activity or three days' physical labor. But semen can, if properly husbanded, be moved upward through the body to the brain and transformed into *ojas*, spiritual and psychic energy; this is the goal of the spiritual aspirant. A seminal economy was not, it should be noted, the peculiar property of Brahminical Hinduism. Its assumptions and calculations were not unknown to vegetarian, hygienic, and health reform movements in western Europe, Russia, and the United States, all of which were absorbed by the question of sex, masturbation, and the ethical entailments of masculinity at a pivotal point in industrial modernity.[76] In his associations with the Vegetarian Society in Britain and in South Africa, Gandhi read more than one article on the physical and spiritual enervation caused by profligate seminal emissions.

The practical efficacy of such a calculus was ardently corroborated by Gandhi, though not without a touch of his characteristic self-mockery: "Many people have told me—and I also believe it—that I am full of energy and enthusiasm, and that I am by no means weak in mind; some even accuse me of strength bordering on obstinacy. . . . It is my full conviction, that if only I had lived a life of unbroken *Brahmacharya* all through, my energy and enthusiasm would have been a thousandfold greater and I should have been able to devote them all to the furtherance of my country's cause as my own."[77] Hence the centrality of fasting as a mode of self-control and, by implication, a more generalized moral and spiritual authority that could exert an influence upon the course of events and upon the actions of others.[78] And if fasting proved efficacious as a means of curbing one's own libido, Gandhi also deployed it as a corrective to the incontinence of others, fasting in protest against the "moral fall" of two students at Phoenix and against the married lover of his twenty-year-old son Manilal.[79] That Gandhi's use of the fast as an instrument of purification of one's own pollution and that of others was at times deployed with a certain moralizing pitilessness is incontestable. But his internalization and deployment of the idioms of purity and pollution were not reducible to the familiar caste-based economies of hierarchy and distance. Moreover, beyond this, as a mode of self-suffering undertaken to purify oneself, to protest against injustice, and to mourn the lapses of one's intimate acquaintances it was affiliated with the emergent mode of politics that came to be called *satyagraha* (literally, persistence in the truth)—a passage in the Gujarati text of *Hind Swaraj* explicitly links satyagraha and fasting—and as such it came to be practiced by some other satyagrahis, including Kasturba, not just by their leader.[80]

But Gandhi possessed from the beginning a gift not just for the bodily act of fasting but for meditating upon its ambivalent ethical terrain. Perhaps it is for this reason that in the days of his mahatma-hood it was Gandhi's fasts rather than those of others that were the cynosure of public attention. But, beyond this, his fasting also had an irreducibly gendered character, signaled partly by its ties to brahmacharya. In fact the pedagogy of abstemiousness and fasting Gandhi learned from his mother contrasts with the masculinization of fasting and renunciation in the orthodox Hindu and Jain traditions and indeed in some of the traditions of fasting in the modern West.[81] The male sage's fasting, says Sally Suther-land Goldman, is a mark of his self-control, especially his control over seminal emissions, a role women can never hope to inhabit. A woman's restraint is, definitionally, externally imposed—neither as daughter, wife, nor widow is her sexuality hers to embrace or abdicate—while a man's is self-imposed. Besides, women's presumed vulnerability to rape (in an economy that presumes men are not rapable), Goldman says, precludes their being ascetics.[82] For his national public, at least, which had detailed knowledge of his concomitant experiments in brahmacharya, Gandhi's great public fasts of the twenties, thirties, and forties were more or less assimilable within the modes of masculine renunciant practice; by then he was a mahatma, a great soul. Sumit Sarkar suggests that Gandhi's renun-ciatory mode might have ensured his popularity among ordinary people, the sadhu (ascetic) being a figure exempted from the usual social and caste hierarchies and an emblem of "controlled rebellion."[83]

Gandhi spent much of his life refining fasting as a corporeal and spiritual process and as an ethicopolitical tactic. Initially he was an in-competent faster, losing his voice and experiencing pain and nausea once the fast was broken. But he proved an adept, innovative pupil, and he learned to drink plenty of water, to have twice-daily enemas, and to exer-cise in bed during his fasts so as to control their effects better. For his pedagogy of fasting he incorporated stratagems and styles from a global canvas, ranging from the fasts familiar to him from the Kathiawad of his youth, where his father had abstained from food in protest against the misconduct of his ruler, to the activities of the Sinn Féin of his early manhood, which were in turn indebted to suffragist modes of activism.[84] Through all this he was singularly cognizant not only of the great power of public fasting but also of its concomitant corporeal temptations and ethical risks. He was mindful of the ways in which voraciousness could be the unwonted auxiliary to gastronomic abstinence. Fasting could serve, for instance, as prelude to or as an incitement to the self-pleasuring of the palate: "I also saw that, the body now being drained more effectively, the food yielded greater relish and the appetite grew keener. It dawned upon me that fasting could be made as powerful a weapon of indulgence as of restraint. Many similar later experiences of mine as well of others can be adduced as evidence of this startling fact" (286–87). Subsequent experi-ments in selecting specific foods and restricting their quantity only un-derlined for him the terrifying potency of the palate, even the gastronomi-cally constricted palate, and the absolute necessity not just of restricting ingestion but of extirpating altogether any form of gustatory gratification. All eating, not just the consumption of meat and alcohol that had been interdicted as a result of the vow to his mother, had to be subjected to a regime of limits and prohibitions before it could be rendered penitential and purified of the violence of enjoyment and therefore "good to eat."

The mahatma was also not unmindful of the status of fasting as a morally ambiguous weapon of satyagraha. He apprehended that the very publicity of fasting could on occasion be inseparable from a violence that was at odds with the professed doctrines of satyagraha. What complicated his own prescriptions for and practice of fasting was the fact that fasting as a form of protest was a practice of long duration in India and was almost invariably coercive rather than persuasive in its character.[85] He was careful to distinguish in his own pronouncements, though perhaps, and inescapably, less successfully in his practice, between the fast proper, an instrument of reputedly feminine mutuality, love, and reconciliation, and the hunger strike, usually undertaken out of vanity or pique or belligerence, "without previous preparation and without adequate thought." He frequently stressed the dangerous moral enticements and costs of fasting and its character as both medicine and poison. It had to be mastered as a form of interlocutory reciprocity before it could be deployed: "Fasting is a fiery weapon. It has its own science. No one, as far as I am aware, has a perfect knowledge of it. Unscientific experimentation with it is bound to be harmful to the one who fasts, and it may even harm the cause espoused. No one who has not earned the right to do so should, therefore, use this weapon. A fast may only be undertaken by him who is associated with the person against whom he fasts. The latter must be directly connected with the purpose for which the fast is being undertaken."[86] Hence his repeated insistence that the potential violence of fasting be leavened and neutralized with affectionate intimacy, that a satyagrahi fast not against a foe but against a "lover." How to guarantee the conspicuous moral force of fasting while reining in its power was one of his continuing preoccupations. In his mind the (reconstellated) practice ideally combined the force of the Hindu and Jain ideas of self-purification, asceticism, and penance and the Christian idea of suffering love.[87] In a very real sense, in its emphasis upon moral and quasi-erotic suasion, it can be said to be an endeavor to "feminize" the practice of public fasting. But in a few instances at least the already available connotations of fasting might have militated, as Joan Bondurant notes, against a Gandhian reinscription: "The very fact of Gandhi's use of traditional methods to effect the education of India in the ways of satyagraha may have functioned as a deterrent in transmitting the full implications of satyagraha to those who participated. Elements which were new in Gandhi's approach—the various emphases upon the well-being of the opponent and of mutual triumph—were sometimes obscured by a ready understanding of the coercive character of traditional methods."[88]

Practice also demonstrated how difficult it was for the mahatma himself to leach out the violence from this weapon of satyagraha and how very contestable and far from self-evident its grounds were. In fact his very first fast for a public cause, undertaken in March 1918 on behalf of striking mill workers in Ahmedabad and against the mill owners, led by his friend and host Ambalal Sarabhai, was marked for him by a moral ambivalence since it could be seen to exploit the mill owners' solicitude for him rather than highlighting the justice of the strikers' demands. Gandhi's great public fasts, like this one, continued to be marked by the irreducibility of their coerciveness *and* their utterly earnest highmindedness. His colleagues and friends and, more importantly, the disputants or "lovers" against whom he fasted, were often uncertain of the moral value and the efficacy of his fasting, and in some instances they were antipathetical to his methods. In the case of the Ahmedabad fast, the mill owners were peevish about Gandhi's pronouncement that they should take the proper stand irrespective of his fast: "[they] even flung keen, delicate bits of sarcasm at me, as indeed they had a perfect right to do," he acknowledges ruefully (389). But they conceded the demand for arbitration after three days of fasting, and they appear to have done it, at least in the faster's telling of it, without rancor. The fact of the fast being partially shared by some "friends and labourers" resulted in the "hearts of the mill-owners [being] touched."

The more famous instance of the fast of 1932, the so-called Epic Fast, against the British government's decision to create separate electorates for untouchables, which would allow them to elect untouchable representatives to provincial legislatures, was at least as ethically indeterminate. Gandhi saw in the decision to grant separate electorates to minority populations a classic instance of the British policy of divide and rule. Even more importantly, he felt the question of the untouchables was internal to the Hindu community; their "statutory separation . . . from the Hindu fold" would undermine the work of reformers who had fought for their acceptance as an integral part of the Hindu community. The fast, he said, was "intended to sting Hindu conscience into right religious action."[89] Many of Gandhi's associates, the British government, and the leaders of the untouchables were baffled by the decision to fast, albeit for different reasons. Rabindranath Tagore, who disagreed with Gandhi on many questions and was generally opposed to fasting as a political tactic, did endorse the moral urgency of this fast. Jawaharlal Nehru, in a moment of extraordinary moral blindness, dismissed the question of untouchability as a "side issue" not worth the "final sacrifice" of the mahatma's life but came around after the commencement of the fast to acknowledging, even if with some bewilderment, "the magic of a fast."[90] Aside from Nehru, many other members of the Congress Party found the fast distasteful in its political style and questionable in its ethical stance.[91] Both the British and the untouchables saw the fast as directed against the empowerment of the latter, whose sole advocate Gandhi claimed to be, in his capacity as the representative of the Congress Party, which in turn claimed to represent all Indians, in contradistinction to the allegedly communal politics of, say, the Muslim League or the untouchable parties. B. R. Ambedkar, the leader of the untouchables and Gandhi's primary antagonist on the question of separate representation of the untouchables, angrily dismissed the fast as "a political stunt" but, in negotiations with Gandhi, reached an agreement known as the Poona or the Yeravda Pact, which abolished the separate electorates granted by Ramsay McDonald's Communal Award but secured a larger number of reserved seats for untouchables. Only untouchables could be candidates for such seats, but these were to be chosen by the general electorate and therefore by the caste Hindu majority. In later years Ambedkar was to characterize this agreement as a "sentimental blunder."[92]

The fast, like all of Gandhi's fasts, had tremendous emotional effect; news of it confirmed his status as a legend, traveling far and wide in a way that no mere newspaper reports or policy statements could have done. As in the case of all his fasts, including the fast of 1924, which had been undertaken (in a Muslim home under the supervision of Muslim physicians) to resolve Hindu–Muslim tensions in the Northwest Frontier Province, it was marked by a particular attentiveness to allegorical gesture. These gestures were mimicked, at least temporarily, by a national audience of Hindus unwilling to assume responsibility for the death of the mahatma. Through much of India temples were thrown open to untouchables, and there were some highly publicized instances of caste Hindu–untouchable commensality. But the drama of the fast alone could not be expected to effect the transformations the fasting mahatma had called for. The iterations of the mahatma's symbolic language proved in a few instances to be mere burlesque, as some of the temples that had admitted untouchables were repurified; certainly there was no appreciable change in the status of the untouchables.[93] Other fasts against intimate antagonists were even less successful in the domain of realpolitik. The Viceroy Lord Linlithgow, for instance, was unmoved by Gandhi's fast in 1943, characterizing it as blackmail and holding its author responsible for the violence of the Quit India movement.[94] The British press likewise refused to concede the moral probity of a fast or hunger strike undertaken against colonial Britain at the height of the Second World War.[95]

The one instance in which Gandhi's fasting appears to have met with success and with approval, even if retrospectively bestowed, was that which was undertaken in Calcutta in 1947 to promote harmony among Hindus, Muslims, and Sikhs in the aftermath of the violence-wracked Partition of the subcontinent. Rioting had broken out in the city, where Gandhi had established a temporary abode in Beliaghata, a poor neighborhood that was the scene of much violence, with the Muslim chief minister of the state. Gandhi was confronted and threatened by irate, violent Hindu mobs. He decided to fast, hoping thereby to touch the hearts of the rioters and of the populace whose unspoken sympathy was with them. The result, after a couple of days' fasting, was a cessation of violence and pledges by leaders of the communal groups to maintain peace. It was a rare triumph of Gandhian fasting, one that justified his moniker, bestowed by the admiring Viceroy Lord Mountbatten, as a "One Man Boundary Force."

Several scholars have pondered the great symbolic power, coupled with the limited practical effectiveness, of the Gandhian strategy of fasting. Bhikhu Parekh, a sympathetic yet not uncritical scholar of Gandhi's life and thought, has seen the fasts as defensive measures, undertaken in the aftermath of the failure of conventional negotiations and conventional modes of persuasion.[96] But the incommensurability of what, for want of a better term, one can call the symbolic and political economies of fasting suggests that the accountancy of success and failure may be an inadequate analytic response to the bodily and philosophical mystery of fasting. Extraordinarily ambiguous in its ethical implications and the cathexes it involves, it is, as Alter remarks, something of a limit for the Gandhian dietetic experiment. If consumption, even to sustain life minimally, is as tainted with violence as sexuality is, then fasting can permit a temporary respite from "the nemesis of nutritional need," becoming a mode of "consuming rather than feeding desire."[97] Such a dynamic is aptly illustrated in the case of the Jain lay ascetic and poet Raychandbhai Mehta. Raychandbhai was Gandhi's contemporary and fellow Gujarati, his counselor on metaphysical questions, diet, and brahmacharya, and the man he named, along with Ruskin and Tolstoy, as the greatest influence on him. Raychandbhai was one of the most prominent instances in the modern period of *samadhi maran* (religiously sanctioned self-annihilation through starvation), transcending his body's appetites and needs through personal seclusion, meditation, celibacy, and a controlled wasting away through fasting; this purified his body of its sins and culminated in his death at the age of thirty-two.[98] Raychandbhai was perhaps the closest thing to a guru Gandhi could expect to find. But Gandhi was no Raychandbhai. His was emphatically what the Rudolphs have denominated a "this-worldly asceticism," and he was possessed of a powerful "desire to serve." And yet he who was given to a painstaking public and occasionally self-justifying scrutiny of his methods was sometimes at a loss to explain the logic and value of fasting except in terms of an existential need that transcended calculability and was its own raison d'être: "I can as well do without my eyes, for instance, as I can without fasts. What the eyes are for the outer world, fasts are for the inner."[99] The sheer inexorability and excess of the act of abstinence is surely worthy of note here.[100] For the impure and guilty body inhabited and harassed by carnality, fasting could not be simply a mode of masculine purification and an affiliated masculine self-assertion. It had to assume the status of an elemental, even a somatic need. The metaphoric substance of the comment above suggests that alimentary abstinence may have functioned, moreover, as a mode of revelation or visionary experience not reducible to the hygienic, mental, and societal benefits Gandhi often adduced as arguments for fasting. The analogy underlines the powerfully positive, and indeed, elemental, valence of the fast as an appetite or a yearning inordinate enough and extra-rational enough to be counterposed to those two overwhelming and perennial antagonists of the male ethical self, the palate and the libido.

Enigmas of Ingestion

Despite the full-throatedness of his denunciation of the violent alimentary order of modernity, Gandhi's engagement with nonviolence, including the nonviolence of vegetarianism, was far from uncomplicated. He was himself hauntingly aware of the sometimes specular relation between aggression and nonviolence. While he had participated as a noncombatant in the Anglo-Boer War and the campaign against the Zulu Rebellion in South Africa on the grounds that imperial citizenship entailed such duties, his decision a decade later, in the aftermath of his formulation of satyagraha, to raise an Indian ambulance corps in London to assist the British war effort during the First World War came as a shock to his associates. This last decision underscores the complexity of Gandhian nonviolence, and his awareness not only of the proximity of violence and nonviolence but also of the coimplication of the nominally nonviolent in structures of violence: "Whilst in England I was enjoying the protection of the British Fleet, and taking shelter as I did under its armed might, I was directly participating in its potential violence" (313). When he returned to India and assumed a leading role in Congress politics there, he was frequently accused—for the most part by British detractors but at times by Indian ones as well, Tagore's disapprobation of the burning of foreign cloth being an illustrious instance—of fomenting hatred and violence, however unwittingly, rather than nonviolence and reminded of the discrepancy between his own elevated ideals and the actions undertaken by his followers.[101] A good part of the mahatma's public correspondence, especially in the 1920s, was devoted to clarifying and controlling the implications of everyday swaraj and satyagrahic practice. In these everyday meditations he reveals himself to be notably open-ended, flexible, and pragmatic with respect to the enactment of ahimsaic principle. In his more mundane communications with correspondents from all over India and the globe, he was possessed by the question of the relative importance of human and animal life, arguing sometimes against an anthropocentric bias and sometimes in favor of the greater moral worth of human beings. A notable controversy about the "mercy-killing" of an injured calf at Sabarmati Ashram was but one instance of the staging of the dilemma, as was that of the killing of rabid dogs in Ahmedabad. In the case of the dogs the mahatma had to remind the readers of Young India in forceful terms that "merely taking life is not always Himsa [violence or injury], one may even say there is sometimes more Himsa in not taking life."[102] Even about meat eating itself, he was usually conscious of the dangers of mandating vegetarianism in a subcontinent notably riven by dietary differences that were inseparable from religious, regional, gendered, and caste identities. With respect to persons not bound to him by familial or quasi-familial contexts, Gandhi could be remarkably accommodating of meat eating.[103]

On his instructions Louis Fischer, Nehru, and Maulana Azad were served meat at Sabarmati Ashram, a practice that upset and confused some of his readers and correspondents.

But Gandhi's meditations upon and experiences of situations that dramatized the limits of nonviolence were, in situations of gendered and familial intimacy, somewhat more troubled and more ironic. Indeed, his account of the toll he imposed as vegetarian patriarch upon a gravely ill Manilal and a postoperative Kasturba speaks to the ambiguity of the dietary gesture and to its immensely complicated moral arithmetic. These bear examining in some detail.

. . .

The crisis involving Manilal occurred when he was ten years old and suffered "a severe attack of typhoid, combined with pneumonia and signs of delirium at night" (219). The doctor prescribed eggs and chicken broth rather than more conventional medicines, which were judged unavailing in his condition. As Gandhi recounts it in his *Autobiography*, the doctor speaks without ambiguity of what is medically requisite: "Your son's life is in danger. . . . I am called in by many Hindu families, and they do not object to anything I prescribe. I think you will be well advised not to be so hard on your son" (219). The ethical decision involved cannot be resolved by a child. Though Manilal refuses the forbidden foods when asked, the father understands the character of the child's obedience: "If I had given him either of these [eggs and chicken broth], he would have taken it" (220). Rejecting the ethically suspect palliative measures proposed by the doctor of biomedicine and accepted without question by his less scrupulous fellow Hindu vegetarians, Gandhi glosses the occasion instead as a true test of vegetarian principle: "To my mind it is only on such occasions that a man's faith is truly tested. Rightly or wrongly it is part of my religious conviction that man may not eat meat, eggs, and the like. There should be a limit even to the means of keeping ourselves alive" (219). Gandhi's repudiation of the therapeutic character of meat might conceivably be read as functioning as a critique of the medical commonsense of the day: "The doctors could not guarantee recovery. At best they could experiment" (220). But his explanation about the refusal of eggs and chicken broth is less skeptical of the curative claims of allopathic medicine than it is desirous of a pure and uncompromised commitment to meatlessness. Hence he refuses not only the medicinal food of the doctor's prescription but also the consolations scripturally available for such situations in the Hindu *dharmashastras* (law books). The doctrine of *apad dharma* (the ethics of extremity or of emergency) is precisely the kind of exemption from right practice that is granted in circumstances when right conduct is perilous or impractical. Of the law book that is the *Manusmriti* Wendy Doniger says, "The concept of *apad* recognizes the inevitability of human fallibility: don't do this, Manu says, but if you *do*, this is what to do to fix it."[104] Indeed, she says, the prescriptive rules of *dharma* (duty, right conduct) in the *Manusmriti* are so extensive and baroque as to be practically paralyzing; therefore much of the lawgiver's text is devoted to supplementing these regulations with emergency codes that can more realistically be applied to ordinary human life. Such an elaboration of prohibitions and permissions has led Brian K. Smith to claim that "Manu is not so much a text on *dharma* as it is on *apad dharma*—the principles of life led in a perpetual state of crisis."[105] Manilal's grave illness is a textbook example of the mise-en-scène of apad dharma, illness being one of the classic instances in which the law permits its own suspension or circumvention. For Gandhi, on the contrary, principle, to retain its character as principle, must prove itself not in conditions of normality but in conditions of crisis. It must be willing, as the words "There should be a limit even to the means of keeping ourselves alive" indicate, to sacrifice life itself in order to be true to itself. This leads to the preservation of life not as a self-evident good but as a terrible temptation that one committed to ahimsaic principle often has to struggle against. As Shetty has pointed out, a willingness to die rather than a will to live becomes the proper response to the crisis of illness: "Vegetarianism then becomes conceivable as a non-violent and therefore ethical mode of dying as much as it is, in times of health, an anti-parasitic remedy against violent living."[106]

These positions are by no means easily arrived at or serenely sustained by the tormented father. Having rejected conventional medical treatment for hydropathic therapy and a minimal, fasting diet of orange juice mixed with water, he wonders both about the opinion of the world and about the advisability of making his son's illness the occasion for a test of vegetarian principle: "What would people say of me? What would my elder brother think of me? Could we not call in another doctor? Why not have an Ayurvedic physician? What right had the parents to inflict their fads on their children?" (220). It is perhaps noteworthy that Kasturba does not feature among Gandhi's imagined interlocutors in his dark night of the soul. Turning away from the persons familiar to him, he turns instead to

God, though without any clear sense of certitude in his faith. Gandhi's crisis is both deeply effortful and a radically lonely experience, marked by a language of anxiety, conflict, haunting, fatigue, and isolation in the midst of others.

Like the Abraham prepared to sacrifice the son he loves in response to a mysterious command from a God whose reasoning is inaccessible to him but whom he feels bound to obey, Gandhi finds himself caught between incommensurable horizons of responsibility and an inability to explain his actions in any reasonable fashion. As Derrida puts it in his reading of Søren Kierkegaard's *Fear and Trembling*, Abraham's absolute responsibility to the other that is God is at violent odds with his duty or his responsibility in general, which forbids filicide and which requires him to be answerable to a community, including his family. A "scandal and a paradox," absolute responsibility cannot provide an accounting, except to the other to whom it is bound, of its actions; in fact, for one bound to silent obedience, the accounting that responsibility in general demands is precisely the temptation he must resist. And yet, in sacrificing responsibility in general, Abraham is not spurning it but conceding its ethical force: "In order for there to be a sacrifice, the ethical must retain all its value; the love for his son must remain intact, and the order of human duty must continue to insist on its rights."[107]

In his terrifyingly absolute fidelity Abraham, though the figure of faith itself, inspires not admiration or a desire for emulation but a kind of horror: his decision to obey God and sacrifice Isaac is calculated to appall. And yet it is his situation that constitutes for Derrida the exemplary rather than the anomalous instance of responsibility itself, especially when we pluralize our sense of the other who demands responsibility of us. Moving away from the notion of God as the single instance of the wholly other who can wrench us away from habits of commonplace and reasonable dutifulness, he suggests a more expansive notion of the wholly other who has a claim on our fidelity. *Tout autre est tout autre*—every other [one] is every [bit] other—is Derrida's way of encapsulating this endless, infinite responsibility. Since we are responsible not to one other but to an innumerable host of others, every act of ethical decision making, every act of fidelity or commitment to one constitutes an inescapable betrayal of all others, human, animal, or divine, who can demand sacrifice of one: "If every human is wholly other [for Gandhi duty to humans would surely have to be supplemented with duty to nonhuman animals], if everyone else, or every other one, is every bit other, then one can no longer distinguish between a claimed generality of ethics that would need to be sacrificed in sacrifice, and the faith that turns towards God alone, as wholly other, turning away from human duty."[108]

Derrida's reading of the enormously risky character of the Abrahamic decision offers a way of understanding Gandhi's trial in all its terrible complexity rather than of construing the right answer to alimentary and medical crisis as pregiven. But in examining the discomfiting limits of the sacrificial logic of a premeditated and thoughtful vegetarianism, the Manilal episode raises some additional questions that Derrida chooses not to pursue in detail. If the vegetarian is one who is willing to sacrifice himself rather than sacrificing the other that is the nonhuman animal, what is indeed properly his own to sacrifice? Who is it who can undertake the responsibility of sacrifice? If sacrifice is a burden it is surely also an entitlement and an assertion of one's rights over one's body and one's actions and those of others. Can a woman be a sacrificer? Is it an accident that it was Abraham alone rather than Sarah or Abraham and Sarah together who was invested with the terrible responsibility of sacrifice? "Does the system of this sacrificial responsibility . . . imply at its very basis an exclusion or sacrifice of woman?," Derrida asks.[109] The virtual absence of Kasturba in the Manilal episode has been noted already. When Gandhi, exhausted by his struggle, goes out for a walk, his son is left "in charge of his mother" (220), but the reader is told nothing of her response to the crisis; the anguish is her husband's alone. Kasturba and her husband often clashed powerfully, especially when the mahatma sought to bend her to his will. But it is difficult to conjecture what she might have felt about this test of vegetarian and medical principle; she was, as Gandhi explains, a vegetarian as a matter of customary practice and might well have shared her husband's distaste for animal foods even in their therapeutic forms. Later in the *Autobiography* Gandhi writes that "she had not much faith in [his] remedies, though she did not resist them" (291), at least when her own well-being was concerned. This submission to a husband under conditions of limited faith captures in some ways the complex character of a woman's (non-)sacrifice. Certainly it is not easy to conjure up a feminine equivalent, at least in the South Asian context, to the mahatma's heroic tale of principle and renunciation.

If Kasturba is very much offstage in the tale about Manilal's illness, she does merit a vegetarian crisis of her own in the *Autobiography*. If the tale of the child's affliction is a parable of his father's incertitude and struggle, hers is a parable of assent. Entitled "Kasturbai's Courage," the chapter describes a rare instance of accord in an otherwise contentious relationship between husband and wife. Quite different in tone from the chapter that describes the episode with Manilal, the conflict here is not so much singular, uncertain, and risky as it is publicly argued and confidently engaged. Gandhi's interlocutor and custodial competitor in this instance is not God or his conscience but a doctor of dubious medical morals who, in her husband's absence and in defiance of his express disapproval of nonvegetarian therapeutics, insists on administering beef tea, a favored food for invalids and convalescents, to a highly debilitated postoperative Kasturba. The possibility of death is broached by Gandhi and Kasturba without any obvious evidence of the heart searching that had marked the crisis with the son, Gandhi saying matter-of-factly at the outset, " 'I would never allow my wife to be given meat or beef, even if the denial meant her death, unless of course she desired to take it' " (289). Occurring in the early days of the satyagraha struggle and Gandhi's commitment to brahmacharya, this test is as much about the incipient mahatma's willingness to sacrifice all to the cause of Truth and to achieve a kind of ethical self-sufficiency as it is about Kasturba's adherence to the principles of right conduct in times of emergency. Nonetheless, the last clause in the statement above invites some notice: while Gandhi has little doubt that Kasturba's death is preferable to a violation of vegetarian principle, she herself must consent to the sacrifice, make it her own, as it were. She has to consent, moreover, not once but again and again in the face of an importunate husband determined to win her free assent in the very midst of extremity. Gandhi is nothing if not self-conscious about the equivocality of his approach to producing a principled refusal of nonvegetarianism: "She was really too weak to be consulted in this matter. But I thought it my painful duty to do so" (289). Nonetheless he is delighted (a word the English-language *Autobiography* generally uses to describe successful engagements with ethical challenges) when, in spite of his scrupulously rehearsed arguments in favor of beef tea, she refuses the temptation of living that such consumption holds out to her. None of this is to suggest that Kasturba was kept from beef tea against her will. An orthodox Hindu, she may well have been willing to die rather than consume forbidden flesh. Indeed, Gandhi suggests that the sacrifice was not a struggle for her and involved no wrestling with principle and therefore was perhaps no real sacrifice at all: "The traditional religion of her forefathers was enough for her" (290). But the litany of repeated, even hyperbolized, renunciations is not without a certain interest and suggests a strenuous endeavor to undo, overwrite, or supplement the husband's decision early in the chapter to forbid meat to an ailing wife to whom it is prescribed.

The insistence upon discussion and consent at the sickbed or death-bed stands in rather striking contrast to Gandhi's more usual mode, which rarely involved discussing with his wife rationales for difficult decisions. Most famously, his vow of brahmacharya was the result of extensive discussions with his coworkers but none at all with his wife. "It is likely that many of my doings have not her approval even today," he says forthrightly in a discussion of the "true friendship" that results from their brahmacharya. "We never discuss them. I see no good in discussing them" (244–45).

In this case, the fact that the writer had to tell what was a version of Manilal's tale again (once more with a happy ending) speaks powerfully to the difficulty of encountering and exorcising the occasionally troubled limits of his vegetarianism and his nonviolence. The story of Kasturba's near-death experience and vegetarian redemption in South Africa features the vegetarian patriarch as one who cannot escape the contingency of violence even or perhaps especially in the exercise of ahimsaic principles.

Gandhi was rarely to be tested again as brutally as he had been in the case of his wife and his son. But the dilemma of ingestion that the event stages—about what may ethically be introduced into the body and how it may be introduced—is articulated with his ambivalence, at a much later point in his career, about letting his grandniece Manu be operated upon for appendicitis rather than being treated by naturopathy.[110] Likewise, when Kasturba became ill with chronic bronchitis while imprisoned at the Aga Khan's palace in Poona and ayurvedic and later biomedical efforts failed to ameliorate her condition, Gandhi ordered all medicines stopped, including a rare supply of penicillin (which had to be administered by injection, a particularly objectionable point for her husband, who de-tested the suspension of moral volition involved in bypassing orality) ordered from Calcutta by his youngest son, Devdas. When she died his testimonial for her was marked by an admixture of heartache and recti-tude: "I cannot imagine life without Ba . . . Her passing has left a vacuum which never will be filled . . . We lived together for sixty-two years . . . If I allowed the penicillin it would not have saved her . . . And she passed away in my lap. Could it be better? I am happy beyond measure."[111] The guilt that shadows, however negligibly, the remark about penicillin is without question the ineluctable experience of all survivors and mourners, but it also resonates somewhat with the South African account of patriarchal austerity in the face of Kasturba's near-death experience.

Gandhi's account of the crisis of ahimsaic principle involving his own body is, interestingly, written under the sign of failure. What his biographer Louis Fischer calls "the first important illness in his life" was a disorder of the alimentary tract, precipitated, in distinction to the ailments of Manilal and Kasturba, by excesses of consumption.[112] Gandhi describes his lapse into dysentery as a result of overindulgence in the delicacies prepared by Kasturba, using terms that carry a quasi-libidinal charge: "She tempted me and I succumbed" (406). Refusing the pharmacological remedies that heal the body at the expense of the soul, he "preferred to suffer the penalty for my folly" (407). Offered the usual eggs and meat broth, combined with the stock ayurvedic advice on the necessary therapeutic violence involved in the cure of illness, he refuses: "How could I relinquish a principle in respect of myself, when I had enforced it relentlessly in respect of my wife, children, and friends?" (408).[113] The language of relentlessness and enforcement Gandhi uses here marks a certain sharp reflexiveness about the fraught intersubjective terrain of ahimsaic practice, and it seals his determination to enact the obedience to the vegetarian virtue he has enforced in others.

His recovery, however, was complicated by his abjuration, sealed with a vow no less, of what is in the subcontinental context a largely innocuous food: milk. His abandonment of cow's milk in South Africa was prompted in part by his horror at the cruelty of the milking process in India and in part by his conviction, derived from the counsel of Raychandbhai, that milk drinking undermined brahmacharya. "[Brahmacharya] has been a matter of very great effort ever since I began to take milk," he says in the *Autobiography* (183). Such a position is in contrast to the generally accepted *sattvic* (calm, pure, cooling rather than heating the passions) character of milk and *ghi* (clarified butter), which is associated with the diet of celibate males and religious aspirants. "In Hindu myth and ritual," says Alter, "milk—particularly cow's milk—is one of the purest fluids."[114] In the face of an unresolvable dilemma, the wife who had tempted him in the first place offers a resolution that is also a temptation, suggesting he drink goat's milk rather than the cow's milk he has specifically abjured. Gandhi's response to this instance of apad dharma, a paradoxical act that preserves life and undermines ethics at the same time, is an acknowledgment of his human frailty: "I succumbed. My intense eagerness to take up the Satyagraha fight [against the repressive

Rowlatt Bills of the colonial government] had created in me a strong desire to live, and so I contented myself with adhering to the letter of my vow only, and sacrificed its spirit" (410).

Despite his compromise, Gandhi continued to feel keenly his deficits in ahimsaic purity: "The will to live proved stronger than the devotion to truth, and for once the votary of truth compromised his sacred ideal by his eagerness to take up the Satyagraha fight. The memory of this action even now rankles in my breast and fills me with remorse, and I am constantly thinking how to give up goat's milk. But I cannot yet free myself from that subtlest of temptations, the desire to serve, which still holds me" (411). Gandhi's alimentary crisis stages for him, in a way the other vegetarian crises could not, the embeddedness of ahimsaic principle in the matrix of other, perhaps equally compelling but incommensurable ethical demands. The absolutism of ahimsaic sacrifice and the autonomy of vegetarianism from other forms of duty and renunciation that marks the tales of Kasturba and Manilal cannot be sustained here. This tale stages the question, in a way different from the others, of what or who is sacrificed in sacrificing oneself to an ideal of vegetarian purity. How is one to assess, for instance, the vegetarian sacrifice of the public man or mahatma in relation to the vegetarianism of the child or the woman/wife/mother? Despite Gandhi's strongly felt conviction that true vegetarianism could not be grounded in calculations of relative profit, such calculations were not always easily ignored or circumvented in practice. The third-person language in the passage above ("the votary of truth compromised his sacred ideal") is an unusual rhetorical instantiation of Gandhi's consciousness of his being something other than a radically isolated individual or even a family man wrestling with ethical dilemmas; it marks, if you will, his awareness of the demands of his mahatma-hood. It both bespeaks a distance from an ideal he has failed to realize and sets up the public figure, with his duties, as not entirely congruent with the private man.

At the same time the speaker is keenly aware of the unforeseen forms of consumption, renunciation, and temptation. The renunciation that is vegetarianism is overcome, not by any gross bodily appetite, but by something more insidious: "the desire to serve." *Seva* (service) is, in the Gandhian moral economy, inseparable from other forms of renunciation, including ahimsaic vegetarianism and *tapasya* (asceticism, including self-suffering). And yet, the powerful affective and bodily investment in such renunciation contributes to a wayward ethical accountancy, sustaining as it does a "desire to live" that cannot but militate against the readiness to die that is the highest form of ethical living. The prospect of competing rather than congruous renunciations thus makes renunciation itself risky rather than straightforward. Moreover, if the desire for renunciation is itself cast in terms of an inexorable drive, the relationship between violence, consumption, and nonattachment is no longer self-evident.

The gendered contours of this third parable of alimentary crisis are notable. An offense implicitly against sexual as well as alimentary purity —since milk serves as an incitement to libidinality—the episode cannot but be as well a lesson on the relationship of the mahatma and his wife. She is an instigator of the crisis, but in giving him permission to transgress she also helps resolve it, though in ways that smack of sophistry rather than unflinching adherence to the solemnity of a vow. As such, she cannot be, as she arguably could not be even in the instance of her own crisis, a full, reflexive participant in the ethical dilemmas staged by Gandhi's near-death experience. Kasturba's wifeliness partakes more of the lesser quality of self-abnegation that Gandhi praised as her most visible virtue, especially in the days of their celibate life together: "As my public life expanded, my wife bloomed forth and lost herself in my work."[115] Notwithstanding Gandhi's insistence that "woman [was] the embodiment of sacrifice and *ahimsa*," this self-abnegation in Kasturba's case, lacking the inexorability of her husband's commitment not to her but to Truth, lacks also the heroic status and purity of sacrifice. In this she participates both in the Hindu wife's dharma, which is the preservation of the life of the husband, and confirms her status as one who is not entitled to offer sacrifice in her own right. Sacrifice is, as I stressed earlier, an entitlement, even a property right, so that the sacrificer proper is ready not just to sacrifice himself but, perhaps just as importantly, to sacrifice others. In contrast, the wife is one who has no rights in her husband and therefore cannot sacrifice him, even to the purest of principles.

Conclusion

A focus on ingestion and abstinence as parabolic form in Gandhi's autobiographical and civic projects allows one, precisely through its reading of the quotidian and the eccentric, to underline the gendered implications of Gandhi's preoccupation with his body and with the bodies he sought to reform. My investigation of two linked loci of Gandhi's dietary practices, namely, the question of meat and modernity and the question of meat in the gendered dynamics of the Hindu vegetarian household, has sought to illuminate the intimate links among meat eating, modern formations of masculine identity, and a national-political aesthetics of the body. It has also sought to show that the history of Gandhi's palate and its transactions with the home and the world demands that one take into account its not inconsiderable ambiguities. The complicated, sometimes unpredictable logic that attends this history serves to emphasize the myriad ways in which the tongue functions as a vehicle of violence both in its abstinences and in its indulgences. A terrain marked by surprise, challenge, and struggle, Gandhian vegetarianism and nonviolence is less a map of fixed ethical and somatic virtue than an unsettled and unsettling practice.

3

Dearth

Accounting for Famine

One cannot but broach the question of famine without a few rehearsals of the obvious. We know altogether too well, for instance, that scarcity, hunger, and famine are metonymically chained to popular conceptions of South Asia. The Indian subcontinent, especially India and Bangladesh, has long been, along with China, Russia, and twentieth-century Ethiopia and the Sahel, one of the proverbial "lands of famine."[1] Such a reputation has become, if anything, more emphatic in the modern period. While the death tolls from particular famines in the last quarter of the nineteenth century did not approach the apocalyptic mortality figures of ten million, about a third of the inhabitants of a densely populated province, of the Bengal famine of 1770, the first great colonial-era famine, their cumulative toll was twice that reckoned in 1770.[2] Even a tale like Kipling's "William the Conqueror," serenely self-congratulatory and historically wide of the mark though it undoubtedly is about the famine relief efforts of the colonial state, is compelled to take note of the recurrent character of famine in British India.[3] Historians, economists, and Indian nationalists have long noted the profound failures of the colonial state in providing famine relief and its role in begetting the conditions, including rigid taxation, neglect of irrigation, prevention of industrialization, and the privileging of the interests of landlords and moneylenders over those of peasants, that produced famine conditions in the first place. R. C. Dutt's *Indian Famines: Their Causes and Prevention* (1901) and Dadabhai Naoroji's *Poverty and Un-British Rule in India* (1901) were only the most prominent among numerous indictments in the late colonial period.[4] As in Ireland in the 1840s, faith in the principles of political economy and in Malthusian theories of population made for a reluctance to interfere with markets and with what were believed to be incontrovertible natural laws of population growth. In the words of Mike Davis, "By official dictate, India like Ireland before it had become a Utilitarian laboratory where millions of lives were wagered against dogmatic faith in omnipotent markets overcoming the 'inconvenience of dearth' [Adam Smith's phrase]."[5] As in the case of the Poor Laws in Victorian Britain a few decades earlier and in the case of Irish famine relief, endeavors to reduce costs and produce efficiencies by reducing famine rations, physically dislocating starving populations from their homes and aggregating them in dormitory camps, demanding hard labor of the recipients as a condition of their receipt of food, and imposing a "distance test" that denied work to able-bodied men and older children within ten miles of their homes made relief odious and often unavailing.[6]

The slow, grudging emergence of a famine code and a corresponding famine insurance fund in the 1870s and 1880s did not necessarily mark a new conception of state responsibility for famine relief. In its early years the fund functioned instead, as William Gladstone complained, as an occasion for raising taxes to finance military ventures in Afghanistan.[7] And while India remained free of major famines, though it suffered eighteen so-called scarcities, between 1908 and 1942, as many as three million people are estimated to have perished in the Bengal famine of 1943–44. Of the two watershed events of the subcontinent's difficult passage into postcoloniality, the Bengal famine of 1943 and the bloodbath associated with the partition of India in 1947, the famine was, for Bengalis, perhaps the more traumatic one. The famine was precipitated at least in part by the "denial policy" of a colonial government at war with Japan, a policy that confiscated stores of rice in coastal areas as well as fishermen's boats so as to forestall an easy takeover of India's eastern front.[8] Not surprisingly, there was a strenuous reluctance on the part of the state, at both the provincial and the federal levels, to concede that there was a subsistence crisis, and in fact the event was never officially designated as a famine. The Statesman was to write scathingly about state-invented euphemisms for starvation and famine in 1943: "The grim word starvation disappeared from the text [of government statistics], remaining only in our own headings; instead, sufferers admitted to hospitals were dubbed 'sick destitutes,' and a laboured appendix contended that most of the 37 deaths on Saturday were due to chronic ailments 'neglected in the past.' "[9] Part of what the famine literature demonstrates, a point that a chronicler of hunger such as Mahasweta Devi underscores with caustic clearsightedness in a novella like *Pterodactyl, Puran Sahay, and Pirtha*, is that the language of state, colonial and postcolonial alike, has recourse to an increasingly baroque lexicon of scarcity and crisis replete with droughts and shortages and relief measures but never, ever famines. This is done to forestall the deployment of the damning term that would index an unexampled experience of inequality, suffering, and exploitation. It also demonstrates that the elision of the term *famine* only serves to guarantee its perilous incipience, its persistence as a secret sharer of the modern, unevenly liberal, self-congratulatory state.

The city of Calcutta, whose workers were protected from the worst effects of famine through food subsidies and rationing, saw the influx of hundreds of thousands of starving people from the countryside. Almost all of them lived on the streets. Some of them were fed at food distribution sites through government-administered feeding centers and private relief societies, though observers as well as famine sufferers often complained about the quality and purity of the food, alleging that it induced or exacerbated stomach problems. For much of the duration of the famine, the government at Delhi remained impervious to the problems of Bengal, accusing Bengalis of overdramatizing the situation and refusing to permit, except briefly, the importation of food from other provinces. Whitehall and the British Parliament, rendered hostile to Indian concerns by the militancy of Indian nationalism, were indifferent as well.[10] The provincial government in Calcutta also proved remarkably inept at dealing with the tragedy. Law and order, however, remained unthreatened through it all. People starved to death in front of food shops guarded by the police, and an efficient, far-flung railway system ensured, not the transportation of food grains into Bengal or the speedy migration of the famine stricken to more prosperous areas, but the transportation of food grains out of famine-stricken areas by hoarders and profiteers.

Partially as a result of official obfuscations, it has been difficult to determine in any precise manner the onset, duration, and costs of the famine. (Mortality figures for famines are generally difficult to determine, since the usual modes of demographic accounting break down in situations of crisis. Besides, diseases continue to claim lives even after famines are officially concluded.) There are differing estimates of the mortality figures for the famine of 1943–44. The Enquiry Commission that was convened in 1944 and charged with investigating the famine arrived at a death toll of 1.5 million, after noting the inaccuracy of public health statistics in India.[11] It was a number that one of its members, W. R. Aykroyd, was later to estimate as being altogether too low.[12] Amartya Sen has examined statistics from the 1943–46 period, rather than simply the 1943–44 span, in order to determine the "excess mortality" attributable to famine. His estimate of 3 million, which takes into account the staggered mortality effect of famine as a consequence of malnutrition and lowered resistance to disease, is generally accepted by historians and economists.[13] The Bengali director Mrinal Sen's screenplay for *Akaler Sandhaney* (*In Search of Famine*, 1980) puts the figure at 5 million. So does Satyajit Ray in *Asani Sanket* (*Distant Thunder*, 1973). All of them caution against a simple, unconsidered opposition between famine and a putative alimentary normality, noting that chronic malnutrition and dearth characterized the lives of peasants, the archetypal victims of famine, in non-famine contexts as well.

I use these events here as a certain irreducible horizon for a reading of Mahasweta's haunting tales "Shishu" ("Children," 1979) and *Pterodactyl, Puran Sahay, and Pirtha* (1982). These tales compel an encounter between the conventional conception of famine as anomalous and exorbitant to the experience of the modern subject of the liberal state and the deranging revelation that subaltern and, more specifically, tribal famine on a genocidal scale remains the inadmissible secret not just of the colonial Indian state, but of the postcolonial one as well.

Another, more immediate context than the famine of 1943–44 for the production of Mahasweta's hunger fictions is unquestionably the breakdown in the legitimacy of the postindependence Indian state, especially as exemplified in its brutal response to peasant uprisings in the 1960s and 1970s and in the suspension of civil liberties in the Emergency of 1975–77. The Naxalite movement took its name and immediate inspiration from a peasant uprising in May 1967 at Naxalbari, a village in West Bengal, though it also owed something to radical struggles in other parts of the world, including Vietnam, Cuba, China, western Europe, and the United States as well as to nineteenth- and twentieth-century peasant struggles for land reform in the subcontinent. Led in armed guerrilla warfare by communist revolutionaries, who would later form the Communist Party of India (Marxist-Leninist), the Naxalites sought a revolution in agrarian relations through an attack on the feudal order in the Indian countryside: landlords, moneylenders, and their enforcers, the state's police force. They received broad support from an unlikely array of political actors, including not only tribal communities in Andhra Pradesh and West Bengal, among the most subalternized in postcolonial India, but also middle-class Bengali students from Calcutta who were inspired by revolutionary idealism and who joined the rural poor in their armed struggle against the state. The state responded with terror on a massive scale, imprisoning, torturing, and killing Naxalite activists and their rural and urban sympathizers in staggering numbers.[14] Facing military and police crackdowns in rural areas and in Calcutta, the extrajudicial assassination of Naxalite leaders by the police, internal conflicts over tactics, and the absence of democratic outlets for claiming rights and expressing grievances, the Naxalites were substantially vanquished by the state by the late seventies.

If the Naxalite movement was the product of the crisis years of 1965– 69 when India's economic, political, and military failures were increasingly apparent, it was followed by more causes of dissatisfaction and modes of unrest on a nationwide basis. By the start of the next decade, the postcolonial state's betrayal of its promises of equity seemed near-complete, as poverty, corruption, inflation, and unemployment rose to critical levels. Protests by workers, peasants, and young people assumed a new centrality on the national stage as more and more people seemed to be responding to the call of the Gandhian socialist leader Jayaprakash Narayan for "total revolution." Much of this opposition was directed against Prime Minister Indira Gandhi, whose crisis of governance was capped by the guilty verdict brought against her in June 1975 by the Allahabad High Court investigating allegations of electoral fraud. Instead of resigning, she declared a state of emergency, suspending fundamental rights, imposing press censorship, jailing activists and members of opposition parties, and permitting her son Sanjay Gandhi to engage in brutal campaigns of slum clearance and forced sterilization of the poor. This state of affairs was to continue until March 1977, when she was decisively defeated at the polls.

These two developments—the breakdown of state legitimacy as exemplified by the Emergency and the rise and suppression of the Naxalite movement—must be reckoned among the political contexts that inform Mahasweta's fiction in the late seventies and early eighties. Mahasweta has written several fictions that are explicitly about the Naxalite movement, including "Hajar Churashir Ma" (1973–74), "Draupadi" (1978), and "Operation Bashai Tudu" (1990). "Shishu" and *Pterodactyl, Puran Sahay, and Pirtha* are not among this number; nonetheless, they cannot be fully understood except through the idioms of crisis inaugurated by these watershed events.

These events also constituted a vital context for the emergence of the Subaltern Studies project of Indian historiography. Ranajit Guha has explicitly described the project as "a child of its times," to be understood as a response to the failure of decolonization.[15] It was the reaction of a conscientized middle-class intelligentsia against the betrayals of the postcolonial state as well as against its perception of its own history of antisubaltern collaboration with a colonial order and its successor regime.[16] One can hardly help noting the ideological continuities between this historiographic enterprise and Mahasweta's literary one, which frequently features the incapacity of the middle-class figure to come to terms with subalternity. Interestingly, it may be precisely her reproof of middle-class obliviousness that makes her a rather popular figure among a largely middle-class Bengali reading public, especially its intelligentsia.

One of the most prominent of contemporary Indian writers, Mahasweta has published, mostly in Bangla, over twenty collections of short stories and over a hundred novels. Her interest in famine is, even more than is customary for Bengalis of her generation, of long standing. She was a student volunteer during the famine of 1943 and was inescapably formed not only by that experience but also by exposure to the ironically rich harvest of fiction, poetry, art, ethnography, and film in Bangla and in English produced by the famine. "It would be hard," says Nikhil Sarkar, "to find a writer in Bengali from those times who had not written a story against the setting of the famine."[17] Among these writers was her first husband, Bijon Bhattacharya, whose play *Nabanna* (*New Rice* [1944]) established a blueprint for politically committed and thematically realistic representation not just for Bangla and left-produced theater but for Indian radical theater in general.[18] Not surprisingly, the ubiquity of hunger among tribal and dalit subjects is a recurring motif in Mahasweta's stories. In "Bichhan (Seeds)" Dulan Ganju grants his stomach the status of a separate and limitless entity: " 'Who can measure our hunger? The empty space in our stomachs keeps expanding!'"[19] Likewise, the Pahan (hereditary priest) in "Daini" (The Witch-Hunt) describes hunger as the one constant of Oraon and Munda life, the only patrimony they can leave their children: "You always cried, 'I'm still hungry.' The same words always. Our children said it. Our grandchildren will say it."[20]

•   •   •

Since the seventies, beginning with *Aranyer Adhikar* (*The Right of/to the Forest*, 1977) Mahasweta has produced a number of works that depict the violent exploitation of tribal, dalit, and other subaltern communities, the devastation of their social order and economic resources, and their struggle against their exploiters.[21] A founder of the Denotified and Notified Tribal Rights Action Group (DNT-RAG) in 1980, she has worked untiringly to improve the living conditions of tribal communities and to help them claim their civil rights through education, outreach, journalism, legal action, and organizing. Because of her long-standing activities as a journalist-ethnographer and tribal activist, she has been seen quite frequently as a brilliant chronicler of a shamefully neglected social reality, as something of a sociologist par excellence; she herself has spoken of the real-life figures who have prompted some of her more memorable characters, Mary Oraon and Crooked Nagesia among others. Such a sociological gloss on her work is also licensed by the fact that her imaginative prose often relies on some of the same indices and figures as her journalistic prose, with its apparatus of details from statistical tables, police reports, and legislative documents.[22] As she has herself noted in her comments about *Bortika* (News), the journal she inherited from her parents and now runs, her objective is to collect "as much data and statistics as can be found."[23] In an interview with Enakshi Chatterjee she insists that she studies "history . . . data, statistics, government gazetteers, human rights laws, laws regarding tribals" rather than fiction or poetry.[24] Thus *Pterodactyl* can enumerate the precise figures of India's tribal disenfranchised: "7.76 percent of the population of India, . . . fifty-nine million, six hundred and thirty-eight persons"; it is little surprise that its protagonist is, like its author, a conscientized journalist.[25] If I focus here on the fact of hunger, starvation, and famine as an intimate part of the landscape of her work it is at least in part because such a focus speaks to the ethnographic, activist, empiricist, and journalistic mode in Mahasweta. As she says in her introduction to *Bitter Soil*, a translation into English of four of her stories, including "Shishu," "I believe in documentation. After reading my work, the reader should face the truth of facts, and feel duly ashamed of the true face of India."[26] She notes, moreover, the empirical, physiological basis for what appears to the middle-class reader as the uncanny phenomenology of shrunken tribal Agariya bodies: "Chronic malnutrition has the result of stunting human and animal bodies. . . . What I wrote in 'Little Ones' ['Shishu'] is correct."[27] Thus in the case of Puran, the journalist-protagonist of *Pterodactyl*, part of the ethical labor demanded of him by his sympathetic and pragmatic civil servant friend Harisharan is factual and journalistic: the public unmasking and indictment of the state's moral failure to recognize and address famine in tribal areas.

Here, though, I seek not to register simply the brutal factuality of this inanition that is the supplement of Indian postcoloniality—the incommensurability, that is, of a moral economy with the political economy of a modern, liberal, and violent state—but to understand famine itself as a figure that, like all figures, exceeds the conventional logic of numeration, accounting, and modularity. For all her passion for facts and data, Mahasweta herself presents a scathing analysis of the subaltern limits of modern forms of computation. In *Pterodactyl*, she provides a barbed rendering of the lack of fit between the overweening character of government statistics and the unremarked but quotidian deprivations of the destitute:

> "The Indian agricultural sector has made remarkable progress." . . . In 1985–86 India has raised between 146 and 148.5 million tons of food grains and 32.6 million tons of oilseed and 175 million tons of sugar-cane; 8.5 million bales of cotton and 11.4 million of jute; and India exports 25 percent of the spices on the international market.
>
> Why is this not reflected from Himachal Pradesh to Tamil Nadu, Maharashtra, Rajasthan to Eastern India?[28]

In this passage official statistics function as a form of willed delusion or self-hypnosis that obviates any reckoning with the less salubrious facts of poverty, inequality, exploitation, and hunger. The following account, from *Douloti*, in which the census takers are rendered delirious by those who subscribe to another system of accounting, gives a more elaborated figuration of positivist, bureaucratic modes of enumeration:

> The census was a hard thing in Seora village. The government people were out of their minds. At first Nagesia, Dusad, Dhobi, Ganju neither opened their mouths, nor spoke. And when they did it was hard to stop them.
>
> —What sort of thing is this? You won't write the names of the children who are dead? Dead or alive they are my children. Their names won't be in the government books?

—Listen sir! Write my mother's brother's name first. Uncle stole my goat and ran off to his daughter's in-laws. You are government people. If you write it up, I will surely get it back.

—You'll write my age? Write, write, maybe ten, maybe twenty, eh? What? I have grandchildren, I can't have so few years? How old are people when they have grandchildren? Fifty, sixty? No, no, how can I be sixty? I have heard that our brave master is fifty. I am Ghasi by caste, and poor. How can I have more years than he? The master has more land, more money, more of everything than me. How can he have fewer years? No, sir, write ten or twenty.

The 1961 census took place in this way.[29]

A brilliantly ironic rendition of the mutual incomprehension of the modern state and the tribal (non-)citizen, this account also poses questions that go to the very heart of calculation: What does it mean to count? Who counts and who is countable? Who is unaccounted for in this enumerated community?[30] What is the status of the nonliving in this aggregation? These are some of the questions Mahasweta takes up in these texts. In both of the works she supplements her customary fact-filled limning of the "silent violence" that Michael Watts has aptly characterized as the famine-inducing policies of some states with a reverie on haunting, with a cast that features the dead, ghosts, specters, demon gods, and a long-extinct creature from the infancy of the earth, the pterodactyl.[31] Such a tropology foregrounds the ways in which the ghost and in some instances the animal become the most urgent figures of famine and the story of the nonhuman visitant its paradigmatic account. Famine provides the figures through which it is possible to contemplate what Derrida has nicely described as a "hauntology" and its attendant ethical claims. It allows one to pose the following questions: What is our debt to the not-human, the once-human, those who are "no longer or who are not yet present and living"?[32] Is it possible to have commerce with a ghost? If, as Avery Gordon has powerfully argued, it is imperative to "learn to talk to and listen to ghosts," how does one recognize a ghost or a ghost's claims?[33] What does it mean to be responsible to, answerable to a ghost, a figure that is not living and not dead, not definitively of the now, the past, or futurity, neither visible nor invisible, neither corporeal nor utterly intangible, in other words, neither something nor someone and therefore not the proper and intelligible subject of rights, redress, and well-doing? For Mahasweta, famine—and the forms of life it produces or makes manifest—incarnates these questions.

A modern, technicized understanding of famine has famously been birthed by Thomas Malthus as a matter of figures: populations growing in geometrical or exponential progression, food resources proceeding according to an arithmetical logic, and the immutable clash between the two. Such an understanding of famine as a problem of reconciling this clash of numbers has been and continues to be pervasive among international relief organizations, in spite of the moral force of Sen's argument that famines, at least in the modern period, are caused not by shortfalls in production or the lack of the transportation that would enable the easy movement of foodstuffs but by powerful social inequalities that he describes as class- and gender-stratified "entitlements." As noted, the famine of 1943–44 is replete with instances in which people starved to death in the midst of plenty. All these details, complete with their sentimental extravagance, are excessively, even wearisomely well known. And yet responses to famine, whether by states or by relief organizations, proceed as if famines were simply a matter of food deficits. "The view of famine as a crisis of food supply and a natural disaster involving mass starvation," says Jenny Edkins, "is so strong, and resonates so deeply, that any other account is liable to go unheard or to be interpreted in more familiar terms."[34]

This prevailing notion of famine as a failure of accountancy is supplemented by other rhetorical evidence that famine as a political or affective phenomenon exceeds this enumerative conceptual and moral frame. Most commonly, famine has functioned in the modern period as a figure itself of the archaic and overwhelming, even of the mythic. As early as in the *Essay on the Principle of Population*, Malthus's sense of the primacy of numbers is shadowed by another, less calculable notion of famine. The rhetoric of the essay, especially as it undergoes changes between the editions of 1798, 1803, and 1806, demonstrates a shifting allegiance between what Mary Poovey has denominated "figures of arithmetic" and "figures of speech," that is, numbers and figurative language as distinct and often competing forms of representation in the early nineteenth century.[35]

In the following famous passage, the logic of arithmetic seems to be held at least temporarily in abeyance, as Malthus's apocalyptic view of the inevitability of overpopulation leads him to apotheosize famine as a terrifyingly preternatural presence far more suited to a medieval landscape than to one produced by political economy, industrialism, and demographic rationality or biopolitics: "Famine seems to be *the last, the most dreadful resource* of nature. The power of population is so superior to the power in the earth to produce subsistence for man, that premature death must *in some shape or other* visit the human race. The vices of mankind are *active and able ministers* of depopulation. They are *the precursors in the great army of destruction, and often finish the dreadful work themselves.* But should they fail in this war of extermination, *sickly seasons, epidemics, pestilence, and plague, advance in terrific array, and sweep off their thousands* and ten thousands. Should success be still incomplete, *gigantic inevitable famine stalks in the rear, and with one mighty blow,* levels the population with the food of the world."[36] What is noteworthy here is a fantasmatic array of images and figures that allegorizes famine as something tremendous, irresistible, and virtually otherworldly, something that outstrips the logic of supply and demand that permeates the analysis of the causes of famine. It is a rhetoric that persisted until well into the twentieth century. Thus famine in Ethiopia and the Sahel in the 1970s and 1980s was routinely spoken of as biblical, as atavistic, as something that could be attributed if not to an angry god or Jehovah of plagues and scourges, then to an inexorable nature that took particularly pitiless forms in the African continent.

Such an apocalyptic view of famine's singular, anomalous, and horrific character can be pressed into service for profoundly conservative ends, wrenching apart as it does the intimately linked questions of hunger, mortality, and quotidian forms of inequality and injustice. Famine, as so many writers on the subject have remarked, is difficult of definition, given its contiguity with quotidian forms of deprivation such as malnutrition, lack of access to health care, and poor sanitation; they caution against a commonsensical deployment of terms like *starvation* and *famine*, where famine is associated primarily with catastrophe and large-scale death.[37] Amrita Rangasami contests the undivided focus on famine mortality as excessively narrow and inhospitable to a comprehensive ethico-political analysis: "The sudden collapse into starvation that has been identified with the famine condition is only . . . the final phase of famine when the stigmata of starvation become visual, and the victims have collapsed. Famine is not an event marked by the death of the victim. The basic failure in the understanding of famine we have today is the inability to recognise the political, social and economic determinants that mark the onset of the process."[38]

And yet, as one reads Mahasweta and other writers on hunger and famine it is also clear that figurality and figurations of the apocalyptic need not necessarily be a symptom of ethical myopia but can also serve as the appropriate tenor for a meditation upon the ethics of responsibility. It is a certain notion of the figurality of famine, its mythic quality, its non-adequation to a simple arithmetical rationality that Mahasweta calls upon in these fictions. It is famine that permits the introduction of a noncalculable responsibility at the limit of subaltern being and subaltern corporeality, in the figure of the specter and the figure of the dying or extinct animal. With this in mind, let us turn to the fictions themselves.

The Specter's Touch

One of Mahasweta's best known tales about famine, "Shishu" owes a significant debt to the literature of the famine of 1943, with its gallery of grotesque and deformed bodies.[39] As in a good deal of literature in Bangla and perhaps in famine literature in general, it draws powerfully upon tales of specters, the living dead, and otherworldly beings; David Lloyd speaks of "[the] phenomenon of haunting that seems indissociable from the [great Irish] Famine."[40] More specifically, it belongs quite emphatically in a certain subclass of the tale of haunting that I have taken the liberty of denominating the bureaucratic gothic. It is a genre that has enjoyed considerable popularity in Bangla and in the Anglo-Indian fictions of colonial India. Among the most prominent examples of the subgenre in English are those produced by Kipling, including "At the End of the Passage," "The Strange Ride of Morrowbie Jukes," and "The Mark of the Beast." In Bangla, the exemplars range from Rabindranath Tagore to Satyajit Ray, with perhaps the best known tale being Tagore's "Kshudito Pashan" (The Hungry Stones).[41] Emerging in the wake of a new, reformed colonial (and metropolitan) bureaucracy, one that has come to uncouple itself from systems of patronage and become a properly Utilitarian institution—meritocratic, efficient, and characterized by notions of transparency and good government—this subgenre marks a certain traumatic excess that is lodged in the heart of the bureaucratic imaginary.[42] Staging the troubled encounter or unexpected juxtapositions of what Dipesh Chakrabarty has named "the time of history" and "the times of gods," the subgenre focuses most commonly on the derangement of the colonial and postcolonial babu-bureaucrat, the functionary who embodies the modern state's dreams of order.[43] Thus Kipling's tales of haunting feature engineers, civil servants, and policemen, while Tagore's famous tale involves an unfinished tale told at a railway station by a cosmopolitan, English-garbed excise collector of cotton.

Like its antecedents, "Shishu" features a bureaucrat, a figure of modern knowledge, rationality, and good conscience, one moreover who in his capacity as civil servant is characterized by a certain class-marked generalizability in the subcontinental landscape. He is assigned to bring relief supplies to a famine-stricken tribal region that has an enigmatic and tormented history of tribal rebellion and the disappearance, massacre, or extermination of tribal populations. The story unfolds against a blasted landscape imprinted with the signs of barrenness and violence and a mythic story of the curse of an Agariya god. Troubled by rumors of the nocturnal theft of supplies by a band of children, the bureaucrat tracks them down, only to discover they are preternaturally stunted adults, the starving and sexually crippled survivors of an earlier tribal rebellion against the postcolonial state. This revelation stupefies him as he realizes that his average Indian body, puny by international standards, is the insignia of an irrefragably cannibalistic, even genocidal voraciousness against a subaltern body politic. He seeks in vain for refuge in a madness that can be the only immunity against such a revelation.

"Shishu" begins not on the terrain of social realism as such but in another space, Lohri, that is mythic and spectrally saturated. Every endeavor is made to note the uncanniness of the place, its dissimilitude, its disjointedness from the familiar grids of a modern Indian or even a terrestrial cartography.[44] At the nexus of three districts of Bihar, Lohri nonetheless cannot be accommodated within them. It is officially a part of Ranchi—described elsewhere in the story as a modern place of "lights, . . . taxis, . . . motor cars" (235), a marketplace of stolen goods intended for the destitute (233), and as the relief officer's comfortable place of residence—but situated on another, discordant, disjointed, visionary map. It is a landscape worked over by historical violence. It is also shot through with unknown latencies: "It looks as if the temperature is extremely high just beneath the surface." All the descriptors, including place names and physical features, are marked by a certain unsureness and indirection: "The place *is called* Lohri," "The entire place *looks like* a burnt out valley" (emphases added). The word "strange," which recurs like a refrain in the story along with cognate terms like "weird," "abnormal," "inhuman," and "bizarre," makes its first appearance here. This literally blasted heath, this place off the edge of the map, is the domain of the Agariya. Blacksmiths by tradition, they will not take to agriculture, a refusal that is an infallible sign, in the lexicon of the state, whether colonial or postcolonial, of backwardness and criminality.[45] And the land itself is not just unamenable to cultivation and civilizing but is positively menacing: "Who knows what's there in the soil? Nothing grows in it. Once my nephew tried to grow some crops, but nothing came of it. The soil grows no rice, no wheat, no maize, no millet, nothing. The plowshare can't enter the soil, as if it's all iron right underneath. It's a cursed land. One look is enough to remove any doubt" (232).

The early pages are devoted to an elaboration of the Agariya tale of origins and of the curse that explains drought and famine and their present destitution. The myth is rendered in a kind of contemptuous officialese—"This is the legend, a primitive one, as you can see" (231)— that is yet tinged with hysteria, as the speakers await from the very opening the appearance or the return of a ghost or ghosts whose existence they can neither confirm nor deny. The massacre of the Agariya inhabitants of Kubha has resulted in a disappearance that, by its very completeness, is unnerving, even unearthly: "Just imagine, Mr. Singh, they vanished in the forest and were lost forever. As if they had metamorphosed into something else!" (232), Now, readers know from *Specters of Marx* (not to mention *Hamlet*) that hauntings are by their nature recursive. A ghost never makes a single visit (or, rather, even its first visit is always gesturing to an anterior history and presence), and its arrivals and actions are both expected and untimely. These recursive returns establish a number of asymmetries among the actors in the tale, not so much the usual asymmetries of power and nutrition that identify the dispensers and receivers of aid, though these are very emphatically present, but the asymmetries that distinguish Agariya subjects who are figures of menace and knowledge and caste Hindu subjects trying to cling to certainty in an alien universe. These are the asymmetries of knowledge that drive caste Hindus to terror, alcohol, and the *prasad* (food offered to a deity and distributed among devotees) of Mahabirji in the uncertainties of a spectral presence that is palpable but ungraspable: "Who knows where they're hiding, to jump on you from who knows where?" (232).

Hence it is that the relief officer, described repeatedly as "an honest and compassionate public servant" (229), is initially made uneasy by the eerie, wraithlike character of the Agariya, "almost naked, emaciated creatures, bellies swollen with worms and sick spleen" (230), all carnality and yet not fully human, who fail to conform to his ersatz visions of tribal life derived from Hindi films. (The frame of reference is not adventitiously chosen. In the Bombay film industry, famine has commonly been deployed as a favored topos of sentimentality, usually to be contrasted with lush and lyrical landscapes and scenes of happy rural folk.) Mahasweta, it should be noted, goes out of her way to confirm the power and the authoritativeness of the Agariya legend and to present it as the frame through which the story's events must be read. She dwells in some detail on the contest of the Agariya hero Jwalamukhi with the sun and the curse this struggle generates. The very environment appears disagreeably palpable, generating a host of comparisons that underline an unpleasant corporeal obtrusiveness that is both uncannily human, sexually menacing in its indeterminacy, and viscous in its tactility: "The night was very dark, black like hair. . . . The darkness was very thick and hot, like some melting and dripping substance, smothering absolutely everything, plugging also the cracks and holes that might let in any light" (233).

This is a tale of a different kind from "Daini" (The Witch-Hunt), which is framed by the diabolical machinations of a Brahman priest who manufactures the tale of a witch as a cover for his son's sexual crimes; its unfolding conforms to the logic of upper-caste exploitation of subaltern vulnerability and desperation.[46] Mahasweta is not given to romanticizing tribal or lower-caste practices or systems of belief. In "Daini," as in so many other stories, she is cleareyed about the ways in which caste Hindu dominance and religious terror have been internalized by those who can only be its victims. And there is sufficient sociological evidence that speaks to the ways in which the hereafter and its inhabitants have been pressed into service for the selfsame caste and feudal superiors who terrorize tribals and low castes in their this-worldly existence. Gyan Prakash provides a finely differentiated account of the hierarchies of gods and ancestral spirits in southern Bihar, the region in which many of Mahasweta's stories, including "Shishu," are set. "A kamia [bonded laborer] was not just a laborer but a Bhuinya [a member of an outcaste group] with a past and a future, with ancestors and descendants, a living person who defined himself in relation to the dead," Prakash notes. "Nor was a malik just a landholder, but a person with a caste status, who also had to define himself in relation to his ancestors. Thus, the spirit-world was a field with highly charged meanings that could not escape from the representations of the malik's power and kamias' subordination."[47] While maliks are occasionally required to propitiate low-caste ghosts, they also function as the purchasers and patrons of malik devatas, exceptionally powerful spirits who protect the lands and crops of landlords.[48] In "Shishu," though, the spirit world is not the unequally shared provenance of exploiters and exploited but the domain of the Agariya alone, alien and threatening in a vaguely menacing way to high-caste Hindus and considerably beyond the protective reach of their deities.

This is not to say that in her focus on Agariya gods, ancestors, and spirits Mahasweta downplays the ideological and physical violence of the postcolonial state, which is ubiquitous and unblushing. The contempt, unease, unexamined privilege, and imperceptiveness of those who herald progress or who administer relief punctuate the entire narrative. The legend of present-day haunting is inaugurated when three emissaries of the state ignore the "junglee" Agariya claims to the hillocks in Lohri as the abode of their *asura deotas* (demon gods) and blast it in search of iron ore. The slaughter of these offenders by the Agariya is followed by the burning of Kubha village by the police and the imposition of punitive taxes on other villages. The tribal welfare officers are themselves scarcely distinguishable from dynamite-deploying geologists and violent policemen. The theft and illegal sale of relief supplies are accepted in matter-of-fact fashion by the dispensers of aid, and the Block Development Officer wields a gun. For the driver of the jeep, the Agariya are mere animals for the way in which they surrender their children to Christian missionaries to keep them from starvation. On the eve of his departure for famine-wracked Lohri the well-intentioned, upright relief officer has a comfortable bath and a meal of unimaginable extravagance that includes "the best quality rice . . . fresh peas in the fried rice, meat, pickles, and dark-brown syrupy *gulabjamuns*," though he is visited in his dreams by visions of violence and uncanniness (234). He is "disturbed and uncomfortable" (230) in a place he has invested with a halo of romantic primitivism. Like the Marabar caves of E. M. Forster's *A Passage to India*, the landscape confounds his demand for spectacle, meaning, or sentiment in terms that are intelligible to him: "There was nothing to see along the way but dusty hills and dull stretches of forest that held old women, who, faced with the prospect of death, didn't even try to live but just sat around in a circle and wailed their chorus of death" (235).[49] Unnerving in their submission to impending death as in their brief and bloody rebellion, they cannot rise to the dignity of impending tragedy. Like the physically decrepit and affectively listless Muselmanner of the best known holocaust of the twentieth century, they are for the official viewer "not only or not so much a limit between life and death; rather, [they mark] the threshold between the human and the inhuman."[50]

Mahasweta, though, is aiming at something more than a denunciation of the insolence, dishonesty, and self-serving ignorance of bureaucrats and their functionaries, important though that task undoubtedly is. The bureaucrat, uncomprehending and superior though he undoubtedly is, is also distinguished unmistakably by his rectitude, growing compassion, and competence: "The relief officer became extremely involved with this work. . . . Its starving destitute people soon assumed top priority in his mind. . . . He promised to help even the doctors and nurses from the mission. Although the regulation allowed for only cholera and typhoid vaccines, he got around that to procure from Ranchi supplies of antibiotics, salves for sores, baby food, even packets of [soy] nutri-nugget" (237). It is difficult to quarrel in any overt way with such a program, notwithstanding the faintly incongruous inclusion of nutri-nugget among the relief supplies. This description seems to confirm the first description of the officer as "honest and compassionate," and it seems as well to point to his moral arousal. A passage such as this stands in pointed contrast to the opening pages of the tale, which highlight the problem of what constitutes right giving and what and how the state and its representatives might give to the Agariya. The Agariya, it seems, are people who baffle all attempts to give them anything that will be fittingly used. The relief officer is told at the outset, "If you gave them land, they would sell it to the moneylender. Then they would glare at you and sullenly complain, 'Where's water? Where's seed? Where's the plow, and the buffalo? How can we cultivate without those?' But even if you gave them those things, they would sell everything to the moneylender and then argue back, 'What are we supposed to eat until the crop is ready? We'd borrowed to eat. We have to repay the loan with the land' " (230).

What is the difference between giving and taking in a context in which all that is received is already mortgaged to one's exploiter? In a situation in which the dominant models of official giving and official investment have failed spectacularly, the relief officer understands that a different formula is required and that he has to give of himself, rather than just distribute goods, if relief efforts are to succeed. But there are just the faintest indications that this condition of loving zeal falls short of what is required. The officer's response follows, indeed exceeds, all the rules of enlightened official conduct: he does not steal supplies, he pays the Agariya wages, he arranges for relief to be provided to all the famine-stricken, he plans for the Agariyas' eventual rehabilitation through farming rather than their traditional occupation of ironsmithing; in this catalogue only this last detail speaks rather too closely to the state's desire to rehabilitate so-called criminal castes and tribes to the settled, respectable pursuit of agriculture. But even more pointedly, one indication that there is some slight deficit in this moral diagram is the notation of the officer's vocabulary of accountancy, which casts its shadow upon what might otherwise have seemed an unimpeachable sentiment: "Its starving destitute people soon assumed *top priority* in his mind" (emphasis added, English in original). Likewise, when he discovers that his youthful Agariya helpers have facilitated the nocturnal removal of supplies despite having addressed him flatteringly as *deota* (god), his outrage takes the form of bafflement that all his moral calculations have failed: "He has been so keen to do good for them. . . . Suddenly he feels he has been tricked, robbed, and left destitute! . . . Is this how they return kindness?" (239).[51] Ingratitude and the stealing of food, no matter how trivial in quantity, are, in this view, a violation of the moral arithmetic and legal prescriptions that bind donor and recipient of aid. In fact, the failure to feel or demonstrate gratitude, to recognize the efforts or gifts of the relief officer, is in this view the symbolic equivalent of theft; indeed, in comparison with the pilfering of two sacks of supplies it might be the more outrageous of the thefts.

The questions of moral economy and moral calculation that such a response raises go to the heart of Mahasweta's elaboration of relations between exploiters and exploited. An economic system of reciprocal relations between officers and tribals, with its notions of debt, repayment, circulation, and symmetry among participants, cannot begin to comprehend the millennially old and systemic forms of oppression that have kept the parties in nonintersecting universes. Moreover, Derrida reminds his readers, the true gift is impossible within the circularity of an exchange economy, whether monetary or symbolic. The circle for him is figurally and definitionally central to any notion of the economic: "Economy implies the idea of exchange, of circulation, of return. . . . The figure of the circle . . . stands at the center of any problematic of *oikonomia*, as it does of any economic field: circular exchange, circulation of goods, products, monetary signs or merchandise, amortization of expenditures, revenues, substitution of use values and exchange values."[52] The gift proper cannot be part of this circular, self-interested, self-absorbed, self-regarding logic of economy; it must interrupt or suspend it. In fact, says Derrida, "if the figure of the circle is essential to economics, the gift must remain *aneconomic*."[53] Logically the gift cannot be thought except in its relation to an exchange economy, but while it cannot be radically outside such an economy it is other to it or holds it in abeyance. And if economy proper is predicated upon a logic of scarcity and the saving and calculation this entails, giving is a nonutilitarian principle of infinite expenditure, of exceeding the economic or calculative relations between persons. As Derrida notes in *The Gift of Death*, true giving is "beyond economy" and indeed must involve the "sacrifice of economy" itself.[54] The fact that such giving is in fact impossible—Derrida says that it "obviously defies commonsense"—is not an argument for jettisoning it; in fact, as Jean-Luc Nancy says about the impossible imperative in Christian ethics to love one's neighbor as oneself, it is "precisely the impossibility of this love [that is] the very thing that produces the very concept, content and reality of this love."[55] That love, or responsibility to the other, is always foreordained to incompleteness or failure also necessitates the sacrifice of self-satisfaction that accomplishment generates.

Such an understanding goes against the grain of received notions of the systemic character of the gift, notably as elaborated by Marcel Mauss. In speaking of economy, exchange, contract, gifts, and countergifts, all of which are calculated to produce symbolic or material returns, Mauss "speaks of everything but the gift," according to Derrida. Rather, he substitutes in its place "the contract of usury."[56] So absolute is the non-contractual, noncircular character of the gift that the slightest hint of calculation, self-consciousness, recognition, or gratitude about it, whether on the part of the giver or the receiver, is sufficient to annihilate its character as gift and to render it counterfeit, mere exchange. On the part of the receiver such recognition functions as the symbolic equivalent of a countergift or an acknowledgment of debt; on the part of the giver, too, self-consciousness functions as a form of recompense, allowing him "to pay himself with a symbolic recognition, to praise himself, to approve of himself, to gratify himself, to congratulate himself, to give back to himself symbolically the value of what he thinks he has given or what he is preparing to give."[57] A certain form of forgetting must necessarily accompany the gift, though a forgetting that does not partake of the psychic economy of repression, which conserves what it represses through displacement.

Derrida's invocation of the language of usury in describing the exchange that masquerades as the gift is not accidental. That the gift is good is not necessarily a given: there are innumerable instances of equivocal or poisoned gifts, as the innumerable stories of boons that are effectively curses amply illustrate. He notes that the gift that enters the system of exchange—of "the gift and the debt, the gift and the cycle of restitution, the gift and the loan, the gift and credit, the gift and the countergift"—is such a poisoned gift or a non-gift.[58] This instrumentalization of giving is "the gift [that] puts the other in debt, with the result that giving amounts to hurting, to doing harm."[59]

• • •

The language of debt and bondage in this accounting of gifting and well-doing connects in a curious, unexpected way to the world of poverty and debt bondage that Mahasweta describes in her fiction. At first the Agariya world seems removed from the traffic in the gift. The Agariyas' most regular economic exchanges are, after all, with the moneylenders who buy up their land, seed, ploughs, and buffaloes. In other fictions, especially "Douloti the Bountiful," Mahasweta has described in unsparing detail the multigenerational slavery prevalent in large portions of southern rural Bihar as a result of the system of bonded labor (kami-yauti).[60] Under this system a kamia (bonded laborer) offers free labor to a boss, landlord, or moneylender in supposed repayment of small loans of money, food, seed, or land incurred at unconscionable rates of interest. Often this debt slavery binds the relatives of the debtor and extends over generations, with the possibility of repayment effectively excluded; a glimpse of this is afforded in the account of the slavery of Shankar's son in Pterodactyl. But while this relationship between the enslaved and the slaveholder is constitutively violent, it is also embedded in a dialectic with an "economy of gentleness and violence" that Prakash designates as characteristic of malik–kamia relations, an economy that makes some approach to the logic of the gift. "Gentle and violent practices of domination [complement] one another," he suggests, and gifts and advances for marriage expenses are dissimulated as "disinterested reciprocity between munificent patrons and dependent subjects."[61] It may seem counterintuitive if not far-fetched to place the honest and zealous relief officer in the company of maliks and moneylenders. And yet, in a story in which no form of consumption, credit, or obligation is unattended by violent inequities and sordid economies, his forms of self-satisfaction at his own well-doing and his reckoning of moral debts accumulated and payment owed cannot but be a prophylactic against the self-forgetting deliverance of oneself to the other that constitutes the ethical relation. In arrogating to himself the power of giving, the relief officer has come to see himself as the deota—a word commonly used in Mahasweta's universe to address feudal superiors—as which he is addressed. The failure of the Agariya to recognize his gift as a gift can only therefore register for him as a theft, as a refusal of the symbolic coin rightfully owed him.

But when the relief officer encounters the no-longer-human survivors of the Kubha massacre, the revelation has the force of something that cannot be subsumed within the ethical calculations he has hitherto undertaken. Neither can it be named as (mere) knowledge. If the entire tale has been structured, as the ghost story commonly is, as a quasi-Barthesian hermeneutic, a set of questions building up toward a period, the narrative ends not in an answer but in a knowledge that is both inconceivable and incommunicable. This nocturnal revelation is a violent, indeed an apocalyptic encounter, unhinging the liberal's dreams of consummation: "The officer repeats to himself that what he is seeing cannot be true. If it is true, then everything else is false: the Copernican system, science, the twentieth century, the Independence of India, the five-year plans, all that he has known to be true" (240).

The relief officer's encounter with the specters of Kubha is a confrontation with a reality that is insistently corporeal and wrenching but at the same time unknowable within the epistemological, ethical, and linguistic grammars available to him. It disallows the comfort of empathy or any will to comprehension. It does not offer any mode of redress; it harbors no solutions. It has no practical transfiguring effect; it allows for neither heroism nor tragedy on his part. Rather, it is a violent assault upon a worldview composed of the verities of science and the state that he has taken as entirely commonsensical ("the Copernican system, science, the twentieth century, the Independence of India, the five-year plans"). It is little wonder that, faced with the trauma of a history he has not come to know but of which he is nonetheless not innocent, he loses one language without being able to find another. The story returns repeatedly to this experience of aphasia: "No sound comes out of his mouth," "the arguments do not manage to find his voice," "Why can't his brain make his voice scream, produce any sound at all?" (240, 241).

Do we chase a ghost? or does a ghost chase us? The officer's first inkling that something is askew in the predictable logic of chaser and chased occurs with the uneasy recognition of sexual difference among the "children" he has been pursuing: "He notices that there are not only boys but also girls. Claws of fear such as he has never known before sink into his chest" (239).[62] The markers of sexual difference here constitute what is unexpected, exorbitant, and yet grimly illuminating about the figures he is pursuing. Why does the fact of the specters' sexual difference, when he had expected a normative, unremarkable maleness, prove so unsettling to the relief officer?[63] Why is it the fact of sexual difference that alerts him to the summons of the other, a summons into a kind of a responsibility he does not desire, understand, or assimilate but cannot refuse? It allows him to perceive, however imperfectly, the scope of the violence of the modern liberal state against the tribal noncitizen, a violence that exceeds the brutal facts of slaughter, ecological violence, and starvation. An important part of the ghostly pedagogy that follows is the revelation of the sexually unproductive genitalia of his accusers, which are "wrinkled, dried up, hanging like a dead object" (240). As happens so often, and as happens particularly in the case of famine narratives, sexual difference functions as the sign of crisis and signals a breakdown in social order and moral authority and in representation itself.[64] The gendered body here becomes the key to a mystery that exceeds supposedly normal modes of brutality, pointing as it does to a holocaust, to ethnocide: "We're down to just these fourteen. Our bodies have shrunk. The men can't do anything with it except piss. The women can't get pregnant."[65] Signs of death and of ethnocide, but also of the ghost's terrifyingly intimate carnality—"they rub their genitals against him, to remind him that they too are adult Indians" (241)—the dead genitals function as a ghostly carapace, as the trace of the human, as what marks the specters of Kubha as both adult human and not-human. They call attention to a responsibility that the officer can neither escape nor sufficiently fulfill. What is most unbearable and enigmatic for the officer in this instance is not, or not just, the encounter with death and holocaust but the fact of his own survival, his living on in the consciousness and the aftermath of this intolerable knowledge.[66] He may wish to pass a sentence of death or madness upon himself—indeed, it is his longed-for quietus in the face of the terrible knowledge with which he is faced—but he cannot make it come to pass: he cannot give himself the gift of death.

Note that Mahasweta makes it a special point to highlight the shock of bodily encounter with ghostly flesh in order to emphasize the limits of mere goodwill. The assault upon the relief officer has less immediately to do with his attitudes or his actions than with the material dimensions of his corporeal being, quite literally with the moral grossness of his five feet and nine inches of growth: "It seems to him that the body of an average Indian, which he has always considered to be puny and short, is the most hideous crime against human civilization, and that he is to blame personally for the hideously stunted forms of these once-proud adults" (241).

His whole physical being is implicated in ethnocide, and his guilt, non-voluntaristic and nonindividualized but deeply intimate and personal, is such as can never be expiated. The violence of a (non-)history he has not understood but of which he is a part cannot be undone by sympathy or knowledge or by seeking to share the life or the privations of the tribals. Such an experience of unwonted touching, in which he experiences his own body as shockingly vulnerable, encroached upon, and strange to himself, merges the sensorial, the epistemological, and the imaginary. But such touching or proximity does not necessarily lead to a passage out of liminality, even though the Agariya are bound with him in a nominally common Indian citizenship; rather, the experience embodies the capacity of touch to produce rupture and displacement. The "incessant rubbing" of Agariya genitalia against his body, keeping pace with the "explosions" in his brain, is like a flagellation, improperly or inadequately sexual, and their touch like that of dried snakeskin. This bodily contact, which is emphatically not a desired intimacy, exposes the radical distances involved in proximity, the limits at which identities are demarcated from one another precisely through a vulnerability to reincarnation. This touch of the other also makes his own body monstrous to himself. More than the ghost's body, it is the body of the definitively living human that is rendered grotesque through this spectral logic.

The Call of the Wild

These aporias of always-unrealized but insistent responsibility and intelligibility must be understood in the light of Mahasweta's dictum in *Pterodactyl, Puran Sahay, and Pirtha*: "From antiquity to today, the long marches of the Aryan and the non-Aryan, of the living and the dead are on parallel ways."[67] In this fiction, as in "Shishu," Mahasweta stresses the impossibility of achieving justice through goodwill and well-doing or of reconciling incommensurable languages and cosmologies. Its protagonist is Puran Sahay, a progressive investigative journalist working in Bihar. Despite the overall integrity of his reporting, he is weak in his personal life, detached from his teenaged son and unable to commit himself to Saraswati, the woman he has loved for years. He is summoned to Pirtha in Madhya Bharat (Middle India) by his ethical bureaucrat friend Harisharan to report on the condition of the tribals there. While there he discovers two related phenomena, one of which can be related to the world and one of which is impossible to convey. He discovers that the tribals live in a condition of perpetual famine, a condition the state is unwilling to name as such. All attempts to secure to the tribals their just rights and to ameliorate their condition falls prey to corruption and brutality, or to condescension at best. Puran also discovers that a dying pterodactyl, which purportedly embodies the soul of the tribal ancestors, has appeared among them. The tribal lad Bikhia, who produces a rock painting of the otherworldly visitant, is rendered mute by his experience. Though the pterodactyl also manifests itself to Puran, he is unable to understand the message it apparently seeks to communicate. After the pterodactyl's passing, he returns to his journalistic duties and produces a scathing report on tribal famine. But he refuses to report on the pterodactyl. Overpowered by a sense of the violence that has exterminated the pterodactyl, he realizes that love alone—tremendous, extreme, earth-shattering love—can be an adequate response to such tragedy.

In this novella Mahasweta juxtaposes the frame narrative of Puran's activities as a journalist, his unfulfilled relationship with Saraswati, the cleareyed and honorable labor of some bureaucrats, and the ubiquity and greater success of the exploiters against the embedded narrative of the appearance and death of the pterodactyl. She makes no overt attempt to reconcile them: Saraswati and the pterodactyl are for the most part held apart, even though Saraswati features occasionally as an off-camera commentator on the relationship of Indian elites to tribal subalterns and though even Puran realizes at one point that his engagement with the people of Pirtha is bound up with his personal life. The world of the dying pterodactyl and the world of twentieth-century India abut one another with no endeavor, as in "Shishu," to provide an explanation that will bring the fantastical, however provisionally, within the ambit of modern reason. Neither does she establish one register as that of documentary realism and the other as that which is purely symbolic, though such a reading is perhaps inescapable. The pterodactyl as the soul of the ancestors cannot not be symbolic, but to imagine that it can be subsumed entirely into a symbolic register is finally a failure of adequation to its reality. To borrow Akira Lippit's terms, it is "animal and metaphor, a metaphor made flesh, a living metaphor that is by definition not a metaphor, antimetaphor,— 'animetaphor.' "[68] As Lippit's language suggests through its simultaneous proliferation and fusion of zoontological terms, the question of the pterodactyl participates in the thinking of several modes, phenomenological, sacred, ecological, and allegorical, of being at once.

Clearly the pterodactyl is an animal like no other, especially in the present, even though it is also a paradigmatic animal—an instance of what Lippit has identified as the "spectral animal" of modernity, existing in a state of *"perpetual vanishing"* in the face of the steadily encroaching onslaught of a modern world featuring an instrumentalist and technologically ruthless humanity.[69] An atavistic creature, out of joint with the relentless tempo of the present, this figure of animality demonstrates no small overlap with the anthropological and popular cultural discourse (in Europe and North America at least and almost certainly in urban middle-class India as well) of the decimation of aboriginal or indigenous populations as a result of their fatal encounters with civilization. Patrick Brantlinger has detailed the ways in which an "extinction discourse" took hold of the imperialist imagination from the early nineteenth century on. Such a discourse imagined the inevitable doom of aboriginal populations that were unable, for a variety of reasons, among them warfare, genocide, disease, often even their own benighted customs, to cope with the demands of conquest, colonization, and settlement. Sometimes melancholic and sometimes serene in the face of the trajectory of development, such a discourse looked to a futurity marked by the disappearance of wilderness and dwellers in the wild, including wild animals and supposedly wild tribes.[70] In the subcontinental context, Ajay Skaria points out, a politics of wildness (an attribute of the *jangal*, the forest or wilderness), articulated by forest communities in complex, often contestatory relationship with the high-caste values of plainsmen, came to be replaced forcibly by the colonial dispensations with a curtailment of older forms of mobility, displacement in the name of development, loss of the forests, and a sponsorship of settled agriculture—all practices that resulted in "marginality, social and ritual inferiority, and political powerlessness."[71] A colonial troping of the aboriginal as anachronistic—as being, like the animal, timeless, nonhistorical, unable to imagine a future and therefore unable to change in substance or over time—came to be adopted by Indian elites in the postcolonial dispensation as well. However, as Skaria also notes, the idiom of anachronism was also capable of being recast into that of autochthony, which has quite another kind of valence in the discourses of nationalism and even of global human rights. Hence, he says, the term *adivasi* (original inhabitant) has found strategic favor among aboriginal populations in India, since it makes a claim to an antiquity that is not predicated upon a notion of primitive inferiority.[72]

 • • •

In her novella Mahasweta brilliantly combines this sense of the moral authority of autochthony or primordiality with a deeply tragic sense of the near extinction of the population of Pirtha and its ways of life.[73] She evokes a geological sense of deep time that is near mythic, almost beyond reckoning. Pirtha on the map is evocative of a moment of geological antiquity prior to the current configuration of the continents: "The survey map of Pirtha Block is like some extinct animal of Gondwanaland. The beast has fallen on its face" (99). A supercontinent that included most of the land masses of the Southern Hemisphere before the continental displacements caused by plate tectonics, and home to a staggering variety of plant and animal life, Gondwanaland is a figure of the primordial ecologies that have formed the planet. Its very name, Gondwana, forest of the tribal Gonds, ties primordiality to autochthony, naming the land mass as wilderness and as the dwelling place of tribals. The autochthony of the tribal exceeds the imagination of the modern nation-state form, binding the proto-Australoid populations of the subcontinent to First Nations in other parts of the planet.[74] At the same time, in tracing this outline of a prehistoric beast on the map, Mahasweta presents a fantastic geography in which marvelous creatures and extinct species still inhabit the earth. Mahasweta's imagination is geological *and* mythic. Her Madhya Bharat, once Gondwanaland, peopled by dying tribals, visited by pterodactyls, is also an imagined universe whose destruction, loss, disappearance, or consignment to amnesia is mourned in a finely calibrated admixture of fury and grief. This is neither modernist nostalgia for the primitive nor an exercise in science fictional time travel; the authorial voice in fact refers contemptuously to the adolescent escapism of the privileged urban youth who consume such fictions of time travel in the belief that one can encounter the otherness of the past without difficulty. The novella's allegorical and mythic thrust is guaranteed, rather, by its sociological exactitude about tribal life. Partaking somewhat of the genre of lost world fictions that perform the work of mourning around what Sumathi Ramaswamy has described as "vanished homelands, hidden civilizations, and forgotten peoples," Mahasweta's novella is nonetheless distinct from them in focusing less on the character of the "unknown and undiscovered" continent than on its pitiless destruction (177).[75] Its tone is less that of nostalgia, however robustly one might inflect that term, than of tragic lament, passionate denunciation, and apocalyptic foreboding.[76] Inveighing against the sentimental fantasy of returning to a lost time, she underlines mournfully "the implacable and cruel truth that time will advance, that the wheels of time will destroy much as they advance. You cannot turn the eighteenth to the seventeenth, however hard you try" (156).

The trope Mahasweta deploys most insistently is that of extinction. The pterodactyl is the most obvious figure of this, entering the narrative under the sign of apocalypse, fated to vanish from the face of the earth. In one sense it is typical of a modern or modernizing world that it is typified by animal disappearance—the character Chotti Munda in another novel by Mahasweta tracks the harsh transition to modernity through animal depopulation in the forests[77]—even though in the post-Cartesian Western metaphysical tradition that grounds modernity animals are believed to have no foreknowledge or fear of death and are therefore unable to experience death proper.[78] How can the impossibility of animal death be reconciled with the marked, even sentimental attentiveness to the idea of animal extinction? In most extinction literature this is managed through the affective device of the last survivor, marked by a radical isolation and singularity, unmated, moving inexorably to extinction.[79] Mahasweta deploys but also exceeds such devices. Her last pterodactyl is dying survivor as well as ancestral soul. Is it animal, god, human, mythic, spectral, reincarnated, a monad, a cosmic flashback, an atavistic survival flashing into the present? Can its passing be designated a death, given its status as a liminal animal/god/specter figure through which we think our relationship to mortality, humanity, and living in general? What might it mean to observe the funeral obsequies of one that is both animal and ghost? The pterodactyl is here a figure of unassimilable alterity, able to inhabit neither past nor present and unable to receive the closure of death in that it is already spectral and otherworldly. We share the ignorance of Puran in the face of its mystery, and like him we must be content to let our desire for certitude and recognition be replaced by wonder and humility.

Even more clear than the fact of ecological holocaust and animal genocide is that of tribal extermination. Pirtha "isn't called a famine area. Pirtha is a place of perennial starvation" (104). Insofar as famine is conventionally understood as an exceptional condition rather than as a chronic one, the famine of Pirtha is unthinkable and unutterable by available dictionaries and ministers of state alike. Instead, money for tribal welfare is appropriated, tribal women and children are purchased as slaves, and famine is generated within the usual economies of exploitation: "In India, famine is being bought and sold 'to whom it may concern.' Man-made famine is always kept going in Kalahandi or Madhopura or any intractable hill or forest area" (125). The one thing the government does supply assiduously to the residents of Pirtha is a plentiful supply of posters on family planning. Mahasweta comments on this with a mordant wit, noting the posters' deployment as insulation and ground covering for those who cannot afford the luxury of "career-planning" and "family-planning." The Malthusian logic that sees overpopulation as the problem of an oversupply of poor people fails spectacularly among those beset by illiteracy, disease, the sale of children, and early mortality. Puran notes bitterly the genocidal logic of the state that would hold them accountable for their failure to perish entirely: "They are themselves guilty as well. With all these arrangements for extinction they are not extinct; don't they have to pay for it?" (170).

. . .

The emphasis on policies of extinction calls to mind Achille Mbembe's well-known gloss on the limits of biopolitical thinking in a universe not defined by First World experience alone—his insistence, most importantly, that political thought come to terms with the fact that dealing, managing, and sometimes spectacularizing death and injury (rather than life alone) for the "*management of the multitudes*" is an important function of the power of contemporary late colonial, postcolonial, and "war machine" orders.[80] Such a necropolitics can often take the form of massacre, torture, and amputation or other forms of mutilation. Of mutilation, practiced widely against noncombatant populations, he says, "The traces of this demiurgic surgery persist for a long time, in the form of human shapes that are alive, to be sure, but whose bodily integrity has been replaced by pieces, fragments, folds, even immense wounds that are difficult to close." Even when the subalternized subjects of such a necropolitical order are not targeted by war machines in such directly visceral ways, they are subject to a more broadly conceived instrumentality of extermination, "new and unique forms of social existence in which vast populations are subjected to conditions of life conferring on them the status of *living dead*."[81] This is nothing if not a precise description of the survivors of the massacre of Kubha, rendered cachectic though not technically dead. Of course their atrophy, like the wasting of the famine victims of Pirtha, is not solely the effect of a necropolitics that targets vulnerable bodies through the direct machinery of war, massacre, and mutilation. These populations are also the addressees of a biopolitical order that seeks to limit population growth, foster interreligious amity, and provide redress to the destitute through relief programs. Indeed,

Mbembe notes that necropolitics rarely functions on its own. Using the case of Palestine as an instance, he notes the "concatenation of multiple powers: disciplinary, biopolitical, and necropolitical" in the "Occupied Territories."[82] Mahasweta's sobering point is that biopolitical management, in the form of family planning, calls for communal harmony, and rural amelioration projects, cannot but be a grim farce at worst and self-delusion at best in a postcolonial state that is complicit in the feudalization of the rural sector and that cannot conceive of the tribal as citizen. Its effects are not really distinguishable from the forms of annihilation that are the domain of necropolitics proper. Whether one considers the shrunken survivors of Kubha, the dying pterodactyl, the sacred mountain in Lohri, or the inhabitants of Pirtha, extermination results in every case.

Animal extinction, ecological violence, and human genocide are hard to hold apart in Mahasweta's prose: all are connected, and none can be reduced to being only an allegorical vehicle for another. Tribals are like the pterodactyl, fragile survivals doomed either to lose their cultural identity through assimilation under unfavorable conditions into mainstream society or to museumization as endangered species in the dubious stewardship of the same society. The second option, the one that might allow for a minimal retention of their distinctiveness, is not without its limits— and its perils: "Even animals preserved behind wire netting are not safe. Somewhere the zookeepers themselves caught and ate the captive deer" (151). But neither can they continue as they are, in the hope of recreating an irrevocably lost landscape: "Who can catch dust-motes from the wind and compose village, forest, field?" (180).

The pterodactyl's decline is the chronicle of a death foretold. Breaching the ordinary limits of time and mortality, the novella retells a familiar story of an already realized extinction even as it imbues the present with the urgency of a tragedy yet to happen.[83] In such a retelling Puran is called upon to recognize the claims upon himself of this past that has already happened but is not yet concluded. This complex, counterintuitive plotting of species time, in which different temporalities, past, present, and apocalyptic future, commingle in the same historical moment, brings this tale within the ambit of the spectral fiction that is "Shishu." As we have seen, specters, like the pterodactyl, are marked by temporal disjunctures; they begin, as Derrida says, "by coming back." Ghostly and animal returns, spectropoetics and zoopoetics, hauntology and zoontology, occupy a terrain devoted to the labors of redress, mourning, and justice to a past that is still unfolding.

What might it mean to be addressed by a pterodactyl? or by a specter? On the one hand, there is a long tradition in modern Western metaphysics that suggests that the animal lacks the capacity for reason, which is almost invariably construed as linguistic reason. Animals possess no language as humans would understand it, language that is sign, that constitutes or expresses subjectivity and is therefore responsive rather than simply reactive. Having no language and being little more than embodied machine or automaton, the animal cannot conclusively be said to have, for Levinas, a face, one with which to solicit the kind of responsibility by which we are bound to other humans.[84] What is substantially true of the Western metaphysical tradition, especially in the last two centuries—though it too has had its notable detractors in the shape of Friedrich Nietzsche, Derrida, and Giorgio Agamben—is not necessarily true of the philosophical traditions, whether "little" or classical, of other parts of the world, especially the Indian subcontinent (or, indeed, of a nonmodern West). In the Hindu, Buddhist, and Jain traditions, animals have consciousness as much as humans do, being part of the same cycle of the transmigration of souls.[85] And even in a Western philosophical and ethical tradition the word *pterodactyl*, in this instance naming an ancestral spirit and a visitant from the beginning of time, cannot be a synonym for *animal*, if indeed *animal* can be a synonym for the nonhuman animal in general. Derrida has coined the term *l'animot*, a "chimerical word" (the chimera being a monster of Greek myth whose monstrosity consisted of her being of varied animal composition, lion, goat, and dragon grafted together) and homonym that puns upon singular and plural forms, *animal* and *animaux*, in order to proffer a critique of the ways in which the multiplicity of animal being is subsumed under a single name (animal) that would encompass all nonhuman animals.[86]

Even if nonhuman animals lack linguistic reason, can they communicate? The anthropological and folkloric literature, even that of a modernized West, suggests that the animal is not necessarily bereft of all possibility of communication and knowledge, even if it does not take linguistic form. Animals, for instance, are often invested with a certain hard-wired truth-discerning capacity, something approximating the telepathic, that exceeds everyday human cognition. Argos, Odysseus's faithful dog, is the only being capable of recognizing him after an absence of two decades. Animals are also commonly believed to have prior warning of disruptions in the order of nature. Such gifts of uncovering secrets and of divining the future—forms of animal perspicuity that are articulated with the transmissions of spectral beings—form the fantasmatic supplement or counterpoint to human reason and human speaking. Mahasweta draws attention to such forms of sensuous, embodied knowledge, to forms of revelation that are not necessarily grounded only in cognition: "This room is telling me, or I am grasping this as I've entered this room . . . this is sensed in the blood, it flows from generation to generation. . . . Why do migratory birds fly in winter to the same distant place, over thousands of years?" (134). To Harisharan this is no more than romanticization. Even for Puran such moments of transmission are rare and fleeting. For the most part he is unable to receive such messages, notwithstanding his keenness to do so: "It is crucial for Puran now to find out what Nature says, what news she gives. . . . But it is breaking your head against an invisible glass wall" (145). It is worth underlining that Nature, conceived here as the (vanishing) other to the human, is the term Puran, citizen of a modernizing order, uses; Shankar, the lone educated tribal and the organic intellectual of his community, does not use the term in his catalogue of the world that the tribals have lost as the result of the brutal incursion of the outsider.

. . .

If communication with Nature is barred, so too is communication with other humans, it seems. The frame narrative is, after all, that of Puran's failure to enter into a relationship with another human being. He is unable in the beginning to understand the subdivisional officer's desperate attempt to describe the unthinkable that has occurred in Pirtha. "This asymptote is a contemporary contagion," the reader is told (102). This nonintersection or noncommunication generally occurs across the tribal–mainstream divide and is most often figured as the breakdown of a common lexicon, even when both parties are speaking what is nominally the same language. Shankar, testifying to the contemporary predicament of Pirtha, cannot make Hindi, the predominant language of northern India and the national language of the Indian state, accommodate the experience of the tribals: "Alas! He speaks Hindi; Puran and Harisharan also speak Hindi, but how can one touch the other?" (118). Speaking across languages only underlines the incommensurability of the worlds they limn. If Hindi is unable to translate the ancient experience of the tribal, in turn the tribal languages stutter when describing contemporary tribal experience. Puran is told by a Ho-speaking translator of the life of the great nineteenth-century tribal rebel leader Birsa Munda, "There are no words for 'exploitation' or 'deprivation' in the Ho language" (118). In such a context the usual logic that ties knowing, experience, language, and value together in an articulated whole comes unraveled. Mainstream languages are implicitly damned for the richness of their vocabularies of lack and terror. Lacking a language of lack, the Ho language, like that of Montaigne's Tupinamba Indians, is the language of the just society precisely because of its deficits, because it cannot give tongue to the experience of injustice.[87] And Puran, who is nothing if not a man of expansive vocabulary and of book learning, is hobbled precisely by an excess of homework and an incapacity to read from anything but a book: "If written by a third person Puran would have got a perspective on the whole thing. There is no one to write" (159). Despite his earnestness and his learning, says Mahasweta,"he has known nothing, for he has wanted to know nothing" (160). The Ho cannot be invited to expand their lexicon; rather, the very extravagance of the mainstream language dictionaries is the sign of an irremediable loss.

And yet it is to such an unlikely figure that the pterodactyl manifests itself. Forcibly dislocated from "the extinct burial-grounds of the vanished settlements . . . the after-world"—this tale, like many others, is about the desecration of tribal burial sites under the onslaught of development—the pterodactyl cannot turn for refuge to its "own" community but must entrust its well-being to its oppressor (182). And this message Puran cannot hear. Time and time again the narrative mocks the modern mainstream Indian's endeavor to reckon with those who are immeasurably ancient and whose sufferings are likewise incalculable, cognitively recessive for those who inhabit another universe. The subdivisional officer likens the urban visitor's attempts to make sense of the tribals to "fathom[ing] the Indian Ocean with a foot-ruler" or to "measur[ing] the distance from the sun by releasing a kite" (104, 106).

"Becoming tribal" or "becoming animal" are options that have been rendered impossible by an intervening history of violence. Humbled by the extraordinary deprivations of the tribals, Puran strives mightily to reduce his own forms of consumption, refusing any but the simplest food and any bedding but a grass mat. Yet such forms of sharing, necessary but inseparable from self-regard, are met with unsentimental impatience by Shankar: "Sir! You people understand nothing. Will our hunger lessen if you don't eat?" (136). Even his solidarity with Bikhia over the guardianship of the pterodactyl—a solidarity that permits him to see the cave paintings of the tribals and to be present at the obsequies for the soul of the ancestors—is unwitting, unwilling on Bikhia's part, temporary, and perhaps even illusory. For a brief, crisis-filled period he can be accepted, not as a tribal but as a guest or a neighbor, one with whom relationship is simultaneously strange and proximate.[88] But however intensely felt, the solidarities of crisis cannot substitute for the painstaking, quotidian labor—what Spivak has called ethical singularity—of transforming the workaday world: "Although their hands were clasped at the end of the episode of danger they realized that they belong to two different worlds" (182).[89] Hence Puran experiences again and again his incapacity to understand either pterodactyl or Bikhia. Unlike the specters of Kubha, who speak in accents understandable by middle-class Indians—indeed, the officer's shock in that story comes from comprehending all too well the enormities that have been committed in his name—the pterodactyl's message to Puran, if there is one, is destined to remain encrypted.

Generally speaking, failures of communication across human and animal worlds are predicated upon the nonspeaking of the animal. Here, though, Mahasweta points to the difficult, effort-laden character of such transactions, the failure being located on the mainstream Hindu side. While Bikhia, despite his illiteracy, his ignorance of the history of evolution, and his unfamiliarity with prehistoric beings, can receive the gift of the pterodactyl, welcoming the creature as the soul of the ancestors, Puran cannot receive what is presumably its message. While he can understand, to some degree at least, Bikhia's ocular communication, the pterodactyl's gray eye can tell him nothing. He is acutely conscious of the failure on his part to understand, straining against the grain of a history of exploitation and cruelty to hear what the other might wish to say. But he cannot learn—and unlearn—fast enough to make a difference.[90] Can one think of the pterodactyl under the sign of subalternity, of whose attempt to solicit a listener Spivak says, "Even when the subaltern makes an effort to the death to speak, she is not able to be heard, . . . speaking and hearing complete the speech act."[91] Can we be addressed by the animal/friend, as Derrida suggests with respect to his cat?[92] Or does an entity such as the pterodactyl partake of an even more complexly compounded form of being, one of whose names might be "divinanimality" and another "humananimality"?[93]

As with the specters in "Shishu," the pterodactyl becomes the occasion to force to the foreground questions about the character of responsibility. When we are called to responsibility, who or what is it that calls to us? Is the other to whom we are responsible merely the human? or are we summoned as well to a responsibility to the nonhuman animal, and in ways that do not permit of strict distinctions between human and non-human beings, whether the latter be nonhuman animal, spectral, or sacred? What is it to be responsible to and for what is not and can never be fully understood or assimilated? Mahasweta suggests, perhaps more powerfully in this novella than in any other of her fictions, that the other who calls to us is nonidentifiable, nonreducible to subjectivity, which is why she has frequent recourse to the idioms of a cosmology that far exceeds the limits of human subjectivity. She says at one point, accentuating the limits of the merely human and the possibility of revelation from sources not entirely subsumed by reason, "See *The Birds*. Look at the group suicide of birds in Jatinga in the state of Assam. How can we tell what birds know or don't know? We have no communication with birds. We cannot know everything of nature's ways" (106). And then, in a move that is neither romanticizing nor slighting, she places the adivasis in a continuum with other exploited, dispossessed inhabitants of the subcontinent, human and nonhuman: "On this labeled sea-girt peninsula, the non-Aryans, the Titans, the demons, the monkeys (how many names for him from the Vedas through the epics, to the later Hindu scriptures) have forever seen land tax being paid in his name, seen influential thugs taking irrigation, fertilizer, and seeds by claiming 'tribal land,' and yet he has no right to that crop" (125).

What is the nature of the responsibility to which we are called? Is responsibility what one does or refrains from doing in response to the call of the other?[94] Is it the fact itself of hearing the address of the other, whether or not one understands what is said or who or what says it? Can Puran be said to have been addressed by this call, notwithstanding his utter failure to understand the character of its appeal, admonition, or warning? What is the nature of this attentiveness, necessary yet always insufficient, this openness that can hear the call without knowing what is being said? Thomas Keenan notes that hearing the call must of necessity be attended by an experience of strangeness rather than any form of familiarity or recognizability; to hear a familiar call is to be exempt from needing to hear the call. Keenan avers, "The call remains irreducibly different, alien, addressed to us . . . but 'like someone else's mail.' "[95]

How can this responsibility be expressed or represented? The pterodactyl's tribal custodian, Bikhia, is rendered mute or puts on muteness, at least where nontribals are concerned, by the fact of his priesthood. And while Puran is permitted to be a witness to the manifestation and the agony of the pterodactyl, he cannot enter into a structure of responsibility with it, responsibility in the literal sense of reciprocity, of responding and being responded to: "The eye [of the pterodactyl] says nothing. . . . It wants to say something, to give some news, Puran does not understand. *No point of communication.* Nothing can be said or written" (158). It is generally speaking true that otherworldly beings are not haphazard in their communications. Often the specter, like that in *Hamlet*, has a single addressee, no matter how many might see it, and its message is secret rather than disseminated. And the specter is not unfailingly a figure of moral clarity nor is its message always unambiguous: the Danish prince's doubts about the bloody-minded and carnally fixated ghost who urges him on to un-Christian murder should dispel any illusions about the invariable moral irreproachability of the revenant. But I do not know of any other instance besides *Pterodactyl* in which the designated recipient of an urgent message fails to understand the message of its otherworldly visitant.

Puran cannot save the pterodactyl, nor indeed can his witnessing be other than a mute and secret one, haunted by the consciousness of his futility; his experience can result in neither knowledge (within the parameters of rationality) nor action. Yet this mute witnessing is also a kind of fidelity. The usual modes of witnessing—newspaper reports, photographs, films, and other forms of the public use of reason—are at best inadequate to the task of rendering justice to Bikhia's people, silent as they are about the causes of the tribals' destitution. In fact, one of Puran's first gestures toward establishing trust among those whose uninvited guest he is consists of handing over his journalist's tools of tape recorder and camera. More importantly, in a context in which famine is a matter of speculation and profit making, publicizing famine can have the ironic effect of facilitating further assault upon those already sentenced to extinction. A mother forced to sell her child to fend off starvation says, "Take a fillim again, people will come again, they'll know famine is going on, again tur-rucks will come. They'll take all the children away" (168). Even those not directly involved in the sale or purchase of human beings are implicated in the traffic in human dignity. Philanthropy is inseparable from a form of entrepreneurship. Shankar understands the activities of the local philanthropist-entrepreneur thus: "Everything finally becomes a deal, even giving food to the hungry. At this moment we're eating his food, in exchange he wants to capture us *in film*. His dictionary cannot include the self-respect of the hungry" (168). Puran realizes that doing good is not only not the same as doing justice, but that doing good can actually function on occasion as a mode of injustice. Justice, as Derrida describes it, speaking of its distinction from law, rule, and well-doing, "is an experience of the impossible. . . . Every time that something comes to pass or turns out well, every time that we placidly apply a good rule to a particular case, to a correctly subsumed example, according to a determinant judgment, we can be sure that law [droit] may find itself accounted for, but not justice. . . . justice is incalculable, it requires us to calculate with the incalculable; and aporetic experiences are the experiences, as improbable as they are necessary, of justice."[96]

What would constitute justice for the tribal? for the pterodactyl? Harisharan understands that the time for justice belongs to a world irrevocably lost: "A civil servant from today's Madhya Pradesh Civil Service cannot give back to an ancient nation the flowing Pirtha, the spreading forest, fields of grain where the only invaders are deer, peacock, and other birds, festival dances not watched and photographed by trippers, burial-grounds where others' shovels and spades won't strike" (121). Inhabiting a present that has been irremediably polluted for them by the presence of diku (Hindu, alien, exploiting) society, the tribals can be saved only through forms that are counterfactual, namely, the undoing of the invasion and the expulsion of the invaders. All that is in Harisharan's power to give in lieu of the justice that is their due is "a little rice, medicine, powdered milk" (121).

. . .

Mahasweta does not trivialize or wish away calculation, bureaucracy, activism, and goodwill. To do so would be to sacrifice the possibility of amelioration in the name of an ethical inexorability that cannot but register as ludicrous. The bureaucrat Harisharan is indispensable to the thinking of responsibility, just as Puran is in his capacity as a journalist. His way of keeping faith with the tribals is to "keep unshaken his faith in paper, pen, and the printing machine" in a world in which journalistic exposés can sometimes move governments to act (186). In a world, moreover, in which tribals and subalterns are bereft of the tools that will allow them to represent themselves, they must, like the pterodactyl, "seek shelter with mainstream writers," open themselves up to the risky possibility of friendship with their enemies rather than seeking it only among fellow sufferers, their own kind (186). As Spivak notes, for Mahasweta there is no bypassing of the "public use of reason," or of the endeavor to insert tribals into citizenship of the postcolonial state, or of the struggle to achieve constitutional rights, change laws, and seek redress in a demo- cratic system.[97] Derrida's point about "calculating with the incalculable" is an important one and demonstrates that while ethics cannot be re- duced to calculation and rule, it is impossible to dismiss calculation. Indeed, calculation can also be a name for the categorical imperative that is collective and activist effort. But both Puran and Harisharan know that the responsibility demands something more, a something more that is not necessarily expressible and not necessarily programmatic. It is signif- icant that the report Puran produces makes no mention of the pterodactyl and of the responsibility it compels. Thinking, acting, and calculating responsibly is not a smoothing over of ambivalences but a wrestling with the undecidability of the ethical crisis where the acting is never free of risk. It is worth stressing that responsibility in the face of the non- knowledge I am naming here is not an entirely arbitrary, uncritical sub- mission to a demand that could be fascist just as easily as it is ethical, as Judith Butler seems at one point to suggest.[98] Such responsibility is the name, rather, of a different relationship to knowledge, one that does not insist on complete intelligibility and mastery as the condition of ethical action. Puran must learn to see and calculate the world "from the ratio of people like Bikhia" even though he has not had communication with the pterodactyl in the way Bikhia apparently has.

In the face of the responsibility grounded in a nonknowledge and nonaction that the specter, whether pterodactyl or ghost, offers, only a radical, world-changing, cosmic unhinging is possible: the longed-for madness of the relief officer or Puran's love. It is notable how often Mahasweta returns to the language of extraordinary trauma—of holo- caust and apocalypse—to describe what has been done to the tribals but also the effect of such a revelation on the well-meaning, self-praising middle-class Indian. If the pterodactyl is described as a figure of histori- cal terror itself, including that of nuclear holocaust, the relief officer's awakening is also described in millennial and apocalyptic terms: "They are adults! No sound comes out of his mouth, but the realization explodes inside his brain, devastating it like Hiroshima and Nagasaki" (240). This can be responded to only with a love, a sense of justice that is likewise abyssal and incalculable: "Only love, a tremendous, excruciating, explo- sive love can still dedicate us to this work when the century's sun is in the western sky, otherwise this aggressive civilization will have to pay a ter- rible price, look at history, the aggressive civilization has destroyed itself in the name of progress, each time. Love, excruciating love, let that be the first step" (196). It is not possible to ignore the triple annotation Mahasweta provides to the notion of love: "excruciating" (*prochondo* [tremendous], *nidaarun* [extreme, unbearable], *bishphorak* [explosive]). This is not a placid emotion but an insistent, wrenching, unquiet one—a ghostly emotion, if you will—one that approximates to some degree the madness that the relief officer seeks to draw upon himself.

In light of this, it is perhaps no accident that the word Mahasweta uses to describe her own labors for tribal justice is *obsession*. She writes with a tremendous sense of urgency and an archiving imperative against an inevitable apocalypse of tribal society. "I had such a great *asthirata* in me, such a restlessness; an *udbeg*, this anxiety; I have to write, somehow I have to document this period which I have experienced because it is going away, it is vanishing," she says about her epic novel about Munda history, *Chotti Munda and His Arrow*.[99] This restless, anxious love, giving of itself without limit, keenly attuned to past and future holocausts, is Mahasweta's mode of calculating the demands of the specter. What kind of acting is loving? And when one gives the gift of such love, what does one give? Nancy, following partly in the track of Jacques Lacan, says that the gift of love is a giving of what one does not have to give away. It consists of a giving of something that cannot be accounted one's own possession, not even one's own person. Love is a certain kind of loss of self-possession; it is a self-abandonment and self-shattering.[100] In this sense it agrees with the Derridean definition of the gift, which breaks with the logic of reciprocity in giving, sacrificing the notion of sacrifice itself. It is this kind of deranging self-abandonment to the irreducibly other, whether spectral, ancestral, or animal, that constitutes for Mahasweta a "remaining accountable to [herself]." In place of the calculations of deficits, resource allocations, and efficiency that normally mark famine talk, Mahasweta gives her readers quite another figuration of accountability.

4

Appetite | SPICES REDUX

Of Khansamas

Rising from my pages comes the unmistakable whiff of chutney. So let me obfuscate no further: I, Saleem Sinai, possessor of the most delicately-gifted olfactory organ in history, have dedicated my latter days to the large-scale preparation of condiments. But now, "A cook?" you gasp in horror, "A khansama merely? How is it possible?" And, I grant, such mastery of the multiple gifts of cookery and language is rare indeed; yet I possess it. You are amazed; but then I am not, you see, one of your 200-rupees-a-month cookery johnnies, but my own master, working beneath the saffron and green winking of my personal neon goddess. And my chutneys and kasaundies are, after all, connected to my nocturnal scribblings—by day among the pickle-vats, by night within these sheets, I spend my time at the great work of preserving. Memory, as well as fruit, is being saved from the corruption of the clocks.

—SALMAN RUSHDIE, *Midnight's Children*

It is by now a commonplace of the literary record that the publication in 1980 of Salman Rushdie's *Midnight's Children* was a landmark event in the history of Anglophone South Asian writing in particular and perhaps of postcolonial fiction in general. That it won the Booker Prize in 1981, followed by the Booker of Bookers in 1993 and the Best of the Bookers in 2008 has served to cement its quasi-mythic status. Beginning "at the precise instant of India's arrival at independence" (*Midnight's Children*, 3)—

a "paradigmatically postcolonial moment," as Deepika Bahri puts it—its ambition and its success "[mark] the inception of Rushdie's career as a postcolonial writer and as founding father for a whole generation of Indian writers to follow."[1] Notwithstanding some invariable carping about the quality of the novel's achievement, its "epic-fabulist" mode, incarnated in a narrative world marked by quasi-Rabelaisian sensory overload, came to be enthusiastically emulated.[2] Among its more notable achievements, and the one most apt given the focus of this book on matters alimentary, was a commitment to "challenging the official, positivist history that constitutes the nation with the unofficial one transmitted unreliably by nerve endings."[3] Tethered by a narrator, Saleem Sinai, whose gifts are gifts not so much of cerebration as of the senses—notably the auditory, the olfactory, and the gustatory—the novel unfolds an experience that Sara Suleri would describe in another context as "[taking] the world on [the] tongue."[4] Utilizing nose, ear, and tongue is inseparable moreover from operations more properly thought of as extrasensory: Saleem's sense of smell, like the voices he hears through his nose-turned-radio, is literally telepathic. At times the senses perform functions that more closely approximate the ideological or the aesthetic or both. Thus Saleem of the preternaturally developed olfactory capacity spurns "[the] flat boiled odours of acquiescence in Karachi," where he spends a troubled adolescence, for "the highly spiced nonconformity of Bombay" (353).

Characteristically, the novel's experiences can be absorbed only through heroic acts of incorporation: "To understand me, you'll have to swallow a world" (458). At the same time, and notwithstanding the imperative for such prodigious forms of consumption, Saleem inhabits a world governed by appropriately strict South Asian rules of ingestion: "One is supposed to digest and swallow only permitted parts of it, the halal portions of the past, drained of their redness, their blood" (62). Such safeguards are necessary in a world in which affect and communication are vectored through cooking and eating and in which many of the women, from Mary Pereira to Saleem's Aunt Alia, stir powerfully negative affect into their dishes, Aunt Alia notably undoing her sister's family through the "birianis of dissension and the nargisi koftas of discord" (395).

Olfaction and ingestion can be curses as much as they are boons. At one point, his olfactory gifts reduce Saleem to the doglike status of a tracker for the Pakistani army in Bangladesh. But at other points he is able to harness such gifts much more creatively to the gastronomic, a humble analogue here for the work of the creative imagination.[5] After an extended phase of amnesia, he is restored to memory through the taste of Mary Pereira's green chutney and comes into his own as the master of chutneys and pickles. In a text in which pickling is likened to storytelling —Saleem's uncle Hanif, for one, plans a filmic "pickle epic" of a neorealist kind—Saleem establishes his creative credentials not so much through the conventional tropes of sexual potency (he is, after all, rendered impotent as a result of his "sperectomy" during the Widow's reign of terror) as through his claim to "the most delicately-gifted olfactory organ in history."

Storytelling, pickling, and chutnification are about more than preservation, though. Such cooking is also about contamination and exaggeration, as Saleem suggests in an extended meditation on the amalgamation of spices: "There is . . . the matter of the spice bases. The intricacies of turmeric and cumin, the subtlety of fenugreek, when to use large (and when small) cardamoms; the myriad possible effects of garlic, garam masala, stick cinnamon, coriander, ginger . . . not to mention the flavorful contributions of the occasional speck of dirt . . . I reconcile myself to the inevitable distortions of the pickling process. To pickle is to give immortality, after all: fish, vegetables, fruit hang embalmed in spice-and-vinegar; a certain alteration, a slight intensification of taste, is a small matter, surely? The art is to change the flavor in degree, but not in kind; and above all (in my thirty jars and a jar) to give it shape and form—that is to say, meaning" (550).

Here, as elsewhere, foods and flavors are, for Rushdie, indices of national or civilizational belonging, though not necessarily in entirely solemn ways.[6] Most famously in *The Moor's Last Sigh* he focuses on the spice trade and on pickling in order to configure the subcontinent as a theater of sensuous plenitude and marvelous fusions, most notably in the "pepper love" of Aurora da Gama and Abraham Zogoiby that produces the protagonist, "a cathjew-nut, a stewpot, a mongrel cur . . a real Bombay mix."[7] In a paradoxical conjoining that is typical of the figural modes he favors, spices function as an authentic emblem of the subcontinent's appetite for hybridization.

Rushdie's turn to spices as a creative and erotic repertoire here is emblematic of a certain strain in the writing, filmmaking, and cultural self-fashioning of a historically recent South Asian diaspora in the global North. For many a writer and filmmaker, spices have served as a favored trope of cultural representation, though few deploy it with the wit and imagination of a Rushdie. Novels like Chitra Divakaruni's *Mistress of Spices* (1997) and films like Mira Nair's *Mississippi Masala* (1991) deploy spices to a number of parabolic ends, to signify, variously, magic, enhantment, healing, and the cultural sedimentations of diaspora. Seeking to re-auratize a subcontinent stripped of its archaic glamour by centuries of colonial rule and associated with poverty and hunger, Divakaruni and Nair deploy spices as "a linguistic and ideological operator rather than an essentialised object," evoking their age-old associations in the West with luxury, cosmopolitanism, and imaginative, erotic, and therapeutic bounty.[8]

Behind this deployment of spices as a favored trope for filtering questions of national and diasporic belonging and affiliation and their econo - mies of taste and consumption looms the figure of the original mistress of spices: Madhur Jaffrey, the single best-known authority on Indian gastronomy in the United States and Britain, the host of three extremely popular cooking shows on the British Broadcasting Corporation (BBC), and the author of fifteen or more books, almost all related to food. Jaffrey's ascendance as an icon is keyed in crucial ways to a mobilization of what some reviewers have described as "the romance of spices." But rather than trading overtly in the exotic aura of spices in the manner of Divakaruni and Nair, she situates spices within an idiom of culinary authenticity, one associated with heterogeneity, complexity, painstaking labor, and home cooking. This authenticity is poised against the culinary corruption represented by curry and curry powder, an invariable shorthand in the West for subcontinental cuisine. Spices, once associated in the medieval European imagination with romance and legend, come to function for her as a reactivated trope of authenticity, distinct from the vulgarizing operations of that homogenizing, gastronomically impoverished, commercially debased quick fix, curry powder. "To me," she says in her first book, *An Invitation to Indian Cooking* (1973), "the word 'curry' is as degrading to India's great cuisine as the term 'chop suey' was to China's. But just as Americans have learned, in the last few years, to distinguish between the different styles of Chinese cooking and between the different dishes, I fervently hope that they will do the same with Indian food instead of lumping it all under the dubious catchall title of 'curry.' "[9] But if curry is a gross flattening of culinary heterogeneity, there is nonetheless something that ties the variegated cuisines of the subcontinent together: "the imaginative use of spices."[10] But how is one to understand the declension from spices to curry? In *An Invitation to Indian Cooking* Jaffrey gives readers the following tableau about the colonial rise of curry powder. It stages the duplicities of nomenclature and of the palate in a parable that implicitly desires, or so it seems, to uncouple the traffic between food and deceit and to establish a hierarchy of pure and polluted foods:

> A British officer in full uniform (possibly a young David Niven) is standing under a palm tree and looking fondly at his bungalow as Indian servants go back and forth carrying heavy trunks from the house into a waiting carriage. When the carriage is loaded, the servants line up on the verandah with tears in their eyes. The officer himself, overcome with emotion, turns to khansamah (cook).
>
> OFFICER: How I shall miss your delicious cooking. My good man, why don't you mix me a box of those wonderful spices that you have been using. I will carry it back with me to Surrey, and therefore, whenever I feel nostalgic about India, I will take out this box and sprinkle some of your aromatic spice mixture into my bubbling pot.
>
> KHANSAMAH: Yes, sa'ab, as you say, sa'ab. (Runs off to kitchen.)
>
> Scene shifts to kitchen, where cook is seen hastily throwing spices into box. He runs back with it to officer.
>
> KHANSAMAH: Here is the box, sa'ab. Sa'ab, if your friend also like, for a sum of two rupees each, I can make more boxes for them as well. . . .
>
> Several years later. Former cook is now successful exporter. He is seen filling boxes marked "Best Curry Powder." When boxes are filled, he puts them in a large crate and stamps it in black: FOR EXPORT ONLY. Then he goes to his money box, opens it, takes out his money, and gleefully counts it. As scene fades away, former cook and present exporter is doing Dance of Joy. . . .
>
> (Invitation)

What is one to make of the absurd scenario played out above? Surely it is a parable of authenticity, of home and of the world, and of the idioms of purity and pollutions that attend the making of nativeness, though Jaffrey is ostensibly ironic not so much about nativeness itself as she is about the colonial practices of commodification and reductiveness. The elaborately campy quality of the tableau is designed to underscore, as no mere sober accounting could do, the comic outrageousness of British trivializations of Indian cuisines. As she has argued in book after book on the cuisines of the subcontinent, the term curry was an invention of early Anglo-Indian sojourners in India rather than an appropriate description of the complexity and variety of Indian cooking; but, she concedes, outside the subcontinent at least the definition "seems to have stuck."[11] Recently Lizzie Collingham has glossed the emergence of curry in the following terms: "Curry became not just a term that the British used to describe an unfamiliar set of Indian stews and ragouts, but a dish in its own right, created for the British in India. One surgeon described curry as 'a most heterogeneous compound of ginger, nutmeg, cinnamon, cloves, cardamoms, coriander, Cayenne pepper, onions, garlic, and turmeric, ground to a powder by a pestle and mortar, made into a paste by ghee, . . . and added to a stewed kid or fowl.' And this was the formula that provided a template for Anglo-Indian curries, most of which were variations on this basic recipe."[12] She notes though that in the eighteenth century curry was not, for Anglo-Indians returning to Britain, the equivalent of curry powder. The emergence of curry powder as a catchall seasoning for Indian food was a later, largely nineteenth-century development, as Anglo-Indians "began to think of curries as variations on one theme." It was then that British cookery books began to call for the addition of curry powder rather than for an assortment of seasonings to dishes they identified as curries.[13]

Modern writers of Indian cookbooks before Jaffrey had bemoaned the reduction of Indian cuisines to curry in most parts of the Western world. In the Time-Life book *The Cooking of India* (1969) Santha Rama Rau had spoken witheringly of this phenomenon: "To most of them [Western minds] curry is simply a floury, yellow cream sauce that can be used indiscriminately with meat or fish or chicken, and served with rice—and, of course, with Major Grey's chutney."[14] In spite of the corrections proffered by Rama Rau's carefully written text, it remained substantially unreviewed by North American food critics and unread by gastronomically adventurous readers. This might have been for reasons having in part to do with the historical moment, as Antoinette Burton has noted: "Given how young the Indian cookbook industry was in the 1960s, Rama Rau may be said to have been present at the beginning of this generic enterprise and to have contributed to the process of converting a largely oral tradition of recipekeeping and culinary narrativizing into a literary genre and, in turn, a transnational phenomenon with a growing (and potentially profitable) diasporic audience."[15]

The crusade against curry would be carried out with more visibility and panache by Jaffrey in the next decade. That the culinary history of the term *curry* is now relatively well known is thanks in no small part to her spirited endeavors to reclaim the multifariousness of Indian cooking from its debased culinary stereotype in the Anglophone West, and her work has resonated for analysts of the traffic in colonial commodities. For scholars like Susan Zlotnick and Uma Narayan, the diminution of Indian cuisines to something called curry is an egregious colonial endeavor to obliterate or refashion the subcontinent's highly differentiated culinary landscapes, akin in its coerciveness to better-known colonial attempts to perform an epistemic overhaul of Indian ways of life.[16] Seeking to let natives represent themselves, rather than be misrepresented by others, such glosses bemoan the reductions entailed in asymmetrical relationships with the other.

But in Jaffrey's case at least, even as she seeks to clarify the strictly British or Anglo-Indian provenance of curry and curry powder, she finds herself pointing to various and prolific *Indian* usages of the term (the Tamil *kari*, the northern Indian *karhi*, and the casual use of the term by English-speaking Indians): " 'Curry' is just a vague, inaccurate word which the world has picked up from the British, *who, in turn, got it mistakenly from us*" (*Invitation*, 5, emphasis added). Moreover, in the richly incongruous moment in which an origin myth is inaugurated under the benevolent tutelage of the sentimental Englishman, it is the Indian *khansamah* who proves to be the most skilled entrepreneur of boxed nostalgia. Is it any wonder that Jaffrey's career should have been bookended by this talismanic term? For one of the later cookbooks, *Quick & Easy Indian Cooking*, extols the timesaving virtues of Bolst's curry powder with nary a backward glance at the David Niven tableau. Jaffrey the purveyor par excellence of appetites in one kind of a box, whether bound as a book or produced as a television show, has further literalized this gustatory fancy, in Britain at least, through a range of culinary products, including jars and boxes, that bear her name.[17] Indeed, she has come to be hailed by no less than the British Tourist Authority's guide as "the Mrs. Beeton [the legendary nineteenth-century author of the bible of British cookery and household management] of the 1990s"[18] and been made an Honorary Commander of the British Empire (CBE) in 2004. Perhaps it is not too fanciful to see in the figure of the khansamah an early self-portrait of the author, who, like her fictional analogue, produced a highly successful culinary commodity in response to demands from eager Westerners and, later, by South Asian diasporic subjects? And it is only apposite to note that the British edition of her recent book, *Madhur Jaffrey's Ultimate Curry Bible* (2003), seized upon the very term she had once held up to derision, even echoing the title of Pat Chapman's *Curry Bible* (1997) and coming to be enlisted (through her publisher in Britain) in a "biblical war" with his claim to the title.[19] In the opening sentences of this book there is even an explicit solicitation, not to be found in the other cookbooks, of a particular kind of British subject. This is not so much the sophisticated, cosmopolitan gastronome hailed in the other writings, but someone with simpler appetites, one who might be called a curry club member: "You think of a curry meal and your mouth lights up. Spices, yet to be tasted, begin tickling the palate. There are visions of kebabs to have with your drinks and then, to accompany your curry, mounds of fluffy rice, sweet and sour chutneys, and relishes."[20] The term *curry* for an Indian or Indian-style dish with a sauce is "not exactly my definition," she notes somewhat ruefully in this introduction. But it belongs to a colonial script that is too overpowering and, eventually, too familiar to be resisted for very long, and she thus comes to incorporate it as a loanword in her own culinary lexicon.

The issue here is not, or not so much, one of misrepresentation by colonizing others against a self-representation by once disempowered subjects, a self-representation that would construct a fuller, more democratic, and generally more affirmative image than that available in dominant representations. What if the long-deferred act of autoethnography produces not a self-evident speaking or a writing back but a confirmation of the logic of a dominant discourse?[21] Representations in any event are never fully the property of their progenitors; they circulate in the world as commodity forms that may be intercepted away from their intended ends. As the campy, commercially savvy artist Vasco Miranda puts it in *The Moor's Last Sigh*, the question is less that of correct representations and misrepresentations than that of "hits" that circulate in the marketplace of representations: " 'hit-take, hit-alliance, hit-conception, hit-terious . . . Opposite of mis-.' "[22] As Jaffrey and others note, the hit-word curry has even entered the lexicon of Anglophone eaters in the subcontinent, being used now to describe dishes with a sauce. On being offered what is touted as " 'the best fish curry of your life' " by an Indian friend in Goa, the food writer Chitrita Banerji responds with some aggravation but also with a keen sense of the futility of insisting on linguistic correctness: "Again, that word—curry. A slippery eel of a word, bent and stretched to cover almost anything with a spicy sauce, a king of misnomers, and yet, to those who use it, the perfect definition for whatever they are trying to describe at that given moment. I've had a beef with curry for many years, long enough now to have quit protesting its application or urging the user to find a more accurate word. If Goanese fish curry was delicious, I was ready to sample it."[23]

A similarly sardonic sense of one's gustatory nativeness and of one's capacity to know it and name it correctly is evident in *Meatless Days*, Suleri's text on gendered national belonging, diasporic displacement, and gastropolitics. It plays off but also transmogrifies both Rushdie's story of the counterinstitutional khansamah in *Midnight's Children* and Jaffrey's culinary entrepreneur in *An Invitation to Indian Cooking*.[24] Indeed, one could say that the Rushdie and Suleri texts provide two distinct but intersecting frames through which Jaffrey's performance of gastronomy can be understood, the first signaling an investment in the imaginative amplitude and distinct Indianness of spices, the second underscoring the performative ironies that trouble the meanings of indigeneity and national reproduction.

In her ironic rewriting of national history's overbearing relationship to women Suleri proffers a genealogical counterpoint to her nationalist father's rapturous litany of masculine heads of state:

> Food certainly gave us a way not simply of ordering a week or a day but of living inside history, measuring everything we remembered against a chronology of cooks. Just as Papa had his own yardstick . . . with which to measure history and would talk about the Ayub era, or the second martial law, or the Bhutto regime, so my sisters and I would place ourselves in time by remembering and naming cooks. "In the Qayuum days," we'd say, to give a distinctive flavor to a particular anecdote, or "in the Allah Ditta era." . . . There is something nourishing about the memory of all those shadow dynasties: we do not have to subsist only on the litany that begins, "After General Ayub came General Yahya; after the Bhutto years came General Zulu Haq," but can also add, "Qayuum begat Shorty and his wife; and they begat the Punjabi poet only called Khansama; he begat Ramzan and Karamdad the bearer; Ramzan begat Tassi-Passi, and he begat Allah Ditta, meanest of them all" (*Meatless Days*, 34).

If Suleri constructs an alternative, albeit equally class-marked, genealogy through cooking and food, she also makes it clear that such gustatory histories, which are in some ways peculiarly tied to conditions of diaspora and migration, are nonetheless saturated with the idioms of national belonging and national purity much like the heroic, relentless histories her father prefers. Migrants preserve their ties to a homeland through their preservation of and participation in traditional customs and rituals of consumption. Food, in the migrant or diasporic subject's cosmos, becomes—whatever it might have been at its place of putative origin—

tenaciously tethered to economies simultaneously and inalienably national and moral.[25] It is precisely through food, through the "poignancies of nourishment," as she so evocatively puts it, that dramas of national and familial duplicity and devotion are enacted. Early in the memoir, the *kapura* incident (which is generated by her sister's unwelcome revelation of the "secret" of the kapura's anatomical origin, an origin quite other than the sweetbreads of her Welsh mother's account) unsettles her confidence in her Pakistani gustatory identity and her capacity to inhabit it as her own:

> Something that had once sat quite simply inside its own definition was declaring independence from its name and nature, claiming a perplexity that I did not like. . . . So, the next time I was in the taut companionship of Pakistanis in New York, I made a point of inquiring into the exact status of *kapura* and the physiological location of its secret, first in the animal and then in the meal. Expatriates are adamant, entirely passionate about such matters as the eating habits of the motherland. Accordingly, even though I was made to feel that it was wrong to strip a food of its sauce and put it back into its bodily belonging, I certainly received an unequivocal response: *kapura*, as naked meat, equals a testicle. . . . "But," and here I rummaged for the sweet realm of nomenclature, "couldn't *kapura* on a lazy occasion also accommodate something like sweetbreads, which is just a nice way of saying that pancreas is not a pleasant word to eat?" No one, however, was interested in this finesse. "Balls, darling, balls," someone drawled, and I knew I had to let go of the subject (22).

Suleri is careful to emphasize, through several reiterations, the parabolic character of this anecdote: "Am I wrong, then, to say that my parable has to do with nothing less than the imaginative extravagance of food and all the transmogrifications of which it is capable?" (34). Reversing and doubling the explanatory logic of the parabolic form, the kapura story comments not simply on the semantic and affective volatilities of food, but on the nature itself of parabolic or allegorical narrative.[26] It is a parable that is interwoven through the characteristic operations of Suleri's figural logic with questions of national origin, authorization, libidinality, and nomenclature.

The kapura fable is also a meditation upon the vexation of origins. Beginnings are fraught in this memoir, not least for Suleri's father, whose tongue always trips over the trisyllabic trap posed by the very word *beginning*, one that seeks to compete with and to unsettle the amplitude of the talismanic name of Pakistan: "There was a word over which he could slow down, to exude ownership as he uttered it! But something like 'beginning'—that is, something more mundane—had to become 'bigning,' a hasty abbreviation that was secretly aware of the comic quality of slapdash, the shorthand through which slapdash begins" (109). This quality of adventitiousness attends all discussion of origins and histories in the memoir, so that, for instance, the author's mother can be buried guiltlessly with a spurious birthplace on her gravestone. Sometimes, and more seriously, though, myths about the purity of beginnings can be sustained only through a calculated form of amnesia, as in the case of Suleri's father's decision to jettison his first wife and daughter and in the instance of his remoteness from the bloody origins of Pakistan. It is no surprise, therefore, that the kapura fable—that which is intimately linked, as Suleri says, to the dilemma of her Pakistaniness—should speak to willed self-delusion and the semantic instabilities of self-knowledge, though it is equally true that such uncertainties are usually resolutely not made part of an aetiology of nostalgia. The figure of her mother, characteristically a little off-center, broods over the inauguration of the palate's transactions with the world and its miscognitions of bodily parts, a telling commentary on the character of what her daughter punningly calls nativity. Not only does she discover her Welsh mother's deceitful production of her Pakistaniness, but she connects these perfidies of nomenclature to the duplicities of food in Pakistan with considerable ironic relish: "To some degree all of us were . . . watchful for hidden trickeries in the scheme of nourishment, for the way in which things would always be missing or out of place in Pakistan's erratic emotional market. . . . Our days and our newspapers were equally full of disquieting tales about adulterated foods and the preternaturally keen eye that the nation kept on such promiscuous blendings" (29).

Producing improper names and "promiscuous blendings" in place of an indisputable story of gastronomic authenticity, the kapura fable is remarkably resonant of Jaffrey's legend of the khansamah and the origin of curry powder.

The Real Thing

The focus in this chapter on the gastronomy of diaspora is inescapably in ironic counterpoint to the limits posed by tribal hunger and immobility in Mahasweta's fiction; as such, this chapter and the previous one constitute the contrasting bookends of a distinctly uneven postcolonial continuum. "[Those] who have stayed in place for thirty thousand years": this is how Spivak would describe the subalterns of Mahasweta's subnational space, for whom the lines of mobility and visibility permitted by socialized capital, legal redress, or nationalism are inconceivable.[27] In rather disjointed places, geographically as well as by virtue of access to citizenship, from such subalterns are those who inhabit the terrain of what one can loosely call the globality of First World immigration and diaspora. Yet, in spite of their lack of access to the symbolic discourses of rights and mobility, these subalterns constitute the invisible but indispensable pole of a world being made over by transnational late capitalism; in this regard, they embody a limit for those that Spivak names the New Immigrants.

An examination of Jaffrey's career as gastronome in a global theater must reckon with her emblematic status among these subjects of postwar migration. As Spivak defines it, New Immigrant figures are produced not by the old transstate and transregional diasporas of slavery, indenture, imperialism, trade, and war, which often involved some forms of subalternalization. They are produced instead through a westward-looking transnational migration of the post–Second World War period; this is a transnationality made possible in many instances by postcolonial class entitlement and fetishized by certain forms of multiculturalist liberalism in the global North.[28] The other relevant difference between the diasporas is that while in the nineteenth century and early twentieth the South Asian diaspora was crucial to the economic interests of the host countries (usually other British colonies) in particular and to the empire in general, its economic importance to the homeland was negligible. The emergence of New Immigrants, on the other hand, occurring as it has in an era of migrant remittances and transnational investment, has seen a significant change in the economic relationship with the home country.[29]

By now this figure, often absorbed within the broad rubric of diaspora, has come to be the focus of critical attention on the part of humanists and social scientists thinking through the uneven relationship among such conditions and terms as postcoloniality, cosmopolitanism, and late capitalist globalization. Perhaps paradoxically, *diaspora*, the term most often used to describe this contemporary figure or phenomenon, is of considerable antiquity. The dilation of its original meaning, Khachig Toloyan suggests, "is due to a change in the prestige of the term, which once connoted deracination, sorrow, and powerlessness."[30] He observes that the term, once reserved for Jewish, Greek, and Armenian experiences of dispersion, has now become part of an arrangement of partial equivalences, "shar[ing] meanings with a larger semantic domain that includes words like immigrant, expatriate, refugee, guest-worker, exile community, overseas community, ethnic community."[31] Thus James Clifford, for one, has sought an updated definition of the term and the phenomenon rather than the prescriptive model offered by William Safran in the inaugural issue of the journal Diaspora. This revised definition would be mindful of the "changing global conditions" of "experiences of displacement, of constructing homes away from home." At the same time Clifford has sought to retain some of the original ethical charge of diaspora by delineating its potentially minoritarian and nonnationalist, even utopian manifestations.[32] This endeavor to invest diaspora and transnationality with the possibility of critique, especially antinationalist critique, has also distinguished the work of Arjun Appadurai. He has famously anatomized the crisis of the nation-state form, arguing that current developments in migration and information technologies worldwide will lead to less territorially bounded forms of identity. In such a postnational world the fate of nationality is to be displaced at least in part by the growth of diasporic public spheres and by a global traffic in images, desires, capital, technologies, and ideologies.[33] He has been criticized, sometimes not entirely fairly, for too celebratory a reading of the postpatriotic and anti-identitarian possibilities of a world reimagined through migrancy; he describes his recent book Fear of Small Numbers as a response, in part, to the questions raised by such critique. The book is a lucid description of the community-building function at the national level of ethnic hatreds that endeavor to exorcise the anxieties unleashed by globalization, though he notes that the "cellular globalization" of contemporaneity has its utopian as well as its dystopian side.[34]

The possibilities of the new forms of late capitalist migration and diaspora have been more unambiguously execrated by Aihwa Ong, who sees the transnationality of overseas Chinese entrepreneurs, particularly those from Hong Kong, Malaysia, and Singapore, as a market-driven form of citizenship far from democratic in its aspirations. The phenomenon of "flexible citizenship" she describes admits of no necessary contradiction between nationalism, including cultural nationalism, and transnationalism; its commitment to "Confucian cultural triumphalism" is not at odds with the self-exoticization required to profit from global schemes of cultural particularity and racial hierarchy.[35] For Timothy Brennan and several other like-minded literary scholars, this censure of opportunistic transnational migrants of the new world order also embraces elite West-based transnationals such as postcolonial theorists (Homi Bhabha is a favorite example) and writers (like Bhabha, Rushdie functions, as Bahri notes, as "the poster child [and therefore sometimes the favored whipping boy] for a certain formulaic postcolonialism")[36] whose very cultural and economic capital is the condition of possibility for their privileging of migrancy, mobility, hybridity, and cosmopolitanism.[37]

Brennan's critique is important to thinking about the serviceability of postcolonial celebrity or iconization for the project of liberal multiculturalism and about what visibility excludes as well as what it renders larger than life. At the same time, an uninflected reading of the sociology of diasporic celebrity tells but a limited story about the modes that diasporic celebrity can assume and the quite varied projects to which it can be attached. And while it is certainly true that Jaffrey's production of a gendered food nostalgia as a condition of diasporic belonging can be said to partake of the fetishistic economies that Brennan describes, such a diagnostic move is not entirely sufficient to the task of analysis. Both nostalgia and fetishism, to be properly understood as complex phenomena, demand a careful parsing of their operations. The tendency to read the political economy of diasporic mobility and visibility in terms of the inequities it obscures and sometimes produces must be matched with an examination of the contexts of its circulation as well of the sometimes counterintuitive particulars textual analysis affords.[38] In their work on the writers of the Anglophone South Asian diaspora, Bahri, Inderpal Grewal, and Bishnupriya Ghosh usefully remark upon the limits of the merely denunciatory reading of the cosmopolitical without a consideration of its various modes.[39] Such a caution is useful to bear in mind even when dealing with the somewhat more modest contours of Jaffrey's gastronomic writing and film career; it is a reminder that, as in the instance of the curry powder tableau, an attentiveness to the metaphoric and allegorical logics that govern the crafting of careers and personae demonstrates that the effects of the prose or of the star image are not necessarily consistent or transparent. It is also to recognize that an attentiveness to tone, including modes of irony and parody, can disturb some of the austere pieties that such a late capitalist figure of diasporic arrival almost inevitably invites. And, finally, Jaffrey's career as gastronome and actress has a quite specifically gendered trajectory, one with potentially interesting implications for thinking about professionalism and mobility in diasporic times and places.

I turn to the prose first. Since I undertake here an examination of the evocation of memory and regional-ethnic Indian identities in conditions of diaspora, I focus on those of Jaffrey's cookbooks that are specifically about Indian food and published in the United States and Britain—*An Invitation to Indian Cooking, Madhur Jaffrey's Indian Cooking, A Taste of India, Flavours of India, Quick & Easy Indian Cooking,* and *Madhur Jaffrey's Ultimate Curry Bible*—while bracketing for the moment her books on other Asian cuisines. When speaking of Indian cookbooks other than those by Jaffrey, I will concentrate not so much upon cookbooks meant for a domestic market as on those intended for consumption outside the subcontinent.

. . .

If Jaffrey has come to assume the place of the virtuosa of Indian cooking in the West, it is not on account of the paucity of Indian cookbooks, either in India or abroad. In his superb analysis of English-language cookbooks in contemporary India, Appadurai describes a novel proliferation of works in this genre in the postwar period. Such a development is a distinct departure from the traditional indifference, in Brahminical thought at least, to the "textualization of the culinary realm" (5). Anthropologists of Hindu food rituals, notably R. S. Khare, have pointed to the fact of the embeddedness of food in medicomoral economies rather than in those of sensory pleasure, consumption, or display.[40] The development of what is now known as Mughlai food in the royal courts of northern India marked something of a shift, though not a sufficiently substantial one, in the public and textual availability of recipes and other culinary instructions. What Appadurai describes, on the other hand, in his scrutiny of postcolonial India is a notable culinary transformation that is indexed by the production and dissemination of English-language cookbooks since the sixties. This transformation signals the construction of a particular kind of sanitized yet culinarily polyglot culture in the context of a recently achieved postcoloniality and the spatial mobility of a professional middle class with aspirations to a worldliness that exceeds earlier limits of caste, religion, and region.[41] Appadurai's contextualization of the rise of the English-language cookbook in postcolonial India also functions as a description of aspects of Jaffrey's gastronomic project, despite her location outside the territorial limits of the Indian nation-space. In fact, her cookbooks can in some ways serve as the most a propos examples of the aspirations to the kind of nationalist cosmopolitanism he describes the cookbooks as enacting. This is partly because of the cookbook's generic indebtedness to the idioms of exilic nostalgia and loss. Many of the Indian cookbooks he describes are written by expatriate subjects, often in response to the social, culinary, and affective contingencies of geographical separation from a motherland.[42] Indeed, Jaffrey's iconic status has a great deal to do with the figuration of a specific kind of gendered life and its consanguinity with the changing national allegories and diasporic losses and demands Appadurai has detailed.[43]

It is now a commonplace that compelling cookbooks are never entirely utilitarian, never examples of an applied science. Susan Leonardi points to the instance of the 1951 edition of *The Joy of Cooking*, in which Irma Rombauer functions as a highly individualized voice, contextualizing recipes and registering individual preferences and dislikes and making no pretense of neutrality. This edition is informal and chatty in style, sprinkled with anecdotes and witticisms, while the edition of 1997, a so-called revision, is really an encyclopedia compiled by a team of experts with little interest in the traditional American food featured by Rombauer.[44] Such a model of cookbook production, as memoir (sometimes fictionalized memoir) and one that muddies the putative oppositions between life and work, appears to be a successful and often markedly gendered subgenre of gastronomic writing. One instance is Chitrita Banerji's superb *Life and Food in Bengal* (1991). Another, perhaps more apposite instance that is also contemporaneous with the work of Jaffrey is Jennifer Brennan's *Curries and Bugles: A Memoir and Cookbook of the British Raj* (1990), a felicitous amalgam of recipes, memories, illustrations, and black-and-white photographs of an India doubly marked, from the title page on, as British and exotic.[45] Brennan's book was exceptionally well received in a Britain steeped in what Rushdie has termed the "Raj nostalgia" ethos; the *Independent on Sunday* called it "the perfect present for anyone who has had connections with the subcontinent, but for those who haven't she also manages to create an aching sense of nostalgia."[46] This ethos was supplemented in notable ways in the eighties and nineties by the spectacular staging of India across a global canvas, sometimes by the Indian state and sometimes by Indian diasporic communities, most notably through the international Festivals of India.[47] It functions as one of the contexts against which Jaffrey's cookbook productions and her iconicity should be understood.

One can call the writing in and of the cookbooks autoethnography in a minor mode. It shares many of the features of autoethnography proper. It has links with personal narrative, fiction, journalism, and performance, and its focus on experience rather than on expertise, its attentiveness to the details of daily life, and its modes of insider observation are mobilized in the service of a distinct kind of cultural explanation or cultural accounting. At the same time it makes no overt claims to ethnographic comprehensiveness or generalizability, being focused rather on actors and phenomena on a very modest scale. Others writers of Indian cookbooks have embraced this model, though few have engaged in it with as much success as Jaffrey. Unlike her books on East and Southeast Asian cooking and Asian vegetarian cooking, the early Indian cookbooks are almost invariably autoethnographic ventures. She is scrupulous about marking, in An Invitation to Indian Cooking, the limits of her ethnic and geographic reach, gastronomically speaking. She defines her recipes as confined not only to Delhi and its environs, but also to the culinary practices of her family; a large number of the recipes are poised in a web of family anecdotes and details. Broad ambition is explicitly renounced through a routing of the content through a specifically personal and recuperative desire: "Some day, I hope, books will be written about all of India's cuisines. . . . But until that happens, my book can introduce you to the smells and tastes which I grew up with as a child in Delhi and which I have struggled over the years to re-create in my American kitchen" (16). She adds that though she offends against ethnic authenticity by including a few recipes not originating in the Delhi region, this is justified by the modest and autobiographical thrust of the book: "I feel very attached to these dishes, and as this is essentially a personal book, I had no compunction about including things that have been adapted in my own kitchen" (14).

Autoethnography, including its minor modes, is almost always characterized by a prior sense of distance and loss, which can nonetheless be made narratively productive. Thus the national tales of the Celtic fringe, newly incorporated into the United Kingdom, and Walter Scott's Waverley novels feature prominently at the start of James Buzard's study of the autoethnographic labors of the nineteenth-century British novel. Written to commemorate a once-separate national identity, these narratives also function through these forms of mnemonic fidelity to produce the lost homelands as imaginable cultural totalities.[48] In Jaffrey's instance, it is An Invitation to Indian Cooking that is most clearly haunted by the strains of exilic poignancy, telling as it does the story of gustatory and familial loss, longing, and return through the ceremonies of gendered homage and enjoyment. While addressed ostensibly to Americans, it is nonetheless also a doubled autobiographical narrative of the citizen and the migrant who learns cooking and learns Indianness retrospectively and with the aid of a geographical distance that, far from impeding, becomes the condition of possibility for epic visions of the homeland and its seductions of the palate.

This first gastronomic narrative treats the intimacy of gustatory and national memories as Jaffrey tracks the emergence of an Indian modernity through the medium of changes in domestic spatial arrangements, food preparation, and gendered mobility. Like *Meatless Days*, Jaffrey's narrative serves to underscore the ways in which the food of a specific urban milieu makes itself part of a historical narrative. Her childhood world, as she remembers it, is marked by the doubleness and liminality characteristic of such a transformation. It is a world poised between something loosely yet incontestably marked as traditional and maternal—life in the Old City, female confinement, Hindi, deference to males, elaborate female labors in the kitchen—and something more recognizably modern and paternal—travel to England, spacious living quarters outside Old Delhi, linguistic competence in English, and increasing educational and even professional opportunities for daughters. The landscape of her past is, in this recollection, Janus-faced, partitioned between spaces that are divided (yet connected) not just geographically but also temporally. That is to say, by the logic of national temporality that Anne McClintock has mapped out, this is also and always a gendered division.[49] Says Jaffrey,

> My father and mother were both born in the heart of the old city of Delhi, where the streets are so narrow that a man and a cow can barely pass each other. Most of the old town houses there are three or four floors high and are built around an inner courtyard. They have many small rooms, niches for closets, and no view, except for other houses, other courtyards, other floors. On all the floors are balconies, running round the courtyard. When my paternal grandfather had become a successful barrister and returned from his travels abroad, being an adventurous and ambitious man, he decided to move out of the area and bought himself a garden estate on the banks of the Jumna. But my mother's people stayed on in the old city. Every now and then my mother would take us to visit her family. Here I must rather shamefacedly admit that I felt, in those days, that I had very little in common with my old-city cousins (10).

The author's desired trajectory in her youth is that of her masculine forebears. Like her barrister grandfather, she leaves home for England in early adulthood to train as an actress. Once she has overcome the danger that the feminine, food-centered, and service-oriented world of her child-hood and adolescence will circumscribe her life choices, she can allow herself to succumb to its seductions and allow it to claim her partially in her migrancy through the medium of cooking. She notes in *Climbing the Mango Trees* [2005], a memoir of her childhood in India, that she had been taught "every last detail of British invalid cookery circa 1930" as part of a bundle of electives in high school but had had no exposure to cooking Indian food.[50] Her stint as a student in England at the Royal Academy of Dramatic Arts is thus the occasion for a twofold education. She does not say much about the training she acquired at the academy, though its importance as a form of credentialing for the celebrity yet to come is indisputable. Like the culinarily constricted Gandhi in late-Victorian London, Jaffrey seems to have staged questions of citizenship, authenticity, and reproduction through a pedagogy of the palate. Unlike the mahatma, the young student in postwar London finds no proximate mentors: the place of the teacher is filled here by the mother, functioning as long-distance guru. A metonymy of maternal presence reveals itself in the mother's letters, written in Hindi, which the daughter consumes over indigestible meals of bland institutional food: "I decided to learn how to cook, and I wrote to my mother in India for recipes. She would answer with long letters in Hindi which I would take with me to school. As I ate my roast and two vegetables, I would ponder her advice . . . put in a pinch of asafoetida—don't let it burn—now put in the cumin and stir for a second or two . . . add the chopped-up tomatoes and fry . . . my mouth would water and the cabbage would stick to my throat" (*Invitation*, 5). The text urges readers to note on the one hand the reciprocity or mutual substitutability of food and words and on the other the reciprocity of the shedding of tears from homesickness and the watering of the mouth. It is a chain of substitutions that operates powerfully in all of Jaffrey's cook-books and that allows food and words, recipe and recollection to com-mingle without constraint.

Unlike the traditions of French gastronomic writing, which is tra-ditionally orchestrated around the masterpieces of the great male chefs—masterpieces that have, in one classic formulation at least, been des-ignated as international and cerebral cuisine in contradistinction to regionally anchored, feminine household cuisines with no aspirations toward or capacity for a like transcendence of the domestic—Jaffrey's own early work unabashedly highlights the familial kitchen and the ma-ternal figure as sources of inspiration.[51] In fact, in this first work she has little to say that is not caustic about the authenticity and quality of the food produced by Indian restaurants in the United States, insisting that private homes alone can provide Indian food that satisfies both the palate and the taste for the real thing. In such a context, her cookbooks can serve as the agent of transformation, bringing India into U.S. domestic space in a manner impossible to reproduce through the institution of the restaurant. The subsequent Indian cookbooks do feature a very small number of recipes from chefs in India, and Jaffrey has served for a number of years as culinary adviser to the Dawat restaurant in New York, but she has nonetheless continued to insist on the indispensability of the domestic hearth to the experience of delectable and regionally unique Indian cooking. "India hides its real food—and the best of its food—in millions of private homes, rich and poor, scattered across its provinces," she writes in A Taste of India.

Such a rhetoric of acknowledgment of familial and usually feminine expertise is a device not entirely unfamiliar: not a few cookbooks, Indian and non-Indian, conceive of cooking as a primarily feminine, domestic activity and give thanks therefore to female fellow travelers. The privileging, moreover, of the refinement of the domestic over that of sham professionals is attributable in part to the absence of a grand restaurant tradition of long duration in India, owing to prohibitions on interdining among Hindus.[52] The class privilege of Jaffrey's family, however, as indexed by the presence of many servants, several cars, shooting and hunting parties, expensive ingredients, and the organization of domestic space—all of which recall the leisured ease of the diegetic space in the Merchant Ivory films in which she has featured so often—can arguably stand in quite persuasively for the aura that attaches in other gastrocultural contexts, for example, the French one, to the person of the chef. Such privileging also indexes the kind of authenticity that the metropolitan reader, whether of South Asian origin or not, expects from a production that claims Indianness. What authenticates such a product is precisely the long memory of the nonmodern and self-effacing line of female forebears that has nourished and disseminated down a female line a sophisticated culinary lore without the aids of cookbooks, formalized recipes, precise measurements, and modern kitchen equipment.[53]

The first cookbook, written to put to rest "a familiar upsurge of guilt and patriotic responsibility" (3), is nevertheless not quite fully nationalist. It rehearses a fairly familiar story of the gendered entry into modernity, an entry that is also a consolidation of tradition; it does this for an

Anglo-American audience eager, in the aftermath of the countercultural movements and global developments of the sixties, to abandon artificiality and to embrace gastronomic authenticity: "Today Americans especially seem to have a great desire to experience the 'real' thing, an authentic taste, a different life style. Anything fake is deplored, fake foods included" (7). Jaffrey's notation of this desire for "the 'real' thing," cordoned off by quotation marks and rhetorically folded into a desire for racial-cultural difference, nicely captures a certain fetishization of authenticity that is part of a new order of ethical or at least reflexive consumption. Lily Cho furnishes an interesting variation on this quest for culinary and gastronomic authenticity in her description of the Western, non-Chinese consumer's persistent suspicion that what he eats in Chinese restaurants in Canada, sweet and sour pork, for example, is not real Chinese food after all: "We've all heard the urban myth about how Chinese restaurants have one menu for white people and another for Chinese people. What the menu makes manifest is the latent suspicion that all is not self-evident. What is maddening about the menu is that it is at once explicitly readable and equivocally illegible. Along the margins of the menu lies the possibility of conspiracy, of another language, of a second menu."[54] In this fantasy of an Eastern inscrutability that poses as its opposite, what is actually on the menu to be glossed by the white diner is the distastefully familiar: "In thinking that he is eating Chinese, the settler colonialist will actually consume *goo lo yok*, white man meat, a version of himself, will engage in a moment of symbolic self-cannibalism."[55] The autoethnographic turn in *An Invitation to Indian Cooking*, allied with the reenchantment of spices as a sign of undissimulated, attractively exotic Indian cooking, constitutes Jaffrey's endeavor to provide a prophylactic against such autophagy.

. . .

The second Indian cookbook, *Madhur Jaffrey's Indian Cooking* (1983), was tied to a BBC television show and became an unexpected success in Britain.[56] Aimed at a slightly wider audience and situated in a different historical moment for India, Britain, and the United States, this text serves up personal narrative that has become far more overtly bound up with a national one. It provides a shorter, if still evocative, account of a childhood in a multitudinous, pluralistic India that is characterized less by the narrow lanes of Old Delhi and female work in the kitchen that had been evoked by the first book than by an achieved Indian modernity distinguished by female mobility and what appears to be a wary and distinctly uneven ethnic-religious tolerance. One could describe it, in other words, as a volume somewhat more in tune with (though by no means reducible to) the somewhat more anxious and assertive nationalism characteristic of Indian communities both in India and abroad in the aftermath of challenges to the legitimacy of the Indian state in the seventies. It is likewise attuned to the imperatives of a contemporaneous North American multiculturalism, a multiculturalism that appears in tandem with the emergence of a late capitalism well attuned to incorporating global conceptions of difference and diversity. And it is also in its element in a Britain that had become, in the wake of Thatcherite nationalism and the Falklands/Malvinas adventure, again curious about once and future empires, as is evidenced in the profusion of such nostalgic productions as *Heat and Dust* (1982), *Gandhi* (1981), *The Far Pavilions* (1984), *A Passage to India* (1984), *Out of Africa* (1984), and *The Jewel in the Crown* (1984). Perhaps in consequence, it is less informed by a gendered critique of cooking, serving, and eating than the first had been. Jaffrey's introduction to this volume is a veritable discovery of India, as she describes the fortuitous diversity that characterizes her circle of friends in school at Delhi: "It so happened that all my friends were of differing faiths and all came, originally, from different regions of the country. Even though we were all Indian, we had hardly any culinary traditions in common. Eating always filled us with a sense of adventure and discovery as we could not always anticipate what the others might bring."[57] While such a carefully orchestrated multicultural spectrum is not entirely anomalous in the nation's capital, which can arrogate to itself certain idioms of national representativeness, the ensemble of friends is too exquisitely balanced not to serve as excellent fodder for a postindependence Nehruvian mode of unity in diversity. The migrant's memory offers a world governed not so much by oppositions as by reconcilable differences articulated within a system that is loosely congruent with national space. The Indian theater offers, within this totality, an infinite multiplication of possibilities and positions.

That this should be so is no surprise; as Appadurai has convincingly demonstrated, it is, paradoxically, the proliferation of cookbooks on *regional* Indian cuisines in postcolonial India that has helped establish the self-conscious and ethnically partitioned Indianness of Indian cooking. Jaffrey's account of culinary sharing among Delhi Hindus, Uttar Pradesh Muslims, Gujarati Jains, Kashmiri Hindus, and Syrian Christians can be seen to enact rituals of nation making through commensality among unlike subjects. Like the subject of spices it serves as a gastronomic analogue for the nation's dizzying powers of serendipitous amalgamation.[58] Such a trope has as its target of address not just the aforementioned Nehruvian paradigm but also the imperatives of a British and North American multiculturalism, the pluralist politics of which promotes the delineation of (culinary) ethnic enclaves as a prior condition for being at home in America, or Canada or Britain, as the case might be, and which is heavily dependent, like the rhetoric of immigrant assimilation it replaced, upon metaphors of culinary processing and prescription. The trope is a favored one for Jaffrey and is equally deployed in describing the condition of the United States ("Such things [as Golden Sesame Corn Bread] are bound to happen when a woman from India who has lived in Europe marries a man from America whose father comes from Kentucky") and India, though an India that is vectored through Britain ("The whole meal was an amazing blend of East and West that only colonial India could produce!").[59]

A *Taste of India* (1985) is the grandest and most ambitious of Jaffrey's endeavors in gastronomic narrative. Taking as its canvas the entire culinary spectrum of the country, it moves systematically from region to region and occasionally across classes, encompassing nawabs in Hyderabad and Koli fisherwomen from the Konkan, while remaining anchored in the gustatory, historical, and architectural remainders of an imperial Mughal Delhi. More than any of the others, this text conveys the sense of India as a totality, a sense that gives it its distinctly monumental, if not epic, flavor. The production values of this text are exceptionally high, and the prose, as one of her reviewers put it, incantatory. If the first cookbook offered a staging of gendered modernity and the second one of national(ist) emergence, this one is a paean to an epic world impossible of reproduction and marked always by yearning and loss. A nostalgic gastronomy is not a notable thing in itself, as we have already seen. Stephen Mennell describes French and English gastronomic literature's stake in the evocation of such yearning: "A . . . final component of gastronomic literature is the nostalgic evocation of memorable meals. Notable menus, lovingly amplified by discussions of why such and such a dish was so remarkable, are often a staple ingredient of gastronomic writing."[60] But rather than seeking to make good this loss, there is in Jaffrey a continual deferral of gastronomic satisfactions. Especially in A *Taste of India* the multiple introductions, regional and national, are peppered with yarns about meals dizzying in their sumptuousness and complete singularity. A few dishes from these memorable meals might find another life as recipes, but most of them are confined to the limits of the introductory prose. Her description of the "spicy fisherman's banquet" prepared by Savitri the Koli fisherwoman, is, she assures readers, "a seafood extravaganza the likes of which no casual tourist to India is ever likely to see." Yet, despite the implicit promise of revelation embedded in such a locution and despite the extended and loving description of the preparation and consumption of pomfret, prawns, squid, *newta* (mudfish), black-eyed peas, and "some of the most scrumptious rice flour breads I have ever eaten," not a single recipe from the feast is anywhere reproduced.[61] The real thing, it seems, is always also located in an oneiric landscape. It is what one must as a reader ever imagine, never possess; like the Barmecide's feast, it is only through words that it can be taken upon the tongue.[62]

Walter Benjamin has described with profound subtlety the transformations that attend the work of art with the advent of forms of mechanical reproduction like printing, photography, and filmmaking. The withering of the aura of the work of art that mechanical reproducibility guarantees coincides with its detachment from ritual and therefore from cult value. One might say that Jaffrey's own paradoxical investment in questions of singularity and reproduction participates in an auratic economy, notwithstanding the fact that by its very form the cookbook is the product par excellence of an age of mechanical reproduction, one that streamlines procedures, calibrates time and ingredients precisely, universalizes a gastro-etiquette, and reaches a mass audience. Yet Jaffrey is at the same time deeply invested in maintaining a sense of Indian cooking as an autonomous and unique pleasure, radically different from the commodification indexed by cookbooks, restaurants, the one-flavor-fits-all curry powder norm, and by the mild-medium-hot Indian restaurant menu norm in the diaspora. Even as she writes cookbooks and produces cooking shows for television audiences, she seeks to insist on cooking as an instrument of magic in the Benjaminian sense and on her own epicurean experience as unduplicable, as is evident in the instance above. Benjamin's analysis of filmic stardom as a response (a response that is close to the "phony spell" of the commodity) to the vanishing of the aura is pertinent here: "The film responds to the shrivelling of the aura with an artificial build-up of the 'personality' outside the studio."[63] Yet in commodity fetishism something of an auratic quality still attaches, in fact must attach, to the commodity in excess of its utilitarian function for it to have any degree of persuasiveness. Hence the status of, for instance, a Marilyn Monroe, whose glamour derives precisely from her availability for commodification, including its forms of mechanical reproducibility.[64]

. . .

The fact that a narrative like the one Jaffrey advances resonates for a certain class-marked expatriate South Asian subject in the First World as well as for a more mainstream, if upscale and culturally savvy audience of non–South Asian Americans and Britons speaks volumes about the ways in which these constituencies are articulated rather than disjunct and the ways in which both are, though to different degrees and with different varieties of affect, invested in The Wonder That Is India.[65] How is it that Jaffrey's limpid prose and impeccable recipes can signify familiarity and comfort *and* exoticism and adventure as part of the same operation? A significant, if unquantifiable, proportion of the pleasure elicited by the star figure might be attributed, I think, to the specific trajectory of her diasporic voyaging. The evocation of the world of a fading British Raj, the descriptions of the landscapes of a still-compelling Mughal Delhi, her status as sojourner in the imperial center—all of these elements manifestly contribute to the nostalgic appeal of the autoethnographic detail and of the recipe. For the expatriate reader, especially one of upper middle-class identifications or aspirations—graduate students, scholars, "English-medium" professionals, and their ilk—moreover, there is the often self-exoticizing thrill of imagining oneself a secret sharer in this gastronomic cornucopia, though this does not on any account detract from the aura of sacerdotal mysteriousness that attaches to Jaffrey. Nor is this pleasure vitiated by the fact that it is by no means uncommon to be transported by nostalgia for foods that are quite unfamiliar and untasted or for a homeland which one may desire precisely because one wishes never to return to it. Nostalgia is certainly capable of being decoupled from personal memory or personal experience, as scholars as diverse as Fredric Jameson and Appadurai have demonstrated. Consider, for instance, Appadurai's analysis of nostalgia as the product and the motor of late capitalist consumerism: "Such nostalgia, as far as mass merchandising is concerned, does not principally involve the evocation of a sentiment to which consumers who really have lost something can respond. Rather, these forms of mass advertising teach consumers to miss things they have never lost. . . . That is, they create experiences of duration, passage, and loss that rewrite the lived histories of individuals, families, ethnic groups, and classes. . . . Rather than expecting the consumer to supply memories while the merchandiser supplies the lubricant of nostalgia, now the viewer need only bring the faculty of nostalgia to an image that will supply the memory of a loss he or she has never suffered. This relationship might be called armchair nostalgia, nostalgia without lived experience or collective historical memory."[66] Appadurai couples the melancholia induced by such an "ersatz nostalgia" with the profound consumerist satisfactions of a loss that is sought, always and necessarily unsuccessfully, to be made good. Renato Rosaldo has spoken, in a somewhat different context, of the nostalgia that attends the recollections or the remainders of what we have willfully lost—or obliterated.[67]

Indeed some of the force of nostalgia might arise from this very paradox of estrangement from experiences that are conventionally claimed as one's own. Postwar immigration to Britain and the United States is not necessarily driven, Sandhya Shukla notes, by an earlier immigrant logic of complete assimilation or by the dream of return to a lost homeland (in spite of the enthusiastic diasporic staging of events like the Festivals of India) but by more intermediate desires for belonging and distance in several places simultaneously.[68] Verne Dusenbery's work on the support for Khalistan, a Sikh homeland in the Punjab, among the Canadian Sikh diaspora suggests, even more fascinatingly, that the nostalgic evocation of a lost homeland is predicated upon unbridgeable distances: "One of the appeals of Khalistan to diasporan Sikhs may be the creation of a publicly recognized 'country of origin,' from which Sikhs may legitimately make claim to their own political voice and to the perquisites of public support for cultural diversity . . . in their countries of residence. If the local logic of multiculturalism in these pluralist polities requires a distinctive 'source culture' derived from a recognized homeland or country of origin, then Sikhs who believe their religion, culture, and politics to be indivisible will endeavor to supply the territorial basis for their 'separate identity as Sikhs.' "[69] Dusenbery here suggests not only that subjects might belong in more than one "imagined community";[70] he also nudges readers toward the possibility that the "imagined community" of the nation might be realizable only in a deterritorialized space and in a temporality that is perpetually deferred.[71] The modality of the imagined community of the diaspora is like the promise of the *post* in postcoloniality, "not yet" and "not there."[72]

Of Munshis

In a recently published memoir, Jaffrey provides another variant on the serialized personal and autoethnographic narrative and its idioms of authenticity and recovery, one that permits her to bind the hybridizations of the new diaspora with a more overtly archaic, caste-bound sense of destiny and disposition. Here she identifies herself pointedly as a Mathur Kayastha of Delhi, an exemplary figure of composite culture produced by successive Mughal and British empires in the subcontinent. If spices had functioned as a master trope in the earlier texts, caste (as Kayastha) fulfills an analogous function here. While she had identified herself as a Delhi Kayastha in her first cookbook, the detail there had served an attenuated sociological function. Here, the sociology of caste is more fully elaborated, not so much in terms of members' relations to other castes or in terms of ritual pollution or scripturally enjoined practices as in terms of male members' changing relations to educational opportunities and professional advancement in various imperial bureaucracies. The organization of such service families as hers, combined in kin groups and marriage alliances transacted within endogamous subcastes, makes up the meaning of caste for this text. But this caste sociology also functions as the vehicle of a certain ontological truth, serving as a continuing autobiographical trope of flexibility, cosmopolitanism, and intellectual aptitude. Chapters 1 and 2 provide a couple of stories of origin, one in an explicitly legendary register and the other in a recognizably historical one. Not warriors, priests, or traders, but freethinking intellectuals devoted to "reading, writing and making laws," Kayasthas as a caste stand outside caste in not belonging to any of the four major varnas (the original Vedic division of all people into four groups marked by distinctions of occupation and status) originally created from the body of the primordial man Purusha. The Kayastha as a figure wielding pen, ink pot, and sword was, in the legend Jaffrey recounts not altogether ironically, specially created by Brahma to be a scribe and to administer justice.[73] She recalls her paternal history as one that exemplifies the particularity of masculine Kayastha culture: urbane, cosmopolitan, affluent, politically loyal yet pragmatic, linguistically gifted, and religiously tolerant.

The most common caste or occupational designation for such a figure is *munshi*. Muzaffar Alam and Sanjay Subrahmanyam note in their history of the munshi (clerk, scribe, or secretary) that this figure was an important intermediary in the early years for an East India Company struggling to come to terms with a linguistically and culturally unfamiliar colony: "The real interlocutor for the Company official . . . was the *munshi*, who was mediator and spokesman (*vakil*), but also a key personage who could both read and draft materials in Persian, and who had a grasp over the realities of politics that men such as Warren Hastings, Antoine Polier, and Claude Martin found altogether indispensable."[74] Munshis, often Hindu Kayasthas, Khatris, or Brahmins, had emerged as consequential civil service personnel in the Mughal period, learning Persian, which had become the language of administration from the time of the emperor Akbar onward, and becoming connoisseurs of the language and its literature. These Persianized Hindu scribal groups came to play an increasingly influential role in the Mughal empire from the seventeenth century on, serving in departments of accountancy, revenue, and draftsmanship and partaking in the "ecumenical learning and religious pluralism" popularized by the great Abul Fazl, Akbar's *wazir* (chief minister) and the author of the *Ain-i-Akbari*, the official history of the emperor's reign.[75] "The term 'composite culture' has been much used and abused in recent years, but arguably one can find it in the life and education of such a [Persianized Hindu] *munshi*," suggest Alam and Subrahmanyam.[76]

Such pragmatism was combined with a genuine enthusiasm for the glories of Indo-Islamic culture, as Kayastha men cultivated a taste for Persian and Urdu poetry, rare books, and miniature paintings and shared modes of clothing and etiquette with *ashraf* (well-born) Muslim gentlemen of refinement and learning. Such tastes and achievements ensured Jaffrey's ancestor Raghunath Bahadur the post of finance minister to the Mughal emperor Aurangzeb. Others migrated in the eighteenth century, during the decline of the Mughal empire, to the newly independent southern princely state of Hyderabad.[77] When British rule came to Delhi, the ever-adaptable Kayastha males added English to their linguistic repertoire, and another ancestor, Munshi Jivanlal, came to be *Mir Munshi* (chief munshi) at the British Residency, in charge of the pensions paid by the British to the family of the Mughal emperor. A confidential messenger between the last Mughal emperor, Bahadur Shah II, and British officialdom before the tumultuous events of 1857, he kept one of the most detailed and best-known accounts of life in Delhi during the Mutiny, as we have seen.

The proverbial Kayastha adaptability offered substantial rewards and protections. While the destruction of the social basis of traditional elite cultures of Delhi in the aftermath of the Mutiny decisively obliterated the Muslim ashraf—Muslims were expelled from the city for over a year after the British recaptured it in 1857, many had their properties seized, and many others were slaughtered indiscriminately—the Kayasthas, who had formed part of the same service and cultural elite of northern India, suffered far fewer negative consequences.[78] The loyalist Jivanlal was rewarded on the resumption of British rule, being made an honorary magistrate and municipal commissioner.

By turns "half-Muslim" and "half-British," Kayastha males are, for Jaffrey, emblematic figures of intellectual curiosity and adaptability, flourishing in moments of historical transition and uncertainty. She herself records her own childhood and adolescence as a time of momentous historical change and transition, encompassing nationalist resistance against the Raj, the Second World War, independence, Partition, and the assassination of Gandhi. Through all of these changes, the Kayasthas survive and even flourish through a combination of political flexibility, nonsectarian tolerance, and a continuing commitment to education and intellectual life that also facilitates career advancement. "Ink is in our blood," Jaffrey says, explicitly naming herself in *Climbing the Mango Trees* as a writer (and not just a cook). It is in these terms that she claims the genealogical weight of an ancestral and caste identity that allows her, finally, to identify with her illustrious *male* forebears; it is a move that allows her to be a munshi in addition to being a khansamah.[79]

Such a summing up of the life and the career interestingly concatenates what one thinks of as discrepant registers of filiation and affiliation —caste, vocation, and career—into one fairly seamless trajectory. Jaffrey's early choice of the theater as vocation remains only partially fulfilled in Britain and the United States, bringing satisfaction but none of the substantive rewards (regularity, income, status, and promotion, most notably) of the career proper. This is perhaps the not altogether surprising arc of the female career professional, for whom a narrative of lack, accidental success, and amateur effort constitutes a fairly familiar script. As in the case of many British, North American, and Indian women before her, women of intelligence and ambition who failed to find a fit domestically between individual aspiration and social exigency, the East offers a career to which she can more successfully lay claim.[80] The memoir's task is to convert happenstance, occasional failure, feminine indirection, and diasporic distance into a patrimonial inheritance of taste, learning, and worldly success. Caste here provides the anamorphic perspective that permits the meaningful reconstitution of what had seemed earlier to be the ad hoc, even discrepant details of gendered life in the diaspora.

It also helps that to be Kayastha, at least of the masculine persuasion, is to be heir to more than the pleasures of reading and writing. For Jaffrey these intellectual and aesthetic proclivities are intimately wedded, within a caste-marked yet cosmopolitan economy of tastes and pleasures, with the more immediately sensuous pleasures of consumption. Thus the Kayastha child being sent to school for the first time has a letter of the alphabet traced on the tongue with honey, in a promise of the sweets of learning. Even more aptly for her purposes of autoethnography and self-fashioning, Kayastha males were famed not only for their status as men of learning but also for their reputation as voluptuaries of the palate, being known as "*sharabi-kebabis*, lovers of alcohol and kebabs."[81]

Of Good Taste and the Masala Film

Perhaps the self-exoticizing turn that marks the mobilization of a Kayastha destiny should not surprise one unduly, since it is not absent from the reenchantment of spices. Neither is it absent from the glamour or aura of the actress associated with Merchant Ivory films in the "Raj nostalgia" mode.[82] No consideration of Jaffrey's alimentary tracts can be complete without a discussion of the work of a parallel filmic trajectory. While many of the cookbooks, especially *An Invitation to Indian Cooking*, juxtapose quite carefully the production of the cook and the actress, Jaffrey in her interviews insists that her dual careers as actress and as writer of cookbooks do not converge in any substantive way: "My grandkids dream of being chefs, but I had no such dreams. . . . I always say I've been dragged kicking and screaming into the world of food. It just happened to me: I kept making a very bad living as an actress and a very good living as a writer about food."[83] Notwithstanding these asseverations of nonintersecting professional arcs, they cannot but be seen as overlapping. Jaffrey may have received her culinary training in New York from James Beard, but the first public notice she received from Craig Claiborne in the *New York Times* inseparably linked the filmic and the culinary. "Indian Actress Is a Star in the Kitchen, Too," his headline proclaimed, coupling her culinary expertise with the success of *Shakespeare Wallah* (1965), the film for which she was to receive a Silver Bear award for best actress at the Berlin Film Festival of 1965.[84]

A brief consideration of the Merchant Ivory filmic oeuvre, and especially its interest in a certain handsome if middle-brow Orientalist cosmopolitanism, might help elucidate the ways in which one persona abuts upon the other. Films like *Shakespeare Wallah* and *Heat and Dust* (1983) stage the by now well-known encounter of the open-minded, curious, and unconventional white woman in the colony or postcolony with the attractive but childlike and untrustworthy Indian male, an encounter that can end only lamentably for the woman because the barriers of gendered culture are too compelling in a Kiplingesque kind of way to be overcome by her goodwill and catholicity. When the English protagonists, customarily female, seek to overturn the violent narrative of empire through the affective reciprocities of usually heterosexual and occasionally homosexual romance (imagining that the trope of "rape" can be reversed into "interracial love," as Jenny Sharpe puts it in *Allegories of Empire*), they discover the unbearably high costs of miscegenation.[85] In these films Jaffrey plays what appears at first glance to be the characteristic role of the seductive and deadly Indian siren uncannily familiar in her inscrutability. She is a figure who, whether as the fabulously bitchy film star and romantic rival in *Shakespeare Wallah* or as decadent dowager queen in *Heat and Dust*, works to thwart the fruition of cross-cultural erotic attraction. Many of the settings likewise—especially in the case of *Heat and Dust* and in the case of *Autobiography of a Princess* (1975), with its Oedipally obsessed and imperious leading figure—help to establish Jaffrey firmly within the ambit of the distinctly royal, romantic, nonmodern India of the princely states, which are already extremely familiar outside the subcontinent through the marketing of upscale tourist packages.[86] The fact that the films are often narratively critical of the inhabitants of such a universe does little to mitigate the loving fascination the camera nonetheless demonstrates for the allure of its milieu. The pleasures of courtly or elite feasting are rarely distant from the economies of taste and consumption that characterize such settings; indeed, elaborately staged and sometimes incongruous meals were to become something of a trademark of Merchant Ivory Productions.[87] It may not be entirely insignificant that Ismail Merchant is himself a gastronome and a writer of cookbooks.[88] Such images are visually fastened to the characters played by Jaffrey, even when she is ostensibly dissociated from specifically aristocratic contexts; *Shake-*

speare Wallah in particular is keenly attentive to the semiotic pliancy and range of the culinary image.

In *Shakespeare Wallah* the Bombay film star Manjula, the character played by Jaffrey, functions as a debased example of an Indian modernity, characterized as it is by the puerile, loutish pleasures of mass culture, including Bombay cinema and cricket, and by the primacy of publicity and the circulation of the image.[89] Her ascendancy is explicitly juxtaposed against the decline of the Shakespearean troupe in postcolonial India and that of the feudal princes who have the good taste but not the economic or cultural capital to function as patrons of the arts. In the vast, darkened dining hall of his palace a cultivated if very faintly pompous maharajah, an urbane connoisseur of the Bard and the film's first audience of the Buckingham Players, the traveling company of Shakespearean performers, listens to suitably melancholy lines ("Let us sit upon the ground / And tell sad stories of the death of kings") from the third act of *Richard II*. "We are all forced to make cuts in the text written for us by destiny," he says, commenting ruefully on the likeness between the Shakespearean text and his own life in a postmonarchical and postimperial India. In its invocation of such a beleaguered patron and such a setting for the performance of the Buckingham Players, the film is faithful to the sociology of Shakespearean performance in early postcolonial India. The patronage of Shakespeare studies and performance inaugurated in the colonial period continued, albeit in attenuated form, in the postcolonial period, and traveling companies such as Geoffrey Kendal's Shakespeareana (upon which the Buckingham Players are clearly based) performed by invitation to audiences of royalty, schoolchildren, college students, and the urban middle classes through the fifties and sixties.[90] These invitations came in large part from the erstwhile princely states of Hyderabad, Gwalior, Patiala, Travancore, and Cochin, the domain of maharajahs with no role but an atavistic one in the postcolonial era.[91] It is one of the film's many ironies, whether witting or unwitting, that the actor playing the maharajah is the brilliant Bengali Marxist actor, director, theater historian, and playwright Utpal Dutt, who began his theatrical training with Shakepeareana but who turned in the fifties to theatrical performances, including Bengali *jatra* (folk theater) adaptations of *Macbeth*, for rural Bengali audiences as part of a self-consciously radical and formally daring theater.[92]

This is not to assert that the film always counterposes an aristocratic and high cultural order against the coarse commercializations of mass culture. Early in the film, the troupe of marooned actors runs into a down-at-heel street entertainer with a pair of performing monkeys, and the most venerable of the British actors explicitly likens their situation to his. And the aristocrats themselves are not all of the same ilk. The charming and faithless young playboy Sanju, who is lover to both Manjula and Lizzie, is, after all, the scion of a feudal aristocracy to which the maharajah also belongs. Despite his professed bardolatry and avowed contempt for the Bombay film industry, his attachment to Shakespeare is inconstant and shallow, while his associations with cricket and with Hindi cinema are quite substantial, even if ambivalent. Manjula herself is conceived in terms that are inseparable from often Orientalist codes of sexual ethics, gendered performance, and class hierarchy; a public and feminized form of Indian modernity is curiously continuous with the traditional forms, as represented, for instance, in Jaffrey's performance as the dowager queen in *Heat and Dust*. The film takes considerable trouble to demarcate the distinctions between the simple and unglamorous but gifted and emancipated Lizzie and her calculating, seductively reactionary Indian counterpart. In one notable scene Manjula condescends to attend a performance of *Othello* by the Buckingham Players but appears during a climactic sequence in the final act and immediately proceeds to draw the attention of the audience away from the stage and toward herself. Given the quasi-Orientalist logic that governs much of the film, it is no contradiction, therefore, to assert that Manjula is simultaneously a representative of Indian modernity in its worst aspects and of Indian tradition, also in its worst aspects and scarcely distinguishable from the former.

From the perspective of hindsight's wry omniscience we can note, with pleasure, that Manjula as a character is acutely conscious of food as a system of gendered meanings and categories, and in practically every scene in which she appears, she deploys food in gendered conflicts and maneuvers.[93] A striking sequence in the film, one of several, signals the kind of charge food preparation, hospitality, and commensality can carry. A bewildered Lizzie Buckingham is virtually kidnapped and forced into a tea-drinking ritual with the redoubtable Manjula, who plays the Oriental *femme fatale* to perfection, dispensing sugar and erotic threats with equal panache. The tea ceremony here indexes multiple and articulated global histories, histories which Sidney Mintz and Piya Chatterjee have detailed. Mintz has tied the increasingly prominent place of sugar in the English diet to England's specifically slave-trading and colonial ascension and to the affiliated regimes of industrial production at home.[94] And in her account of the complicated metropolitan allure of tea Chatterjee notes that it becomes a medium through which the chronicles of global expansion and conquest can be told. Yet, layered into these more visible political economies of European expansion are tales of imagination and desire which fuelled the burgeoning demand for tea, and sparked its journey into the grandest parlours of Europe. From the late sixteenth century, tea's allure for European palates emerged from its consummate connection to the riches of the celestial kingdom itself: the secret and shadow-Empire of the great "Orient" which would keep at bay European trade incursions for over two centuries. Curtailed supply would make the commodity more dear, and indeed, more desirable. Tea thus signified the imagined Orient: exotic, scarce, and magical in its connection to such secret and vast territories.[95]

These multifarious valences are carefully elaborated in this scene, identified as "tea with a tiger" in the DVD of the film. The tea ceremony stage managed by Manjula is marked not simply by the aesthetics of leisure that its protocols came to denote in the narrative of an upper-class Victorian femininity but also by a theatrically corrupt elegance that is unmistakably tied to the image of the zenana. Beginning with the camera's pan from left to right across a set of elaborately carved *jaalis* (latticed wooden screens), an architectural signifier of gendered concealment and voyeurism, before coming to rest on Manjula and Lizzie, the scene deploys all the tropes of the zenana: its conspiring and deadly women, its establishment of mute female slaves, its diaphanous sartorial style, and opulent domestic interiors. It is little wonder that Lizzie overturns the proffered cup of tea.[96] Commensality is here metaphorized as the occasion of corporeal, including erotic, violation in a moment that nicely braids together British colonial fears of bodily proximity to natives and indigenous fears of caste pollution (see chapter 1 on the Mutiny's narratives of purity and pollution). The fluid in the cup is the locus of a profoundly libidinal cross-racial traffic: to drink is invariably to gesture toward other, more dangerous interminglings and infusions.

The transactional logic of giving, receiving, and refusing food in this scene is, as we have seen, inseparable from often Orientalist formulations of sexual–racial rivalry, intimacy, and hierarchy. And yet it is impossible not to note as well the sardonic, indeed campy, aura with which Jaffrey's characters are often imbued. Merchant's early fascination with the Bombay cinema cult of stardom and his proximity to some of its leading players, especially the actress Nimmi, manifest themselves in this film as in some of the other feature films and documentaries made by Merchant

Ivory Productions, most notably *Bombay Talkie* (1970) and *Helen: Queen of the Nautch Girls* (1973). John Pym is right to note that the films' response to the Bombay film industry is not so much disdain as "half-spellbound, half-aghast curiosity."[97] These shifting modes of affective and aesthetic response are certainly on view in *Shakespeare Wallah* as well. Manjula is capable occasionally of deploying the conventions of Bollywood melodramatic dialogue to considerable self-mocking effect, just as she is capable of deploying her star power ruthlessly in other contexts. In one of her early scenes, a scene of conventionally played romantic separation and anguish, a staple of Bollywood cinema—Sanju has lingered at the theater, missed dinner, and come home late to a hungry, aggrieved Manjula—is followed by a parodic enactment by the two lovers of the conventions of romantic love on the Indian screen. Thus the very fact of her role in the satirization of the Hindi *masala* film—she plays the role of the highly commodified actress thoroughly inserted into the narratives of a vulgar, extravagant melodrama that is worlds apart from the restraint and the affective depth of the Shakespearean stage—bears a complex and layered relationship, rather than an invariably predictable one, to the idioms of food and theatricality that constitute the grammar of the Merchant Ivory film. That the role of Sanju is played by Shashi Kapoor, himself an actor in the Bombay film industry and the scion of one of the most distinguished film families in the industry, only underlines the self-mocking character of this scene.

Rosie Thomas provides a useful capsule summary of the ingredients of the masala film: "A form has evolved in which narrative is comparatively loose and fragmented, realism irrelevant, psychological characterization disregarded, elaborate dialogues prized, music essential, and both the emotional involvement of the audience and the pleasures of sheer spectacle privileged throughout the three-hour duration of the entertainment. Crucially, it involves the skillful blending of various modes— song and dance, fights, comedy, melodrama, romance, and more—into an integrated whole that moves its audience."[98] The term *masala* (spice; mixture of spices) itself refers, however, not simply to this tried and tested repertoire (as in *curry powder*, perhaps?) of filmic ingredients, but in filmic as in nonfilmic contexts in South Asia also indexes a modality of embellishment and raillery. To the culturally alert reader, the term yokes in a taut conjuncture the idioms of culinary commercialization and of filmic hyperbole; it looks forward prophetically to the persona of the mistress of spices even as it showcases a debased yet droll popular

Indian sensibility. Reading this film retrospectively, in the context of the cookbooks' success, is to give a proleptic cast to Manjula's sardonic performance of stardom; it is to anticipate the jaunty perspicacity of the khansamah.

Curry in a Hurry

In the concluding chapter of *Meatless Days*, Suleri presents a series of ironic meditations on writing, revelation, and closure: "Last year, when I decided to sit down and write a series of short tales, I imagined those tales would wend their way into a final story, to be titled 'The Last Cigarette.' Renouncing vice seemed like a suitable accoutrement of finality, a gesture of purity perhaps, making me anticipate the triumph with which I could write, 'I have smoked my final cigarette.' Apparently, I hadn't" (180). The cigarette comes instead to mark dailiness and evanescence, concretizing as it does her mother's rituals of reclusive proximity and the author's own experience of the detachments, the "intense perfunctoriness," of acting: "The theater knew full well the joy of taking something into the body that can within a second be removed, smoke behaving then like someone else's lines" (180). Instead of the finality of bodily virtue and purposeful consummation, she discovers, as in the parable of the kapura, the deferral and vexation of beginnings and endings. What she uncovers in the place of the terminus are erasures, iterations, and remnants. Writing, nominally the vehicle of purposiveness and meaning, is both palimpsestic and fugitive; thus the daily inscriptions and washings away of Urdu script on *takhts* (boards) are both sensually palpable and as ephemeral as cigarettes. Writing "disappears" (184), she asserts, in books unwritten and unread, such as her father's unwritten memoirs (with a title—*Boys Will Be Boys*—that teases as much as an untold Sherlock Holmes tale does), and in her friend Dale's book on breastfeeding.[99] Her mother's failure to write a book enhances the poignancy of her passing, though Suleri can, in a bow to "the sentimental honor of the east" (184), transform such an absence into a reconstellation of her own status as one of her mother's compositions. Writing disappoints any desire for the undisguised revelation; but this disappointment is itself a gift, forcing an attentiveness to the stealthy and ironic exertions of metaphor.

"The Last Cigarette" turns out to be a parable about the banality and unfulfilled promises that ensure the failure of the life to assume parabolic closure. It seems an apposite consummation as well to a chapter on

Jaffrey to end, however provisionally, with one of her late-career Indian works, *Quick & Easy Indian Cooking* (1996), which constitutes something of a departure from her narrative and culinary norms, denuded as it is of the account of the extended natal family and having only the briefest of acknowledgments to take the place of personal narrative or autoethnography and hardly any narrative gloss on the recipes. It is not surprising therefore to note its reliance upon new kinds of shortcuts, including, perhaps most significantly, the use of curry powder. "In the interests of speed," says Jaffrey matter-of-factly, "I have turned to a rather good brand of curry powder, Bolst's."[100] In its narrative spareness the work perhaps comes closest to the curry powder recommended here or to the bottled sauces Jaffrey has created and promoted. This fact alone enacts a certain distance from the monumentality of the feasts that have marked texts like *A Taste of India*. Like Suleri's last cigarette, it gestures toward a world of evanescence, quick fixes, habit, and quotidian practices, a world in which cooking, like meaning, is done in order to be undone every day.

Quick & Easy Indian Cooking, though, is hardly a reversal of a gastronomic career erected on the scaffolding of authenticity, specificity, and labor-intensive processes. As I have suggested throughout, curry powder always has been the secret sharer of the narrative of subcontinental culinary authenticity, always unsettling its favored trope, spices. Patrons of subcontinental restaurants in the West are well aware that a large number of cheaper Indian restaurants rely on the "one-curry sauce" for their operations[101]—or indeed that this is an image that up-market restaurants have sought quite ostentatiously to shun. But a merely censorious reading of curry powder's staying power, or a derisive gloss on Jaffrey's turn to it, is, as we have seen, always inadequate to the task of understanding its tropological complexities and the parables it has managed to generate, including those of its own origins. The career of Madhur Jaffrey and of her fabulous khansamah proves that despite manifold repressions and disavowals, curry powder repeatedly returns to the scene of Indian cooking, even if it is in the partially comic and partially guilty guise of Curry in a Hurry.

Remains ┊ A CODA

Flavor of my infancy, my mother, still be food: I want
my hunger as it always was, neither flesh nor fowl!
—*Meatless Days*, 160

From its title on, *Meatless Days* elaborates a phenomenology of postcolonial encounter and relationship through cooking and eating. Inescapably enmeshed in violence, eating in some instances takes the familiar (and familiarly gendered) form of predation. Thus Suleri's father, a devotee of the idea of Pakistani nationhood and a chronicler of official discourse, is a "consumer of context," whose "eating . . . up alive" of inconvenient historical and personal details in the service of his patriotic and journalistic work situates him firmly, if sometimes absurdly, within a cannibal economy of victimization. "[No] audience that came his way departed without feeling slightly stripped," says Suleri, the daughter, of his acts of simultaneous incorporation and purgation.

If the father's cannibalism partakes of a customary metaphoric logic, much else in Suleri's text is devoted to the question of what it might mean to think cannibalism both literally and metaphorically. There is an extraordinary literalism to the way in which food functions in the novel—the *kapura* parable of the preceding chapter is a vivid instance of this—and the obstinacy with which it refuses to sequester itself in a purely metaphoric or allegorical realm or to subordinate itself to a world of abstractions. Thus the kapura (or the pancreas, or the kidney, or the mother's breast) is both word and flesh, to be spoken as well as eaten. We all begin, Suleri says, as cannibals, feeding upon our mothers' bodies inside and outside the womb. As ur-food, mother's milk does not admit of substitutions or indeed of any kind of comparison, being "neither flesh nor fowl." Thus the "slippage . . . from nipple to bottle" as we are wrenched from our primordial source of food and made over to "the shoddy metaphors of Ostermilk and Babyflo" is the first shock of the alimentary tract, as grievous as it is inevitable (23). Maternal nourishment can also take less sentimental forms. When the mother seeks to school her children in habits of detachment and nonpossession rather than mawkish clinging, her gift—"Take disappointment, child, eat disappointment from me"— can be a difficult one to accept.

This figuration of the mother as source and purveyor of food provides something of a template for the text's explorations of love, dependence, vulnerability, conflict, and transubstantiation. Eating can be a dangerous business, as can the simple fact of inhabiting a body, especially in a book in which it is profoundly difficult to distinguish the flesh of the body from meat that is dressed for the table. A kitchen accident nearly castrates her younger brother Irfan, turning his genitals into something akin to a consumable, "a blanched and fiery grape" (11). Even more spectacularly, on Eid, the feast of the Abrahamic sacrifice, the continguity between the ritual killing of sons and the ritual killing of goats is underlined with a literalism that insists we pay attention to the sacrificial character of eating, which involves consuming the remains of living beings: "[On] the appointed day, the animals are chopped, in place of sons, and neighbors graciously exchange silver trays heaped with raw and quivering meat" (4). Elsewhere, less violently perhaps but still pointedly, readers are invited to contemplate a gustatory landscape of brain-shaped cauliflower and kidneys that are an inescapable reminder of their bodily function and of their status as (animal, human) remains even as they appear in the innocuous company of lentils on the table.

This traffic in food and body parts also has a tender side. The profoundest form of love, that between mothers and children and between sisters, is troped as cannibalism. Thus, Suleri's sister Ifat becomes milk on the festival of Shab-e-miraj, her other sister Tillat's breasts produce chocolate milk that leaves her children unable to consume any other food, and Ifat swallows her babies in order to expel them after a nine-month interval. In the novel's most spectacular account of cannibalistic affection, the dreaming Sara, a mourner turned body snatcher, tucks away a piece of her mother's corpse under her tongue as an act of poignant and violent daughterly faithfulness:

A blue van drove up: I noticed it was a refrigerated car and my father was inside it. He came to tell me that we must put my mother in her coffin, and he opened the blue hatch of the van to reach inside, where it was very cold. What I found were hunks of meat wrapped in cellophane, and each of them felt like Mamma, in some odd way. It was my task to carry those flanks across the street and to fit them into the coffin at the other side of the road, like pieces in a jigsaw puzzle. Although my dream will not let me recall how many trips I made, I know my hands felt cold. Then, when my father's back was turned, I found myself engaged in rapid theft—for the sake of Ifat and Shahid and Tillat and all of us, I stole away a portion of the body. It was a piece of her foot I found, a small bone like a knuckle, which I quickly hid inside my mouth, under my tongue. Then I and the dream dissolved, into an extremity of tenderness (44).

If eating is rarely separable from death in Suleri's work, the relationship is not necessarily an unpleasant or even an ambivalent one. In this instance, the eating of the maternal remains is the best form of memorialization, making the child once again flesh of her mother's flesh.

Meatless Days is a matchless example of the text that illustrates the potential and the challenges of thinking colonialism and postcoloniality through and with alimentation. Wonderfully attentive to the particular, the eccentric, and the contingent, it enables at the same time—and precisely through such attentiveness—an engagement with the larger questions of violence, desire, and transformation; it provides an exemplary instance of the coalescence of the small detail and the philosophically expansive. Suleri's sense of the ways in which cooking, eating, shunning, and thinking about food constitute a complex grammar not only of everyday gendered and raced postcolonial life but of subjectivity itself instantiates powerfully the lessons of my own text. Eating, and not eating, as the preceding chapters have shown, are powerfully implicated in the politics of empire and decolonization. But they are not, or not only, the by-products of these processes of historical and epistemic overhaul: they are also fundamentally constitutive of it, at the level of ideas, practices, figures, debates, and conflicts. If diet and digestion furnish a narrative arc for the subject's emergence, they can also serve (as in the case of the kapura fable) to satirize or at least to perplex any notion of heroic consolidation or genealogical continuities. A text such as Suleri's (or, for that matter, any others of the texts discussed here) also stages the subject's incapacity to master the food she eats; thus she may be called upon to chasten her palate through a punitive consumption of kidney, or she might have to take gravel upon the tongue in absorbing her mother's pedagogy of disappointment. The alimentary occasion may even underline her own susceptibility to becoming food. Eating is thus more than an exercise in self-augmentation or self-possession; it can be an experience of vulnerability, uncertainty, and dependence, in ways that are not always incongruous with the experience of not eating. As such, the body in alimentation stages the fraught relationship between an inside and an outside whose boundaries are not always known or fixed, and between subject and object status.

Above all, alimentation involves us in relationship with others, whether human, animal, or otherworldly. In conditions of alimentary (and other) inequality, these are often relationships of individual or structural rapaciousness; it matters little whether they are willed or not. But if the experience of feeding with and upon others is constitutively violent, the ethical entailments of this violence can also be less than clear-cut. Suleri's tale of the slaughtered goat is not so much a plea to renounce meat eating—she is decidedly ironic about her father's insistence on a "civilized" posture that accepts carnivory but not the gross visibility of slaughter—as it is to confront rather than evade the ineluctable violence entailed in all eating and perhaps in all kinship. It is this double insistence on the entailments of sensuous life, which cannot be rendered into abstraction without some loss, and the complexities of the ethical lessons that might be drawn from it that makes this anecdote an emblematic moment in *Meatless Days*. As a parable of the vexed politics of embodied relationship in general and of the alimentary nexus in particular, it is also an apt coda to *Alimentary Tracts*.

Notes

Introduction

1. Jack Goody, "Industrial Foods: Towards the Development of a World Cuisine."

2. E. M. Forster, *A Passage to India*, 48–49. I use the term *Anglo-Indian* as it was commonly used in the nineteenth century and early twentieth, to refer to those of British origin who were domiciled in the subcontinent for the duration of their service or employment there (and sometimes beyond it).

3. Sanjay Subrahmanyam has suggested, however, that notwithstanding the rush to find sea routes to the east, Vasco da Gama's voyage of 1498 was less conclusive in establishing the conduit of the spice trade than has been commonly thought (Keynote lecture, 22nd Annual South Asia Conference, UC Berkeley, 16 February 2007). For a learned and engaging account of Vasco da Gama's career, see his *The Career and Legend of Vasco da Gama*. Rushdie is mobilizing a more conventional as well as a more obviously counterfactual historiography here, one that permits a certain plotting of linked world historical events.

4. Wolfgang Schivelbusch, *Tastes of Paradise: A Social History of Spices, Stimulants, and Intoxicants*, trans. David Jacobson, 13.

5. Om Prakash, "Restrictive Trading Regimes: VOC and the Asian Spice Trade in the Seventeenth Century."

6. For a short history of the British East India Company, see Philip Lawson, *The East India Company: A History*.

7. Timothy Morton, *The Poetics of Spice: Romantic Consumerism and the Exotic*, 10.

8. James L. Hevia, "Opium, Empire, and Modern History," 311.

9. Sidney W. Mintz, *Sweetness and Power: The Place of Sugar in Modern History* and "Time, Sugar, and Sweetness."

10. Hevia, "Opium, Empire, and Modern History," 313.

11. Ibid., 311.

12. For Marx, capital is "dead labour which, vampire-like, lives only by sucking living labour, and lives the more, the more labour it sucks" (*Capital: A Critique of Political Economy*, 3 vols., trans. Ben Fowkes, 1:342).

13. Avital Ronell, *Crack Wars: Literature Addiction Mania*. On the difficulty of disentangling addiction from desire, see David L. Clark, "Heidegger's Craving: Being-on-Schelling."

14. For the boycott in Britain on Caribbean sugar, see Charlotte Sussman, "Women and the Politics of Sugar, 1792"; and Timothy Morton, "Blood Sugar."

15. Piya Chatterjee, *A Time for Tea: Women and Postcolonial Labor on an Indian Plantation*. Also see Roy Moxham, *Tea: Addiction, Exploitation, and Empire*.

16. Gayatri Chakravorty Spivak, "Three Women's Texts and a Critique of Imperialism," 244, 248. Mark Sanders has noted Spivak's indebtedness to Keats for this language of pedagogic instruction and imaginative transformation. See *Gayatri Chakravorty Spivak: Live Theory*, 22.

17. David Arnold, *Colonizing the Body: State Medicine and Epidemic Disease in Nineteenth-Century India*.

18. The bhadralok (literally, respectable people) is a term used to denote the administrative, professional, and landed middle classes, of largely upper-caste Hindu origin, of nineteenth-century Bengal. They were associated with Western-style education, employment with the colonial government, and a high degree of self-consciousness, sometimes bordering on abjection, about their association with the changes inaugurated by colonialism. See Tithi Bhattacharya, *Sentinels of Culture: Class, Education, and the Colonial Intellectual in Bengal, 1848–85*.

19. Tapan Raychaudhuri, *Europe Reconsidered: Perceptions of the West in Nineteenth-Century Bengal*, 27.

20. On this, see Sudipta Kaviraj, *The Unhappy Consciousness: Bankimchandra Chattopadhyay and the Formation of Nationalist Discourse in India*; Indira Chowdhury, *The Frail Hero and Virile History: Gender and the Politics of Culture in Colonial Bengal*; John Rosselli, "The Self-Image of Effeteness: Physical Education and Nationalism in Nineteenth-Century Bengal"; and Milind Wakankar, "Body, Crowd, Identity: Genealogy of a Hindu Nationalist Ascetics."

21. On the politics of dress and diet in the biography of Anandibai Joshi, see Sandhya Shetty, "Dying to Be a Doctor."

22. Of course such asceticism is a mark of principle *and* privilege in ways that are not easy to disentangle. The instances cited here are a powerful reminder of the extraordinarily large numbers of people who lie at least partly outside the orbit of such moral economies. To some of them, becoming the subject of such a renunciation of consumption can be counterintuitive in light of their experience of dearth. To others, free of the dietary proscriptions of caste Hindus, the denunciation of beef and alcohol is fully consonant with the aversive logic of caste Hindu politics.

23. Claude Lévi-Strauss, "The Culinary Triangle."

24. Edmund Leach, *Claude Lévi-Strauss*.

25. Diana Fuss, "Fashion and the Homospectatorial Look," 730.

26. Christopher Craft, " 'Kiss Me with those Red Lips': Gender and Inversion in Bram Stoker's *Dracula*," 109.

27. Jacques Derrida, "Economimesis," trans. Richard Klein, 20.

28. Descriptions of anthropophagy are also found in the texts of the classical world. These were mobilized assiduously by travelers to the Americas and other far-off places, as Claude Rawson remarks ("Unspeakable Rites: Cultural Reticence and the Cannibal Question"). On the serviceability of the cannibal trope from 1492 onward, see Francis Barker et al., eds., *Cannibalism and the Colonial World*. There are exceptions to this figuration of anthropophagy in an economy of repugnance, Michel de Montaigne's essay on cannibals being the best known instance.

29. Geoffrey Sanborn, *The Sign of the Cannibal: Melville and the Making of a Postcolonial Reader*, 24, 26. This horror was the more necessary to avow in light of the belief in the early nineteenth century that once tasted, human flesh was an addictive rather than a revolting substance (27).

30. Ibid., 41. Peter J. Kitson notes that "[unlike] the ritual variety, survival or famine cannibalism, sometimes referred to as 'white cannibalism,' appears to need no explanation other than of necessity" (" 'The Eucharist of Hell'; or, Eating People Is Right: Romantic Representations of Cannibalism").

31. Denise Gigante, *Taste: A Literary History*, 118–24. Tales of Irish cannibalism were not uncommon in the seventeenth century, as Rawson confirms (*God, Gulliver, and Genocide: Barbarism and the European Imagination, 1492–1945*).

32. Edmund Burke, *Reflections on the Revolution in France*. Gigante notes that the cannibalism of the French revolution had for Burke a literal character and not just a figural one (*Taste*, 63).

33. Alan Bewell, *Romanticism and Colonial Disease*, 143.

34. For an analysis of this phenomenon in contemporary cultural criticism, see Richard C. King, "The (Mis)uses of Cannibalism in Contemporary Cultural Critique."

35. Sigmund Freud, *Totem and Taboo*, trans. James Strachey.

36. Catherine Gallagher, "The Potato in the Materialist Imagination." Gallagher notes that part of the revulsion aroused by the potato among English workers had to do with its advocacy as a miracle food by a number of political economists, including Arthur Young. Also see E. P. Thompson, "The Moral Economy of the English Crowd in the Eighteenth Century." It bears noting though that measure and quality were regulated for bread in a way that may have been unique in the history of British food regulation; to give up bread therefore was not to give up a food like any other but one undergirded by symbolic and legal protections.

37. Nupur Chaudhuri, "Memsahibs and Motherhood in Nineteenth-Century

Colonial India," 528. Writers from Jean-Jacques Rousseau and Mary Wollstone-craft on had extolled the virtues of breastfeeding, but the practice had not been uniformly adopted by bourgeois women in nineteenth-century Britain.

38. Sara Suleri, *The Rhetoric of English India*, 80. Such ambivalence was not unique to the colony—bourgeois mothers in Britain felt similar anxieties about the potential for contagion in the rented or commodified breast of the lowborn wet nurse—but was felt with particular acuteness there. Katie Trumpener notes "the crucial, if paradoxical, continuities between British nationalist and imperialist fiction, the ways in which the cultural anxieties accompanying the internal coloniza-tion of Britain (particularly the subjugation of Ireland) are both displaced and reformulated once the area of imperial conquest becomes the overseas empire" (*Bardic Nationalism: The Romantic Novel and the British Empire*, 216).

39. High mortality rates for wet nurses' infants occurred in Britain as well. See Valerie Fildes, *Wet Nursing: A History from Antiquity to the Present*, 190–204, cited by Gail Turley Houston, "Broadsides at the Board: Collations of *Pickwick Papers* and *Oliver Twist*," 753.

40. Flora Annie Steel and Grace Gardiner, *The Complete Indian Housekeeper and Cook*, 179.

41. Ann Laura Stoler, "Domestic Subversions and Children's Sexuality."

42. Rudyard Kipling, "Baa Baa Black Sheep."

43. See, for instance, Philip Mason, *The Men Who Ruled India*.

44. Hindu South Asia has long enjoyed a favored place in anthropologies and histories of diet and its ensembles of permissions and prohibitions. For instance, the codes of food preparation and commensality in Brahminical Hinduism receive some attention, along with the dietary practices of Orthodox Jewish communities, in Mary Douglas's classic work *Purity and Danger: An Analysis of the Conception of Pollution and Taboo*, on pollution and taboo as well as in Julia Kristeva's *Powers of Horror: An Essay on Abjection*, trans. Leon S. Roudiez.

45. Arjun Appadurai, "Is Homo Hierarchicus?" 745.

46. Appadurai, "Putting Hierarchy in Its Place," 41; Ronald Inden, chap. 2, *Imagining India*; Gloria Goodwin Raheja, "India: Caste, Kingship, and Dominance Reconsidered"; and Nicholas Dirks, *The Hollow Crown: Ethnohistory of an Indian Kingdom* and *Castes of Mind: Colonialism and the Making of Modern India*.

47. Wendy Doniger notes that while Hindus had a great deal of regard for the *Manusmriti*, which came to be deployed in the colonial period as the source of Hindu law, they did not necessarily see it as a text allowing for direct application, especially in courts of law, nor did they consider it the only authoritative source of rules of right conduct. Hence when British administrators tried to make the basis of a system of jurisprudence they had a difficult time of it and had to resort to the numerous commentaries that had been produced about it. See Doniger, "Why Should a Priest Tell You Whom to Marry? A Deconstruction of the Laws of Manu."

48. Cited in Raheja, "India: Caste, Kingship, and Dominance Reconsidered," 499.

49. Milind Wakankar, "The Anomaly of Kabir: Caste and Canonicity in Indian Modernity," 103 n. 9.

50. Raheja, "India: Caste, Kingship, and Dominance Reconsidered," 501–2.

51. See, for example, Rosalind O'Hanlon, *Caste, Conflict and Ideology: Mahatma Jotirao Phule and Low Caste Protest in Nineteenth-Century Western India* and "Issues of Widowhood: Gender and Resistance in Colonial Western India"; M. S. S. Pandian, *Brahmin and Non-Brahmin: Genealogies of the Tamil Political Present*; Anupama Rao, ed., *Gender and Caste*; V. Geetha and S. V. Rajadurai, *Towards a Non-Brahmin Millennium: From Iyothee Thass to Periyar*; Gopal Guru, *Dalit Cultural Movement and Dialectics of Dalit Politics in Maharashtra*; Eleanor Zelliot, *From Untouchable to Dalit: Essays on the Ambedkar Movement*; and Vasant Moon, ed. *Dr. Baba Saheb Ambedkar: Writings and Speeches*, 18 vols.

52. Raheja, "India: Caste, Kingship, and Dominance Reconsidered," 519.

53. McKim Marriott, "Hindu Transactions: Diversity Without Dualism," 111.

54. Appadurai, "Putting Hierarchy in Its Place," 36–40.

55. Louis Dumont, *Homo Hierarchicus: The Caste System and Its Implications*, trans. George Sainsbury et al.

56. See Lucy Carroll, "Law, Custom, and Statutory Social Reform: The Hindu Widows' Remarriage Act of 1856."

57. Anupama Rao, "Introduction," *Gender and Caste*, 17.

58. It is true that Hurree Babu can read caste too; but his reading is, as far as one can tell, a result of Lurgan's training rather than the untutored canniness seen in Kim.

59. See, for instance, Michael Edwardes, *Bound to Exile: The Victorians and India*.

60. See David Arnold, "Hunger in the Garden of Plenty: The Bengal Famine of 1770." Arnold notes that the sufferings of the famine-stricken in 1770 helped produce a colonial vision that blamed the victims as passive and fatalistic.

61. Amartya Sen has characterized famines as "highly divisive phenomena. . . . It is rare [in the twentieth century] to find a famine that affected more than 5 or 10 per cent of the population. There are, to be sure, alleged accounts of famines in which nearly everyone in a country had to go hungry. But most of these anecdotes do not bear much scrutiny" (*Development as Freedom*, 168). For a caustic analysis of the profitability of famines and their sometimes deliberate causation or prolongation, see Amrita Rangasami, " 'Failure of Exchange Entitlements' Theory of Famine: A Response," and David Keen, *The Benefits of Famine: A Political Economy of Famine and Relief in Southwestern Sudan, 1983–1989*. Sen has insisted that scholars avoid focusing, in their analysis of famine, on negative freedoms as an explanatory horizon for its causation. Thus, to ask if starving Bengali peasants were legally barred from buying rice or from moving to cities for employment is to

misunderstand the cause and course of famine. His emphasis rather is on positive freedoms, what he calls "capabilities." In "Equality of What?" he insists that crisis conditions like famine can be crucial for elaborating a robust conception of rights as something provided and guaranteed rather than simply as something that cannot be taken away. In the absence of a welfare economics that actively develops human capabilities and well-being, the capabilities that will make for a meaningful rather than a nominal exercise of freedom, events such as famines will end up reproducing if not exacerbating forms of inequality and injustice ("Equality of What?").

62. The succinct phrasing is Rajeswari Sunder Rajan's. See *The Scandal of the State: Women, Law, and Citizenship in Postcolonial India*, 7.

63. Partha Chatterjee, "Introduction: A Political History of Independent India," 21.

64. Niraja Gopal Jayal, "The Gentle Leviathan: Welfare and the Indian State," 21.

65. Partha Chatterjee, *The Politics of the Governed: Reflections on Popular Politics in Most of the World*, 136. Chatterjee ignores the unevenness in rights of citizenship in the West in order to highlight the "postcolonial difference" in thinking the contours of non-Western democratic governance. Nonetheless, his formulation of the category of "population" or "political society" in India remains an important one, not least for the light it sheds on the ways in which claims can be made and met, albeit to a limited degree, outside the structures of legitimacy and rights.

66. Ranajit Guha, *Dominance without Hegemony: History and Power in Colonial India*.

67. On the ab-human, see Kelly Hurley, *The Gothic Body: Sexuality, Materialism, and Degeneration at the Fin-de-Siècle*.

68. Christopher Herbert draws attention to the discrepancy between the low mortality figures (on the Anglo-Indian and British side) and the "epochal importance" granted it by contemporaries in Britain and Anglo-India (*War of No Pity: The Indian Mutiny and Victorian Trauma*, 1–3).

69. For a history of the Naxalite movement, begun in Naxalbari in 1967 and still extant as an ideology and as a guerrilla movement in India and Nepal, see Sumanta Banerjee, *India's Simmering Revolution: The Naxalite Uprising*.

70. James Laidlaw, *Riches and Renunciation: Religion, Economy, and Society among the Jains*.

1. Disgust

1. E. P. Thompson, "The Moral Economy of the English Crowd in the Eighteenth Century."

2. Homi K. Bhabha, "By Bread Alone: Signs of Violence in the Mid-Nineteenth Century," 202.

3. Ron Inden, *Imagining India*.

4. See, for instance, R. C. Majumdar, *The Sepoy Mutiny and the Revolt of 1857*, and S. N. Sen, *Eighteen Fifty-Seven*. In fairness to Kaye and to many other nineteenth-century British commentators on the Mutiny, it must be said that the greased cartridge affair had a symptomatic rather than a causative cast for them.

5. Ranajit Guha, *Elementary Aspects of Peasant Insurgency in Colonial India*, 242.

6. Ibid., 226 ff. For more on the peasant character of the uprising, see Eric Stokes, *The Peasant and the Raj: Studies in Agrarian Society and Peasant Rebellion in Colonial India* and *The Peasant Armed: The Indian Revolt of 1857*; Abani Lahiri, *The Peasant and India's Freedom Movement*; Gautam Bhadra, "Four Rebels of Eighteen Fifty-Seven"; Tapti Roy, *The Politics of a Popular Uprising: Bundelkhand in 1857*; and Rudrangshu Mukherjee, *Awadh in Revolt, 1857–1858: A Study of Popular Resistance*.

7. Guha, *Elementary Aspects of Peasant Insurgency*, 256–69.

8. Bhabha, "By Bread Alone," 206.

9. Jacques Derrida, " 'Eating Well,' or the Calculation of the Subject: An Interview with Jacques Derrida."

10. I maintain a certain looseness of appellation in my use of such terms as *Anglo-Indian*, *Briton*, *sahib*, and even *Indian*; this is not accidental. The community of whites of British origin resident in India used a variety of designations for itself, a variety that marks its ambivalent sense of belonging and legitimacy in the subcontinent. Occasionally these subjects were identified as Indians, though distinct from the so-called natives of the subcontinent, in metropolitan writing. Kipling delighted in calling himself a Punjabi. (And then, for some real and fictional whites such as Richard Burton and Kipling's Kim, Englishness was marked by the access it provided to racialized theater, to the capacity to assume brown or black masks.) During the Mutiny years the community of whites in India was augmented significantly by military personnel requisitioned from Britain.

11. Bhabha, "By Bread Alone."

12. My thanks to Sandhya Shetty for suggesting this term.

13. Rudrangshu Mukherjee notes ongoing efforts to build up an archive of Urdu and Persian sources (*Awadh in Revolt*, xvii n. 39). Tapti Roy draws attention to the little-studied publications of the popular vernacular press in Bareilly and Lucknow and to the writings of the rebels of 1857, in the shape of "proclamations, brief announcements, *ishtihars* [bulletins], *farmans* [decrees], pamphlets, letters, appeals and circulars," and disseminated over numerous archives ("Rereading the Texts: Rebel Writings in 1857–58," 222). Commenting on the surprisingly high volume of production in a year of acute crisis, she observes, "There was supposed to be something compelling about the written word, which, when read or read out, had the force of turning people into partisans" (22).

14. Charles Theophilus Metcalfe, *Two Native Narratives of the Mutiny in Delhi, translated from the originals*.

15. For a translation of Ghalib's *Dastanbu*, see Ralph Russell and Khurshidul Islam, trans., *Oxford India Ghalib: Life, Letters, and Ghazals*.

16. Sir Syed Ahmed Khan, *The Causes of the Indian Revolt*, trans. by "two European friends" and with an introduction by Francis Robinson.

17. See Rudrangshu Mukherjee, "The Evidence," *Spectre of Violence: The 1857 Kanpur Massacres*, 82–122.

18. Sisir Kumar Das notes that the educated middle classes of the subcontinent, whether Muslim or Hindu, did not sympathize, for the most part, with the uprising, even though they might have been appalled by Anglo-Indian and British reprisals, and did not produce any significant literature in the immediate aftermath of the revolt. He cites two of the most prominent of the eyewitness accounts in the Indian languages: Durgadas Bandyopadhyay's *Bidrohe Bangali* (Calcutta, 1891) and Vishnubhat Godse's *Majha Pravas* (Pune, 1907). See *A History of Indian Literature, 1800–1910: Western Impact, Indian Response*, 125–26 and 379–80 n. 12. While Das's conclusion about the slimness of the record of educated opinion is factually correct, it is not sufficiently attentive to the conditions of censorship under which the vernacular press in the British territories operated. See Henry Scholberg, *The Indian Literature of the Great Rebellion*, for a useful list of primary sources, especially in Urdu.

19. William Dalrymple, *The Last Mughal–The Fall of a Dynasty: Delhi, 1857*. I am unable to assess Dalrymple's role as "discoverer" of the Mutiny materials in the National Archives; nonetheless, his work remains useful in providing a detailed and compulsively readable account of life in Delhi in 1857, both within the court and outside it. Also see Narayani Gupta, *Delhi between Two Empires*, for an account of courtly and common life in Delhi in this period.

20. Members of the other ranks and their families were exceptions to this mania for testimony—though George M. Fenn's *Begumbagh* (1879) does assume the voice of a common soldier. Kipling's unpublished story "The Little House at Arrah" affects the voice of an Indian *khansamah* (steward, cook). My thanks to Anjali Arondekar for bringing the Kipling text to my attention.

21. Mahasweta Devi, *The Queen of Jhansi*. Pankaj Rag has underlined the need to supplement elite sources of information on 1857 with popular and folk materials and has furnished an instance of how this can be achieved for the regions of eastern Uttar Pradesh and western Bihar; see his "1857: Need for Alternative Sources." More recently, Charu Gupta has taken note of the dalit heroes of the Mutiny—"some constructed, some exaggerated, some 'discovered' "—celebrated in dalit communities in north India; see "Dalit 'Viranganas' and the Reinvention of 1857," 196.

22. Opium was, like salt, an East India Company monopoly, accounting for 16–17 percent of revenues in British India in 1850, "stanching the flow of New World silver into China, ... [and sending] vast quantities of silver bullion back to Britain" (James Hevia, "Opium, Empire, and Modern History [review essay]," 312). While a medicalized lexicon of drug addiction was some decades away even in Britain, and opinions about the recreational and medicinal use of opium and

bhang far from unanimous from Anglo-Indian medical personnel, these substances sometimes were seen to fuel the fury demonstrated in 1857 by the antagonists of the company's rule. James Mills suggests it was not until the 1870s that opium usage came to be regarded with alarm; it was then, he suggests, that it came to be tied much more firmly with various forms of political violence, including that of 1857 (*Madness, Cannabis, and Colonialism*).

23. Rudrangshu Mukherjee, *Mangal Pandey: Brave Martyr or Accidental Hero?*, 53.

24. Ibid., 53.

25. See, for instance, Sita Ram Pande, *From Sepoy to Subedar; Being the Life and Adventures of Subedar Sita Ram*, trans. Lieutenant-Colonel Norgate, ed. James Lunt. Some scholars have cast doubts on the authenticity of this narrative, but the broad institutional changes it details are not in doubt.

26. As C. A. Bayly notes in his summary of Eric Stokes's conclusions, what occurred in 1857 "was not one movement, be it a peasant revolt or a war of national liberation; it was many." Moreover, peasants themselves did not constitute a single category; they fought on both sides of the revolt. The same can be said about the other constituencies that feature in the historiography of 1857. See "Editor's Concluding Note" in Eric Stokes, *The Peasant Armed: The Indian Revolt of 1857*.

27. C. A. Bayly, *The New Cambridge History of India, II.1: Indian Society and the Making of the British Empire*, 170.

28. See J. W. Kaye and G. B. Malleson, *History of the Indian Mutiny of 1857–8*, new edition, 6 vols., vol. 1.

29. Ibid., 1:159. These concerns must be understood in terms of sartorial codes that were binding, though in different ways, upon Anglo-Indians and Indians alike. C. A. Bayly has described the " 'moral' and 'transformative' " properties of cloth in the precolonial Indian context; see "The Origins of Swadeshi (home industry): Cloth and Indian Society, 1700–1930." Bernard Cohn suggests that dress codes were not epiphenomenal but central to an understanding of modesty, honor, and respect; sartorial prestations (*khilats*) in the Mughal court bound recipients in relationships of incorporation and obligation to the body of the sovereign, a fact that caused considerable unease to British officials who wished to assert their independence even as they maintained the fiction of the emperor's sovereignty over Hindustan ("Cloth, Clothes, and Colonialism: India in the Nineteenth Century"). (They themselves were to insist on certain "Indian" forms of sartorial deference, compelling Indians, even those of high status, to take off their shoes in their presence.) Emma Tarlo notes that missionary activities often included the presumed civilizing of native dress. The Poona missionary E. F. Elwin, she notes, spoke sarcastically of Christianization as "a matter of trousers" (*Clothing Matters: Dress and Identity in India*, 35).

30. For a full account, see Maya Gupta, "The Vellore Mutiny: July 1806." Also see Devadas Moodley, "Vellore 1806: The Meanings of Mutiny."

31. Kaye and Malleson, *History of the Indian Mutiny*, 1:181.

32. See Gautam Bhadra, "Four Rebels of Eighteen Fifty-Seven"; and Ranajit Guha, *Elementary Aspects of Peasant Insurgency*.

33. Such tales of pollution continued to be a common feature of anticolonial mobilization well after 1857–58. Ranajit Guha notes that during the Swadeshi agitation of the early twentieth century, sugar, salt, and cotton textiles were designated as impure "not merely because of their alien origin but also because the salt and the sugar were believed to have been adulterated with ground cow-bone powder, while the Manchester textiles were said to have been made out of yarn processed with the fat and blood of the same sacred species" (*Dominance Without Hegemony: History and Power in Colonial India*, 113).

34. Tanika Sarkar, *Bengal, 1928–1934: The Politics of Protest*, 80.

35. Sudipta Sen has described the ways in which the East India Company struggled, until 1857, to assert its own authority of conquest while maintaining the Mughal throne as "a source of visible, if not always legitimate, authority" (*Distant Sovereignty: National Imperialism and the Origins of British India*, xiv).

36. Thompson, "The Moral Economy of the English Crowd." Thompson's description of the "bread nexus"—that which binds authorities and populace in a web of mutual obligation—as a cornerstone of the moral economy is important here. It is opposed to an emerging, contractually based, and putatively more efficient cash nexus beloved of political economists.

37. Kaye and Malleson, *History of the Indian Mutiny*, 1:147.

38. Quoted by Mukherjee, *Awadh in Revolt*, 172.

39. Edward Thompson, *The Other Side of the Medal*, 117–19. Talbot Mundy's novella about a loyalist Risaldar during the Mutiny is entitled *For the Salt He Had Eaten* (1920).

40. Ian Baucom, *Out of Place: Englishness, Empire, and the Locations of Identity*, 106.

41. Karl Marx, "The Future Results of the British Rule in India [July 22, 1853]."

42. T. Rice Holmes, *A History of the Indian Mutiny, and of the Disturbances which Accompanied It among the Civil Population*, 5th ed., 78–79.

43. W. J. Shepherd states that mutineers and rebels were persuaded by Azimullah Khan, who had traveled to Britain and to the Crimean battlefields, that Britain was a small, sparsely populated country, the bulk of whose manpower was already stationed in India (*A Personal Narrative of the Outbreak and Massacre at Cawnpore, during the Sepoy Revolt of 1857*, 2d ed.).

44. Mukherjee, *Awadh in Revolt*, 59–63. James C. Scott suggests that the minimal security of a subsistence ethic can lead peasant subjects in so-called traditional or precapitalist societies to prefer the relations of exploitation in a paternalist order to the insecurities of commercialized agriculture and contractual agrarian relations in a capitalist order.

45. Sarkar, *Bengal, 1928–1934*, 80–81.

46. Roy Moxham, *The Great Hedge of India*.

47. See Mark Kurlansky, *Salt: A World History*, and Moxham, *The Great Hedge*.

48. Seema Alavi, *The Sepoys and the Company: Tradition and Transition in Northern India, 1770–1830*, 75, 44–45.

49. Ibid., 76. See Nicholas Dirks's suggestion that caste in its present form is "a modern phenomenon, that is, specifically, the product of an historical encounter between India and Western colonial rule" (*Castes of Mind: Colonialism and the Making of Modern India*, 5). Sanskritization is the term given by M. N. Srinivas to a process of vertical mobility within the jati/varna hierarchy that is widespread in the subcontinent, including groups both within the caste Hindu community and outside it. It is defined as the process by which a lower-ranked caste, tribe, or other community emulates the customs, rituals, beliefs, ways of life, and even the caste denomination of a higher, particularly a dwija ("twice-born": Brahman, Kshatriya, or Vaishya) caste; such a move, says Srinivas, generally follows upon the improvement in political or economic status of the lower-ranked group or from its increased exposure to and self-consciousness about the "Great Tradition" of Hinduism. Sanskritization involves, among other things, changes in forms and objects of worship, the adoption of the sacred thread, new restrictions upon women's sexuality, mobility, and economic activity, and changes in diet (*The Cohesive Role of Sanskritization and Other Essays*).

50. Kaye and Malleson, *History of the Indian Mutiny*, 1:360. Also see Sen, *Eighteen Fifty-Seven*, 41, and Majumdar, *The Sepoy Mutiny and the Revolt of 1857*, 69.

51. These two versions are juxtaposed in J. A. B. Palmer, *The Mutiny Outbreak at Meerut in 1857*, 15.

52. Marriott, "Hindu Transactions: Diversity without Dualism," 111.

53. Edward Leckey, *Fictions Connected with the Indian Outbreak of 1857 Exposed*. The Crimean War forms an important global context for the Mutiny, though I cannot take up here the questions of colonial crisis and colonial vulnerability that are highlighted by these events.

54. Gujars were stigmatized as hereditary thieves and marauders in a British typology of caste and criminality; see the entry on "Goojur" in Henry Yule and A. C. Burnell, *Hobson-Jobson*, ed. William Crooke, new edition, 386. This disdain is shared by some Indian historians. Majumdar's repudiation of the Mutiny as a genuine anticolonial rebellion has to do with the participation in it of these debased social actors (*The Sepoy Mutiny and the Revolt of 1857*).

55. Dalrymple, *The Last Mughal*, 19, 21, 144, 195, and passim.

56. Kaye and Malleson, *History of the Indian Mutiny*, 1:385.

57. Ibid., 1:416–17.

58. Guha, *Elementary Aspects of Peasant Insurgency*, 263.

59. Nana Saheb, on the other hand, ordered the hands of a Muslim butcher chopped off for having slaughtered cattle. The man bled to death, and the Nana was confronted by angry Muslim sepoys who demanded that he rescind his ban on cow slaughter. Despite the ecumenical character of the rumors, which played

on Muslim and Hindu fears alike, and despite the earnest endeavors of Bahadur Shah and Hazrat Mahal to reach both communities through a carefully considered gastropolitics, there were these occasional fractures among the rebels on questions of dietary permission and prohibition.

60. See S. A. A. Rizvi and M. L. Bhargava, eds., *Freedom Struggle in Uttar Pradesh*, 1:257–64.

61. Satadru Sen, *Disciplining Punishment: Colonialism and Convict Society in the Andaman Islands*.

62. Anand A. Yang, "The Lotah Emeutes of 1855: Caste, Religion and Prisons in North India in the Early Nineteenth Century." Yang stresses that these reforms were introduced to achieve efficiencies in prison administration and also, quite explicitly, to deprive prisoners of the pleasures of purchasing food and cooking it, pleasures deemed peculiarly Indian (111). On the other side, caste and religion could serve as "powerful and effective 'weapons of the weak,'" he notes, and should not be read as a simple expression of caste outrage (113).

63. On missionary activity in the subcontinent and aid to missionary education by the government, see Thomas Metcalf, *The Aftermath of Revolt: India, 1857–1870*, esp. chap. 3 ("Education and Social Reform"). It is possible though to exaggerate the extent to which the Mutiny was the antagonistic religious encounter of subcontinental Islam and evangelical Christianity; this is one of the entailments of reading backward from the events of September 11, 2001. Sabyasachi Bhattacharya is surely correct to note that "in the fluid situation of that turbulent year, many identities formed the bases of alliance and conflict. . . . It is more often than not incorrect to privilege one particular identity above all others as the key to understand what 1857 is about" ("Rethinking 1857," xvi).

64. Dirks, *Castes of Mind*, 131.

65. On this act, see Gauri Viswanathan, *Outside the Fold: Conversion, Modernity, and Belief*. Her chapter on converts' rights of inheritance makes it abundantly clear how ambivalent the British themselves were about this issue.

66. Azimullah Khan, Nana Saheb's adviser, was admitted into the mission school at Cawnpore as a starving boy during the famine of 1837–38.

67. Kaye and Malleson, *History of the Indian Mutiny*, vol. 1.

68. Pratul Chandra Gupta, *Nana Sahib and the Rising at Cawnpore*, 36. Also see Rizvi and Bhargava, eds., *Freedom Struggle in Uttar Pradesh*, vol. 1.

69. Mark Thornhill, *The Personal Adventures and Experiences of a Magistrate During the Rise, Progress, and Suppression of the Indian Mutiny*, 2. J. G. Farrell's *The Siege of Krishnapur* commences with the unannounced delivery of chapatis to the dispatch box of the Collector of Krishnapur.

70. Palmer, *The Mutiny Outbreak at Meerut in 1857*, 3.

71. Palmer states that the cholera epidemic of northern India occurred in 1856, well before the months leading up to the Mutiny (*The Mutiny Outbreak at Meerut in 1857*, 2–3). A few observers who looked beyond the events of 1857–58 noted that

the circulation of chapatis recurred in 1862, well after the Mutiny was suppressed (Gupta, *Nana Sahib and the Rising at Cawnpore*, 37–38).

72. T. Rice Holmes was one of the proponents of the theory of the fiery cross. G. B. Malleson was perhaps the best-known promulgator of this conspiracy theory, naming the Maulvi of Faizabad as the originator of a chapati plot. See Kaye and Malleson, *History of the Indian Mutiny* 5:292. Benjamin Disraeli was unwilling to name conspirators with the confidence Malleson displayed, but he too was convinced that the transmission of chapatis and lotus flowers were "outward and visible signs of confederacy." See Benjamin Disraeli, "Military Mutiny or National Revolt?" 21.

73. Roy Porter, Preface to Piero Camporesi, *Bread of Dreams: Food and Fantasy in Early Modern Europe*, trans. David Gentilcore, 13. On bread riots in Europe, also see E. P. Thompson, "Moral Economy"; and George Rude, *The Crowd in the French Revolution*.

74. Kaye and Malleson, *History of the Indian Mutiny*, vol. 6.

75. In Roger Luckhurst's *The Invention of Telepathy, 1870–1901*, the mysterious chapatis are discussed in terms of their place in Victorian narratives of the colonial occult.

76. C. A. Bayly, "Knowing the Country: Empire and Information in India." Bayly mentions the panic of 1907, when Anglo-Indians were convulsed at the phenomenon of holy men smearing cow dung on trees. They saw this as a sign that all Europeans were to be slaughtered on the fiftieth anniversary of the Mutiny.

77. Gautam Chakravarty, *The Indian Mutiny and the British Imagination*, 167–69. In G. A. Henty's *In Times of Peril*, one of the boy heroes even passes as a bear for a short period of time! Practically no Eurasians or Anglo-Indians successfully passed as natives during the Mutiny, though several attempted to do so. Henry Kavanaugh made his way in Indian clothes from the Lucknow Residency to Sir Colin Campbell's camp in the Alambagh in the company of the Indian spy Kanauji Lal, a feat for which he received the Victoria Cross. A few Anglo-Indian women who escaped the carnage at Satichaura Ghat in Cawnpore were sheltered by Indians and may have assumed Indian clothing while under their hosts' protection.

78. Narrative of Mainoddin Khan, in Metcalfe, *Two Native Narratives of the Mutiny in Delhi*, 40, 9. In John Masters's *The Nightrunners of Bengal* (a novel named for the carriers of the chapatis) the chapatis, along with pieces of goat's flesh, circulate in a sublunary world ruled by Hindu gods and threats of malediction. The protagonist Rodney Savage deciphers its meaning but only in a dream after the event: "Can't you read the messages? A chupatti in five parts, signifying the fifth month. A chupatti in ten parts, for the tenth day. Flesh, white-skinned on white side, raw on the other—a big piece for a sahib, a smaller piece for a memsahib, and a little piece for a child. On May tenth kill all the white skins—or they kill us!" (*The Nightrunners of Bengal*, 183).

79. Palmer, *The Mutiny Outbreak at Meerut in 1857*, 2.

80. Flora Annie Steel, *The Garden of Fidelity, Being the Autobiography of Flora Annie Steel*, 213.

81. Ibid., 214.

82. Bhabha, "By Bread Alone," 202, 204, 206.

83. Jenny Sharpe, *Allegories of Empire: The Figure of Woman in the Colonial Text*. This is not to suggest that no rapes of Anglo-Indian or Eurasian women or girls occurred. Amy Horne was certainly raped, as perhaps was Ulrica Wheeler (P. J. O. Taylor, ed., *A Companion to the "Indian Mutiny" of 1857*, 46–48, 345). The *Times* correspondent William Howard Russell encountered two Eurasian girls who spoke to him of their experiences of rape (*My Indian Mutiny Diary*, ed. Michael Edwardes, 124). The focus on the purportedly violated body of the English lady effectively precluded, in Anglo-Indian texts at least, any consideration of the sexual violence visited upon the bodies of Indian women during the mutineers' sojourn in Delhi or the British recapture of the capital city; for Urdu-language accounts of these violations, see Dalrymple, *The Last Mughal*, 302, 427.

84. Sharpe, *Allegories of Empire*, 61–69.

85. Nancy Paxton, *Writing Under the Raj: Gender, Race, and Rape in the British Colonial Imagination, 1830–1947*, 110.

86. Sharpe, *Allegories of Empire*, 61.

87. Frantz Fanon, *The Wretched of the Earth*, trans. Constance Farrington, 38–39.

88. In the seventeenth century and the eighteenth soldiers' liaisons and marriages with local women were encouraged by the Company as a cost-saving device, though the children of such liaisons were their mothers' charges and not necessarily provided for by their fathers. See Percival Spear, *The Nabobs: A Study of the Social Life of the English in Eighteenth-Century India*. On the slave-concubinage practiced by representatives of the Company in the eighteenth century and the early nineteenth, see Indrani Chatterjee, "Colouring Subalternity: Slaves, Concubines and Social Orphans in Early Colonial India."

89. See, most famously, Samuel Foote, *The Nabob: A Comedy in Three Acts*. Edmund Burke's indictment of Company employees as "birds of prey and passage, with appetites continually renewing for a food that is continually wasting" is among the most searing indictments of the venality and ruthlessness of these figures (speech on Fox's East India Bill, 1 December 1783, *Writings and Speeches of Edmund Burke*, 5:403).

90. See Spear, *The Nabobs*; and Kenneth Ballhatchet, *Race, Sex, and Class Under the Raj*.

91. Sudipta Sen, *Distant Sovereignty*, 134.

92. C. J. Hawes, *Poor Relations: The Making of a Eurasian Community in British India, 1773–1833*. Also see Betty Joseph, "The Politics of Settlement," *Reading the East India Company, 1720–1840: Colonial Currencies of Gender*, 92–122. The work of Anglo-Indian writers of the late nineteenth century such as Kipling and Steel suggests that concubinage did not disappear despite official disapproval.

93. Durba Ghosh, *Sex and the Family in Colonial India: The Making of Empire*. Richard Burton's approving gloss on the still-extant institution of the Indian mistress in the Anglo-India of the 1840s is well known: "The Bibi (white woman) was at that time rare in India; the result was the triumph of the Bubu (coloured sister). I found every officer in the corps more or less provided with one of these helpmates. We boys naturally followed suit. . . . [The Bubu] is all but indispensable to the student, and she teaches him not only Hindostani grammar, but the syntaxes of native Life. She keeps house for him, never allowing him to save money, or, if possible, to waste it. She keeps the servants in order. She has an infallible recipe to prevent maternity, especially if her tenure of office depends on such compact. She looks after him in sickness and is one of the best of nurses, and, as it is not good for man to live alone, she makes him a manner of home" (Isabel Burton, *Life of Sir Richard F. Burton, K.C.M.G., F.R.G.S., by His Wife*, 2 vols., 135). Burton had nothing but contempt and revulsion, though, for the hybrid offspring produced by these interracial sexual arrangements; for evidence of this, see *Goa, and the Blue Mountains; or, Six Months on Sick Leave*, ed. Dane Kennedy.

94. See Bart Moore-Gilbert, *Kipling and "Orientalism,"* for a study of Anglo-Indian assertions of distinctiveness from metropolitan Britons.

95. Rudyard Kipling, "The Tomb of His Ancestors."

96. Sudipta Sen, *Distant Sovereignty*, xiii.

97. Nicholas Dirks, *The Scandal of Empire: India and the Creation of Imperial Britain*, 182.

98. Thomas Metcalf argues for the Mutiny's transformative character in the relationship of Anglo-India to India (*The Aftermath of Revolt: India, 1857–1870*). One need not agree in toto with this diagnosis to concede that the Mutiny, generating as it did a novel vocabulary of loyalty and betrayal, did inaugurate a significant insistence on racial distance as a matter of policy and as part of an Anglo-Indian psychic landscape.

99. Eric Stokes, *The English Utilitarians and India*, xiii; also see E. M. Collingham, *Imperial Bodies: The Physical Experience of the Raj, c. 1800–1947*, 6–7, 50–92.

100. Julia Kristeva, *Powers of Horror: An Essay on Abjection*, trans. Leon S. Roudiez.

101. Dominique Laporte notes the Renaissance rediscovery of and admiration for Roman sanitation, including the institution of the cloaca maxima (*History of Shit*, trans. Nadia Benabid and Rodolphe el-Khoury, 14).

102. Norbert Elias, *The Civilizing Process: Sociogenetic and Psychogenetic Investigations*, rev. ed., trans. Edmund Jephcott and ed. Eric Dunning, Johan Goudsblom, and Stephen Mennell. Also see Pierre Bourdieu, *Distinction: A Social Critique of the Judgment of Taste*, trans. Richard Nice.

103. Peter Stallybrass and Allon White, *The Politics and Poetics of Transgression*, 148. Also see Mary Poovey, *Making a Social Body: British Cultural Formation, 1830–1864*; Christopher Hamlin, ed., *Public Health and Social Justice in the Age of Chadwick: Britain, 1800–1854*; Pamela K. Gilbert, *Mapping the Victorian Social Body*; Seth

Koven, *Slumming: Social and Sexual Politics in Victorian Britain*, on hygiene and sanitary reform in nineteenth-century Britain. See Alain Corbin and Georges Vigarello (*Concepts of Cleanliness: Changing Attitudes in France Since the Middle Ages*, trans. Jean Birrell) for a history of dirt, cleanliness, and olfaction in nineteenth-century France. Also see Anne McClintock's discussion of "the Victorian poetics of racial hygiene and imperial progress" in *Imperial Leather: Race, Gender and Sexuality in the Colonial Contest*, 209.

104. Quoted by David Arnold, *Colonizing the Body: State Medicine and Epidemic Disease in Nineteenth-Century India*, 98. In the 1890s, Kipling was to evoke the Calcutta Stink as a reality and a rebuke to the windy effusions of the would-be legislators at a meeting of the city's municipal council ("The City of Dreadful Night").

105. Erin O'Connor, *Raw Material: Producing Pathology in Victorian Culture*, 226–27.

106. Arnold, *Colonizing the Body*, 89–90.

107. Rosemary George, "The Authoritative Englishwoman: Setting up Home and Self in the Colonies." Also see Swati Chattopadhyay, " 'Goods, Chattels and Sundry Items': Constructing 19th-Century Anglo-Indian Domestic Life."

108. On the development of the bungalow as a model dwelling for Anglo-Indian rulers, see Anthony D. King, *The Bungalow: The Production of a Global Culture*. Flora Annie Steel's *Complete Indian Housekeeper and Cook*, written in the 1880s, summarizes Anglo-Indian housekeeping practices perfected over more than half a century.

109. Collingham, *Imperial Bodies*, 171.

110. See Dane Kennedy, *The Magic Mountains: Hill Stations and the British Raj*.

111. Collingham, *Imperial Bodies*, 156–59. Mary Procida suggests that on private occasions Anglo-Indians did enjoy Indian food ("Feeding the Imperial Appetite: Imperial Knowledge and Anglo-Indian Domesticity").

112. On British soldiers' susceptibility to venereal disease in the colonies, see Philippa Levine, *Prostitution, Race and Politics: Policing Venereal Disease in the British Empire*.

113. Collingham, *Imperial Bodies*, 112.

114. Cited by Saul David, *The Indian Mutiny, 1857*, 67–68.

115. Charles Malamoud, *Cooking the World: Ritual and Thought in Ancient India*, trans. David White, 8. On one of the most famous tales of *jootha* in the Hindu sacred narratives, see Philip Lutgendorf, "Dining Out at Lake Pampa: The Shabari Episode in Multiple Ramayanas."

116. McKim Marriott, "Caste Ranking and Food Transactions: A Matrix Analysis,"142. As Arun Prabha Mukherjee suggests in her introduction to *Joothan*, the Hindi-language autobiography of the contemporary dalit writer Omprakash Valmiki, "The Hindi word *joothan* literally means food left on a plate, usually destined for the garbage pail in a middle-class urban home. However, such food would be

characterized *joothan* only if someone else were to eat it. The word carries the connotations of ritual purity and pollution, because *jootha* means polluted. I feel that words such as *leftovers* or *leavings* are not adequate substitutes for *joothan*. *Leftovers* has no negative connotations and can simply mean food remaining in the pot that can be eaten at the next meal; *leavings*, although widely used by Ambedkar and Gandhi, is no longer in the active vocabulary of Indian English. *Scraps* and *slops* are somewhat closer to *joothan*, but they are associated more with pigs than with humans" (Introduction, Omprakash Valmiki, *Joothan: A Dalit's Life*, trans. Arun Prabha Mukherjee, xxxix).

117. In general high-caste Hindus in mid-nineteenth-century India did not dine with casteless Europeans. Neither did respectable Muslims, who were concerned about the presence of pork and alcohol on the sahib's table. Anglo-Indians often complained of this; their own racially exclusionary practices in dining and entertainment were generally explained in terms of the local practices that treated Christians as polluting because of their failure to abide by dietary restrictions.

118. Mukherjee, *Spectre of Violence*, 60–62; and Rudrangshu Mukherjee, *Awadh in Revolt, 1857–1858*, ix–x. Anglo-Indians were not the only ones to be subjected to these practices of inversion. The mutineers were highhanded and coercive even with those traditional leaders—Bahadur Shah, Nana Saheb, the Rani of Jhansi—whom they had chosen as the leaders of their uprising.

119. Alexander Duff, *The Indian Rebellion: Its Causes and Results*, 63.

120. Leckey's skepticism about Mutiny fictions was matched by that of his contemporary Marx, who wrote with pointed indignation about eyewitness accounts of sexual humiliation emanating from over a thousand miles from the scene of the purported outrages (Karl Marx and Friedrich Engels, *The First Indian War of Independence, 1857–1859*).

121. Marina Warner, "Fee Fie Fo Fum: The Child in the Jaws of the Story."

122. Christopher Hibbert, *The Great Mutiny, India 1857*, 213.

123. Kaye and Malleson, *History of the Indian Mutiny*, 2:250.

124. Hibbert, *The Great Mutiny*, 329. Alimentary deprivation was experienced by Indians as well, it should be noted. Dalrymple describes the starvation suffered by the inhabitants of Delhi, not so much on account of British efforts, which were confined to the Ridge, but because of the new levies imposed by Gujars on goods coming into or leaving the city (*The Last Mughal*, 294).

125. W. J. Shepherd, *A Personal Narrative of the Outbreak and Massacre at Cawnpore*, 64.

126. Mowbray Thomson, *The Story of Cawnpore*.

127. For Shepherd, a significant part of the injury he believed himself to have suffered during his few weeks' captivity in a Cawnpore jail was caused by having to eat parched gram. After his experiences in the entrenchment and jail—he lost his wife, two children, and several members of his extended family to injuries at the entrenchment and the massacres at Satichaura Ghat and the Bibighar—he was,

understandably, in a "shattered state of body and mind" and unfit for sustained exertion. His catalogue of distresses lists his digestive disorder ahead of his failing memory, his suddenly tender conscience, and his incapacity to concentrate (*A Personal Narrative of the Outbreak and Massacre at Cawnpore*, appendix C, xxiv).

128. George Otto Trevelyan, *Cawnpore*, 278.

129. Ibid., 284. J. W. Sherer, *Daily Life During the Indian Mutiny: Personal Experiences of 1857*.

130. Trevelyan, *Cawnpore*, 281.

131. Ibid., 278–79.

132. Ibid., 277–84. Shepherd, on the other hand, subscribes to the notion that the Nana's interest in his captives was unequivocally sexual and that they were supplied with clean clothes and superior victuals, including beer, wines, rum, milk, and meat, so as to facilitate their sexual surrender to him (*A Personal Narrative*, 94–95).

133. Trevelyan, *Cawnpore*, 280. Honoria Lawrence noted that many Anglo-Indians shared the distaste for low-caste figures that high-caste Hindus displayed (Philip Mason, *A Matter of Honour: An Account of the Indian Army, Its Officers and Men*).

134. Vivian Dering Majendie, *Up Among the Pandies: A Year's Service in India*, 223.

135. Patrick Brantlinger, "The Well at Cawnpore: Literary Representations of the Indian Mutiny of 1857," *Rule of Darkness: British Literature and Imperialism, 1830–1914*, 204.

136. On the Black Hole's status as "founding trauma" for the East India Company in the eighteenth century, see Betty Joseph, "Archival Fictions: Memories of Violence in the Age of Sensibility," *Reading the East India Company, 1720–1840: Colonial Currencies of Gender*, 61–91. Also see Kate Teltscher's " 'The Fearful Name of the Black Hole': Fashioning an Imperial Myth." (J. Z. Holwell's account of the Black Hole experience may have had a "limited impact" in Britain, as Linda Colley claims [in *Captives: Britain, Empire, and the World, 1600–1850*, 255], but this was not true with respect to Anglo-Indians in the subcontinent.) It is curious to speculate on the ways in which the well has continued to feature in a subcontinental landscape of gendered atrocity and martyrdom, as witnessed by the well at Jallianwala Bagh and the countless wells in which Sikh and Hindu women lost their lives during Partition. My thanks to Bishnupriya Ghosh for drawing my attention to this last point.

137. Russell, *My Indian Mutiny Diary*, 34. My thanks to Catherine Robson for raising the question of the well in the Mutiny's gastropoetics.

138. Pierre Nora, "Between History and Memory: Les Lieux de Memoire."

139. I have not read the reports Russell wrote for the *Times* and so cannot tell if they differ in emphasis from the published *Diary*.

140. For Kristeva the two are linked in terms of their operations and affect: "The corpse (or cadaver: *cadere*, to fall), that which has irremediably come a

cropper, is cesspool, and death;. . . . refuse and corpses *show me* what I permanently thrust aside in order to live" (*Powers of Horror*, 3).

141. Alain Corbin, *The Foul and the Fragrant: Odor and the French Social Imagination*. See Warwick A. Anderson, "Excremental Colonialism: Public Health and the Poetics of Pollution," and Joshua Esty, "Excremental Postcolonialism," on the metaphoric slide between improper modes of defecation and the racially marked primitive subject.

142. Sigmund Freud, *Civilization and Its Discontents* trans. James Strachey, 51–52 n. 1. Also see William Ian Miller, *The Anatomy of Disgust*, 66–79.

143. Immanuel Kant, *Anthropology from a Pragmatic Point of View*, trans. Victor Lyle Dowdell, 45.

144. Frederick Cooper, *The Crisis in the Punjab*; quoted by Thompson, *The Other Side of the Medal*, 66. Counterinsurgent atrocities were invariably justified in terms of their status as imitation or retaliation or both; Indian atrocities were said to have spawned British ones.

145. Christopher Herbert, *War of No Pity: The Indian Mutiny and Victorian Trauma*. While Herbert is rightly critical of literary analyses that paper over the ambivalent responses of Britain and Anglo-India to the Mutiny, he is by no means free of instances of selective citation and tendentious reading.

146. Bholanauth Chunder, *The Travels of a Hindoo to Various Parts of Bengal and Upper India*, 2 vols.

147. Carl Schmitt, *The Nomos of the Earth in the Jus Publicum Europaeum*, trans. G. L. Umen, cited in Ian Baucom, "The Disasters of War: On Inimical Life,"178; and Achille Mbembe, "Necropolitics," trans. Libby Meintjes.

148. Baucom, "The Disasters of War." Baucom's essay is an important supplement to the work of Schmitt and Mbembe; it establishes the way in which the figure of the bandit or the robber accommodated the exercise of the state of exception and of extrajudicial violence in nineteenth-century Europe itself, not just in the colonies.

149. Mbembe, "Necropolitics," 21.

150. Diana L. Paton, "Punishment, Crime, and the Bodies of Slaves in Eighteenth-Century Jamaica," 942.

151. Mukherjee, *Spectre of Violence*, 32–34.

152. Michael Edwardes, *Red Year: The Indian Rebellion of 1857*, 87–88.

153. Pankaj Rag, "1857: Need for Alternative Sources," 143. One should not overlook the temporary empowerment of untouchables in this operation.

154. Mukherjee, *Spectre of Violence*, 32.

155. Russell, *My Indian Mutiny Diary*, 161. The tradition of attributing British lapses to the contagion of the Indian environment was a hoary one; see, for instance, T. B. Macaulay's essay on Clive.

156. I am indebted to Sandhya Shetty for this turn of phrase.

157. For a fine elaboration of reverse colonization, see Stephen Arata, "The Occidental Tourist: Bram Stoker's *Dracula* and the Anxiety of Reverse Colonization."

158. Trevelyan, *Cawnpore*, 332.

159. Steel, *On the Face of the Waters*; Kaye and Malleson, *History of the Indian Mutiny*, vol. 1.

160. Bernard Cohn, "Representing Authority in Victorian India," 179. Pilgrimages or tours to Mutiny sites continue to be offered by British outfits with an interest in military history.

161. David Arnold, "Deathscapes: India in an Age of Romanticism and Empire, 1800–1856," 343.

162. Robert Travers, "Death and the Nabob: Imperialism and Commemoration in Eighteenth-Century India," 90–92, 114.

163. Ibid., 121.

164. Cohn, "Representing Authority," 178.

165. Nayanjot Lahiri, "Remembering 1857: The Revolt in Delhi and Its Afterlife." Also see Narayani Gupta, *Delhi Between Two Empires*. Lahiri notes that some restorations of historical buildings were undertaken in the early twentieth century by the Viceroy Lord Curzon, who had an interest in archaeology as well as a desire to represent colonial rule in its enlightened form.

166. Ian Baucom, "The Path from War to Friendship: E. M. Forster's Mutiny Pilgrimage," *Out of Place: Englishness, Empire, and the Locations of Identity*, 112.

167. Trevelyan, *Cawnpore*.

168. A beautiful carved marble figure placed over the Bibighar well head in February 1863, the statue was commissioned by Viceroy and Lady Canning and carved by Baron Carlo Marochetti (P. J. O. Taylor, *A Companion to the "Indian Mutiny" of 1857*, 210).

2. Abstinence

1. Lloyd I. Rudolph and Susanne Hoeber Rudolph, *The Modernity of Tradition: Political Development in India*; Joseph Alter, *Gandhi's Body: Sex, Diet, and the Politics of Nationalism*; and Leela Gandhi, *Affective Communities: Anticolonial Thought, Fin-de-Siècle Radicalism, and the Politics of Friendship*.

2. Despite the occasionally defensive tendency of his study of Gandhi's positions, B. R. Nanda is surely right to insist on their evolving and experiential character, and he quotes N. K. Bose to good effect: "The secret of Gandhi's greatness lay not in the absence of human failings and foibles, but in his inner restlessness, ceaseless striving and intense involvement in the problems of mankind. He was not a slave to ideas and concepts, [which] were for him aids in grappling with human problems, and were to be reconsidered if they did not work" (*Gandhi and His Critics*, 146).

3. Joseph Alter, "Celibacy, Sexuality, and the Transformation of Gender into

Nationalism in North India," 61. Alter's more recent *Gandhi's Body* gestures toward a few of the questions I broach in this chapter. Gender, though, is not a central analytic optic in Alter's chapters on Gandhi in the way it is in this work.

4. Jawaharlal Nehru's *An Autobiography* is the most easily cited and the most ideologically appropriate counterexample to Gandhi's venture.

5. Mohandas K. Gandhi, *Autobiography: The Story of My Experiments With Truth*, trans. Mahadev Desai, 197 (subsequent citations will be incorporated parenthetically into the text). On Gandhi's response to his first Congress meeting, see Sandhya Shetty's manuscript on Gandhi and sanitation.

6. Bhikhu Parekh, *Gandhi*, 9.

7. Rudolph and Rudolph, *The Modernity of Tradition*, 170–71.

8. Rajmohan Gandhi, *The Good Boatman: A Portrait of Gandhi*, 199.

9. See James Laidlaw, *Riches and Renunciation: Religion, Economy, and Society Among the Jains*, esp. chaps. 7–12.

10. Ibid., 170. On Jain dietary practices also see Padmanabh S. Jaini, "Fear of Food? Jain Attitudes on Eating." On Gandhi and Jainism, see Stephen N. Hay, "Jain Influences on Gandhi's Early Thought," and Chandran D. S. Devanesen, *The Making of the Mahatma*.

11. Gandhi was born in Porbandar and educated in Rajkot, both princely states nominally governed by Indian princes but acknowledging the paramountcy of the British Crown. British rule in Kathiawad, the peninsula where Gandhi was born and lived until his departure for London, was of relatively recent date, though, at the time of Gandhi's childhood and adolescence.

12. For an analysis of this phenomenon, see Mrinalini Sinha, *Colonial Masculinity: The "Manly Englishman" and the "Effeminate Bengali" in the Late Nineteenth Century*, and Ashis Nandy, *The Intimate Enemy: Loss and Recovery of Self Under Colonialism*.

13. Thomas B. Macaulay, "Robert Clive" and "Warren Hastings." Also see Kipling, especially "The Head of the District" and "The Trials of Padgett, M.P."

14. John Rosselli, "The Self-Image of Effeteness: Physical Education and Nationalism in Nineteenth-Century Bengal."

15. Milind Wakankar, "Body, Crowd, Identity: Genealogy of a Hindu Nationalist Ascetics," 49.

16. To cite but one example: Katherine Mayo's *Mother India* (1927) specifically exempts the manly and meat-eating Muslim from her indictment of the sins of caste Hindu (and especially Bengali) males: feebleness, cowardice, licentiousness, patriarchal cruelty, seditiousness.

17. Rudolph and Rudolph, *The Modernity of Tradition*, 175.

18. Jacques Derrida, " 'Eating Well': An Interview," 113–14.

19. As a vegetarian by conviction in England, Gandhi was to reverse himself on the question of meat eating and bodily might: "It is easy to see that Vegetarianism is not only not injurious, but on the contrary is conducive to bodily strength and that attributing the Hindu weakness to Vegetarianism is simply based on a fal-

lacy" (Essay in *The Vegetarian*, 28 February 1891, reprint. *Collected Works of Mahatma Gandhi*, 1:33).

20. Sigmund Freud, *Totem and Taboo*, trans. James Strachey.

21. G. C. Spivak, "Three Women's Texts and a Critique of Imperialism."

22. Louis Fischer, *The Life of Mahatma Gandhi*, 82.

23. I thank Barbara Metcalf for pointing this out to me.

24. Erik Erikson, *Gandhi's Truth: On the Origins of Militant Nonviolence*, 135. A few latter-day commentators such as Sudhir Kakar have followed Erikson's lead in understanding Mehtab's role in Mohandas's psychic development; see "Gandhi and Women," *Intimate Relations: Exploring Indian Sexuality*. Rajmohan Gandhi suggests it was Mehtab's "stand for the new [social reform] against the old" that appealed to the boyish, reform-minded Gandhi (*Mohandas: A True Story of a Man, His People, and an Empire*, 16).

25. Erikson, *Gandhi's Truth*, 140. Gandhi himself saw in Harilal an embodiment of an earlier self he had cast off: "I have always felt that the undesirable traits I see today in my eldest son are an echo of my undisciplined and unformulated early life" (*Autobiography*, 175). The equivocal character of the phrase "in some locality" (see the passage on p. 9) is also telling: was this a locality characterized by illicit sexual traffic? Was it a Muslim neighborhood? I thank Piya Chatterjee for drawing my attention to the nuances of this phrase. For a biography of Harilal, see Chandulal Bhagubhai Dalal, *Harilal Gandhi: A Life*, trans. Tridip Suhrud.

26. Bernard S. Cohn, "Cloth, Clothes, and Colonialism: India in the Nineteenth Century."

27. Emma Tarlo, *Clothing Matters: Dress and Identity in India*, 44.

28. For one example see Mulk Raj Anand, *The Coolie*. Lawrence Cohen has also drawn my attention to *Sookha Patta*, the Hindi novel by Amarkant, in which a character comments on the immodesty of tight-fitting Western-style trousers, rather than loosely tailored Indian-style ones.

29. See, for instance, Meredith Borthwick, *The Changing Role of Women in Bengal*.

30. See, for instance, Madhu Kishwar, "Gandhi on Women"; and Ashis Nandy, *The Intimate Enemy*. Vinay Lal goes so far as to speak of Gandhi's desire to rid himself of masculine heterosexual desire by becoming a woman (who is invested with no desire of her own) as "vulva envy" ("Nakedness, Nonviolence, and Brahmacharya: Gandhi's Experiments in Celibate Sexuality,"128).

31. M. K. Gandhi, *Bapu's Letters to Mira* [1924–1948], 12–13.

32. Nirmal Kumar Bose, *My Days with Gandhi*, 206.

33. Julia Twigg, "Vegetarianism and the Meanings of Meat," 27–28; and Maud Ellmann, *The Hunger Artists: Starving, Writing, and Imprisonment*, 12. As we shall see later, not all vegetarians were sympathetic to feminism; some were ferociously critical of the new regime of modernity, with its reconstellation of gendered relations—a reconstellation of which the feminist movement was one index. And vegetarianism was not associated only with femininity, whether in India or

in the United Kingdom or in the United States in the late nineteenth century and the early twentieth; the historical and conceptual links between vegetarianism and masculine self-consolidation will be established in greater detail later in the chapter.

34. Tarlo, *Clothing Matters*, 71–82.

35. Ibid., 67.

36. His own experiments in what was called reform after his return from England were marked by a simultaneous attentiveness to sartorial and culinary proprieties. He introduced oatmeal and cocoa in his Kathiawad home and knives and forks to his unwilling family in Natal; at the same time he also made them wear shoes and socks, which they found tight-fitting and smelly.

37. *The Collected Works of Mahatma Gandhi*, 1:15.

38. V. S. Naipaul, *India: A Wounded Civilization*, 102–5. I borrow the term "carnivoracity" from Maggie Kilgour, *From Communion to Cannibalism: An Anatomy of Metaphors of Incorporation*.

39. M. K. Gandhi, "London Diary" and *Satyagraha in South Africa*.

40. For a careful account of the character and purpose of the *Autobiography*, see chapter 8 ("Indianisation of Autobiography") of Bhikhu Parekh's, *Colonialism, Tradition and Reform: An Analysis of Gandhi's Political Discourse*.

41. Gandhi, *Collected Works of Mahatma Gandhi*, vol. 1. Nanda, *Gandhi and His Critics*, 26.

42. James D. Hunt, *Gandhi in London*, 9. This Dalpatram Shukla was a different figure from the famous nineteenth-century Gujarati poet.

43. B. R. Nanda, *Mahatma Gandhi: A Biography*, 24.

44. Javed Majeed, writing on the thematics of embarrassment and adolescence in the *Autobiography*, has noted the "paradox of Gandhi's self-empowerment through self-reduction" (*Autobiography, Travel and Postnational Identity: Gandhi, Nehru and Iqbal*, 231).

45. Vows of silence are not uncommon for Hindu and Jain ascetics.

46. Scholars have occasionally noted the global or the diasporic provenance of some of the core elements of Gandhi's philosophical-political agenda; see Peter van der Veer, "Introduction," *Nation and Migration: The Politics of Space in the South Asian Diaspora*. Richard G. Fox, in "East of Said," speaks of the (European) "affirmative Orientalism" Gandhi deployed in his excoriation of modern civilization (*Edward Said: A Critical Reader*; also see his *Gandhian Utopia: Experiments With Culture*). But the banal practices of diet and clothing have always been coded as the irrefragably local.

47. For an instructive account of the gastropolitics of Percy Bysshe Shelley and his circle, see Timothy Morton, *Shelley and the Revolution in Taste: The Body and the Natural World*. Shelley was to remain an important figure for the British vegetarian movement throughout the nineteenth century.

48. Colin Spencer, *The Heretic's Feast: A History of Vegetarianism*, 272–74.

49. Stephen Hay, "The Making of a Late-Victorian Hindu: M. K. Gandhi in London, 1888–1891," 92.

50. For an account of some of these figures, see Hillel Schwarz, *Never Satisfied: A Cultural History of Diets, Fantasies and Fat*, and James Whorton, *Crusaders for Fitness: The History of American Health Reformers*. Note, too, that the ideological importance accorded to vegetarianism in the 1890s by Hindu reformist bodies like the Arya Samaj emerged in the context of a distinctly late nineteenth-century modality of self-fashioning. On the vegetarianism of the Arya Samaj, see Kenneth W. Jones, *The New Cambridge History of India, Vol. III: Socio-Religious Reform Movements in British India*, 95–103, and J. T. F. Jordens, *Dayananda Saraswati: His Life and Ideas*.

51. Ronald D. LeBlanc, "Tolstoy's Way of No Flesh: Abstinence, Vegetarianism, and Christian Physiology."

52. Henry S. Salt, *A Plea for Vegetarianism and Other Essays*; Howard Williams, *The Ethics of Diet*; Anna Kingsford, *The Perfect Way in Diet*. For an account of some fellow travelers in late nineteenth-century Britain, see Stephen Winsten, *Salt and His Circle*. For an exhaustive and reverential account of the affinities between Tolstoy and Gandhi, see Martin Green, *The Challenge of the Mahatmas* and *The Origins of Nonviolence: Tolstoy and Gandhi in Their Historical Settings*.

53. Chandran D. S. Devanesen provides perhaps the best account of the late Victorian milieu of the London whose denizen Gandhi was for three years (*The Making of the Mahatma*). Also see Martin Green, *Gandhi: Voice of a New Age Revolution*, 79–117.

54. Green, *Gandhi: Voice of a New Age Revolution*, 95.

55. Françoise Lionnet and Shu-mei Shih, eds., *Minor Transnationalism*.

56. Leela Gandhi, *Affective Communities*, 20, 67–114.

57. Tristram Stuart, *The Bloodless Revolution: A Cultural History of Vegetarianism from 1600 to Modern Times*.

58. James D. Hunt, *Gandhi in London*, 34.

59. M. K. Gandhi, *Collected Works of Mahatma Gandhi* 1:34.

60. Gandhi, *Hind Swaraj and Other Writings*, 63–64. Gandhi's showcasing of disease and medicine owes a good deal to his reading in 1909 of Carpenter.

61. Sandhya Shetty, " 'The Quack Whom We Know': Illness and Nursing in Gandhi." Shetty notes (as does Alter, in *Gandhi's Body*) that Gandhi was no less critical of ayurvedic medicine than he was of modern biomedicine.

62. Mehta, *Mahatma Gandhi and His Apostles*, 202. Alter (*Gandhi's Body*) provides an excellent account of nonallopathic therapies in early twentieth-century India and Europe.

63. Joan Jacobs Brumberg, "The Appetite as Voice," 166. Also see, for a notable elaboration of the gendered character of ingestion and fasting in another historical period, Caroline Walker Bynum, *Holy Feast and Holy Fast: The Religious Significance of Food to Medieval Women*.

64. Ellmann, *The Hunger Artists*, 18.

65. Gang Yue, *The Mouth That Begs: Hunger, Cannibalism, and the Politics of Eating in Modern China*, 47.

66. Franz Kafka, "A Hunger Artist."

67. Tim Pratt and James Vernon, " 'Appeal from This Fiery Bed': The Colonial Politics of Gandhi's Fasts and Their Metropolitan Reception," 94.

68. Prabhudas Gandhi describes the contrast between the "special dishes" and parties of the early days at Phoenix, when Gandhi "relished good food," and the subsequent regime for children and adults alike of "long days of work and saltless food," relieved only by the prospect of salted and spiced meals on Sundays (*My Childhood With Gandhiji*, 45, 108, and passim).

69. Kishwar, "Gandhi on Women," part 3, 1754.

70. William Ian Miller, "Gluttony," 97.

71. See Maggie Kilgour, *From Communion to Cannibalism*, esp. 85–102, for an analysis of the traffic between eating and aggression.

72. Amartya Sen, *Poverty and Famines: An Essay on Entitlement and Deprivation*.

73. Harindranath Chattopadhyaya, "Sarojini Naidu: A Sketch," 2. She was perhaps the most skeptical, dietarily speaking, of the mahatma's associates; she dismissed his diet as "grass and goat's milk" and noted, in her inimitably waggish mode, the enormous expenditure of resources required to shepherd Gandhi safely through his fasts. See Sarojini Naidu, *Selected Letters, 1890s to 1940s*, ed. Makarand Paranjpe, 291–93. Also see Madeleine Slade (Mirabehn) for an account of some of the less successful dietary experiments at Sabarmati Ashram (*The Spirit's Pilgrimage*, 82–85).

74. As Robert P. Goldman points out in his study of hunger and lust in the *Valmiki Ramayana*, the link between the control of sexual and dietary appetites is of very ancient provenance in India ("Ravana's Kitchen: A Testimony of Desire and the Other"). Sally Goldman notes that, in the *dharmashastras*, the act of sexual intercourse constituted a violation of the fast.

75. Joseph Alter, *The Wrestler's Body: Identity and Ideology in North India*, 129.

76. See, for instance, Stephen Nissenbaum, *Sex, Diet, and Debility in Jacksonian America: Sylvester Graham and Health Reform*.

77. Gandhi, *Collected Works of Mahatma Gandhi*, vol. 85:216; Parekh, *Gandhi*, 276. The elaboration of a seminal economy is curiously silent about women, a silence Gandhi shares; can it be because he, in contrast to the tradition in which this economy is grounded, saw women as substantially free of sexual desire?

78. Rudolph and Rudolph, *The Modernity of Tradition*: "If Gandhi lived his private life in public, it was because both he and those who observed him believed that a man's claim to be just, to command others, to attain wisdom, was proportional to his capacity for self-rule" (196).

79. See Fischer, *Mahatma Gandhi*, for a brief reference to the Manilal episode.

80. M. K. Gandhi, *Hind Swaraj and Other Writings*, ed. Anthony J. Parel, 91 n. 180.

81. See Marie Griffith for an account of the ways in which fasting was deployed by male reformers of the Progressive era in the United States to purge fat, restore virility, and promote well-being ("Apostles of Abstinence: Fasting and Masculinity during the Progressive Era").

82. See Goldman's "Soul Food: Consumption, Conception, and Gender in Early Sanskrit Literary Texts," manuscript. The complex and insistently gendered terrain of food refusal, specifically anorexia, and its far from self-evident relation to heroic assertion, is elaborated by Deepika Bahri, "Disembodying the Corpus: Postcolonial Pathology in Tsitsi Dangarembga's 'Nervous Conditions.'" Also see Françoise Lionnet, "'She Breastfed Reluctance into Me': Hunger Artists in the Global Economy."

83. Sumit Sarkar, "The Conditions and Nature of Subaltern Militancy: Bengal from Swadeshi to Non-Co-operation, c. 1905–22," *Subaltern Studies III*, ed. Ranajit Guha, 314–15.

84. For the father's fast, see Pyarelal, *Mahatma Gandhi—The Early Phase*.

85. For an account of Gandhi's borrowing of modes of protest from Kathiawadi and more broadly Gujarati contexts, see Howard Spodek, "On the Origins of Gandhi's Political Methodology: The Heritage of Kathiawad and Gujarat." Also see David Hardiman, *Gandhi in His Time and Ours: The Global Legacy of His Ideas*, 39–51.

86. N. K. Bose, *Studies in Gandhism*, 2d ed., 175; quoted in Joan V. Bondurant, *Conquest of Violence: The Gandhian Philosophy of Conflict*, rev. ed., 37. Derrida on the *pharmakon*.

87. Parekh, *Gandhi*, 11. Also see Parekh, *Colonialism, Tradition and Reform*, 99–100.

88. Bondurant, *Conquest of Violence*, 119.

89. Fischer, *The Life of Mahatma Gandhi*, 385–87. For a detailed account of the fast, see Pyarelal, *The Epic Fast*.

90. Nehru, *Autobiography*.

91. See Judith M. Brown, *Gandhi: Prisoner of Hope*, 266–67, for an account of the Indian (primarily Congress) opposition to the fast.

92. B. R. Ambedkar, *Gandhi and Gandhism*, xxiv. Also see his *What Congress and Gandhi Have Done to the Untouchables*. See Gauri Viswanathan, *Outside the Fold: Conversion, Modernity, and Belief*, 211–39, for a discussion of Ambedkar's views on electoral reform.

93. In her analysis of two fictional works, Mulk Raj Anand's *Untouchable* and Shanta Rameshwar Rao's *Children of God*, Viswanathan discusses the ambivalent response of the novels' untouchables, familiar with the quotidian experience of hunger, to Gandhi's fasting (*Outside the Fold*, 223). The moral nonequivalence of hunger and fasting implied by such a response constitutes a powerful critique of Gandhi's fasting; but it also omits the religious and therapeutic contexts of his

practice. For Gandhi the action of fasting could not simply be reduced to the experience of bodily hunger.

94. Ved Mehta, *Mahatma Gandhi and His Apostles*, 153–54.

95. Pratt and Vernon, " 'Appeal from This Fiery Bed,' " 106–12.

96. Parekh, *Colonialism, Tradition and Reform*, 202.

97. Alter, *Gandhi's Body*, 41, 37, 48.

98. Laidlaw, *Riches and Renunciation*, 233–41.

99. Gandhi, *Collected Works of Mahatma Gandhi*, v. 29:290. Brown 122.

100. For a discussion of the relationship between eagerness and renunciation, see my "Transits, Transformations, and Body Talk: Gandhi's Passages from India."

101. Shahid Amin, "Gandhi as Mahatma: Gorakhpur District, Eastern UP, 1921–2," does a fine job of detailing the ways in which the legend of Gandhi circulated among subjects prompted by considerations rather distinct from those of the Congress Party.

102. M. K. Gandhi, *Young India*, 21 October 1926.

103. As Wendy Doniger notes, "Arguments about whether or not to kill, sacrifice, and/or eat animals were often at the heart of interreligious violence, sometimes the grounds on which human beings attacked other human beings (usually with words, though occasionally with blows)" (*The Hindus: An Alternative History*, 10). It is probably fair to say that Gandhi was more insistent about prescribing sexual abstinence to large numbers of people than he was to prescribing vegetarianism. His vegetarianism found its primary theater of enactment in the ashrams, especially in South Africa, and within the familial circle.

104. Wendy Doniger, "Rationalizing the Irrational Other: 'Orientalism' and the Laws of Manu," 36.

105. Cited ibid., 37–38.

106. Shetty, " 'The Quack Whom We Know,' " 17.

107. Jacques Derrida, *The Gift of Death*, trans. David Wills, 66.

108. Ibid., 84.

109. Ibid., 76.

110. Pyarelal, *Mahatma Gandhi—The Last Phase*, 2:191–95.

111. Fischer, *The Life of Mahatma Gandhi*, 491.

112. Ibid., 203.

113. On violence and therapeutics in the ayurvedic texts, see Francis Zimmerman, *The Jungle and the Aroma of Meats: An Ecological Theme in Hindu Medicine*.

114. Alter, *The Wrestler's Body*, 148. Milk is symbolically linked to semen and is consumed by men to build up seminal reserves, though these are designed to be converted into spiritual power rather than being expended in sexual activity. Alter writes, "Milk builds up a wrestler's semen reserve, but it also cools his passion, just as milk neutralizes poison. Having built up his supply of semen, however, a wrestler is not only able to neutralize the poison of passion; like the *sannyasi* [male religious ascetic or renunciant], he can turn poison back into semen. He is hyper-

virile but sexually passive and controlled. Milk contributes directly to this powerful conundrum" (*The Wrestler's Body*, 151).

115. M. K. Gandhi, "Introduction," Sushila Nayyar, *Kasturba: Wife of Gandhi*.

3. Dearth

1. There is a vast literature on subcontinental famines, especially those of the nineteenth century and the twentieth. The following is a very partial list: David Arnold, *Famine: Social Crisis and Historical Change* and "Famine in Peasant Consciousness and Peasant Action: Madras, 1876–78"; B. M. Bhatia, *Famines in India: A Study in Some Aspects of the Economic History of India (1860–1965)*; Mike Davis, *Late Victorian Holocausts: El Niño Famines and the Making of the Third World*; Romesh Chunder Dutt, *Indian Famines: Their Causes and Prevention* and *Famines and Land Assessments in India*; Kali Charan Ghosh, *Famines in Bengal, 1770–1943*; Paul Greenough, *Prosperity and Misery in Modern Bengal: The Famine of 1943–1944*; Arup Maharatna, *The Demography of Famines: An Indian Historical Perspective*; Aditee Nag Chowdhury Zilly, *The Vagrant Peasant: Agrarian Distress and Desertion in Bengal 1770 to 1830*; Amartya Sen, *Poverty and Famines: An Essay on Entitlement and Deprivation*; Sanjay Sharma, *Famine, Philanthropy and the Colonial State: North India in the Early Nineteenth Century*; Navtej Singh, *Starvation and Colonialism: A Study of Famines in the Nineteenth-Century British Punjab, 1858–1901*; Hari Shanker Srivastava, *The History of Indian Famines and Development of Famine Policy (1858–1918)*; and James Vernon, *Hunger: A Modern History*, chap. 3 ("Hunger as Political Critique").

2. W. W. Hunter's *Annals of Rural Bengal*, 7th ed., remains to this day the best source of information for the famine of 1770.

3. Rudyard Kipling, "William the Conqueror." In light of what is known now of some of the proximate causes of famine in colonial India Kipling's decision to make his leading man Scott an official in the Irrigation Department is an unwittingly ironic one.

4. Romesh Chunder Dutt, *Famines and Land Assessments in India* and *The Economic History of India*, 2 vols.; and Dadabhai Naoroji, *Poverty and Un-British Rule in India*.

5. Davis, *Late Victorian Holocausts*, 31. This was not the only occasion on which India was used as a testing ground for Utilitarian ideas; see Eric Stokes, *The English Utilitarians and India*.

6. For an analysis of political economy and the Irish famine of the 1840s, see Cecil Woodham-Smith, *The Great Hunger: Ireland, 1845–1849*; Mary Daly, *The Great Famine in Ireland*; Christine Kinealy, *This Great Calamity: The Irish Famine, 1845–1852*; Terry Eagleton, *Heathcliff and the Great Hunger: Studies in Irish Culture*; Christopher Morash, *Writing the Irish Famine*; Cormac Ó Gráda, *Black '47 and Beyond: The Great Irish Famine in History, Economy, and Memory*; and David Lloyd, "The Political Economy of the Potato."

7. Davis, *Late Victorian Holocausts*, 57.

8. The following is a rough chronology of the famine: At the beginning of the 1940s, the colonial government in New Delhi decided to prioritize Britain's war aims. The Congress Party, in protest against the subordination of Indian interests, withdrew from the running of the elected provincial governments and therefore from cooperation with British rule. The Muslim League ministry in Bengal, however, did not resign; but it remained distinctly subordinate to the British governor of the province as well as to British military authorities and civil servants.

The Japanese conquest of Burma in 1942 cut off imports of coarse Burmese rice into Bengal and induced terror in the colonial government. The "boat denial" scheme, which was undertaken in response to fears of a Japanese invasion, removed or destroyed tens of thousands of boats in coastal areas, thus effectively eliminating the means of livelihood of large numbers of fishermen and the mode of transportation of people and goods in an area where rivers were widely used for transportation. This was matched by a "rice denial" scheme, through which cultivators were forced to sell tens of thousands of tons of grain to the government for the purpose of supplying the military and the industrial workers who were essential to the war effort.

These exercises in boat denial and rice denial induced widespread panic and an epidemic of hoarding. Prices increased exponentially over the course of 1943; growers and traders withheld their stocks from the market, either out of fear of requisitioning or price controls or in the hope of making large profits in the face of rapidly rising prices. Developments such as these led to the widespread sense that the famine of 1943–44 (1350 in the Bangla calendar) was a man-made event rather than one precipitated by agricultural shortages or natural calamities. As massive price increases put rice out of the reach of peasants, sharecroppers, fishermen, and others of the rural poor, they sold what land and other goods they possessed in distress sales. Rural refugees poured into the cities, especially Calcutta, in the hundreds of thousands. The clumsy, erratic, and inefficient interventions of the beleaguered provincial government, combined with the indifference of Delhi and of Whitehall, meant that very little famine relief reached the affected rural areas. The refugees were fed in "gruel kitchens" run in Calcutta by private charities and by the Revenue Department. But this was far from sufficient to feed the large numbers of starving people in the city, many of whom perished. The *aman* (winter) harvest of rice in 1943–44 was unprecedentedly large, and this lured some refugees back to their rural homes, as did the forced repatriation schemes of the government. But the period of recovery was prolonged and uncertain, as the rural population contended with epidemics of smallpox, cholera, and malaria. Scholars such as Greenough and Sen suggest that the endpoint of the famine should properly be seen as mid-1946 rather than 1944.

9. The *Statesman*, Calcutta, 14 September 1943; reprinted in Ian Stephens, *Monsoon Morning*, 188. See Nancy Scheper-Hughes, *Death Without Weeping: The Violence of Everyday Life in Brazil*, for a scathing analysis of the ways in which the modern

Brazilian state colludes with the biomedical health care system to recode chronic hunger as a psychological problem requiring medication rather than food: "Nervos, a rich folk conceptual scheme for describing relations among body, mind, and social body, is appropriated by medicine and transformed into something other: a biomedical disease that alienates mind from body and that conceals the social relations of sickness" (169).

10. Amartya Sen, *Development as Freedom.*

11. *Famine Inquiry Commission Report on Bengal* (1944), 108–46.

12. W. R. Aykroyd, *Conquest of Famine,* 77.

13. Amartya Sen, *Poverty and Famines,* especially "Appendix D, Famine Mortality: A Case Study," 217–49. Sugata Bose and Ayesha Jalal suggest that between 3.5 and 3.8 million people were killed as a result of the famine; see *Modern South Asia: History, Culture, Political Economy,* 157. Also see Sugata Bose, "Starvation amidst Plenty: The Making of Famine in Bengal, Honan, and Tonkin, 1942–45."

14. For a history of the Naxalite movement, see Sumanta Banerjee, *India's Simmering Revolution: The Naxalite Uprising.*

15. Ranajit Guha, "Introduction," *A Subaltern Studies Reader, 1986–1995,* xiii. Also see C. A. Bayly, "Rallying Around the Subaltern," reprinted in *Mapping Subaltern Studies and the Postcolonial,* ed. Vinayak Chaturvedi.

16. Henry Schwarz describes the concept of the subaltern in the Subaltern Studies project as "a provocation, a theoretical fiction designed to prod the middle class into awareness of its own historic complicity in disciplining the masses it could never learn to represent" ("Subaltern Studies: Radical History in the Metaphoric Mode"; reprint. David Ludden, ed. *Reading Subaltern Studies: Critical History, Contested Meaning and the Globalization of South Asia,* 322). For a summary of the bhadralok's production as a figure of simultaneous assimilation and discontent in nineteenth- and early twentieth-century India, see my "Bhadralok/bhadramahila."

17. Nikhil Sarkar, *A Matter of Conscience: Artists Bear Witness to the Great Bengal Famine of 1943,* trans. Satyabrata Dutta, 22.

18. Bijon Bhattacharya, *Nabanna.*

19. "Bichhan (Seeds)," in *Women, Outcastes, Peasants, and Rebels,* ed. and trans. Kalpana Bardhan, 165.

20. "Daini (The Witch-Hunt)," in ibid., 258.

21. The term *tribe,* used to denominate the aboriginal peoples of the subcontinent, is a standard one in South Asian sociology, being used to distinguish such communities from those subsumed under the Hindu term *caste.* Occasionally the term *adivasi* is used as a synonym for the tribal subject. These are not necessarily rigidly bounded categories, though, and the history of subaltern social transformation notes instances of the absorption ("sanskritization," in Srinivas's terms) of tribals into caste Hindu society (at the bottom rungs, needless to say). In recent years, a resurgent and high-caste Hindu fundamentalism has sought to recruit

tribal subjects into a caste Hindu fold. For an account of the colonial and late nationalist understanding of tribe and caste, see Ajay Skaria, "Shades of Wildness: Tribe, Caste, and Gender in Western India."

22. See, for instance, *Dust on the Road: The Activist Writings of Mahasweta Devi*, ed. Maitreya Ghatak.

23. Mahasweta Devi in *Mahasweta Devi: Witness, Advocate, Writer* (dir. Shashwati Talukdar, 2001). Maitreya Ghatak has described *Bortika* as "the first significant effort in alternative literature in Bengali" ("Introduction," *Dust on the Road*).

24. Mahasweta Devi in conversation with Enakshi Chatterjee, 171.

25. Journalists appear repeatedly in Mahasweta's fiction as figures of the crisis of postcolonial liberalism; see the journalist Kali Santra in "Operation Bashai Tudu."

26. Mahasweta Devi, " 'Palamau Is a Mirror of India': An Introduction," *Bitter Soil*, vii.

27. Ibid., ix.

28. Mahasweta Devi, "Pterodactyl, Puran Sahay, and Pirtha," 127.

29. Mahasweta Devi, "Douloti the Bountiful," 31–32. I have made a couple of minor modifications to the translation.

30. I have borrowed the term *enumerated community* from Sudipta Kaviraj, though I cannot subscribe to his somewhat romantic notions of what constitutes its opposite, the premodern "fuzzy community"; see "The Imaginary Institution of India." Also see Benedict Anderson, "Census, Map, Museum," for a fine account of the ways in which the national subject is called into being as individual, identifiable, and fixed (*Imagined Communities: Reflections on the Origin and Spread of Nationalism*, rev. ed.). Viswanathan demonstrates that the census has always been marked by vexatious deficits in exactitude and by the often peremptory exercise of the census taker's classificatory authority; see her *Outside the Fold: Conversion, Modernity, and Belief*, 159–63. On the nineteenth-century history of the census in India, see Bernard Cohn, "The Census, Social Structure, and Objectification in South Asia." As Anderson, Cohn, and Appadurai have noted, demography was never politically innocent, especially in colonial contexts; see, for instance, Appadurai, "Number in the Colonial Imagination." In distinction to Appadurai, Sussman has drawn attention to the ways in which "most of the groundbreaking work in human statistics was done among colonial or subaltern populations—in Scotland, Ireland, the New World, and among the urban poor," and was thus already ideologically inflected before its export to colonies in Africa, southeast Asia, and the Indian subcontinent ("The Colonial Afterlife of Political Arithmetic: Swift, Demography, and Mobile Populations," 111).

31. Michael Watts, *Silent Violence: Food, Famine and Peasantry in Northern Nigeria*.

32. Jacques Derrida, *Specters of Marx: The State of the Debt, the Work of Mourning, and the New International*, trans. Peggy Kamuf. Also see Avery F. Gordon's answer to

the question, "What kind of case is the case of a ghost?": "It is often a case of inarticulate experiences, of symptoms and screen memories, of spiraling effects, of more than one story at a time, of the traffic in domains of experience that are anything but transparent and referential" (*Ghostly Matters: Haunting and the Sociological Imagination*, 24, 25).

33. Gordon, *Ghostly Matters*, 23. Despite the somewhat awkward rhetoric of talking and listening to ghosts, Gordon's project is not a liberal one.

34. Jenny Edkins, *Whose Hunger? Concepts of Famine, Practices of Aid*, 13.

35. Mary Poovey, *A History of the Modern Fact: Problems of Knowledge in the Sciences of Wealth and Society*, 307–28. Poovey notes that it was the jettisoning of the providential language in the 1806 edition, combined with the addition of what were conceived as secular, nontheological "numbers: tables of annuities, population growth, and food prices, which were assembled from records as diverse as bills of mortality, census returns, and agricultural records," that made Malthus immensely unpopular with the reading public (290).

36. Thomas Robert Malthus, *An Essay on the Principle of Population*, ed. Geoffrey Gilbert, 61.

37. Sen has been accused of this in the distinction he seeks to draw for his reading of crisis: "Starvation is used here in the wider sense of people going without adequate food, while famine is a particularly virulent manifestation of its causing widespread death" (*Poverty and Famines*, 40). Notwithstanding his detractors, some of whom read him rather hastily, Sen is a subtle thinker and writer. He states this about the distinction he makes between starvation and famine, "The definitional exercise is more interesting in providing a pithy description of what happens in situations clearly diagnosed as one of famine than in helping us do the diagnosis—the traditional function of a definition" (*Poverty and Famines*, 40 n. 3).

38. Amrita Rangasami, " 'Failure of Exchange Entitlements' Theory of Famine: A Response," 1800. Also see David Arnold, *Famine: Social Crisis and Historical Change*, 44–45: "Sen's hypothesis, . . . has drawn attention to famine's uneven and discriminatory impact. . . . But, for all the unquestionable impact of his work, it must be doubted whether Sen has really provided a theory of famine *causation*, as he contends in challenging the 'food availability decline' argument, so much as given an explanation of how famines develop once they have (for whatever reason) been set in motion." In fairness to Sen, it should be stated that he has persuasively *disproved* (in taking on the "food availability decline" argument) what was believed to be the cause of famine. Alex de Waal uses local perceptions of famine in Darfur, Sudan, to discriminate between famines, which cause disruptions, including death, in a way of life, and "famines that kill," which involve excess mortality. Even if famine is distinguished by death alone, its mortality figures are notoriously difficult to calculate, especially as a relatively small percentage of deaths in a given famine are explicitly attributable to starvation; most famine deaths are

attributable to diseases such as cholera, malaria, and dysentery (Alex de Waal, *Famine That Kills: Darfur, Sudan, 1984–1985*).

39. The work of Manik Bandopadhyay and Zainul Abedin are good examples of these. My thanks to Sudipta Sen for reminding me of this.

40. David Lloyd, "The Indigent Sublime: Specters of Irish Hunger," 156.

41. Rabindranath Tagore, *Rabindra Rachanabali*, vol. 11. Rabindranath was something of a master of the ghost story, a popular genre in Bengali literary and folk traditions. I am grateful to Amitav Ghosh for alerting me to the resonances between "Kshudito Pashan" and a tale such as "Shishu."

42. On the vexed reform of the civil service in Victorian Britain, see Lauren Goodlad, " 'A Middle Class Cut into Two': Historiography and Victorian National Character." Civil service reforms in colonial India were themselves the subject of ambivalence and criticism, as the discussions about "competitionwallahs" demonstrated.

43. Dipesh Chakrabarty, "The Time of History and the Times of Gods."

44. Mahasweta Devi, "Strange Children," 229 (subsequent citations will be incorporated parenthetically into the text).

45. See Sandria Freitag, "Collective Crime and Authority in North India" and "Crime in the Social Order of Colonial North India"; Sanjay Nigam, "Disciplining and Policing the 'Criminals by Birth' "; and Radhika Singha, " 'Providential' Circumstances: The Thuggee Campaign of the 1830s and Legal Innovation."

46. Mahasweta Devi, "The Witch-Hunt," in *Of Women, Outcastes, Peasants, and Rebels*, ed. and trans. Kalpana Bardhan.

47. Gyan Prakash, *Bonded Histories: Genealogies of Labor Servitude in Colonial India*, 200.

48. Prakash, *Bonded Histories*, 210–11.

49. See David Lloyd's work on the Great Famine in Ireland for a splendid analysis of the uncertainty induced in the English observer by the Irish practice of keening and by the Irish "emotional economy" generally ("The Memory of Hunger").

50. Giorgio Agamben, *Remnants of Auschwitz: The Witness and the Archive*, trans. Daniel Heller-Roazen, 55. The fact that the Muselmann is a figure of " 'Oriental' agony" (70) is not inconsequential to his being rendered as a figure on his way to becoming inhuman. For a further, fascinating gloss on the religio-cultural and political implications of the use of the term, see Gil Anidjar, *The Jew, the Muslim: A History of the Enemy*.

51. In Mahasweta's fictional universe, tribal and low-caste subjects routinely address their feudal superiors as devta or deota. The relief officer's sense of his singularity in being so addressed is misplaced, to say the least.

52. Jacques Derrida, *Given Time: 1. Counterfeit Money*, trans. Peggy Kamuf, 6.

53. Ibid., 7. Also see "Economimesis."

54. Jacques Derrida, *The Gift of Death*, trans. David Wills, 95.

55. Jean-Luc Nancy, "Love and Community: A round-table discussion with Jean-Luc Nancy, Avital Ronell and Wolfgang Schirmacher," August 2001.

56. Derrida, *Given Time*, 24, 26.

57. Ibid., 14.

58. Ibid., 13.

59. Ibid., 12.

60. See Gayatri Spivak, "Woman in Difference: Mahasweta Devi's 'Douloti the Bountiful,'" for a gendered analysis of bond slavery in modern India.

61. Prakash, *Bonded Histories*, 185.

62. Derrida is not explicitly attentive to the gender of the specter, whether in *Hamlet* or in *The German Ideology*, even though both texts are centrally about patrimonial legacies, whether of a Danish or Hegelian variety. In "Marx and Sons," though, he insists that "the question of woman and sexual difference is at the heart of [the] analysis of spectral filiation" (231). (This is more than can be said for the rest of the cast of *Ghostly Demarcations*.) Also see Gayatri Spivak's "Ghostwriting" for a notation of the gender of ghosts.

63. Prakash notes that for Bhuinyas and caste Hindus in southern Bihar, "the only female ghosts that existed were those who were believed to be evil" (*Bonded Histories*, 203).

64. Margaret Kelleher, *The Feminization of Famine: Expressions of the Inexpressible?* 6–7.

65. It is perhaps not too much of a stretch to link this to the representations of the breakdown of maternality in accounts of the famine of 1943.

66. See Cathy Caruth's description of the nature of trauma: "At the core of these stories [of trauma], I would suggest, is . . . a kind of double telling, the oscillation between a *crisis of death* and the correlative *crisis of life*: between the story of the unbearable nature of an event and the story of the unbearable nature of its survival" (*Unclaimed Experience: Trauma, Narrative, and History*, 7).

67. Mahasweta Devi, "Pterodactyl, Puran Sahay, and Pirtha," 142.

68. Akira Lippit, *Electric Animal: Toward a Rhetoric of Wildlife*, 165.

69. Ibid., 1.

70. Patrick Brantlinger, *Dark Vanishings: Discourse on the Extinction of Primitive Races, 1800–1930*.

71. Ajay Skaria, *Hybrid Histories: Forests, Frontiers and Wildness in Western India*, xi.

72. Ibid., 277–81. In the subcontinent, Hindu nationalism has long sought to distinguish so-called Aryans, the putative ancestors of caste Hindus, from Muslims, who are cast as outsiders and invaders. Not surprisingly, its adherents are made uncomfortable, as Skaria notes, by the popularity of the term *adivasi* to designate non-Hindu groups.

73. These claims to autochthony are asserted in the present moment in terms of attachment to sacred ecologies of dwelling and subsistence and against the en-

croachments and deracinating initiatives of mainstream populations and states. They should not be seen as a valorization of autochthony under all circumstances. For a well-considered caution against the mystifications of autochthonist arguments (as distinct from historical ones), especially in the instance of Zionism, see Daniel Boyarin and Jonathan Boyarin, "Diaspora: Generation and the Ground of Jewish Identity."

74. As Gayatri Spivak notes, "The sentiment of an entire nation as place of origin is not a statement within aboriginal discursive formations, where locality is of much greater importance" (A Critique of Postcolonial Reason: Toward a History of the Vanishing Present, 141–42 n. 43).

75. Sumathi Ramaswamy, The Lost Land of Lemuria: Fabulous Geographies, Catastrophic Histories, 1.

76. This is not to dismiss all deployments of nostalgia as regressive, but only to suggest that it is not part of Mahasweta's apparatus for imagining the possibility of an alternative, just future for the tribals. For a reading of the productive uses of reflective nostalgia, see Gaurav Desai, "Old World Orders: Amitav Ghosh and the Writing of Nostalgia."

77. Mahasweta Devi, Chotti Munda and His Arrow, trans. Gayatri Chakravorty Spivak.

78. Akira Lippit, "The Death of an Animal" and Electric Animal, 27–54.

79. Simon A. Cole, "Do Androids Pulverize Tiger Bones to Use as Aphrodisiacs?"

80. Achille Mbembe, "Necropolitics," trans. Libby Meintjes. The "war machine" he describes combines the functions of a mobile, disaggregated militia, a political organization, and a mercantile company (32–33).

81. Ibid., 35, 40.

82. Ibid., 29.

83. Bliss Cua Lim identifies this uncanny temporality as characteristic of the way in which the ghost film in the Philippines takes on the question of historical justice; see her "Spectral Times: The Ghost Film as Historical Allegory."

84. "You ask at what moment one becomes a face. I do not know at what moment the human appears, but what I want to emphasize is that the human breaks with pure being, which is always a persistence in being. This is my principal thesis. A being is something that is attached to being, to its own being. That is Darwin's idea. The being of animals is a struggle for life. A struggle of life without ethics. It is a question of might" ("The Paradox of Morality: An Interview with Emmanuel Levinas," trans. Andrew Benjamin and Tamara Wright, in The Provocation of Levinas: Rethinking the Other, ed. Robert Bernasconi and David, 169; reprint. Animal Philosophy: Essential Readings in Continental Thought, 50). It should be admitted that Levinas's refusal to concede the possibility of an animal face is not an easy position for him to maintain; it is a conclusion reached after very obvious struggle.

85. See Wendy Doniger's reflections on J. M. Coetzee, *The Lives of Animals*, ed. Amy Gutmann.

86. "*Ecce animot*. Neither a species nor a gender nor an individual, it is an irreducible living multiplicity of mortals, and rather than a double clone or a portmanteau word, a sort of monstrous hybrid, a chimera waiting to be put to death by its Bellerophon" (Jacques Derrida, "The Animal That Therefore I Am (More to Follow)," trans. David Wills, 409).

87. Michel de Montaigne: "It is a nation, . . . that hath no kind of traffic, no knowledge of letters, no intelligence of numbers, no name of magistrate nor of politic superiority, no use of service, of riches or of poverty, no contracts, no successions, no partitions, no occupation but idle, no respect of kindred but common, no apparel but natural, no manuring of lands, no use of wine, corn, or metal. The very words that import lying, falsehood, treason, dissimulations, covetousness, envy, detraction, and pardon were never heard of amongst them" ("Of Cannibals," trans. John Florio, 1603).

88. For a discussion of "the double connotation of proximity and strangeness" in the neighbor, see Kenneth Reinhard, "Kant with Sade, Lacan with Levinas."

89. Spivak gives the name of "ethical singularity" to this individual, everyday, one-on-one (rather than crisis-driven) encounter with the subaltern: " 'Ethical singularity' is neither 'mass contact' nor engagement with 'the common sense of the people.' . . . the object of ethical action is not an object of benevolence, for here responses flow from both sides. It is not identical with the frank and open exchange between radicals and the oppressed in times of crisis, or the intimacy that anthropologists often claim with their informant groups, although the importance of at least the former should not be minimized. This encounter can only happen when the respondents inhabit something like normality. Most political engagements fail in the long run because of the absence of this engagement" ("Translator's Preface," *Imaginary Maps*, xxv).

90. I have borrowed the idiom of "unlearning" from Spivak, from her aphorism that we, as subjects of privilege and exploitation, must "unlearn our privilege as our loss."

91. Gayatri Chakravorty Spivak, "Subaltern Talk: Interview with the Editors," 191.

92. See Derrida, "The Animal That Therefore I Am (More to Follow)," for the question of the animal address. In an otherwise admiring reading of this essay, David Wood cautions against domesticating the animal's address, associating it first and foremost with "companion species" such as the cat: "One of my concerns is that there is, if only in a residual way, a certain hubris, in insisting on being addressed by an animal (once we have discovered that this is possible!). Much of that to which we do violence has no name, and does not address us. We must perhaps begin with the ruptures in the familiar, with the uncanny we find at home. But we must also step off the porch and reflect on the violence that is being done in our name, without our knowing it, and the violence happening behind the

back of history merely as an exaggerated consequence of the individually reason-able things we do" (David Wood, "Thinking with Cats,"143). The just caution Wood proffers here can also be brought to bear upon texts like Donna Haraway's *The Companion Species Manifesto: Dogs, People, and Significant Otherness.*

93. On "divinanimality" see Jacques Derrida, "And Say the Animal Re-sponded?" 134. On "humananimality," see Steven Connor, "Thinking Perhaps Begins There: The Question of the Animal."

94. On this question, see Petar Ramadanovic, "When 'To Die in Freedom' Is Written in English."

95. Thomas Keenan, *Fables of Responsibility: Aberrations and Predicaments in Ethics and Politics,* 28.

96. Derrida, "Force of Law: The 'Mystical Foundation of Authority,'" trans. Mary Quaintance, 16.

97. See Spivak's gloss on this in "Righting Wrongs": "[The] real effort should be to access and activate the tribals' 'indigenous' democratic structures to *parlia-mentary* democracy by patient and sustained efforts to learn from below. *Activate* is the key word here. There is no tight cultural fabric (as opposed to group soli-darity) among these disenfranchised groups after centuries of oppression and neglect" ("Righting Wrongs," 548).

98. Judith Butler, "Ethical Ambivalence."

99. Mahasweta Devi, "Telling History: Gayatri Chakravorty Spivak Interviews Mahasweta Devi," *Chotti Munda and His Arrow,* x.

100. Jean-Luc Nancy, "Love and Community." Also see "Shattered Love."

4. Appetite

1. Deepika Bahri, *Native Intelligence: Aesthetics, Politics, and Postcolonial Literature,* 155.

2. Of English-language fiction in India before *Midnight's Children,* Meenakshi Mukherjee says, "It was as if the burden of English was too heavy and the entire enterprise was grinding to a halt. Unlike novels in the other Indian languages which had lively constituencies comprising people from different walks of life, the novel in English seemed to be a walled-in entity, constructed and sustained by the academics of English departments, in an attempt to give some local relevance to their own profession which was otherwise largely dependent on foreign sources" ("Introduction," *Rushdie's Midnight's Children: A Book of Readings,* 11).

3. Ankhi Mukherjee, "Fissured Skin, Inner-Ear Radio, and a Telepathic Nose: The Senses as Media in Salman Rushdie's *Midnight's Children,*" 61.

4. Sara Suleri, *Meatless Days,* 28 (subsequent citations will be incorporated parenthetically into the text).

5. Patricia Merivale, "Saleem Fathered by Oskar: Intertextual Strategies in *Midnight's Children* and *The Tin Drum,*" 127.

6. In *The Ground Beneath Her Feet*, Ormus Cama deploys bad puns to allegorize his turn to the West in terms of allegiances to different forms of bread: "Ormus Cama plunges into this new world, betraying, without a backward glance, the fabled breads of home. . . . East is East, thinks Ormus Cama; ah, but yeast is West" (289–90).

7. Salman Rushdie, *The Moor's Last Sigh*, 104 (future citations will be incorporated parenthetically into the text).

8. Timothy Morton, *The Poetics of Spice: Romantic Consumerism and the Exotic*, 18.

9. Madhur Jaffrey, *An Invitation to Indian Cooking*, 5 (future citations will be incorporated parenthetically into the text).

10. Madhur Jaffrey, *Madhur Jaffrey's Indian Cookery*, 9.

11. Madhur Jaffrey, *From Curries to Kebabs: Recipes from the Indian Spice Trail*, 8. This was originally published in the United Kingdom as *Madhur Jaffrey's Ultimate Curry Bible*.

12. Lizzie Collingham, *Curry: A Tale of Cooks and Conquerors*, 118.

13. Ibid., 141.

14. Cited in Antoinette Burton, *The Postcolonial Careers of Santha Rama Rau*, 109.

15. Ibid., 130.

16. Susan Zlotnick, "Domesticating Imperialism: Curry and Cookbooks in Victorian England," and Uma Narayan, "Eating Cultures: Identity, Incorporation, Indian Food."

17. She has produced for the Tilda food products company a number of pickles and cook-in sauces.

18. Shrabani Basu, *Curry in the Crown: The Story of Britain's Favourite Dish*, xvi. Basu provides a detailed account of "currymania" in Britain in the 1980s and 1990s. (Appropriately, the favorite so-called curry dish of most Britons is chicken tikka masala, a dish created in London by Bangladeshi restaurateurs in response to local demand for a sauce to accompany the tikkas.) The magnum opus of Isabella Beeton, Jaffrey's nineteenth-century predecessor, is *The Book of Household Management*. It is appropriate that in postimperial London Jaffrey's likeness should hang in the National Portrait Gallery.

19. Pat Chapman, the founder of the British-based Curry Club, notes on his Web site his unavailing endeavors to patent the term "curry bible" as his own: www.patchapman.co.uk, visited 26 November 2007).

20. Jaffrey, *From Curries to Kebabs*, 7.

21. For a discussion of some the difficulties of autoethnography, see James Buzard, "On Auto-Ethnographic Authority."

22. Rushdie, *The Moor's Last Sigh*, 150. My attention was drawn to this passage by Deepika Bahri's fine reading of the anxieties about representation in postcolonial literature (*Native Intelligence: Aesthetics, Politics, and Postcolonial Literature*, 160).

23. Chitrita Banerji, *Eating India: An Odyssey into the Food and Culture of the Land of*

Spices, 38. Jaffrey herself uses the term in her autobiography, *Climbing the Mango Trees: A Memoir of a Childhood in India.*

24. *Meatless Days*, nominally similar to *Midnight's Children* in many of its themes and metaphoric investments—both depict the strange interanimation of private and public histories, both are poised between autobiography and fiction, and both turn to the sensory and the culinary as heuristic devices—cannot, however, be linked to it through a simple copula. If anything it is a brilliant departure from the epic-fabulist mode of Rushdie's novel and the grandiloquence and verbosity of its narrator, Saleem. Its relative modesty is an effect of its scale; it is also an effect of its focus upon the everyday gendered politics of the Pakistani household. What Gayatri Spivak identifies as Rushdie's "anxiety to write woman into the narrative of history" is recast productively by Suleri ("Reading *The Satanic Verses*"). Hence her "translation" of Rushdie produces both recognition and disorientation.

25. Arjun Appadurai, "How to Make a National Cuisine: Cookbooks in Contemporary India," 11.

26. Inderpal Grewal describes the metaphorizability of food and body in the book in the following terms: "Pregnancy, eating, motherhood, and injury . . . become metaphors for the elasticity of the boundaries of this subject made up of unstable parts. The prevalence of the metaphor of food all through the narrative emphasizes the notion of incorporation and multiplicity, rather than a complete whole" ("Autobiographic Subjects and Diasporic Locations: *Meatless Days* and *Borderlands*," 241).

27. Gayatri C. Spivak, *A Critique of Postcolonial Reason: Toward a History of the Vanishing Present*, 402.

28. Gayatri C. Spivak, "Diasporas Old and New: Women in the Transnational World." It is crucial to take cognizance of the nonuniformity in class terms of a late capitalist westward migration; Spivak's focus on the class-marked New Immigrant (rather than all immigrants) is a result of this figure's emblematic status not only as upwardly mobile model minority but also as "the unexamined referent for all postcoloniality" ("Poststructuralism, Marginality, Postcoloniality, and Value," 228). On older South Asian diasporas in Britain and the United States, see Rozina Visram, *Ayahs, Lascars, and Princes: Indians in Britain, 1700–1947*; Antoinette Burton, *At the Heart of the Empire: Indians and the Colonial Encounter in Late Victorian Britain*; Sukanya Banerjee, *Becoming Imperial Citizens*; Shompa Lahiri, *Indians in Britain: Anglo-Indian Encounters, Race and Identity, 1880–1930*; Karen Leonard, *Making Ethnic Choices: California's Punjabi-Mexican-Americans*; Brian Keith Axel, *The Nation's Tortured Body: Violence, Representation, and the Formation of a "Sikh" Diaspora*; and Tony Ballantyne, *Between Colonialism and Diaspora: Sikh Cultural Formations in an Imperial World.*

29. Susan Koshy, "Introduction," *Transnational South Asians: The Making of a Neo-Diaspora*, 16.

30. Khachig Tololyan, "The Contemporary Discourse of Diaspora Studies," 648.

31. Khachig Tololyan, "The Nation-State and Its Others: In Lieu of a Preface," 4.

32. James Clifford, "Diasporas."

33. Arjun Appadurai, *Modernity at Large: Cultural Dimensions of Globalization.*

34. Arjun Appadurai, *Fear of Small Numbers: An Essay on the Geography of Anger.*

35. Aihwa Ong, *Flexible Citizenship: The Cultural Logics of Transnationality*, 135.

36. Bahri, *Native Intelligence*, 159.

37. Timothy Brennan, *Salman Rushdie and the Third World: Myths of the Nation* and *At Home in the World: Cosmopolitanism Now.* Also see Aijaz Ahmad, *In Theory*; and Revathi Krishnaswamy, "Mythologies of Migrancy: Postcolonialism, Postmodernism, and the Politics of (Dis)Location." While Pheng Cheah's disapprobation of the "discrepant cosmopolitanism" examined by Clifford and Bhabha does not share Brennan's privileging of biography, it, too, insists on the politically dubious claims of migrancy talk (as against that of a progressive "popular nationalism" of a global periphery): "[Is] it not obvious, from the start, that the paradigm for these radical cosmopolitanisms is not really decolonized space but the metropolitan scenario of migracy and mobility?" ("Given Culture: Rethinking Cosmopolitical Freedom in Transnationalism," 300). For a response to criticisms of his work, see James Clifford, "Mixed Feelings."

38. For a salutary caution against a zero sum logic that insists on an exact match between privilege at the core and underdevelopment at the periphery, see Bruce Robbins's "Comparative Cosmopolitanisms."

39. Deepika Bahri, *Native Intelligence*; Inderpal Grewal, "Becoming American: The Novel and the Diaspora," *Transnational America: Feminisms, Diasporas, Neoliberalisms*, 35–79; and Bishnupriya Ghosh, *When Borne Across: Literary Cosmopolitics in the Contemporary Indian Novel.*

40. R. S. Khare, *Culture and Reality: Essays on the Hindu System of Managing Foods* and *The Hindu Hearth and Home.*

41. These cookbooks hailed a relatively novel constituency of cooks and consumers who read in order to learn how to cook. As Jaffrey observes in *Invitation to Indian Cooking* and as Keya Ganguly confirms, "Cookbooks are . . . largely inessential; they represent the refuge of the untrained" (*States of Exception: Everyday Life and Postcolonial Identity*, 129).

42. In a similar vein, see Roland Barthes on French food advertising: "[It] assigns to food a function that is, in some sense, commemorative: food permits a person (and I am here speaking of French themes) to partake each day of the national past. In this case, the historical quality is obviously linked to food techniques (preparation and cooking). . . . They are, we are told, the repository of a whole experience, of the accumulated wisdom of our ancestors. . . . it is fair to say that through his food the Frenchman experiences a certain national continuity. By way of a thousand detours, food permits him to insert himself daily into his own

past and to believe in a certain culinary 'being' of France" ("Towards a Psychosociology of Contemporary Food Consumption," 24).

43. Jaffrey is not necessarily unique in her production of the cookbook as national allegory. Rombauer's *The Joy of Cooking* has functioned as an American institution, a resource consulted over several generations on the basics for its ease of use and its compilation of time-honored, quintessentially American recipes. (The fact that it was chosen by the New York Public Library in 1995 as one of the 150 most consequential books of the century is evidence enough of its talismanic status.) In Britain, Beeton's *Book of Household Management* has served a similar function (though it is not as much in current use as *The Joy of Cooking* is), dedicated as it is to "plain English" food, complete with a preference for overdone vegetables, and to a careful sequestration of deleterious French influences. On the content and impact of Beeton's work, see Elizabeth David, "Isabella Beeton and Her Book," and Graham Nown, *Mrs. Beeton: 150 Years of Cookery and Household Management*. The national imaginary features more overtly in Jaffrey than in Rombauer or Beeton, an inescapable corollary of the diasporic production of her work.

44. Susan J. Leonardi, "Recipes for Reading: Summer Pastas, Lobster à la Riseholme, and Key Lime Pie." The informality of the earlier editions of Rombauer's book is underscored in its title: *The Joy of Cooking: A Compilation of Reliable Recipes, with an Occasional Culinary Chat.*

45. Chitrita Banerji, *Life and Food in Bengal*; Jennifer Brennan, *Curries and Bugles: A Memoir and Cookbook of the British Raj.*

46. Jacket blurb for Jennifer Brennan, *Curries and Bugles.*

47. On the Festivals of India, see Sandhya Shukla, *India Abroad: Diasporic Cultures of Postwar America and England*. This decade also saw an assiduous cultivation by the Indian state, through advertising, filmmaking, and investment opportunities, of that favored diasporic subject, the Non-Resident Indian (NRI), a term commonly reserved for erstwhile citizens now resident in the First World. Facing a balance of payments crisis in the early 1970s, the Indian state created the category of the NRI in order to solicit remittances from economically successful Indian immigrants in the United Kingdom, North America, Hong Kong, and Singapore; see Shukla, *India Abroad*, 59. Bakirathi Mani and Latha Varadarajan explain that the NRI "was meant to signify the professional migrant in Europe and North America, whereas 'person of Indian origin' (PIO)—a category that became more prominent in the late 1990s—was meant to be an umbrella term that included third- and fourth-generation immigrants in southeast Asia, the Caribbean, and Africa whose forebears had initially left the Indian subcontinent during the period of colonial occupation to provide unskilled and semi-skilled labor in other colonial territories" ("'The Largest Gathering of the Global Indian Family': Neoliberalism, Nationalism, and Diaspora at Pravasi Bharatiya Divas," 71).

48. James Buzard, *Disorienting Fiction: The Autoethnographic Work of Nineteenth-Century British Novels.*

49. Anne McClintock, "Family Feuds: Gender, Nation and the Family."

50. Jaffrey, *Climbing the Mango Trees*, 217.

51. Jean-François Revel, *Culture and Cuisine: A Journey Through the History of Food*, trans. Helen R. Lane.

52. See Frank F. Conlon, "Dining Out in Bombay," for a description of the development of public dining in Bombay over the course of the century.

53. Luce Giard describes her stake in the study of everyday cooking practices in terms that are analogous, if more romantic: "A will to learn to consider the fleeting and unpretentious ways of operating that are often the only place of inventiveness available to the subject: they represent precarious inventions without anything to consolidate them, without a language to articulate them, without the acknowledgment to raise them up; they are bricolages subject to the weight of economic constraints, inscribed in the network of concrete determinations" ("Doing-Cooking," 155–56).

54. Lily Cho, "On Eating Chinese: Chinese Restaurants and the Politics of Diaspora," 73.

55. Ibid., 72.

56. Jaffrey was told that the day after she made Lemony Chicken with Coriander on the BBC show, all the cilantro in Manchester sold out (*From Curries to Kebabs*, 32).

57. Madhur Jaffrey, *Madhur Jaffrey's Indian Cookery*, 8.

58. It would be instructive to juxtapose against these fictions of culinary amalgamation the many Indian texts, mostly though not exclusively in Indian languages (from Tagore's *Gora* [1910] to U. R. Ananthamurthy's *Samskara* [1965]), that stage the difficulties rather than the pleasures of commensality.

59. Madhur Jaffrey, *Madhur Jaffrey's Cookbook: Easy East/West Menus for Family and Friends*, 225, 255.

60. Stephen Mennell, *All Manners of Food: Eating and Taste in England and France from the Middle Ages to the Present*, 271. See Krishnendu Ray, *The Migrant's Table: Meals and Memories in Bengali–American Households*, for an account of the nostalgic imperative in expatriate investments, often imaginative and affective rather than practically realized, in the foods of home.

61. Madhur Jaffrey, *A Taste of India*, 107–8.

62. For a related discussion of food processing that serves to distance the viewer from the recipe, though in a distinctly different class context, see Barthes, "Ornamental Cookery": "This ornamental cookery is indeed supported by wholly mythical economics. . . . It is, in the fullest meaning of the word, a cuisine of advertisement, totally magical, especially when one remembers that this magazine [*Elle*] is widely read in small-income groups. The latter, in fact, explains the former: it is because *Elle* is addressed to a genuinely working-class public that it is very careful not to take for granted that cooking must be economical" (Roland Barthes, *Mythologies*, trans. Annette Lavers, 79). Stephen Mennell's criticism of

Barthes's errors about the empirical details of the food publications he compares (*All Manners of Food*, 250–55) does not invalidate Barthes's larger point about the irreducibility of many forms of gastronomic writing to serviceability alone.

63. Walter Benjamin, "The Work of Art in the Age of Mechanical Reproduction," 231. Also see "The Storyteller" and "On Some Motifs in Baudelaire."

64. On Benjamin's ambivalence about the vanishing of the aura, see Miriam Hansen, "Benjamin, Cinema and Experience: 'The Blue Flower in the Land of Technology.' "

65. A. L. Basham, *The Wonder That Was India*.

66. Appadurai, *Modernity at Large*, 77–78. See, too, his analysis of this question elsewhere in the same volume: "The past is not now a land to return to in a simple politics of memory. It has become a synchronic warehouse of cultural scenarios, a kind of temporal central casting, to which recourse can be taken as appropriate, depending on the movie to be made, the scene to be enacted, the hostages to be rescued" (30). See also Fredric Jameson, "Postmodernism and Consumer Society" and "Nostalgia for the Present."

67. Renato Rosaldo, "Imperialist Nostalgia."

68. Shukla, *India Abroad*, 12.

69. Verne A. Dusenbery, "A Sikh Diaspora? Contested Identities and Constructed Realities," 33–34.

70. Benedict Anderson, *Imagined Communities: Reflections on the Origin and Spread of Nationalism*, rev. ed.

71. On the often awkward fit between the terms space and culture, see Akhil Gupta and James Ferguson, "Beyond 'Culture': Space, Identity, and the Politics of Difference."

72. Sangeeta Ray captures this temporal, geographic, and psychic disjunction succinctly: "*We are here but not quite. We want to be home but not yet*" ("Through the Looking Glass").

73. Jaffrey, *Climbing the Mango Trees*, 6–7.

74. Muzaffar Alam and Sanjay Subrahmanyam, "The Making of a Munshi," 61. In the colonial period the term also encompassed those who tutored their colonial rulers in the languages of the subcontinent.

75. Ibid., 62, 71.

76. Ibid., 71.

77. Jaffrey, *Climbing the Mango Trees*, 15. For a magisterial history of the Kayasthas of Hyderabad, see Karen Isaksen Leonard, *Social History of an Indian Caste: The Kayasths of Hyderabad*.

78. On the destruction of ashraf Muslim communities after 1857, see Aamir R. Mufti, *Enlightenment in the Colony: The Jewish Question and the Crisis of Postcolonial Culture*, 111–12.

79. Madhur Jaffrey, interview by Malcolm Jolley.

80. The scholarship on this topic is immense. For starters, see Antoinette

Burton, *Burdens of Empire: British Feminists, Indian Women, and Imperial Culture, 1865–1915*; Sandhya Shetty, "(Dis)locating Gender Space and Medical Discourse in Colonial India"; Vron Ware, *Beyond the Pale: White Women, Racism and History*; Deirdre David, *Rule Britannia: Women, Empire, and Victorian Writing*; Chandra Mohanty, "Under Western Eyes: Feminist Scholarship and Colonial Discourses"; and Spivak, "Three Women's Texts and a Critique of Imperialism."

81. Jaffrey, *Climbing the Mango Trees*, 179.

82. The phrase is Salman Rushdie's. See his "Outside the Whale," 92.

83. Madhur Jaffrey, interview by Malcolm Jolley.

84. Craig Claiborne, "Indian Actress Is a Star in the Kitchen, Too."

85. Sharpe, *Allegories of Empire: The Figure of Woman in the Colonial Text.*

86. See Barbara Ramusack, "The Indian Princes as Fantasy: Palace Hotels, Palace Museums, and Palace on Wheels."

87. John Pym, *The Wandering Company: Twenty-One Years of Merchant Ivory Films*, 52.

88. Interestingly, Ismail Merchant and James Ivory were introduced to one another by Madhur Jaffrey and her first husband, Saeed Jaffrey. See Saeed Jaffrey, *Saeed: An Actor's Journey*, 110–11.

89. The fact of Satyajit Ray's involvement in the film (he was responsible for the musical score) and that of Subrata Mitra, his early photographer, is no surprise, given Ray's trenchant critiques of popular Bombay cinema and his own endeavors to establish a cinematic alternative to its nonrealist, melodramatic codes of representation.

90. Ania Loomba, *Gender, Race and Renaissance Drama*, 30–31.

91. Nandi Bhatia, " 'Shakespeare' and the Codes of Empire in India," 103. Also see Sudipto Chatterjee, "Utpal Dutt 1929–1993."

92. Jyotsna Singh, "Different Shakespeares: The Bard in Colonial/Postcolonial India," 454.

93. See Arjun Appadurai's "Gastro-politics in Hindu South Asia" for an account of the ways in which food can serve as the medium or the message of conflict in South Indian Brahmin households.

94. Sidney W. Mintz, *Sweetness and Power: The Place of Sugar in Modern History*: "[Increased consumption of sugar in Britain] represent[s] an extension of empire outward, but on the other [it also] mark[s] an absorption, a kind of swallowing up, of sugar consumption as a national habit. Like tea, sugar came to define English 'character' " (39). Also see Sussman, "Women and the Politics of Sugar, 1792."

95. Piya Chatterjee, *A Time for Tea: Labor, Gender, and History on an Indian Plantation*. Elizabeth Kowaleski-Wallace elaborates the ways in which tea, sugar, and china, all ingredients of a genteel tea-drinking ritual, came to signify, in eighteenth-century Britain, gendered allure and gendered degeneracy; see *Consuming Subjects: Women, Shopping and Business in the Eighteenth Century.*

96. The scene seeks to hyperbolize and to repudiate Manjula's solicitations; Lizzie's contact with Manjula is far more phobically charged than any of her encounters with Sanju ever is. The almost delirious character of such a repudiation makes it possible to suggest that while the scene unquestionably harks back to the prototypical colonial scene of romance between the Eastern man and the Western (white) woman, it also supplements it in ways that are worthy of note. The visual and performative conjuration of the *zenana* within the tea-drinking frame is evocative of another and more perverse libidinal possibility in which a depraved Eastern patriarch is present and yet bracketed: the scene cannot but recall the Orientalist fantasies of lesbian eroticism that are inescapably associated with the sexual politics of the harem—especially since so many of the film's scenes of commensality between two actors, whether incipient or actual, are rendered in an explicitly erotic register: the *pan* (betel leaf) eating when Lizzie and Sanju first meet, Sanju's and Manjula's coupling and quarreling over delayed meals and shared delicacies, and the erotic tensions of eating on the road. (The feast in the maharaja's palace early in the film is obviously exempt from this logic.) In the sexually and racially anxious economy of the film, the fascination and terror of such interminglings is the more potent for being articulated through modes of indirection. For an elaboration of the associative continuum between the harem and lesbian eroticism, see Felicity Nussbaum, *Torrid Zones: Maternity, Sexuality, and Empire in Eighteenth-Century English Narratives*; and Gayatri Gopinath, "Theorizing Transnational Sexualities: Nostalgia, Desire, Diaspora." To my mind, the best reading to date of the erotics of the zenana/harem and the *hammam* is Srinivas Aravamudan's "Lady Mary in the *Hammam*," in *Tropicopolitans: Colonialism and Agency, 1688–1804*, 159–89.

97. Pym, *The Wandering Company*, 62.

98. Rosie Thomas, "Melodrama and the Negotiation of Morality in Mainstream Hindi Film," 162. Also see the following: Rosie Thomas, "Indian Cinema: Pleasures and Popularity"; Ravi Vasudevan, "The Melodramatic Mode and the Commercial Indian Cinema"; and Erik Barnouw and S. Krishnaswamy, *Indian Film*, 2d ed.

99. As it happens, *Boys Will Be Boys* was eventually written, though by Suleri herself (as "a daughter's elegy") and not by her father. But it was perhaps more resonant unwritten than written.

100. Madhur Jaffrey, *Quick & Easy Indian Cooking*, 134.

101. Basu, *Curry in the Crown*, 121. Basu attributes the use of this sauce to the unfamiliarity of the mostly Bangladeshi owners of Indian restaurants in Britain with the northern Indian dishes they were forced to serve.

Select Bibliography

Agamben, Giorgio. *Remnants of Auschwitz: The Witness and the Archive.* Translated by Daniel Heller-Roazen. New York: Zone Books, 2002.

Ahmad, Aijaz. *In Theory: Classes, Nations, Literatures.* London: Verso, 1994.

Alam, Muzaffar, and Sanjay Subrahmanyam. "The Making of a Munshi." *Comparative Studies of South Asia, Africa and the Middle East* 24, no. 2 (2004): 61–72.

Alavi, Seema. *The Sepoys and the Company: Tradition and Transition in Northern India, 1770–1830.* Delhi: Oxford University Press, 1995.

Alter, Joseph. "Celibacy, Sexuality, and the Transformation of Gender into Nationalism in North India." *Journal of Asian Studies* 53, no. 1 (February 1994): 45–66

———. *Gandhi's Body: Sex, Diet, and the Politics of Nationalism.* Philadelphia: University of Pennsylvania Press, 2000.

———. *The Wrestler's Body: Identity and Ideology in North India.* Berkeley: University of California Press, 1992.

Amarkant. *Sookha Patta.* Rajkamal Prakashan, 2004.

Ambedkar, B. R. *Gandhi and Gandhism.* Jullundur: Bheem Patrika Publications, 1970.

———. *What Congress and Gandhi Have Done to the Untouchables.* Bombay: Thacker, 1945.

Amin, Shahid. "Gandhi as Mahatma: Gorakhpur District, Eastern UP, 1921–2." *Subaltern Studies III,* ed. Ranajit Guha, 1–61. Delhi: Oxford University Press, 1984.

Anand, Mulk Raj. *The Coolie.* London: Lawrence and Wishart, 1936.

———. *Untouchable.* London: Wishart, 1935.

Ananthamurthy, U. R. *Samskara.* Translated by A. K. Ramanujan. New Delhi: Oxford University Press, 1978.

Anderson, Benedict. *Imagined Communities: Reflections on the Origin and Spread of Nationalism.* Revised edition. London: Verso, 1991.

Anderson, Warwick A. "Excremental Colonialism: Public Health and the Poetics of Pollution." *Critical Inquiry* 21 (spring 1995): 640–69.

Anidjar, Gil. *The Jew, the Muslim: A History of the Enemy*. Stanford: Stanford University Press, 2003.

Appadurai, Arjun. *Fear of Small Numbers: An Essay on the Geography of Anger*. Durham: Duke University Press, 2006.

——. "Gastro-politics in Hindu South Asia." *American Ethnologist* 8, no. 3 (August 1981): 494–511.

——. "How to Make a National Cuisine: Cookbooks in Contemporary India." *Comparative Studies in Society and History* 30, no. 1 (1988): 3–24.

——. "Is Homo Hierarchicus?" *American Ethnologist* 13, no. 4 (November 1986): 745–61.

——. *Modernity at Large: Cultural Dimensions of Globalization*. Minneapolis: University of Minnesota Press, 1996.

——. "Putting Hierarchy in Its Place." *Cultural Anthropology* 3, no. 1 (February 1988): 36–49.

Arata, Stephen. "The Occidental Tourist: Bram Stoker's *Dracula* and the Anxiety of Reverse Colonization." *Victorian Studies* 33, no. 1 (summer 1990): 621–45.

Aravamudan, Srinivas. "Lady Mary in the Hammam." *Tropicopolitans: Colonialism and Agency, 1688–1804*. Durham: Duke University Press, 1999.

Arnold, David. *Colonizing the Body: State Medicine and Epidemic Disease in Nineteenth-Century India*. Berkeley: University of California Press, 1993.

——. "Deathscapes: India in an Age of Romanticism and Empire, 1800–1856." *Nineteenth-Century Contexts* 26, no. 4 (December 2004): 339–53.

——. "Famine in Peasant Consciousness and Peasant Action: Madras, 1876–78." *Subaltern Studies III*, ed. Ranajit Guha, 62–115. Delhi: Oxford University Press, 1984.

——. *Famine: Social Crisis and Historical Change*. Oxford: Basil Blackwell, 1988.

——. *Gandhi*. Harlow, Essex: Longman/Pearson Higher Education, 2001.

——. "Hunger in the Garden of Plenty: The Bengal Famine of 1770." *Dreadful Visitations: Confronting National Catastrophe in the Age of Enlightenment*, ed. Alessa Johns, 81–111. New York: Routledge, 1999.

Axel, Brian Keith. *The Nation's Tortured Body: Violence, Representation, and the Formation of a "Sikh" Diaspora*. Durham: Duke University Press, 2001.

Aykroyd, W. R. *Conquest of Famine*. New York: Reader's Digest Press, 1975.

Bahri, Deepika. "Disembodying the Corpus: Postcolonial Pathology in Tsitsi Dangarembga's 'Nervous Conditions.'" *Postmodern Culture* 5, no. 1 (September 1994).

Ballantyne, Tony. *Between Colonialism and Diaspora: Sikh Cultural Formations in an Imperial World*. Durham: Duke University Press, 2006.

Ballhatchet, Kenneth. *Race, Sex, and Class Under the Raj*. New York: St. Martin's, 1980.

Banerjee, Sukanya. *Becoming Imperial Citizens*. Durham: Duke University Press, 2010.

Banerjee, Sumanta. *India's Simmering Revolution: The Naxalite Uprising*. London: Zed Press, 1984.

Banerji, Chitrita. *Eating India: An Odyssey into the Food and Culture of the Land of Spices.* New York: Bloomsbury USA, 2007.

——. *Life and Food in Bengal.* 1991; reprint. New Delhi: Rupa, 1993.

Barker, Francis, et al., eds. *Cannibalism and the Colonial World.* Cambridge: Cambridge University Press, 1998.

Barnouw, Erik, and S. Krishnaswamy. *Indian Film.* 2d. ed. New York: Oxford University Press, 1980.

Barthes, Roland. "Ornamental Cookery." *Mythologies.* Translated by Annette Lavers. New York: Hill and Wang, 1972.

——. "Towards a Psychosociology of Contemporary Food Consumption." *Annales: Economies, Societies, Civilisations,* no. 5 (1961); reprinted in Carolyn Counihan and Penny Van Esterik, eds., *Food and Culture: A Reader,* 20–27. London: Routledge, 1977.

Basham, A. L. *The Wonder That Was India.* AMS Press, 1911.

Basu, Shrabani. *Curry in the Crown: The Story of Britain's Favourite Dish.* New Delhi: Harper Collins India, 1999.

Baucom, Ian. "The Disasters of War: On Inimical Life." *Polygraph* 18 (2006): 166–90.

——. *Out of Place: Englishness, Empire, and the Locations of Identity.* Princeton: Princeton University Press, 1999.

Bayly, C. A. "Knowing the Country: Empire and Information in India." *Modern Asian Studies* 27, no. 1 (February 1993): 3–43.

——. *The New Cambridge History of India, II.1: Indian Society and the Making of the British Empire.* Cambridge: Cambridge University Press, 1988.

——. "The Origins of Swadeshi (Home Industry): Cloth and Indian Society, 1700–1930." *The Social Life of Things: Commodities in Cultural Perspective,* ed. Arjun Appadurai, 285–321. Cambridge: Cambridge University Press, 1988.

——. "Rallying Around the Subaltern." *Journal of Peasant Studies* 16, no. 1 (1988): 110–20; reprinted in *Mapping Subaltern Studies and the Postcolonial,* ed. Vinayak Chaturvedi, 116–26. London: Verso, 2000.

Beeton, Isabella. *The Book of Household Management.* London: S. O. Beeton, 1861.

Benjamin, Walter. "On Some Motifs in Baudelaire." *Illuminations,* ed. Hannah Arendt and trans. Harry Zohn. New York: Schocken Books, 1968.

——. "The Storyteller." *Illuminations,* ed. Hannah Arendt and trans. Harry Zohn. New York: Schocken Books, 1968.

——. "The Work of Art in the Age of Mechanical Reproduction." *Illuminations,* ed. Hannah Arendt and trans. Harry Zohn. New York: Schocken Books, 1968.

Bewell, Alan. *Romanticism and Colonial Disease.* Baltimore: Johns Hopkins University Press, 1999.

Bhabha, Homi. *The Location of Culture.* London: Routledge, 1994.

Bhadra, Gautam. "Four Rebels of Eighteen Fifty-Seven." *Subaltern Studies IV,* ed. Ranajit Guha, 229–75. Delhi: Oxford University Press.

Bhatia, B. M. *Famines in India: A Study in Some Aspects of the Economic History of India* (1860–1965). Delhi: Asia Publishing House, 1967.

Bhatia, Nandi. " 'Shakespeare' and the Codes of Empire in India." *Alif: Journal of Comparative Poetics*, no. 18 (1998): 96–126.

Bhattacharya, Bijon. *Nabanna*. 1944; reprint. Calcutta: Prama, 1984.

Bhattacharya, Sabyasachi. "Rethinking 1857." *Rethinking 1857*, ed. Sabyasachi Bhattacharya, ix–xl. Hyderabad: Orient Longman, 2007.

Bhattacharya, Tithi. *Sentinels of Culture: Class, Education, and the Colonial Intellectual in Bengal, 1848–85*. New York: Oxford University Press, 2007.

Bondurant, Joan V. *Conquest of Violence: The Gandhian Philosophy of Conflict*. Rev. ed. Berkeley: University of California Press, 1965.

Borthwick, Meredith. *The Changing Role of Women in Bengal*. Princeton: Princeton University Press, 1984.

Bose, Nirmal Kumar. *My Days with Gandhi*. Calcutta: Nishana, 1953.

——. *Studies in Gandhism*. 2d. ed. Calcutta: Indian Associated Publishing, 1947.

Bose, Sugata. "Starvation amidst Plenty: The Making of Famine in Bengal, Honan, and Tonkin, 1942–45." *Modern Asian Studies* 24.4 (October 1990): 699–727.

Bose, Sugata, and Ayesha Jalal. *Modern South Asia: History, Culture, Political Economy*. London: Routledge, 1998.

Bourdieu, Pierre. *Distinction: A Social Critique of the Judgment of Taste*. Translated by Richard Nice. Cambridge: Harvard University Press, 1987.

Boyarin, Daniel, and Jonathan Boyarin. "Diaspora: Generation and the Ground of Jewish Identity." *Critical Inquiry* 19, no. 4 (summer 1993): 693–725.

Brantlinger, Patrick. *Dark Vanishings: Discourse on the Extinction of Primitive Races, 1800–1930*. Ithaca: Cornell University Press, 2003.

——. *Rule of Darkness: British Literature and Imperialism, 1830–1914*. Ithaca: Cornell University Press, 1988.

Brennan, Jennifer. *Curries and Bugles: A Memoir and Cookbook of the British Raj*. London: Viking, 1990.

Brennan, Timothy. *At Home in the World: Cosmopolitanism Now*. Cambridge: Harvard University Press, 1997.

——. *Salman Rushdie and the Third World: Myths of the Nation*. New York: St. Martin's Press, 1989.

Brown, Judith M. *Gandhi: Prisoner of Hope*. New Haven: Yale University Press, 1989.

Brumberg, Joan Jacobs. "The Appetite as Voice." *Food and Culture: A Reader*, ed. Carole Counihan and Penny Van Esterik, 159–79. London: Routledge, 1997.

Burke, Edmund. *Reflections on the Revolution in France*, ed. L. G. Mitchell. 1790; New York: Oxford University Press, 1999.

——. *Speech on Fox's East India Bill, December 1, 1783*. *Writings and Speeches of Edmund Burke*. Volume 5. Oxford: Clarendon Press, 1981.

Burton, Antoinette. *At the Heart of the Empire: Indians and the Colonial Encounter in Late Victorian Britain*. Berkeley: University of California Press, 1998.

——. *Burdens of Empire: British Feminists, Indian Women, and Imperial Culture, 1865–1915.* Chapel Hill: University of North Carolina Press, 1994.

——. *The Postcolonial Careers of Santha Rama Rau.* Durham: Duke University Press, 2007.

Burton, David. *The Raj at Table: A Culinary History of the British in India.* London: Faber and Faber, 1994.

Burton, Isabel. *Life of Sir Richard F. Burton, K.C.M.G., F.R.G.S., by His Wife.* 2 vols. London: Chapman and Hall, 1893.

Burton, Richard F. *Goa, and the Blue Mountains; or, Six Months on Sick Leave,* ed. Dane Kennedy. 1851; Berkeley: University of California Press, 1991.

Butler, Judith. "Ethical Ambivalence." *The Turn to Ethics,* ed. Marjorie Garber, Beatrice Hanssen, and Rebecca L. Walkowitz, 15–28. London: Routledge, 2000.

——. *Precarious Life: The Powers of Mourning and Violence.* London: Verso, 2004.

Buzard, James. "On Auto-Ethnographic Authority." *Yale Journal of Criticism* 16, no. 1 (2003): 61–91.

——. *Disorienting Fiction: The Autoethnographic Work of Nineteenth-Century British Novels.* Princeton: Princeton University Press, 2005.

Bynum, Caroline Walker. *Holy Feast and Holy Fast: The Religious Significance of Food to Medieval Women.* Berkeley: University of California Press, 1987.

Carroll, Lucy. "Law, Custom, and Statutory Social Reform: The Hindu Widows' Remarriage Act of 1856." *Women in Colonial India,* ed. J. Krishnamurthy, 1–26. Delhi: Oxford University Press, 1988.

Caruth, Cathy. *Unclaimed Experience: Trauma, Narrative, and History.* Baltimore: Johns Hopkins University Press, 1996.

Chakrabarty, Dipesh. "The Time of History and the Times of Gods." *The Politics of Culture in the Shadow of Capital,* ed. Lisa Lowe and David Lloyd, 35–60. Durham: Duke University Press, 1997.

Chakravarty, Gautam. *The Indian Mutiny and the British Imagination.* Cambridge: Cambridge University Press, 2005.

Chapman, Pat. Web site www.patchapman.co.uk. Visited 26 November 2007.

Chatterjee, Indrani. "Colouring Subalternity: Slaves, Concubines and Social Orphans in Early Colonial India." *Subaltern Studies X,* eds. Gautam Bhadra, Gyan Prakash, and Susie Tharu, 49–97. New Delhi: Oxford University Press, 1999.

Chatterjee, Partha. "Introduction: A Political History of Independent India." *State and Politics in India.* Delhi: Oxford University Press, 1997.

——. *The Politics of the Governed: Reflections on Popular Politics in Most of the World.* New York: Columbia University Press, 2004.

Chatterjee, Piya. *A Time for Tea: Women and Postcolonial Labor on an Indian Plantation.* Durham: Duke University Press, 2001.

Chatterjee, Sudipto. "Utpal Dutt 1929–1993." *TDR* 38, no. 1 (spring 1994): 29–30.

Chattopadhyay, Swati. " 'Goods, Chattels and Sundry Items': Constructing 19th-

Century Anglo-Indian Domestic Life." *Journal of Material Culture* 7, no. 3 (2002): 243–71.

Chattopadhyaya, Harindranath. "Sarojini Naidu: A Sketch." *Perspectives on Sarojini Naidu*, ed. K. K. Sharma, 1–4. Ghaziabad: Vimal Prakashan, 1989.

Chaudhuri, Nupur. "Memsahibs and Motherhood in Nineteenth-Century Colonial India." *Victorian Studies* 31, no. 4 (summer 1988): 517–35.

Cheah, Pheng. "Given Culture: Rethinking Cosmopolitical Freedom in Trans-nationalism." *Cosmopolitics: Thinking and Feeling Beyond the Nation*, eds. Pheng Cheah and Bruce Robbins, 290–328. Minneapolis: University of Minnesota Press, 1998.

Cho, Lily. "On Eating Chinese: Chinese Restaurants and the Politics of Diaspora." Ph.D. diss., University of Alberta, 2003.

Chowdhury, Indira. *The Frail Hero and Virile History: Gender and the Politics of Culture in Colonial Bengal*. Delhi: Oxford University Press, 1998.

Chunder, Bholanauth. *The Travels of a Hindoo to Various Parts of Bengal and Upper India*. 2 vols. London: N. Trubner, 1869; Elibron Classics, 2005.

Claiborne, Craig. "Indian Actress Is a Star in the Kitchen, Too." *New York Times*, 7 July 1966.

Clifford, James. "Diasporas." *Cultural Anthropology* 9, no. 3 (August 1994): 302–38.

——. "Mixed Feelings." *Cosmopolitics: Thinking and Feeling Beyond the Nation*, eds. Pheng Cheah and Bruce Robbins, 262–270. Minneapolis: University of Minnesota Press, 1998.

Cohen, William A., and Ryan Johnson, eds. *Filth: Dirt, Disgust, and Modern Life*. Minneapolis: University of Minnesota Press, 2004.

Cohn, Bernard S. "The Census, Social Structure, and Objectification in South Asia." *An Anthropologist among the Historians and Other Essays*. Delhi: Oxford University Press, 1987.

——. "Cloth, Clothes, and Colonialism: India in the Nineteenth Century." *Colonialism and Its Forms of Knowledge*. Princeton: Princeton University Press, 1996.

——. "Representing Authority in Victorian India." *The Invention of Tradition*, eds. Eric Hobsbawm and Terence Ranger, 165–209. Cambridge: Cambridge University Press, 1992.

Cole, Simon A. "Do Androids Pulverize Tiger Bones to Use as Aphrodisiacs?" *Social Text*, no. 42 (spring 1995): 173–93.

Colley, Linda. *Captives: Britain, Empire, and the World, 1600–1850*. New York: Random House, 2002.

Collingham, E. M. (Lizzie). *Curry: A Tale of Cooks and Conquerors*. New York: Oxford University Press, 2006.

——. *Imperial Bodies: The Physical Experience of the Raj, c. 1800–1947*. Cambridge: Polity Press, 2001.

Conlon, Frank F. "Dining Out in Bombay." *Consuming Modernity: Public Culture in a*

South Asian World, ed. Carol A. Breckenridge, 90–128. Minneapolis: University of Minnesota Press, 1995.

Connor, Steven. "Thinking Perhaps Begins There: The Question of the Animal." Downloaded from Steven Connor's home page at Birkbeck College, London. Visited 5 August 2007.

Conrad, Joseph. Heart of Darkness, ed. Robert Kimbrough. New York: Norton, 1988.

Corbin, Alain. The Foul and the Fragrant: Odor and the French Social Imagination. Cambridge: Harvard University Press, 1986.

Craft, Christopher. " 'Kiss Me with those Red Lips': Gender and Inversion in Bram Stoker's Dracula." Representations 8 (autumn 1984): 107–33.

Dalal, Chandulal Bhagubhai. Harilal Gandhi: A Life. Edited and translated by Tridip Suhrud. 1977; reprint. Hyderabad: Orient Longman, 2007.

Dalrymple, William. The Last Mughal—The Fall of a Dynasty: Delhi, 1857. New York: Alfred A. Knopf, 2007.

Daly, Mary. The Famine in Ireland. Dundalk: Dublin Historical Association, 1986.

Das, Sisir Kumar. A History of Indian Literature, 1800–1910: Western Impact, Indian Response. New Delhi: Sahitya Akademi, 2005.

David, Deirdre. Rule Britannia: Women, Empire, and Victorian Writing. Ithaca: Cornell University Press, 1996.

David, Elizabeth. "Isabella Beeton and Her Book." Wine and Food, no. 109 (1961): 3–8.

David, Saul. The Indian Mutiny, 1857. London: Viking, 2002.

Davis, Mike. Late Victorian Holocausts: El Niño Famines and the Making of the Third World. London: Verso, 2000.

Dawson, Graham. Soldier Heroes: British Adventure, Empire and the Imagining of Masculinities. London: Routledge, 1994.

Deleuze, Gilles, and Felix Guattari. A Thousand Plateaus: Capitalism and Schizophrenia. Translated by Brian Massumi. Minneapolis: University of Minnesota Press, 1987.

Derrida, Jacques. "And Say the Animal Responded?" Zoontologies: The Question of the Animal. Edited by Cary Wolfe, 121–46. Minneapolis: University of Minnesota Press, 2003.

——. "The Animal That Therefore I Am (More to Follow)." Translated by David Wills. Critical Inquiry 28, no. 2 (winter 2002): 369–418.

——. " 'Eating Well,' or the Calculation of the Subject: An Interview with Jacques Derrida." Who Comes After the Subject? Edited by Eduardo Cadava, Jean-Luc Nancy, and Peter Connor, 96–119. New York: Routledge, 1991.

——. "Economimesis." Translated by Richard Klein. diacritics 11, no. 2 (summer 1981): 2–25.

——. "Force of Law: The 'Mystical Foundation of Authority.' " Translated by Mary Quaintance. Deconstruction and the Possibility of Justice, eds. Drucilla Cornell, Michel Rosenfeld, and David Gray Carlson, 3–67. London: Routledge, 1992.

———. *The Gift of Death*. Translated by David Wills. Chicago: University of Chicago Press, 1995.

———. *Given Time: 1. Counterfeit Money*. Translated by Peggy Kamuf. Chicago: University of Chicago Press, 1992.

———. "Marx and Sons." *Ghostly Demarcations: A Symposium on Jacques Derrida's Specters of Marx*, ed. Michael Sprinker, 213–69. London: Verso, 1999.

———. *Specters of Marx: The State of the Debt, the Work of Mourning, and the New International*. Translated by Peggy Kamuf. New York: Routledge, 1994.

Desai, Gaurav. "Old World Orders: Amitav Ghosh and the Writing of Nostalgia." *Representations* 85 (winter 2004): 125–48.

Devanesen, Chandran D. S. *The Making of the Mahatma*. Madras: Orient Longman, 1969.

de Waal, Alex. *Famine That Kills: Darfur, Sudan, 1984–1985*. Oxford: Clarendon Press, 1989.

Dirks, Nicholas. *Castes of Mind: Colonialism and the Making of Modern India*. Princeton: Princeton University Press, 2001.

———. *The Hollow Crown: Ethnohistory of an Indian Kingdom*. Ann Arbor: University of Michigan Press, 1993.

———. *The Scandal of Empire: India and the Creation of Imperial Britain*. Cambridge: Harvard University Press, 2006.

Disraeli, Benjamin. "Military Mutiny or National Revolt?" *India in 1857: The Revolt Against Foreign Rule*, ed. Ainslie Embree. 1963, 9–21; reprint. Delhi: Chanakya Publications, 1987.

Divakaruni, Chitra Banerjee. *The Mistress of Spices*. New York: Anchor Books, 1998.

Doniger, Wendy. *The Hindus: An Alternative History*. New York: Penguin, 2009.

———. "Rationalizing the Irrational Other: 'Orientalism' and the Laws of Manu." *New Literary History* 3, no. 1 (winter 1992): 25–43.

———. "Reflections on J. M. Coetzee." *The Lives of Animals*, ed. Amy Gutmann, 93–106. Princeton: Princeton University Press, 1999.

———. "Why Should a Priest Tell You Whom to Marry? A Deconstruction of the Laws of Manu." *Bulletin of the American Academy of Arts and Sciences* 44, no. 6 (March 1991): 18–31.

Douglas, Mary. *Purity and Danger: An Analysis of the Conception of Pollution and Taboo*. 1966; reprint. London: Routledge, 1992.

Duff, Alexander. *The Indian Rebellion: Its Causes and Results*. New York: Robert Carter and Brothers, 1858.

Dumont, Louis. *Homo Hierarchicus: The Caste System and Its Implications*. Translated by George Sainsbury et al. Revised English edition. 1966; reprint. Chicago: University of Chicago Press, 1981.

Dusenbery, Verne A. "A Sikh Diaspora? Contested Identities and Constructed Realities." *Nation and Migration: The Politics of Space in the South Asian Diaspora*, ed.

Peter van der Veer, 17–42. Philadelphia: University of Pennsylvania Press, 1995.

Dutt, Romesh Chunder. *The Economic History of India*. 2 vols. 1906; reprint. New Delhi: Publications Division, Ministry of Information and Broadcasting, Government of India, 1960.

——. *Famines and Land Assessments in India*. 1900; reprint. New Delhi: B. R. Publishing, 1985.

——. *Indian Famines: Their Causes and Prevention*. London: P. S. King and Son, 1901.

Eagleton, Terry. *Heathcliff and the Great Hunger: Studies in Irish Culture*. London: Verso, 1995.

Edkins, Jenny. *Whose Hunger? Concepts of Famine, Practices of Aid*. Minneapolis: University of Minnesota Press, 2000.

Edwardes, Michael. *Bound to Exile: The Victorians and India*. London: Sidgwick and Jackson, 1969.

——. *Red Year: The Indian Rebellion of 1857*. London: Hamish Hamilton, 1973.

Elias, Norbert. *The Civilizing Process: Sociogenetic and Psychogenetic Investigations*. Rev. ed. Translated by Edmund Jephcott; eds. Eric Dunning, Johan Goudsbloum, and Stephen Mennell. 1939; Oxford: Blackwell Publishers, 2000.

Ellmann, Maud. *The Hunger Artists: Starving, Writing, and Imprisonment*. Cambridge: Harvard University Press, 1993.

Erikson, Erik. *Gandhi's Truth: On the Origins of Militant Nonviolence*. New York: Norton, 1969.

Esty, Joshua. "Excremental Postcolonialism." *Contemporary Literature* 40, no. 1 (spring 1999): 22–59.

Famine Inquiry Commission. *Famine Inquiry Commission Report on Bengal*. 1944.

Fanon, Frantz. *The Wretched of the Earth*. Translated by Constance Farrington. New York: Grove Weidenfeld, 1963.

Fenn, George M. *Begumbagh*. London, 1879.

Fildes, Valerie. *Wet Nursing: A History from Antiquity to the Present*. Oxford: Basil Blackwell, 1988.

Fischer, Louis. *The Life of Mahatma Gandhi*. 1951; reprint. New Delhi: Indus/Harper Collins, 1992.

Foote, Samuel. *The Nabob: A Comedy in Three Acts*. 1778; reprint. New York: D. Longworth, 1813.

Forster, E. M. *A Passage to India*. 1924; reprint. San Diego: Harcourt Brace, 1984.

Foucault, Michel. *The History of Sexuality, Volume 1: The Use of Pleasure*. Translated by Robert Hurley. reprint. New York: Vintage Books, 1985.

Fox, Richard G. "East of Said." *Edward Said: A Critical Reader*, ed. Michael Sprinker, 144–56. Oxford: Blackwell, 1992.

——. *Gandhian Utopia: Experiments With Culture*. Boston: Beacon Press, 1989.

Freitag, Sandria. "Collective Crime and Authority in North India." *Crime and Crimi-*

nality in British India, ed. Anand Yang, 140–56. Tucson: University of Arizona Press, 1985.

———. "Crime in the Social Order of Colonial North India." *Modern Asian Studies* 25, no. 2 (1991): 227–61.

Freud, Sigmund. *Civilization and Its Discontents.* Translated by James Strachey. New York: W. W. Norton, 1961.

———. *Totem and Taboo.* Translated by James Strachey. 1913; reprint. London: Routledge and Kegan Paul, 1950.

Fuss, Diana. "Fashion and the Homospectatorial Look." *Critical Inquiry* 18, no. 4 (summer 1992): 713–37.

———. *Identification Papers.* London: Routledge, 1996.

Gallagher, Catherine. "The Potato in the Materialist Imagination." *Practicing New Historicism*, eds. Catherine Gallagher and Stephen Greenblatt, 110–35. Chicago: University of Chicago Press, 2001.

Gandhi, Leela. *Affective Communities: Anticolonial Thought, Fin-de-Siècle Radicalism, and the Politics of Friendship.* Durham: Duke University Press, 2006.

Gandhi, Mohandas K. *Autobiography: The Story of My Experiments with Truth.* Translated by Mahadev Desai. 1948; reprint. New York: Dover, 1983.

———. *Bapu's Letters to Mira (1924–1948).* Ahmedabad: Navajivan Publishing House, 1949.

———. *Collected Works of Mahatma Gandhi.* Volume 1 (1884–96). Delhi: Ministry of Information and Broadcasting, Government of India, 1958.

———. *Hind Swaraj and Other Writings.* Edited by Anthony J. Parel. Cambridge: Cambridge University Press, 1997.

———. "London Diary." *Collected Works of Mahatma Gandhi*, vol. 1, 3–21.

———. *Satyagraha in South Africa.* Ahmedabad: Navajivan, 1928.

———. *Young India.* 21 October 1926.

Gandhi, Prabhudas. *My Childhood With Gandhiji.* Ahmedabad: Navajivan Press, 1957.

Gandhi, Rajmohan. *The Good Boatman: A Portrait of Gandhi.* New Delhi: Viking Penguin, 1995.

———. *Mohandas: A True Story of a Man, His People, and an Empire.* New Delhi: Viking, 2006.

Ganguly, Keya. *States of Exception: Everyday Life and Postcolonial Identity.* Minneapolis: University of Minnesota Press, 2001.

Geetha, V., and S. V. Rajadurai, *Towards a Non-Brahmin Millennium: From Iyothee Thass to Periyar.* Calcutta: Samya, 1998.

George, Rosemary Marangoly. "The Authoritative Englishwoman: Setting Up Home and Self in the Colonies." *The Politics of Home: Postcolonial Relocations and Twentieth-Century Fiction.* Cambridge: Cambridge University Press, 1996.

Ghalib, Mirza Asadullah Khan. *Oxford India Ghalib: Life, Letters, and Ghazals.* Translated by Ralph Russell and Khurshidul Islam. New York: Oxford University Press, 2003.

Ghosh, Bishnupriya. "On Grafting the Vernacular: The Consequences of Postcolonial Spectrology." *boundary 2* 31, no. 2 (2004): 197–218.

——. *When Borne Across: Literary Cosmopolitics in the Contemporary Indian Novel*. New Brunswick, N.J.: Rutgers University Press, 2004.

Ghosh, Durba. *Sex and the Family in Colonial India: The Making of Empire*. Cambridge: Cambridge University Press, 2006.

Ghosh, Kali Charan. *Famines in Bengal, 1770–1943*. Calcutta: Indian Associated Publishing, 1944.

Giard, Luce. "Doing-Cooking." *The Practice of Everyday Life*. Volume 2: *Living and Cooking*. Translated by Timothy J. Tomasik; ed. Michel de Certeau, Luce Giard, and Pierre Mayol. Minneapolis: University of Minnesota Press, 1998.

Gigante, Denise. *Taste: A Literary History*. New Haven: Yale University Press, 2005.

Gilbert, Pamela K. *Mapping the Victorian Social Body*. Albany: SUNY Press, 2004.

Goldman, Robert P. "Ravana's Kitchen: A Testimony of Desire and the Other." *Questioning Ramayanas*, ed. Paula Richman, 105–16. Berkeley: University of California Press, 2000.

Goldman, Sally Sutherland. "Soul Food: Consumption, Conception, and Gender in Early Sanskrit Literary Texts." Manuscript.

Goodlad, Lauren. " 'A Middle Class Cut into Two': Historiography and Victorian National Character." *ELH* 67 (2000): 143–78.

Goody, Jack. "Industrial Foods: Towards the Development of a World Cuisine." *Food and Culture: A Reader*, eds. Carole Counihan and Penny Van Esterik, 338–56. London: Routledge, 1997.

Gopinath, Gayatri. "Theorizing Transnational Sexualities: Nostalgia, Desire, Diaspora." *positions* 5, no. 2 (winter 1998): 467–89.

Gordon, Avery. *Ghostly Matters: Haunting and the Sociological Imagination*. Minneapolis: University of Minnesota Press, 1997.

Goswami, Manu. " 'Englishness' on the Imperial Circuit: Mutiny Tours in Colonial South Asia." *Journal of Historical Sociology* 9, no. 1 (March 1996): 54–84.

Green, Martin. *The Challenge of the Mahatmas*. New York: Basic Books, 1978.

——. *Gandhi: Voice of a New Age Revolution*. New York: Continuum, 1993.

——. *The Origins of Nonviolence: Tolstoy and Gandhi in Their Historical Settings*. University Park: Pennsylvania State University Press, 1986.

Greenough, Paul. *Prosperity and Misery in Modern Bengal: The Famine of 1943–1944*. Oxford: Oxford University Press, 1982.

Grewal, Inderpal. "Autobiographic Subjects and Diasporic Locations: *Meatless Days* and *Borderlands*." *Scattered Hegemonies: Postmodernity and Transnational Feminist Practices*, eds. Inderpal Grewal and Caren Kaplan, 231–54. Minneapolis: University of Minnesota Press, 1994.

——. *Transnational America: Feminisms, Diasporas, Neoliberalisms*. Durham: Duke University Press, 2005.

Griffith, Marie. "Apostles of Abstinence: Fasting and Masculinity during the Progressive Era." *American Quarterly* 52, no. 4 (2000): 599–638.

Guha, Ranajit. *Dominance without Hegemony: History and Power in Colonial India.* Cambridge: Harvard University Press, 1997.

———. *Elementary Aspects of Peasant Insurgency in Colonial India.* Delhi: Oxford University Press, 1983.

———. "Introduction." *A Subaltern Studies Reader, 1986–1995,* ix–xxii. Minneapolis: University of Minnesota Press, 1997.

Gupta, Akhil, and James Ferguson, "Beyond 'Culture': Space, Identity, and the Politics of Difference." *Cultural Anthropology* 7, no. 1 (February 1992): 6–23; reprinted in Akhil Gupta and James Ferguson, eds. *Culture, Power, Place: Explorations in Critical Anthropology,* 33–51. Durham: Duke University Press, 1997.

Gupta, Charu. "Dalit 'Viranganas' and the Reinvention of 1857." *1857: Essays from Economic and Political Weekly,* 193–212. Hyderabad: Orient Longman, 2008.

Gupta, Maya. "The Vellore Mutiny: July 1806." *Defying Death: Struggles Against Imperialism and Feudalism,* eds. Maya Gupta and Amit Kumar Gupta, 18–38. New Delhi: Tulika, 2001.

Gupta, Narayani. *Delhi Between Two Empires.* Delhi: Oxford University Press, 1981.

Guru, Gopal. *Dalit Cultural Movement and Dialectics of Dalit Politics in Maharashtra.* Mumbai: Vikas Adhyayan Kendra, 1997.

Hamlin, Christopher, ed. *Public Health and Social Justice in the Age of Chadwick: Britain, 1800–1854.* Cambridge: Cambridge University Press, 1988.

Hansen, Miriam. "Benjamin, Cinema and Experience: 'The Blue Flower in the Land of Technology.' " *New German Critique* 40 (winter 1987): 179–224.

Hardiman, David. *Gandhi in His Time and Ours: The Global Legacy of His Ideas.* New York: Columbia University Press, 2003.

Hawes, C. J. *Poor Relations: The Making of a Eurasian Community in British India, 1773–1833.* Richmond, Surrey: Curzon Press, 1996.

Hay, Stephen N. "Jain Influences on Gandhi's Early Thought." *Gandhi, India, and the World,* ed. S. Ray, 14–23. Bombay: Nachiketa Publishers, 1970.

———. "The Making of a Late-Victorian Hindu: M. K. Gandhi in London, 1888–1891." *Victorian Studies* 33.1 (autumn 1989): 75–98.

Henty, G. A. *In Times of Peril: A Tale of India.* London: Griffith and Farran, 1881.

Herbert, Christopher. *War of No Pity: The Indian Mutiny and Victorian Trauma.* Princeton: Princeton University Press, 2008.

Hevia, James L. "Opium, Empire, and Modern History." *China Review International* 10, no. 2 (fall 2003): 307–26.

Hibbert, Christopher. *The Great Mutiny, India 1857.* Harmondsworth: Penguin Books, 1978.

Holmes, T. Rice. *A History of the Indian Mutiny, and of the Disturbances which Accompanied It among the Civil Population.* 5th ed. London: Macmillan, 1904.

Houston, Gail Turley. "Broadsides at the Board: Collations of *Pickwick Papers* and

Oliver Twist." *Studies in English Literature, 1500–1900* 31, no. 4 (autumn 1991): 735–55.

Hunt, James D. *Gandhi in London*. New Delhi: Promilla, 1978.

Hunter, W. W. *Annals of Rural Bengal*. 7th ed. Reprint. London: Smith, Elder, 1897.

Hurley, Kelly. *The Gothic Body: Sexuality, Materialism, and Degeneration at the Fin-de-Siècle*. Cambridge: Cambridge University Press, 1997.

Inden, Ronald. *Imagining India*. London: Blackwell, 1990.

Ivory, James, dir. *Shakespeare Wallah* (1965).

Jaffrey, Madhur. *Climbing the Mango Trees: A Memoir of a Childhood in India*. London: Ebury Press, 2005.

——. Interview by Malcolm Jolley, Toronto, February 2007, *Gremolata* 112: www.gremolata.com. Visited 28 November 2007.

——. *An Invitation to Indian Cooking*. 1973. Reprint. New York: Vintage Books, 1975.

——. *Madhur Jaffrey's Cookbook: Easy East/West Menus for Family and Friends*. New York: Harper and Row, 1987.

——. *Madhur Jaffrey's Indian Cookery*. Woodbury, N.Y.: Barron's, 1983.

——. *Madhur Jaffrey's Ultimate Curry Bible*. London: Ebury Press, 2003.

——. *Quick & Easy Indian Cooking*. San Francisco: Chronicle Books, 1996.

——. *A Taste of India*. London: Pavilion Books, 1985.

Jaffrey, Saeed. *Saeed: An Actor's Journey*. New Delhi: Harper Collins India, 1999.

Jaini, Padmanabh S. "Fear of Food? Jain Attitudes on Eating." *Jain Studies in Honour of Jozef Deleu*, eds. Rudy Smet and Kenji Watanabe, 339–53. Tokyo: Ho-no-tomosha, 1993.

Jameson, Fredric. "Nostalgia for the Present." *Postmodernism, or The Cultural Logic of Late Capitalism*. Durham: Duke University Press, 1991.

——. "Postmodernism and Consumer Society." *The Anti-Aesthetic: Essays on Postmodern Culture*, ed. Hal Foster, 111–25. Port Townsend, Wash.: Bay Press, 1983.

Jayal, Niraja Gopal. "The Gentle Leviathan: Welfare and the Indian State." *Social Scientist* 22, no. 9/12 (September–December 1994): 18–26.

Jones, Kenneth W. *The New Cambridge History of India*. Volume 3: *Socio-Religious Reform Movements in British India*. Cambridge: Cambridge University Press, 1989.

Jordens, J. T. F. *Dayananda Saraswati: His Life and Ideas*. Delhi: Oxford University Press, 1997.

Joseph, Betty. *Reading the East India Company, 1720–1840: Colonial Currencies of Gender*. Chicago: University of Chicago Press, 2004.

Kafka, Franz. "A Hunger Artist." *Norton Anthology of Short Fiction*, ed. R. V. Cassill, 714–21. New York: Norton, 1978.

Kakar, Sudhir. *Intimate Relations: Exploring Indian Sexuality*. New Delhi: Penguin Books, 1989.

Kant, Immanuel. *Anthropology from a Pragmatic Point of View*. Translated by Victor Lyle Dowdell. 1798; reprint. Carbondale: Southern Illinois University Press, 1978.

Kaviraj, Sudipto. "The Imaginary Institution of India." *Subaltern Studies VII*, ed. Partha Chatterjee and Gyanendra Pandey, 1–39. Delhi: Oxford University Press, 1992.

———. *The Unhappy Consciousness: Bankimchandra Chattopadhyay and the Formation of Nationalist Discourse in India*. Delhi: Oxford University Press, 1995.

Kaye, J. W., and G. B. Malleson. *History of the Indian Mutiny*. 6 vols. London, 1897.

Keen, David. *The Benefits of Famine: A Political Economy of Famine and Relief in South-western Sudan, 1983–1989*. Princeton: Princeton University Press 1994.

Keenan, Thomas. *Fables of Responsibility: Aberrations and Predicaments in Ethics and Politics*. Stanford: Stanford University Press, 1997.

Kelleher, Margaret. *The Feminization of Famine: Expressions of the Inexpressible?* Durham: Duke University Press, 1997.

Kennedy, Dane. *The Magic Mountains: Hill Stations and the British Raj*. Delhi: Oxford University Press, 1996.

Khan, Sir Syed Ahmed. *The Causes of the Indian Revolt*. Translated by "two European friends"; introduction by Francis Robinson. 1873. Reprint. Oxford: Oxford University Press, 2000.

Khare, R. S. *Culture and Reality: Essays on the Hindu System of Managing Foods*. Simla: Indian Institute of Advanced Study, 1976.

———. *The Hindu Hearth and Home*. Durham: Carolina Academic Press, 1976.

Kilgour, Maggie. *From Communion to Cannibalism: An Anatomy of Metaphors of Incorporation*. Princeton: Princeton University Press, 1990.

Kincaid, Jamaica. *Annie John*. New York: Farrar, Straus and Giroux, 1985.

Kinealy, Christine. *This Great Calamity: The Irish Famine, 1845–1852*. Dublin: Gill and Macmillan, 1994.

King, Anthony D. *The Bungalow: The Production of a Global Culture*. London: Routledge and Kegan Paul, 1984.

King, Richard C. "The (Mis)uses of Cannibalism in Contemporary Cultural Critique." *diacritics* 30, no. 1 (spring 2000): 106–23.

Kingsford, Anna. *The Perfect Way in Diet*. London, 1881.

Kipling, Rudyard. "Baa Baa Black Sheep." *Wee Willie Winkie*, ed. Hugh Haughton. 1888. Reprint. London: Penguin Books, 1988.

———. "The City of Dreadful Night." *From Sea to Sea: Letters of Travel*. New York: Doubleday & McClure, 1899.

———. "The Enlightenments of Padgett, M.P." *Under the Deodars*. 1890; London: Edinburgh Society, 1899.

———. "The Head of the District." *Life's Handicap*. London: Macmillan, 1891.

———. *Kim*. Norton Critical Edition, ed. Zoreh T. Sullivan. New York: W. W. Norton, 2002.

———. "The Little House at Arrah." *The Reader's Guide to Rudyard Kipling's Work*, ed. Reginald Engledow Harbord, 1972–79. Canterbury: Gibbs and Sons, 1961–72.

———. "The Mark of the Beast." *Life's Handicap*, ed. P. N. Furbank. London: Penguin, 1987: 195–207.

———. "The Strange Ride of Morrowbie Jukes." *Wee Willie Winkie*, ed. Hugh Haughton. 1888. Reprint. London: Penguin, 1988.

———. "The Tomb of His Ancestors." *The Day's Work*, ed. Constance Phipps. 1898. Reprint. Harmondsworth: Penguin Books, 1988.

———. "William the Conqueror." *The Day's Work*, ed. Constantine Phipps. 1898. Reprint. London: Penguin, 1988.

Kishwar, Madhu. "Gandhi on Women." *Economic and Political Weekly*, 5 October 1985, 1691–1702; 12 October 1985, 1753–58.

Kitson, Peter J. " 'The Eucharist of Hell'; or, Eating People Is Right: Romantic Representations of Cannibalism." *Romanticism on the Net* 17 (February 2000). www.users.ox.ac.uk. Visited 8 September 2008.

Koshy, Susan, and R. Radhakrishnan, eds. *Transnational South Asians: The Making of a Neo-Diaspora*. New York: Oxford University Press, 2008.

Koven, Seth. *Slumming: Social and Sexual Politics in Victorian Britain*. Princeton: Princeton University Press, 2004.

Kowaleski-Wallace, Elizabeth. *Consuming Subjects: Women, Shopping, and Business in the Eighteenth Century*. New York: Columbia University Press, 1997.

Krishna, Srinivas, dir. *Masala* (1991).

Krishnaswamy, Revathi. "Mythologies of Migrancy: Postcolonialism, Postmodernism, and the Politics of (Dis)Location." *Ariel* 26, no. 1 (1995): 125–46.

Kristeva, Julia. *Powers of Horror: An Essay on Abjection*. Translated by Leon S. Roudiez. New York: Columbia University Press, 1982.

Kurlansky, Mark. *Salt: A World History*. New York: Penguin, 2002.

Lahiri, Abani. *The Peasant and India's Freedom Movement*. New Delhi: V. V. Giri National Labour Institute, 2001.

Lahiri, Nayanjot. "Remembering 1857: The Revolt in Delhi and Its Afterlife." *World Archaeology* 35, no. 1 (June 2003): 35–60.

Lahiri, Shompa. *Indians in Britain: Anglo-Indian Encounters, Race and Identity, 1880–1930*. London: Routledge, 1999.

Laidlaw, James. *Riches and Renunciation: Religion, Economy, and Society among the Jains*. Oxford: Clarendon Press, 1995.

Lal, Vinay. "Nakedness, Nonviolence, and Brahmacharya: Gandhi's Experiments in Celibate Sexuality." *Journal of the History of Sexuality* 9, no. 1/2 (January–April 2000): 105–36.

Laporte, Dominique. *History of Shit*. Translated by Nadia Benabid and Rodolphe el-Khoury. Cambridge: MIT Press, 2000.

Lawson, Philip. *The East India Company: A History*. London: Longman, 1993.

LeBlanc, Ronald D. "Tolstoy's Way of No Flesh: Abstinence, Vegetarianism, and Christian Physiology." *Food in Russian History and Culture*, eds. Musya Glants and Joyce Toomre, 81–102. Bloomington: Indiana University Press, 1997.

Leckey, Edward. *Fictions Connected with the Indian Outbreak of 1857 Exposed*. Bombay: Chesson and Woodhall, 1859.

Leonard, Karen Isaksen. *Making Ethnic Choices: California's Punjabi-Mexican-Americans.* Philadelphia: Temple University Press, 1992.

——. *Social History of an Indian Caste: The Kayasths of Hyderabad.* Berkeley: University of California Press, 1978; Hyderabad: Orient Longman, 1994.

Leonardi, Susan J. "Recipes for Reading: Summer Pastas, Lobster à la Riseholme, and Key Lime Pie." *PMLA* 104, no. 3 (summer 1989): 340–47.

Levinas, Emmanuel. "The Paradox of Morality: An Interview with Emmanuel Levinas." Translated by Andrew Benjamin and Tamara Wright. *The Provocation of Levinas: Rethinking the Other*, eds. Robert Bernasconi and David Wood, 168–80. London: Routledge, 1988; reprinted in *Animal Philosophy: Essential Readings in Continental Thought*, eds. Matthew Calarco and Peter Atterton, 49–50. New York: Continuum, 2004.

Levine, Philippa. *Prostitution, Race and Politics: Policing Venereal Disease in the British Empire.* London: Routledge, 2003.

Lévi-Strauss, Claude. "The Culinary Triangle." *Food and Culture: A Reader*, eds. Carole Counihan and Penny Van Esterik, 28–35. London: Routledge, 1997.

Lim, Bliss Cua. "Spectral Times: The Ghost Film as Historical Allegory." *positions* 9, no. 2 (2001): 281–329.

Lionnet, Françoise. " 'She Breastfed Reluctance into Me': Hunger Artists in the Global Economy." *Women, Culture, and Practices of Development*, eds. Celeste Schenck and Susan Perry, 214–34. London: Zed Press, 2001.

Lionnet, Françoise, and Shu-mei Shih, eds. *Minor Transnationalism.* Durham: Duke University Press, 2005.

Lippit, Akira. "The Death of an Animal." *Film Quarterly* 56, no. 1 (autumn 2002): 9–22.

——. *Electric Animal: Toward a Rhetoric of Wildlife.* Minneapolis: University of Minnesota Press, 2000.

Lloyd, David. "The Indigent Sublime: Specters of Irish Hunger." *Representations* 92, no. 1 (November 2005): 152–85.

——. "The Memory of Hunger." *Loss: The Politics of Mourning*, eds. David L. Eng and David Kazanjian, 205–28. Berkeley: University of California Press, 2003.

——. "The Political Economy of the Potato." *Nineteenth-Century Contexts* 29, nos. 2–3 (June–September 2007): 311–35.

Luckhurst, Roger. *The Invention of Telepathy, 1870–1901.* Oxford: Oxford University Press, 2002.

Lutgendorf, Philip. "Dining Out at Lake Pampa: The Shabari Episode in Multiple Ramayanas." *Questioning Ramayanas: A South Asian Tradition*, ed. Paula Richman, 119–36. Berkeley: University of California Press, 2001.

Macaulay, Thomas B. "Robert Clive." Edited by Vincent A. Smith. London: Oxford University Press, 1921.

——. "Warren Hastings." *Critical and Historical Essays*, ed. Hugh Trevor-Roper. New York: McGraw-Hill, 1965.

Maharatna, Arup. *The Demography of Famines: An Indian Historical Perspective.* Delhi: Oxford University Press, 1996.

Mahasveta Devi. In conversation with Enakshi Chatterjee. *The Wordsmiths,* ed. Meenakshi Sharma. Delhi: Katha, 1996.

Mahasweta Devi. "Operation Bashai Tudu." *Bashai Tudu.* Translated by Samik Bandyopadhyay and Gayatri Chakravorty Spivak. Calcutta: Thema, 1990.

———. "Bichhan (Seeds)." *Of Women, Outcastes, Peasants, and Rebels.* Edited and translated by Kalpana Bardhan. Berkeley: University of California Press, 1990.

———. *Bitter Soil.* Translated by Ipsita Chanda. Calcutta: Seagull Books, 1998.

———. "Daini (The Witch-Hunt)." *Women, Outcastes, Peasants, and Rebels.* Edited and translated by Kalpana Bardhan. Berkeley: University of California Press, 1990.

———. "Douloti the Bountiful." *Imaginary Maps: Three Stories by Mahasweta Devi.* Translated and introduced by Gayatri Chakravorty Spivak. London: Routledge, 1995.

———. *Dust on the Road: The Activist Writings of Mahasweta Devi.* Edited by Maitreya Ghatak. Calcutta: Seagull Books, 1997.

———. *The Queen of Jhansi.* Translated by Mandira and Sagaree Sengupta. Calcutta: Seagull Books, 2000.

———. "Pterodactyl, Puran Sahay, and Pirtha." *Imaginary Maps.* Translated by Gayatri Spivak. London: Routledge, 1995.

———. "Strange Children." *Of Women, Outcastes, Peasants, and Rebels: A Selection of Bengali Short Stories.* Edited and translated by Kalpana Bardhan, 229–41. Berkeley: University of California Press, 1990.

———. "Telling History: Gayatri Chakravorty Spivak interviews Mahasweta Devi." *Chotti Munda and His Arrow.* Translated by Gayatri Chakravorty Spivak. New York: Blackwell, 2003.

———. "The Witch-Hunt." *Of Women, Outcastes, Peasants, and Rebels.* Edited and translated by Kalpana Bardhan, 242–71. Berkeley: University of California Press, 1990.

Majeed, Javed. *Autobiography, Travel and Postnational Identity: Gandhi, Nehru and Iqbal.* Basingstoke: Palgrave Macmillan, 2007.

Majendie, Vivian Dering. *Up among the Pandies: A Year's Service in India.* London: Routledge, Warne, and Routledge, 1859.

Majumdar, R. C. *The Sepoy Mutiny and the Revolt of 1857.* Calcutta: Firma K. L. Mukhopadhyay, 1957.

Malamoud, Charles. *Cooking the World: Ritual and Thought in Ancient India.* Translated by David White. Delhi: Oxford University Press, 1996.

Malthus, Thomas Robert. *An Essay on the Principle of Population,* ed. Geoffrey Gilbert. 1798. Reprint. Oxford: Oxford University Press, 1993.

Mani, Bakirathi, and Latha Varadarajan. " 'The Largest Gathering of the Global Indian Family': Neoliberalism, Nationalism, and Diaspora at Pravasi Bharatiya Divas." *Diaspora* 14, no. 1 (2005): 45–74.

Marriott, McKim. "Caste Ranking and Food Transactions: A Matrix Analysis." *Structure and Change in Indian Society*, eds. Milton Singer and Bernard Cohn, 133–71. Chicago: Aldine, 1968.

——. "Hindu Transactions: Diversity without Dualism." *Transaction and Meaning: Directions in the Anthropology of Exchange and Symbolic Behavior*, ed. Bruce Kapferer, 109–42. Philadelphia: Institute for the Study of Human Issues, 1976.

Marx, Karl. *Capital: A Critique of Political Economy*. 3 vols. Translated by Ben Fowkes. London: Penguin, 1990.

Marx, Karl, and Friedrich Engels. "The Future Results of the British Rule in India [July 22, 1853]." *The First Indian War of Independence, 1857–1859*. Moscow: Foreign Languages Publishing House, 1959.

Mason, Philip. *A Matter of Honour: An Account of the Indian Army, Its Officers and Men*. London: Cape, 1974.

——. *The Men Who Ruled India*. London: Jonathan Cape, 1985.

Masters, John. *The Nightrunners of Bengal*. New York: Viking, 1951.

Mayo, Katherine. *Mother India*. New York: Harcourt, Brace & Company, 1927.

Mbembe, Achille. "Necropolitics." Translated by Libby Meintjes. *Public Culture* 15, no. 1 (winter 2003): 11–40.

McClintock, Anne. "Family Feuds: Gender, Nation and the Family." *Feminist Review* 44 (summer 1993): 61–80.

——. *Imperial Leather: Race, Gender, and Sexuality in the Colonial Contest*. New York: Routledge, 1995.

Mehta, Ved. *Mahatma Gandhi and His Apostles*. New Haven: Yale University Press, 1976.

Mennell, Stephen. *All Manners of Food: Eating and Taste in England and France from the Middle Ages to the Present*. 2d. ed. Urbana: University of Illinois Press, 1996.

Merivale, Patricia. "Saleem Fathered by Oskar: Intertextual Strategies in Midnight's Children and The Tin Drum." *Ariel: A Review of International English Literature* 21, no. 3 (July 1990): 7–21.

Metcalf, Thomas. *The Aftermath of Revolt: India, 1857–1870*. Princeton: Princeton University Press, 1964.

Metcalfe, Charles Theophilus. *Two Native Narratives of the Mutiny in Delhi, Translated from the Originals*. 1898. Reprint. Delhi: Seema Publications, 1974.

Michie, Helena. *The Flesh Made Word: Female Figures and Women's Bodies*. New York: Oxford University Press, 1987.

Miller, William Ian. *The Anatomy of Disgust*. Cambridge: Harvard University Press, 1997.

——. "Gluttony." *Representations* 60 (fall 1997): 92–112.

Mills, James. *Madness, Cannabis, and Colonialism*. New York: St. Martin's Press, 2000.

Mintz, Sidney W. *Sweetness and Power: The Place of Sugar in Modern History*. New York: Viking, 1985.

——. "Time, Sugar, and Sweetness." *Food and Culture: A Reader*, eds. Carole Counihan and Penny Van Esterik, 357–69. London: Routledge, 1997.

Mohanty, Chandra. "Under Western Eyes: Feminist Scholarship and Colonial Discourses." *Feminist Review* 30 (1988): 61–88.

Montaigne, Michel de. "Of Cannibals." Translated by John Florio. 1603; London: David Nutt, 1892.

Moodley, Devadas. "Vellore 1806: The Meanings of Mutiny." *Rebellion, Repression, Reinvention: Mutiny in Comparative Perspective*, ed. Jane Hathaway, 87–101. Westport, Conn.: Praeger, 2001.

Moon, Vasant, ed. *Dr. Baba Saheb Ambedkar: Writings and Speeches*. 18 vols. Bombay: Government of Maharashtra, [1990–2003].

Moore-Gilbert, Bart. *Kipling and "Orientalism."* London: Croom Helm, 1986.

Morash, Christopher. *Writing the Irish Famine*. Oxford: Clarendon Press, 1995.

Morton, Timothy. *The Poetics of Spice: Romantic Consumerism and the Exotic*. Cambridge: Cambridge University Press, 2000.

———. *Shelley and the Revolution in Taste: The Body and the Natural World*. Cambridge: Cambridge University Press, 1994.

Moxham, Roy. *The Great Hedge of India*. New York: Carroll and Graf, 2001.

———. *Tea: Addiction, Exploitation, and Empire*. New York: Carroll and Graf, 2004.

Mufti, Aamir R. *Enlightenment in the Colony: The Jewish Question and the Crisis of Postcolonial Culture*. Princeton: Princeton University Press, 2007.

Mukherjee, Arun Prabha. Introduction to Omprakash Valmiki, *Joothan: A Dalit's Life*. Translated by Arun Prabha Mukherjee. New York: Columbia University Press, 2003.

Mukherjee, Rudrangshu. *Awadh in Revolt, 1857–1858*. Wimbledon: Anthem Press, 2002.

———. *Mangal Pandey: Brave Martyr or Accidental Hero?* New Delhi: Penguin Books, 2005.

———. *Spectre of Violence: The 1857 Kanpur Massacres*. New Delhi: Viking, 1998.

Naidu, Sarojini. *Selected Letters, 1890s to 1940*. Edited by Makarand Paranjpe. New Delhi: Kali for Women, 1996.

Naipaul, V. S. *India: A Wounded Civilization*. 1976; reprint. New York: Vintage Books, 1978.

Nair, Mira, dir. *Mississippi Masala* (1991).

Nair, Rukmini Bhaya. "History as Gossip in *Midnight's Children*." *Midnight's Children: A Book of Readings*, ed. Meenakshi Mukherjee, 49–68. Delhi: Pencraft International, 1999.

Nancy, Jean-Luc. "Love and Community: A Round Table Discussion with Jean-Luc Nancy, Avital Ronell and Wolfgang Schirmacher." August 2001. www.egs.edu. Visited 25 July 2007.

———. "Shattered Love." *The Inoperative Community*, ed. Peter Connor, trans. Peter Connor, Lisa Garbus, Michael Holland, and Simona Sawhney. Minneapolis: University of Minnesota Press, 1991.

Nanda, B. R. *Gandhi and His Critics*. Delhi: Oxford University Press, 1985.

———. *Mahatma Gandhi: A Biography*. Delhi: Oxford University Press, 1958.

Nandy, Ashis. *The Intimate Enemy: Loss and Recovery of Self under Colonialism*. Delhi: Oxford University Press, 1983.

Naoroji, Dadabhai. *Poverty and Un-British Rule in India*. London: S. Sonnenchein, 1901.

Narayan, Uma. "Eating Cultures: Identity, Incorporation, Indian Food." *Dislocating Cultures: Identities, Traditions, and Third-World Feminism*. London: Routledge, 1997.

Nayyar, Sushila. *Kasturba: Wife of Gandhi*. Wallingford, Pa.: Pendle Hill, 1948.

Nehru, Jawaharlal. *An Autobiography*. London: Bodley Head, 1958.

Nigam, Sanjay. "Disciplining and Policing the 'Criminals by Birth.'" Parts I and II, *Indian Economic and Social History Review* 27, no. 2 (1990): 131–64, and 27, no. 3 (1990): 259–87.

Nissenbaum, Stephen. *Sex, Diet, and Debility in Jacksonian America: Sylvester Graham and Health Reform*. Westport, Conn.: Greenwood Press, 1980.

Nora, Pierre. "Between History and Memory: Les Lieux de Memoire." *Representations* 26 (spring 1989): 7–25.

Nown, Graham. *Mrs. Beeton: 150 Years of Cookery and Household Management*. London: Ward Lock, 1986.

Nussbaum, Felicity. *Torrid Zones: Maternity, Sexuality, and Empire in Eighteenth-Century English Narratives*. Baltimore: Johns Hopkins University Press, 1995.

O' Connor, Erin. *Raw Material: Producing Pathology in Victorian Culture*. Durham: Duke University Press, 2000.

Ó Gráda, Cormac. *Black '47 and Beyond: The Great Irish Famine in History, Economy, and Memory*. Princeton: Princeton University Press, 1999.

O'Hanlon, Rosalind. *Caste, Conflict and Ideology: Mahatma Jotirao Phule and Low Caste Protest in Nineteenth-Century Western India*. Cambridge: Cambridge University Press, 2002.

———. "Issues of Widowhood: Gender and Resistance in Colonial Western India." *Contesting Power: Resistance and Everyday Social Relations in South Asia*, ed. Douglas Haynes and Gyan Prakash, 62–108. Berkeley: University of California Press, 1992.

Palmer, J. A. B. *The Mutiny Outbreak at Meerut in 1857*. Cambridge: Cambridge University Press, 1966.

Pande, Sita Ram. *From Sepoy to Subedar; Being the Life and Adventures of Subedar Sita Ram*. Translated by Lieutenant-Colonel Norgate. Edited by James Lunt. 1873. Reprint. Hamden, Conn.: Archon Books, 1970.

Pandian, M. S. S. *Brahmin and Non-Brahmin: Genealogies of the Tamil Political Present*. Delhi: Permanent Black, 2007.

Parekh, Bhikhu. *Colonialism, Tradition and Reform: An Analysis of Gandhi's Political Discourse*. New Delhi: Sage Publications, 1989.

———. *Gandhi*. Oxford: Oxford University Press, 1997.

Paton, Diana L. "Punishment, Crime, and the Bodies of Slaves in Eighteenth-Century Jamaica." *Journal of Social History* 34, no. 4 (summer 2001): 923–54.

Paxton, Nancy. *Writing Under the Raj: Gender, Race, and Rape in the British Colonial Imagination, 1830–1947.* New Brunswick, N.J.: Rutgers University Press, 1999.

Poovey, Mary. *A History of the Modern Fact: Problems of Knowledge in the Sciences of Wealth and Society.* Chicago: University of Chicago Press, 1998.

———. *Making a Social Body: British Cultural Formation, 1830–1864.* Chicago: University of Chicago Press, 1995.

Porter, Roy. Preface to Piero Camporesi, *Bread of Dreams: Food and Fantasy in Early Modern Europe.* Translated by David Gentilcore. Chicago: University of Chicago Press, 1989.

Prakash, Gyan. *Another Reason: Science and the Imagination of Modern India.* Princeton: Princeton University Press, 1999.

———. *Bonded Histories: Genealogies of Labor Servitude in Colonial India.* Cambridge: Cambridge University Press, 1990.

Prakash, Om. "Restrictive Trading Regimes: VOC and the Asian Spice Trade in the Seventeenth Century." *Spices in the Indian Ocean World,* ed. M. N. Pearson, 317–36. Aldershot: Variorum Press, 1996.

Pratt, Tim, and James Vernon, " 'Appeal from This Fiery Bed': The Colonial Politics of Gandhi's Fasts and Their Metropolitan Reception." *Journal of British Studies* 44 (January 2005): 92–114.

Procida, Mary. "Feeding the Imperial Appetite: Imperial Knowledge and Anglo-Indian Domesticity." *Journal of Women's History* 15, no. 2 (summer 2003): 123–49.

Pyarelal. *The Epic Fast.* Ahmedabad: Navajivan Publishing House, 1932.

———. *Mahatma Gandhi—The Early Phase.* Ahmedabad: Navajivan Press, 1965.

———. *Mahatma Gandhi—The Last Phase.* Volume 2. Ahmedabad: Navajivan Press, 1958.

Pym, John. *The Wandering Company: Twenty-One Years of Merchant Ivory Films.* London: British Film Institute and New York: Museum of Modern Art, 1983.

Rag, Pankaj. "1857: Need for Alternative Sources." *Social Scientist* 26, no. 1/4 (January–April 1998): 113–47.

Raheja, Gloria Goodwin. "India: Caste, Kingship, and Dominance Reconsidered." *Annual Review of Anthropology* 17 (1988): 497–522.

Ramadanovic, Petar. "When 'To Die in Freedom' Is Written in English." *diacritics* 28, vol. 4 (winter 1998): 54–67.

Ramanujan, A. K. "Translator's Note." U. R. Ananthamurthy, *Samskara.* Delhi: Oxford University Press, 1976.

Ramaswamy, Sumathi. *The Lost Land of Lemuria: Fabulous Geographies, Catastrophic Histories.* Berkeley: University of California Press, 2004.

Ramusack, Barbara. "The Indian Princes as Fantasy: Palace Hotels, Palace Museums, and Palace on Wheels." *Consuming Modernity: Public Culture in a South Asian World,* ed. Carol A. Breckenridge, 66–89. Minneapolis: University of Minnesota Press, 1995.

Rangasami, Amrita. " 'Failure of Exchange Entitlements' Theory of Famine: A Response." *Economic and Political Weekly* 20, nos. 41, 42 (October 1985): 1747–52, 1797–1801.

Rao, Anupama, ed. *Gender and Caste.* Delhi: Kali for Women, 2003.

Rawson, Claude. *God, Gulliver, and Genocide: Barbarism and the European Imagination, 1492–1945.* Oxford: Oxford University Press, 2001.

——."Unspeakable Rites: Cultural Reticence and the Cannibal Question." *Social Research* 66.1 (Spring 1999): 167–93.

Ray, Krishnendu. *The Migrant's Table: Meals and Memories in Bengali–American Households.* Philadelphia: Temple University Press, 2004.

Ray, Sangeeta. "Through the Looking Glass." *Seminar* 538, The Diaspora: Indian-Americans and the Motherland, June 2004; www.india-seminar.com. Visited 5 December 2006.

Ray, Satyajit, dir. *Asani Sanket* (Distant Thunder). (1973).

Raychaudhuri, Tapan. *Europe Reconsidered: Perceptions of the West in Nineteenth-Century Bengal.* Delhi: Oxford University Press, 1988.

Reinhard, Kenneth. "Kant with Sade, Lacan with Levinas." *MLN* 110, no. 4, Comparative Literature Issue (September 1995): 785–808.

Revel, Jean-François. *Culture and Cuisine: A Journey through the History of Food.* Translated by Helen R. Lane. New York: Doubleday, 1984.

Rizvi, S. A. A., and M. L. Bhargava, eds. *Freedom Struggle in Uttar Pradesh.* Volume 1. Lucknow: Publications Bureau, Information Department, Uttar Pradesh, 1957.

Robbins, Bruce. "Comparative Cosmopolitanisms." *Secular Vocations: Intellectuals, Professionalism, Culture.* London: Verso, 1993.

Rombauer, Irma. *The Joy of Cooking: A Compilation of Reliable Recipes, with an Occasional Culinary Chat.* Indianapolis: Bobbs-Merrill, 1943.

Ronell, Avital. *Crack Wars: Literature Addiction Mania.* Lincoln: University of Nebraska Press, 1992.

Rosaldo, Renato. "Imperialist Nostalgia." *Representations* 26 (1989): 107–22.

Rosselli, John. "The Self-Image of Effeteness: Physical Education and Nationalism in Nineteenth-Century Bengal." *Past and Present* 86 (February 1980): 121–48.

Roy, Parama. "Bhadralok/bhadramahila." *Keywords in South Asian Studies,* ed. Rachel M. Dwyer. School of Oriental and African Studies (SOAS), University of London online publication (March 2006). www.soas.ac.uk.

——. "Transits, Transformations, and Body Talk: Gandhi's Passages from India." *Pacific Coast Philology* 42, no. 2 (2007): 133–55.

Roy, Tapti. *The Politics of a Popular Uprising: Bundelkhand in 1857.* New Delhi: Oxford University Press, 1986.

——. "Rereading the Texts: Rebel Writings in 1857–58." *Rethinking 1857,* ed. Sabyasachi Bhattacharya, 221–36. Hyderabad: Orient Longman, 2007.

Rude, George. *The Crowd in the French Revolution.* London: Oxford University Press, 1959.

Rudolph, Lloyd I., and Susanne Hoeber Rudolph. *The Modernity of Tradition: Political Development in India*. Chicago: University of Chicago Press, 1967.

Rushdie, Salman. *The Ground Beneath Her Feet*. London: Picador Books, 1999.

———. *Midnight's Children*. London: Jonathan Cape, 1980.

———. *The Moor's Last Sigh*. New York: Knopf, 1997.

———. "Outside the Whale." *Imaginary Homelands: Essays and Criticism, 1981–1991*. London: Penguin, 1991.

Russell, William Howard. *My Indian Mutiny Diary*. Edited by Michael Edwardes. 1858. Reprint. London: Cassell, 1957.

Salt, Henry S. *A Plea for Vegetarianism and Other Essays*. Manchester, 1886.

Sanborn, Geoffrey. *The Sign of the Cannibal: Melville and the Making of a Postcolonial Reader*. Durham: Duke University Press, 1998.

Sanders, Mark. *Gayatri Chakravorty Spivak: Live Theory*. London: Continuum, 2006.

Sarkar, Nikhil. *A Matter of Conscience: Artists Bear Witness to the Great Bengal Famine of 1943*. Translated by Satyabrata Dutta. Calcutta: Punascha, 1998.

Sarkar, Sumit. "The Conditions and Nature of Subaltern Militancy: Bengal from Swadeshi to Non-Co-operation, c. 1905–22." *Subaltern Studies III*, ed. Ranajit Guha, 271–320. Delhi: Oxford University Press, 1984.

Sarkar, Tanika. *Bengal, 1928–1934: The Politics of Protest*. Delhi: Oxford University Press, 1987.

Scheper-Hughes, Nancy. *Death without Weeping: The Violence of Everyday Life in Brazil*. Berkeley: University of California Press, 1992.

Schivelbusch, Wolfgang. *Tastes of Paradise: A Social History of Spices, Stimulants, and Intoxicants*. Translated by David Jacobson. New York: Vintage, 1992.

Schmitt, Carl. *The Nomos of the Earth in the Jus Publicum Europaeum*. Translated by G. L. Umen. New York: Telos Press, 1983.

Scholberg, Henry. *The Indian Literature of the Great Rebellion*. New Delhi: Promilla, 1993.

Schwarz, Henry. "Subaltern Studies: Radical History in the Metaphoric Mode." *Writing Cultural History in Colonial and Post-colonial India*. Philadelphia: University of Pennsylvania Press, 1997. Reprint. David Ludden, ed. *Reading Subaltern Studies: Critical History, Contested Meaning and the Globalization of South Asia*, 304–39. London: Anthem Press, 2002.

Schwarz, Hillel. *Never Satisfied: A Cultural History of Diets, Fantasies, and Fat*. New York: Free Press/Macmillan, 1986.

Scott, James C. *The Moral Economy of the Peasant: Rebellion and Subsistence in Southeast Asia*. New Haven: Yale University Press, 1977.

Sen, Amartya. *Development as Freedom*. New Delhi: Oxford University Press, 1999.

———. "Equality of What?" *Equal Freedom: Selected Tanner Lectures on Human Values*, ed. Stephen Darwall, 307–30. Ann Arbor: University of Michigan Press, 1995.

———. *Poverty and Famines: An Essay on Entitlement and Deprivation*. Oxford: Clarendon Press, 1982.

Sen, Ela. *Darkening Days, Being a Narrative of Famine-Stricken Bengal.* Calcutta: Susil Gupta, 1944.

Sen, Mrinal. *Akaler Sandhaney* (In Search of Famine). Script reconstructed and translated by Samik Bandyopadhyay. Calcutta: Seagull Books, 1983.

Sen, S. N. *Eighteen Fifty-Seven.* Delhi: Publications Division, Ministry of Information and Broadcasting, 1957.

Sen, Satadru. *Disciplining Punishment: Colonialism and Convict Society in the Andaman Islands.* New York: Oxford University Press, 2000.

Sen, Sudipta. *Distant Sovereignty: National Imperialism and the Origins of British India.* London: Routledge, 2002.

Sharma, Sanjay. *Famine, Philanthropy and the Colonial State: North India in the Early Nineteenth Century.* Delhi: Oxford University Press, 2001.

Sharpe, Jenny. *Allegories of Empire: The Figure of Woman in the Colonial Text.* Minneapolis: University of Minnesota Press, 1993.

Shepherd, W. J. *A Personal Narrative of the Outbreak and Massacre at Cawnpore.* Lucknow: London Printing Press, 1879.

Sherer, J. W. *Daily Life During the Indian Mutiny: Personal Experiences of 1857.* 1898; reprint. Allahabad: Legend Publications, 1974.

Shetty, Sandhya. "(Dis)locating Gender Space and Medical Discourse in Colonial India." *Genders* 20. 188–230. New York: New York University Press, 1994.

——. "Dying to Be a Doctor: Remembering Anandibai and Gopalrao in India and America." *Archive and Pharmacy* (forthcoming).

——. " 'The Quack Whom We Know': Illness and Nursing in Gandhi." *Rethinking Gandhi and Nonviolent Relationality: Global Perspectives,* eds. Debjani Ganguly and John Docker, 38–65. London: Routledge and New Delhi: Orient Longman, 2007.

Singh, Jyotsna. "Different Shakespeares: The Bard in Colonial/Postcolonial India." *Theater Journal* 41, no. 4 (December 1989): 445–58.

Singh, Navtej. *Starvation and Colonialism: A Study of Famines in the Nineteenth-Century British Punjab, 1858–1901.* New Delhi: National Book Organisation, 1996.

Singha, Radhika. " 'Providential' Circumstances: The Thuggee Campaign of the 1830s and Legal Innovation." *Modern Asian Studies* 27 (February 1993): 83–146.

Sinha, Mrinalini. *Colonial Masculinity: The "Manly Englishman" and the "Effeminate Bengali" in the Late Nineteenth Century.* Manchester: Manchester University Press, 1995.

Skaria, Ajay. *Hybrid Histories: Forests, Frontiers and Wildness in Western India.* Delhi: Oxford University Press, 1999.

——. "Shades of Wildness: Tribe, Caste, and Gender in Western India." *Journal of Asian Studies* 56, no. 3 (August 1997): 726–45.

Slade, Madeline. *The Spirit's Pilgrimage.* New York: Coward-McCann, 1960.

Spear, Percival. *The Nabobs: A Study of the Social Life of the English in Eighteenth-Century India.* 1932. Reprint. Delhi: Oxford University Press, 1998.

Spencer, Colin. *The Heretic's Feast: A History of Vegetarianism*. Hanover, N.H.: University Press of New England, 1995.

Spivak, Gayatri Chakravorty. *A Critique of Postcolonial Reason: Toward a History of the Vanishing Present*. Cambridge: Harvard University Press, 1999.

———. "Ghostwriting." *diacritics* 25, no. 2 (summer 1995): 65–84.

———. "Poststructuralism, Marginality, Postcoloniality, and Value." *Literary Theory Today*, ed. Peter Collier and Helga Geyer-Ryan, 219–44. Cambridge: Polity Press, 1990.

———. "Reading *The Satanic Verses*." *Outside in the Teaching Machine*. London: Routledge, 1993).

———. "Righting Wrongs." *South Atlantic Quarterly* 103, no. 2/3 (spring–summer 2004): 523–81.

———. "Subaltern Talk: Interview with the Editors." *The Spivak Reader: Selected Works of Gayatri Chakravorty Spivak*, eds. Donna Landry and Gerald MacLean. London: Routledge, 1996.

———. "Three Women's Texts and a Critique of Imperialism." *"Race," Writing, and Difference*, ed. Henry Louis Gates Jr., 262–280. Chicago: University of Chicago Press, 1986.

———. "Woman in Difference: Mahasweta Devi's 'Douloti the Bountiful.'" *Cultural Critique*, no. 14, The Construction of Gender and Modes of Social Division II (winter 1989–90): 105–28.

Spodek, Howard. "On the Origins of Gandhi's Political Methodology: The Heritage of Kathiawad and Gujarat." *Journal of Asian Studies* 30, no. 2 (February 1971): 361–72.

Srinivas, M. N. *The Cohesive Role of Sanskritization and Other Essays*. Delhi: Oxford University Press, 1989.

Srivastava, Hari Shanker. *The History of Indian Famines and Development of Famine Policy (1858–1918)*. Agra: Sri Ram Mehra, 1968.

Stallybrass, Peter, and Allon White. *The Politics and Poetics of Transgression*. Ithaca: Cornell University Press, 1986.

Steel, Flora Annie, and Grace Gardiner. *The Complete Indian Housekeeper and Cook*. 1888. Reprint, rev. ed., London, 1921.

———. *The Garden of Fidelity, Being the Autobiography of Flora Annie Steel*. London: Macmillan, 1929.

Stephens, Ian. *Monsoon Morning*. London: Ernest Benn, 1966.

Stokes, Eric. *The English Utilitarians and India*. Delhi: Oxford University Press, 1989.

———. *The Peasant and the Raj: Studies in Agrarian Society and Peasant Rebellion in Colonial India*. Cambridge: Cambridge University Press, 1978.

———. *The Peasant Armed: The Indian Revolt of 1857*. Edited by C. A. Bayly. Oxford: Clarendon Press, 1986.

Stoler, Ann Laura. "Domestic Subversions and Children's Sexuality." *Race and the Education of Desire*. Durham: Duke University Press, 1995.

Stuart, Tristram. *The Bloodless Revolution: A Cultural History of Vegetarianism from 1600 to Modern Times*. New York: Norton, 2006.

Subrahmanyam, Sanjay. *The Career and Legend of Vasco da Gama*. Cambridge: Cambridge University Press, 1997.

——. Keynote lecture, 22nd. Annual South Asia Conference, University of California, Berkeley, 16 February 2007.

Suleri Goodyear, Sara. *Boys Will Be Boys: A Daughter's Elegy*. Chicago: University of Chicago Press, 2003.

——. *Meatless Days*. Chicago: University of Chicago Press, 1989.

——. *The Rhetoric of English India*. Chicago: University of Chicago Press, 1992.

Sunder Rajan, Rajeswari. *The Scandal of the State: Women, Law, and Citizenship in Postcolonial India*. Durham: Duke University Press, 2003.

Sussman, Charlotte. "Women and the Politics of Sugar, 1792." *Consuming Anxieties: Consumer Protest, Gender, and British Slavery, 1713–1833*. Stanford: Stanford University Press, 2000.

Tagore, Rabindranath. *Gora*. 1910. Reprint. London: Macmillan, 1924.

——. "Kshudito Pashan." *Rabindra Rachanabali*. Volume 11. Calcutta: Visva Bharati, 1979.

Talukdar, Shashwati, dir. *Mahasweta Devi: Witness, Advocate, Writer*. (2001).

Tarlo, Emma. *Clothing Matters: Dress and Identity in India*. Chicago: University of Chicago Press, 1996.

Taylor, P. J. O. *A Companion to the "Indian Mutiny" of 1857*. Delhi: Oxford University Press, 1996.

Teltscher, Kate. " 'The Fearful Name of the Black Hole': Fashioning an Imperial Myth." *Writing India, 1757–1990: The Literature of British India*, ed. Bart Moore-Gilbert, 30–51. Manchester: Manchester University Press, 1996.

Thomas, Rosie. "Indian Cinema: Pleasures and Popularity." *Screen* 26, nos. 3–4 (May–August 1985): 116–31.

——. "Melodrama and the Negotiation of Morality in Mainstream Hindi Film." *Consuming Modernity: Public Culture in a South Asian World*, ed. Carol Breckenridge, 157–82. Minneapolis: University of Minnesota Press, 1995.

Thompson, E. P. "The Moral Economy of the English Crowd in the Eighteenth Century." *Past and Present* 50, no. 1 (1971): 76–136.

Thompson, Edward. *The Other Side of the Medal*. London: Hogarth Press, 1925.

Thomson, Mowbray. *The Story of Cawnpore*. London, 1859.

Thornhill, Mark. *The Personal Adventures and Experiences of a Magistrate during the Rise, Progress, and Suppression of the Indian Mutiny*. London: John Murray, 1884.

Tololyan, Khachig. "The Contemporary Discourse of Diaspora Studies." *Comparative Studies of South Asia, Africa and the Middle East* 17, no. 3 (2007): 647–55.

——. "The Nation-State and Its Others: In Lieu of a Preface." *Diaspora: A Journal of Transnational Studies* 1, no. 1 (Spring 1991): 3–7.

Travers, Robert. "Death and the Nabob: Imperialism and Commemoration in Eighteenth-Century India." *Past and Present* 196 (August 2007): 83–124.

Trevelyan, George Otto. *Cawnpore*. 1865. Reprint. London: Macmillan, 1886.

Trumpener, Katie. *Bardic Nationalism: The Romantic Novel and the British Empire*. Princeton: Princeton University Press, 1997.

Twigg, Julia. "Vegetarianism and the Meanings of Meat." *The Sociology of Food and Eating: Essays on the Sociological Significance of Food*, ed. Anne Murcott, 18–30. Aldershot: Gower, 1983.

Van der Veer, Peter. "Introduction." *Nation and Migration: The Politics of Space in the South Asian Diaspora*. Philadelphia: University of Pennsylvania Press, 1995.

Vasudevan, Ravi. "The Melodramatic Mode and the Commercial Indian Cinema." *Screen* 30, no. 3 (summer 1989): 29–50.

Vernon, James. *Hunger: A Modern History*. Cambridge: Harvard University Press, 2007.

Vigarello, Georges. *Concepts of Cleanliness: Changing Attitudes in France since the Middle Ages*. Translated by Jean Birrell. Cambridge: Cambridge University Press, 1988.

Visram, Rozina. *Ayahs, Lascars, and Princes: Indians in Britain, 1700–1947*. London: Pluto Press, 1986.

Viswanathan, Gauri. *Outside the Fold: Conversion, Modernity, and Belief*. Princeton: Princeton University Press, 1998.

Wakankar, Milind. "Body, Crowd, Identity: Genealogy of a Hindu Nationalist Ascetics." *Social Text* 45 (winter 1995): 45–73.

——. "The Anomaly of Kabir: Caste and Canonicity in Indian Modernity." *Muslims, Dalits, and the Fabrications of History*, eds. Shail Mayaram, M. S. S. Pandian, and Ajay Skaria, 99–139. Calcutta: Seagull Books, n.d.

Ware, Vron. *Beyond the Pale: White Women, Racism and History*. London: Verso, 1992.

Warner, Marina. "Fee Fie Fo Fum: The Child in the Jaws of the Story." *Cannibalism and the Colonial World*, eds. Francis Barker, Peter Hulme, and Margaret Iversen, 158–82. Cambridge: Cambridge University Press, 1998.

Watts, Michael. *Silent Violence: Food, Famine and Peasantry in Northern Nigeria*. Berkeley: University of California Press, 1983.

Whorton, James. *Crusaders for Fitness: The History of American Health Reformers*. Princeton: Princeton University Press, 1984.

Williams, Howard. *The Ethics of Diet*. Manchester: John Heywood, 1883.

Winsten, Stephen. *Salt and His Circle*. London: Hutchinson, 1951.

Wood, David. "Thinking with Cats." *Animal Philosophy: Essential Readings in Continental Thought*, eds. Matthew Calarco and Peter Atterton, 129–44. London: Continuum, 2004.

Woodham-Smith, Cecil. *The Great Hunger: Ireland, 1845–1849*. London: Harper and Row, 1962.

Yang, Anand A. "The Lotah Emeutes of 1855: Caste, Religion and Prisons in North India in the Early Nineteenth Century." *Confronting the Body: The Politics of Physicality in Colonial and Post-Colonial India*, eds. James H. Mills and Satadru Sen, 102–17. London: Anthem Press, 2004.

Yue, Gang. *The Mouth that Begs: Hunger, Cannibalism, and the Politics of Eating in Modern China*. Durham: Duke University Press, 1999.

Yule, Henry, and A. C. Burnell. *Hobson-Jobson*. Edited by William Crooke. 1903. Reprint. New Delhi: Munshiram Manoharlal, 1994.

Zelliot, Eleanor. *From Untouchable to Dalit: Essays on the Ambedkar Movement*. 1992. Reprint. New Delhi: Manohar, 2001.

Zilly, Aditee Nag Chowdhury. *The Vagrant Peasant: Agrarian Distress and Desertion in Bengal 1770 to 1830*. Wiesbaden: Franz Steiner Verlag, 1982.

Zimmerman, Francis. *The Jungle and the Aroma of Meats: An Ecological Theme in Hindu Medicine*. Berkeley: University of California Press, 1987.

Zlotnick, Susan. "Domesticating Imperialism: Curry and Cookbooks in Victorian England." *Frontiers: A Journal of Women Studies* 16, no. 2/3 (1996): 51–68.

Index

Begum Hazrat Mahal, 49

Benjamin, Walter, 74, 177–78

Besant, Annie, 91–92

Bewell, Alan, 13

Bhabha, Homi, 31, 33–34, 53–55, 167

Bhadralok, 8–9, 196 n. 18, 224 n. 16

Bhang (cannabis), 37, 58, 73, 203 n. 22

Bhattacharya, Bijon, 121

Bhudev Mukhopadhyay, 8–10

Biopolitics, 125, 143–44

Black Hole of Calcutta, 68, 212 n. 136. See also Prisons

Blyton, Enid, 2–3

Body as colonial contact zone, 7, 24, 33

Bondurant, Joan, 100

Brahamacharya. See Celibacy

Brahmin. See Caste

Brantlinger, Patrick, 67–86, 140

Bread, 3, 28, 33, 232 n. 6; cash nexus vs. nexus of, 25, 31, 204 n. 36; of English as unclean, 48, 50, 197 n. 36; riots for, in Europe, 15, 51, 207 n. 73

Breastfeeding, 41, 197 n. 37; anxiety of Anglo-Indians about, 15–16, 19, 60, 197 n. 38; in Meatless Days, 189, 191–92. See also Milk

Brennan, Jennifer, 169

Brennan, Timothy, 166–67, 234 n. 37

Brumberg, Joan, 94

Bureaucracy, 123–24, 151, 180; bureaucratic gothic and, 127; civil servants and, 113, 127–29, 151

Burke, Edmund, 13, 197 n. 32, 208 n. 89

Burton, Antoinette, 159

Burton, Richard, 201 n. 10, 209 n. 93

Butler, Judith, 152

Buzard, James, 170

Cannabis. See Bhang

Cannibalism, 7, 12–14, 20, 53, 128, 174; breastfeeding in Meatless Days as, 191–92; Derrida on, 1–2, 11–13, 20, 29, 81; in history of otherness, 13, 197 nn. 28–32; as Mutiny trope, 62–63

Carnivory, 26, 30, 76, 80–83, 93, 105; as feature of Western cuisine, 10, 94–96; muscular masculinity and, 80, 215 n. 16. See also Vegetarianism

Carpenter, Edward, 91–93, 218 n. 60

Cartridges, greased. See Indian Mutiny of 1857

Caste: Brahmins and, 8–9, 16–19, 46–47, 60, 97, 168, 191, 198 n. 44; British appropriations of, 17–19, 45–46; envy and, 35; Kayasthas and, 180–83; permeability of, 18–19, 35; purity and pollution of, 8–10, 16–17, 35, 46–47, 187; untouchables/dalit and, 18, 60, 62, 71, 101–3, 121–22, 180, 188, 202 n. 21; Widow Remarriage Act of 1856 and, 19

Celibacy, 75–76, 89, 94, 97–99, 104, 110–12. See also Masculinity: seminal withholding and

Chakrabarty, Dipesh, 127

Chakravarty, Gautam, 52

Chapatis, 31–34, 50–53, 63–65, 207 nn. 71–72, 207 n. 75, 207 n. 78; in On the Face of the Waters, 53, 55; in The Siege of Krishnapur, 206 n. 69

Charter Act of 1813, 49–50

Chatterjee, Partha, 23, 200 n. 65

Chatterjee, Piya, 186–87

Cheah, Pheng, 244 n. 37

Cho, Lily, 174

Christianity, 16, 34, 56, 71, 73, 74, 91, 100, 134, 150, 175, 211 n. 117; Caste Disabilities Removal Act of 1850 and, 50; masculinity and, 80–81, 90;

Kierkegaard, Søren, 108
Kim (Kipling), 19, 57, 199 n. 58, 201 n. 10
Kincaid, Jamaica, 3
Kipling, Rudyard, 16, 19, 57, 68, 77, 116, 127, 184, 201 n. 10, 208 n. 92, 210 n. 104, 222 n. 3
Kishwar, Madhu, 96

Laidlaw, James, 29–30, 79
Leach, Edmund, 11
Leckey, Edward, 63
Leftovers, 61–62, 210 n. 116
Leonardi, Susan, 169
Levinas, Emmanuel, 145, 229 n. 84
Lévi-Strauss, Claude, 11
Lionnet, Françoise, 91
Lippit, Akira, 139–40
Lloyd, David, 127, 227 n. 49, 226 n. 35

Macaulay, Thomas B., 89, 213 n. 155
Mahasweta Devi, 23, 27, 36, 118, 126–27, 164; apocalypse and extinction in works of, 139, 141–44, 152; narrative forms and, 127, 139, 146; nostalgia in, 141; Pterodactlyl, Puran Sahay, and Pirtha, 123–24, 138–51; radical love in works of, 139, 153; representations by, of labor/slavery, 130–32, 135; semiotic difficulty/ambiguity in works of, 141; sexual difference as problem in works of, 136–37; "Shishu," 127–38; sociological realism in works of, 119–22, 141; tribal advocacy in works of, 122, 139, 141, 151–52
Malamoud, Charles, 62
Malthus, Thomas, 117, 125–26, 143
Marriott, McKim, 18
Marx, Karl, 6, 12, 43, 96 n. 12, 211 n. 120
Masala: as food, 3, 156, 188, 232 n. 18; in Indian film lexicon, 188–89

Masculinity: British vs. Indian/Bengali, 58, 79–80; seminal withholding and, 80, 90, 97–99, 221 n. 114
Masters, John, 207 n. 78
Mauss, Marcel, 134
Mbembe, Achille, 70, 143–44
McClintock, Anne, 171
Meat eating. See Carnivory
Meatless Days (Sara Suleri), 155, 171, 162; kapura (testicle) fable in, 163–64, 189–94
Medicine: Ayurvedic, 94, 107, 111–12, 218 n. 61; "modern"/Western, 7, 91, 93–94, 106, 111, 223 n. 9
Mehta, Raychandbhai, 104, 112–13
Mehtab, Sheikh, 80, 92–93, 226 n. 24
Merchant, Ismail, 184, 187–88. See also Merchant Ivory Productions
Merchant Ivory Productions, 183–88, 238 n. 88
Metcalfe, Sir Charles Theophilus, 35, 53
Midnight's Children (Rushdie), 154–57, 162, 231 n. 2, 243 n. 24
Milk, 16, 66, 97, 151, 212 n. 132; abstinence from, of Gandhi, 112–14, 219 n. 73; semen and, 221 n. 114. See also Breastfeeding
Mill, James, 93, 203 n. 22
Mintz, Sidney, 5, 186
Missionaries. See Christianity
"A Modest Proposal" (Swift), 13
Montaigne, Michel de, 14, 147, 230 n. 87
Morton, Timothy, 5, 217 n. 47
Mughal Empire, 35–37, 41–42, 47–48, 57, 73, 176, 180–82, 203 n. 29, 204 n. 35
Munshis, 180–82, 237 n. 74
Mukherjee, Rudrangshu, 37, 201 n. 13
Muslims. See Islam
Mutiny. See Indian Mutiny of 1857; Vellore Mutiny of 1806

Tribes and tribals, 27, 52, 119–24, 140–41, 146–47, 149–50, 224 n. 21, 228 n. 72; Agariya as, 123, 128–33, 135, 138; Gondwanaland and, 141

Trocki, Carl A., 5–6

Untouchable (dalit). See Caste

Vampirism, 6, 12, 43, 196 n. 12

Vegetarianism, 20, 75, 81, 87, 170; as radical movement, 87–92, 217 n. 47, 218 n. 50, 218 n. 52; Gandhi and, 9, 75–81, 83, 93–95, 97–98, 104–7, 109–13, 115, 215 n. 19, 221 n. 103; gender and, 26, 76, 85, 216 n. 33. See also Carnivory

Vellore Mutiny of 1806, 40–41, 48

Vernon, James, 95

Violence: eating as, 11, 22, 24, 26, 29, 93, 101, 115, 201, 192–94; epistemic and political modes of, 14, 70, 124, 128, 131, 135, 137–39, 144, 147

Vivekananda, Swami, 79

Waste, bodily, 58, 60, 65, 74; excrement as, 67, 69, 213 n. 141

Watts, Michael, 124

Wells, 39, 48, 64, 67–70, 74, 114 n. 168, 212 nn. 136–37

Wet nursing. See Breastfeeding

Wheeler, General Hugh, 65, 67

Witnessing, 27, 149, 150, 227 n. 50; eyewitness accounts as act of, 35–36, 48, 66

Wright, J. A., 46

Yang, Anand, 49, 206 n. 62

Yue, Gang, 95

Zlotnick, Susan, 160

Parama Roy is professor of English at the
University of California, Davis. She is the author
of *Indian Traffic: Identities in Question in Colonial and
Postcolonial India* (1997) and editor, with Manali Desai
and Piya Chatterjee, of *States of Trauma* (2009).

. . .

Library of Congress Cataloging-in-Publication Data
Roy, Parama.
Alimentary tracts : appetites, aversions, and the
postcolonial / Parama Roy.
p. cm. — (Next wave)
Includes bibliographical references and index.
ISBN 978-0-8223-4788-0 (cloth : alk. paper)
ISBN 978-0-8223-4802-3 (pbk. : alk. paper)
1. Postcolonialism—India. 2. British—India—
History. 3. Food habits—Political aspects—India.
4. Politics and culture. I. Title. II. Series: Next wave.
DS479.R785 2010
954.03—dc22   2010023400